ELIZABETH I's
SECRET LOVER

ELIZABETH I's SECRET LOVER

THE ROYAL AFFAIR WITH ROBERT DUDLEY, EARL OF LEICESTER

ROBERT STEDALL

PEGASUS BOOKS
NEW YORK LONDON

ELIZABETH I'S SECRET LOVER

Pegasus Books, Ltd.
West 37th Street, 13th Floor
New York, NY 10018

First Pegasus Books hardcover edition July 2020

Typeset in Times New Roman 11.5/14 by
Aura Technology and Software Services, India.

ISBN: 978-1-64313-472-7

10 9 8 7 6 5 4 3 2 1

Printed in the United States of America
Distributed by Simon & Schuster

Contents

Part 3: Political Adviser And Military Commander

Also by the same author

Hunting from Hampstead: The Story of Henry and Lucy Stedall and their children, Book Guild Publishing, 2002

A two-volume history of Mary Queen of Scots:

The Challenge to the Crown, Volume I: The Struggle for Influence in the Reign of Mary Queen of Scots 1542-1567, Book Guild Publishing, 2012

The Survival of the Crown, Volume II: The return to Authority of the Scottish Crown following Mary Queen of Scots' Deposition from the Throne, Book Guild Publishing, 2014

Men of Substance: The London Livery Companies' Reluctant Part in the Plantation of Ulster, Austin Macauley Publishers, 2016

Mary Queen of Scots' Downfall: The Life and Murder of Henry, Lord Darnley, Pen & Sword Books Limited, 2017

The Roots of Ireland's Troubles, Pen & Sword Books Limited, 2019

Website: www.maryqueenofscots.net

List of Illustrations

Maps

Picture section

List of Illustrations

Map of England

Map of the Netherlands c. 1586

Drawn by David Atkinson, Hand Made Maps Limited

Family Trees

1. The English Succession

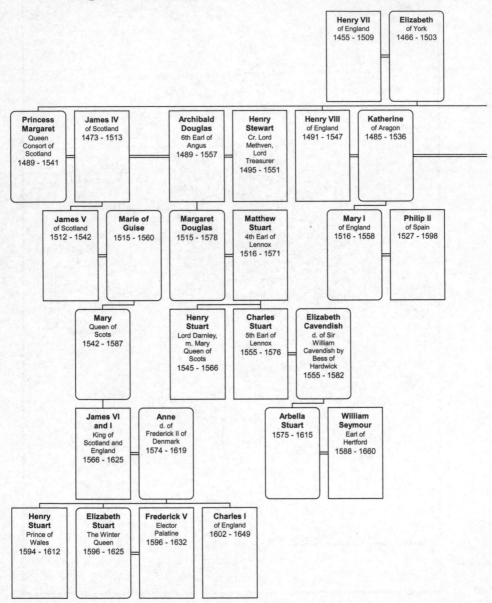

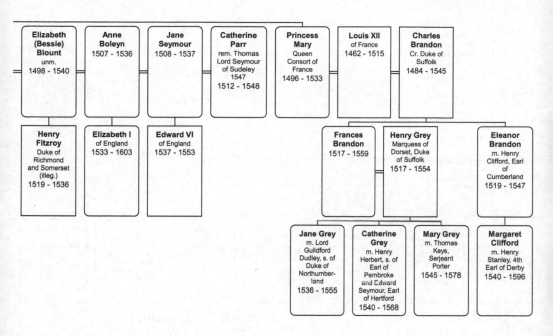

2. The Dudley Family

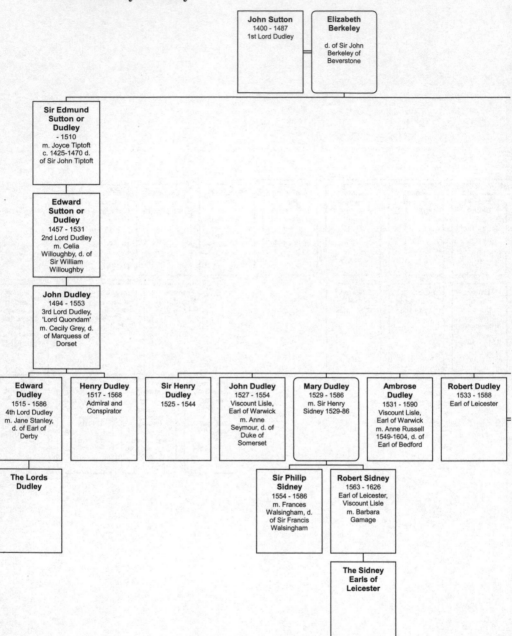

John Sutton
1400 - 1487
1st Lord Dudley

Elizabeth Berkeley
d. of Sir John Berkeley of Beverstone

Sir Edmund Sutton or Dudley
- 1510
m. Joyce Tiptoft
c. 1425-1470 d. of Sir John Tiptoft

Edward Sutton or Dudley
1457 - 1531
2nd Lord Dudley
m. Celia Willoughby, d. of Sir William Willoughby

John Dudley
1494 - 1553
3rd Lord Dudley, 'Lord Quondam'
m. Cecily Grey, d. of Marquess of Dorset

Edward Dudley
1515 - 1586
4th Lord Dudley
m. Jane Stanley, d. of Earl of Derby

Henry Dudley
1517 - 1568
Admiral and Conspirator

Sir Henry Dudley
1525 - 1544

John Dudley
1527 - 1554
Viscount Lisle, Earl of Warwick
m. Anne Seymour, d. of Duke of Somerset

Mary Dudley
1529 - 1586
m. Sir Henry Sidney 1529-86

Ambrose Dudley
1531 - 1590
Viscount Lisle, Earl of Warwick
m. Anne Russell 1549-1604, d. of Earl of Bedford

Robert Dudley
1533 - 1588
Earl of Leicester

The Lords Dudley

Sir Philip Sidney
1554 - 1586
m. Frances Walsingham, d. of Sir Francis Walsingham

Robert Sidney
1563 - 1626
Earl of Leicester, Viscount Lisle
m. Barbara Gamage

The Sidney Earls of Leicester

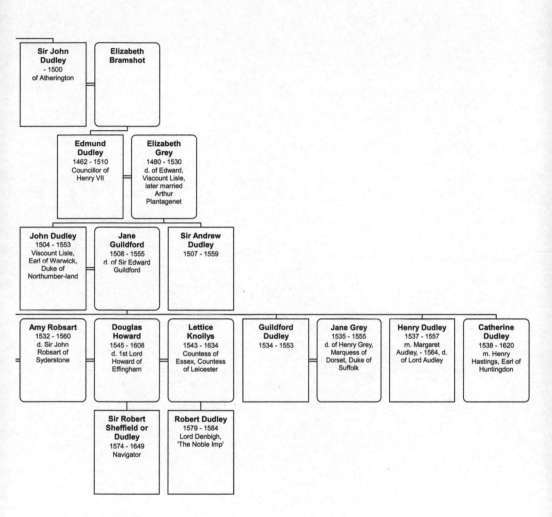

Introduction

I have spent the last sixteen years making an intensive study of Tudor history, and my lack of any academic preconception has allowed me to stand back from the accepted paradigm of the period. The copious records of the political brilliance of William Cecil, Lord Burghley, focus entirely on his undoubted skills but gloss over his devious methods used to belittle his opponents. One example of the praise showered on this preeminent Elizabethan political figure can be found in *The Great Lord Burghley; A Study in Elizabethan Statecraft* by Martin Andrew Sharp Hume written in 1898. Hume can see no wrong in Cecil and he makes corresponding attacks on his enemies. One of the casualties is Mary Queen of Scots, the Catholic heir to the English throne. Most of the evidence for the murder of Lord Darnley emanates from Cecil's records and can be shown to have been falsified, but conventional historians of the past have tied themselves in knots attempting to link together conflicting pieces of unsupportable evidence. In his effort to prevent Mary from succeeding the childless Elizabeth, Cecil encouraged a plot for the murder of her husband, Lord Darnley. He then connived with the Scottish lords opposing her to persuade her to marry the Earl of Bothwell, known to have masterminded the murder. This made their marriage appear like a crime of passion, when she had played no part in the murder or its planning. It was the marriage not the murder which tarnished her name, leading to her imprisonment. Cecil later tried to entrap her into supporting apparently treasonable plots, which he had fabricated, to provide grounds for her execution. It was Lady Antonia Fraser who started to dispel criticism of Mary in her ground-breaking history of 1969, but even she failed to point out Cecil's Machiavellian role in the process of defaming her.

It was not just Mary Queen of Scots. Cecil saw Lord Robert Dudley as a threat to his position as Elizabeth's Secretary of State. It was Cecil who hinted that the untimely death of Robert's first wife, Amy Robsart, might be murder, the motive for which was to enable him to marry the English Queen. It was Cecil who cajoled Elizabeth into pulling back from the marriage, perhaps preventing a Tudor heir from succeeding to the English Crown. As the ultimate politician, he believed that the ends justified the means. Dudley's name has been further tarnished by a libellous Catholic tract, later known as *Leicester's Commonwealth* designed to highlight his Puritan shortcomings. Nevertheless, traditional historians, including William Camden, accepted its scurrilous content at face value.

As with my histories of Mary Queen of Scots, this biography attempts to redress the balance by rehabilitating another of Cecil's victims. No one would pretend that Dudley was faultless any more than was Mary Queen of Scots, despite Lady Antonia's sanitising efforts. Nevertheless, Dudley's shortcomings should not prevent him from standing out as the most interesting and influential personality of the Elizabethan age.

Surprisingly there have been only two histories of Dudley in more recent years, Elizabeth Jenkins's *Elizabeth and Leicester,* published by Victor Gollancz in 1961 and Derek Wilson's *Sweet Robin,* published by Allison & Busby Ltd. in 1981. I owe a debt to both authors for their meticulous research. I have also benefited from research on Lady Jane Grey and on Lettice Knollys by Nicola Tallis and on many other histories of the Tudor period. As always, I have reached my own conclusions from the plausible evidence to provide a fresh assessment of Dudley and his achievements and of the personalities that surrounded him. He was a man of many qualities.

I am most grateful to Claire Hopkins at Pen & Sword History for her advice and support on the production of this biography, and to Karyn Burnham, who has edited the text. Most importantly, I have to thank Liz for putting up with my disappearance for long periods into Tudor history and to my son Oliver, who has rescued me when my computer has failed to respond as promptly as I would like to a well-deserved dose of chastisement!

Robert Stedall

PART 1

PRE-ELIZABETHAN
UPS AND DOWNS

Prologue

There can be no surprise that after the death of a monarch as dominant as Henry VIII, there was the risk of a power vacuum when it came to establishing government for his 9-year-old son, now Edward VI. Under his will, Henry had proposed a Council of Regency of sixteen equals to govern until Edward came of age. Nevertheless, ruling by committee would never be a viable option for those ambitious men, who now surrounded the Crown. The only real hope for the future was Edward's quite extraordinary intellect, moral rectitude, and grasp of politics from a very early age.

The family traditionally dominating positions around the English Crown were the Howards of Norfolk. Thomas Howard, the 3rd Duke had enjoyed glittering early military success with his father, the 2nd Duke, in defeating the Scots at Flodden in 1513. Although he remained among the first choice of military commander for much of Henry's reign, Cardinal Wolsey criticised his belligerent foreign policy. Norfolk also conflicted with rival courtiers by promoting family members as spouses for the ageing King. Initially these marriages gained him royal favour, but when his nieces, Anne Boleyn and Catherine Howard, failed to provide Henry with either hoped-for male heirs or matrimonial harmony, they lost their heads. Norfolk shuffled quickly to disassociate himself from their shortcomings, blaming other members of the voluminous Howard clan for their perceived faults.

A second problem for Norfolk was his adherence to the Roman Catholic faith at a time when Henry was seeking a divorce from Katherine of Aragon. His rearguard Catholic stance was supported by Henry FitzAlan, 19th Earl of Arundel; Thomas Wriothesley, the Lord Chancellor; Stephen Gardiner, Bishop of Winchester and Edmund Bonner, Bishop of London. Even Henry was a traditionalist at heart. As a young man, he had written *Assertio Septem Sacrimentorum* defending the Seven Sacraments of the Catholic faith. In 1521, he was created *Fidei Defensor* (Defender of the Faith) by Pope Leo X. He wanted to retain Catholic dogma but needed the Crown at the head of the English church rather than the Pope. Although Thomas Cranmer, Archbishop of Canterbury, who masterminded Henry's break with Rome and divorce from Katherine of Aragon, leaned the Henrican church towards Reformist thinking, Henry hung tenaciously to traditional worship.

Cranmer, with the Council's support, made several attempts to provide a liturgy to satisfy all sides, but the King remained wary of Reformist dogma. It was only after his marriage to Catherine Parr in 1543 that Reform gained the upper hand. Catherine was devoutly Evangelical (the word 'Protestant' was not used until the 1550s) and she surrounded the court with likeminded thinkers, all of whom supported Cranmer's views. These included her brother, William Parr, 1st Marquess of Northampton; Edward Seymour, 1st Earl of Hertford and his brother Thomas Seymour, the uncles of Prince Edward; Henry Grey, 3rd Marquess of Dorset, married to Frances Brandon, the King's niece, and John Dudley, Viscount Lisle, whose mother was a first cousin of the 1st Marquess of Dorset. This caucus was careful not to challenge the views of the ageing King, but Catherine took Henry's younger children, Elizabeth and Edward, under her wing to ensure that they became well-grounded in Reformed beliefs. With Catherine as queen consort, her allies were able to isolate the traditionalists led by Norfolk, keeping them away from the King.

Henry's focus was on the military abilities of his advisers. By now, it was Hertford and Lisle, who were considered the two most accomplished military commanders in England. Henry had no respect for Dorset. In 1536, he had been sent north to restore order during the Pilgrimage of Grace, a Yorkshire uprising opposing the break with Rome. Dorset had demonstrated complete incompetence, singularly failing in his objectives.

The Howards remained out in the cold. In late 1546, with the King surrounded by Catherine Parr's allies, Norfolk and his son, Henry, Earl of Surrey, 'the most foolish proud boy that ever was in England',[1] attempted a Catholic coup to seize Prince Edward and gain control of the Regency. Not only did this fail, but Surrey had provocatively assumed the royal arms of Edward the Confessor as part of his personal heraldry. They were both arrested and sent to the Tower on charges of treason. On 19 January 1547, Surrey was beheaded and Norfolk was attainted by statute without trial. Although Henry reportedly approved Norfolk's execution on his deathbed, his life was saved by the King's demise on the following day. He was lucky. Henry had been quoted as saying: 'I never spared man in my anger nor woman in my lust.'[2]

Norfolk's fall from grace enabled Catherine's Evangelical allies to surround the new King, Edward VI, who was not yet 10 years old. Although it was the custom for those condemned by the late King to be included in a general amnesty at his successor's coronation, Norfolk remained imprisoned in the Tower of London throughout Edward's reign. During this time his estates fell prey to members of the young King's Council. He was only released and pardoned in 1553, when Mary Tudor became Queen. Meanwhile, his grandson and heir, Thomas, was left to spend his young manhood disgraced in the country.

Although they had been close allies, Henry's death set the stage for a showdown between Hertford and Lisle. It was never a contest, as Hertford was the uncle of the young King, and Lisle had no immediate ambition to supersede him. Nevertheless, Hertford was extremely suspicious of his rival's motives. He did his best to demean him, putting their former warm friendship under pressure. What had been extraordinary was Lisle's mercurial rise from most unpromising beginnings to become the second man behind the throne.

Chapter 1

John Dudley, Viscount Lisle

During the medieval era, the Sutton family was of no great substance or significance, but in the reign of Edward II (1308–27), it acquired the impregnable Dudley Castle as a perquisite of John Sutton's marriage to Margaret de Somery. In addition to the Lordship of Dudley, Margaret provided estates in Worcestershire and Staffordshire.[1] Although family members were initially known as the Suttons of Dudley, by the 1450s they had dropped the Sutton name, so that the 1st Baron called himself John 'Dudley'. Quite remarkably, he tiptoed unscathed round the pitfalls of the Wars of the Roses and lived to welcome Henry VII as King after the Battle of Bosworth. He was by then aged 84 and had outlived his eldest son. On his death two years later, the title passed to his grandson, Edward. It was John's second son, Sir John Dudley of Atherington, who demonstrated all the ambition that his nephew, Edward Lord Dudley, lacked. With Henry VII being King, Sir John was picked as Sheriff of Sussex and served the Tudors in local government capacities until his death in 1500.[2]

Sir John's eldest son, Edmund, was born in about 1462. Although his father and grandfathers had been soldiers, he had an aptitude for the law and was educated at Oxford University and Gray's Inn. By 1485, he was already an up-and-coming lawyer, enjoying the patronage of Sir Reginald Bray, one of the most influential of the new King's advisers. Bray was a member of 'the King's Council Learned in the Law',[3] which acted as a special court for trying financial cases, but in practice operated as a royal debt collection agency. Through Bray's connections, Edmund became Under-Sheriff of London in about 1499 and Speaker of the House of Commons in 1504. Before the year was out, he was a member of the Privy Council and had also joined the Council Learned in the Law in his own right.[4] These posts were lucrative, and he soon extended his estates into Sussex and Hampshire and acquired extensive acreages elsewhere.

He also had a fine house in Candlewick Street in London, next door to his fellow Council colleague, Sir Richard Empson.

With Henry VII's thirst to augment the royal coffers, Dudley and Empson had the task of pressurising wealthier subjects by ferreting among private papers to establish land and other revenue sources that had been concealed. 'They devised ways to exploit long defunct feudal laws to the advantage of the exchequer.'[5] Despite being well rewarded by a grateful sovereign, 'no mean quantity stuck to their fingers'.[6] They perverted justice for their own ends as the representatives of a grasping and despotic King. In 1509, when Henry VII lay dying, they took measures for their own protection. 'At their petition, the Council entered into a recognizance to hold no individual member guilty of crimes permitted in pursuance of Royal policy.'[7] Although they had agreed to muster in Candlewick Street in the event of trouble, the new King, Henry VIII, was ready 'to disembarrass the government of unpopular members'[8] and acted quickly to sacrifice them before they could escape.

The Council's recognisance was deemed 'contrary to law, reason and good conscience'[9] and was set aside. Dudley and Empson were charged with treason on the absurd grounds of having conspired 'to seize the King and his Council by force and to govern according to [their] will'.[10] After conviction, they were confined to the Tower to await attainder and possible execution. It had been Henry VII, in his effort to benefit the Royal exchequer, who had encouraged them to act as they did, shutting 'his eyes to the way they performed'. This made them 'rightly the victim[s] of public hatred'.[11] Their execution 'was the only imaginable retribution for a career of enthusiastic villainy'.[12]

Dudley remained in the Tower for sixteen months, during which time he wrote *The Tree of Commonwealth,* an allegorical political treatise of advice for the new King. It is a book of breadth and wisdom, revealing the humanity of a man 'who had thought deeply about the affairs of kings and subjects, a brilliant lawyer, capable of marshalling his thoughts to achieve the utmost clarity and impact'.[13] He admitted that his 'own life hath been so wicked and so openly known',[14] and demonstrated that loyalty to King and loyalty to country could not always be combined.[15] He advised Henry VIII 'to avoid the avarice and the manipulation of the law which had been his father's weaknesses'.[16] The young King disregarded Dudley's treatise, and it remained hidden in the Royal Archives for centuries, although Dudley's son held a transcript. On 17 August 1510,

Empson and Dudley were beheaded at Tower Hill, but there was some sympathy for their predicament. Edmund avoided a traitor's grave and was buried at the Church of Blackfriars in the City, with his attainder being reversed.

Dudley left a widow, Elizabeth Grey, and five children. She was the daughter of Viscount Lisle and, within fifteen months as a relatively wealthy lady, she remarried Arthur Plantagenet, an illegitimate son of Edward IV. In 1523, following the deaths of her elder siblings, Arthur became Viscount Lisle in right of his wife. With the Tudors keeping tabs on their Plantagenet rivals, even though illegitimate, Arthur was retained at court as an esquire to the bodyguard of the King with a quarterly salary of £6 13*s*. 4*d*. With Edmund's attainder having been reversed, Arthur received the benefit of most of the Dudley lands. With Elizabeth's eldest son, John Dudley, being aged only 8 at his father's execution, he was made a ward of the Crown. In accordance with usual practice, the wardship was acquired by Sir Edward Guildford, an old friend of his father's. This entitled Guildford to the benefit of John's inheritance until he reached his majority in return for providing him with a home and education.

Guildford was a major landowner in Kent and Sussex; he was also Master of the Ordnance and later Warden of the Cinque Ports and Marshal of Calais.[17] When he was 9, John Dudley moved to live with Guildford's family at High Halden near Tenterden in Kent. Guildford 'was the ideal man to give his young ward a solid grounding both in estate management and also the accomplishments of a courtier'.[18] With no sons of his own, he developed a strong bond with his ward, doing much to restore the Dudley family fortunes. 'At an early age, John was betrothed to Sir Edward's daughter, Jane, and when they were old enough they were married.'[19] Despite this being an arranged marriage, they developed 'a deep and lasting affection',[20] during which she bore him thirteen children.[21] On Guildford's death, the couple inherited his substantial estates.

Although John arrived at court as a man of comparatively modest means, he soon made his mark. 'In 1521 he was a member of Cardinal Wolsey's entourage on a diplomatic mission to France.'[22] Yet it was as a soldier that he first achieved recognition. In 1523, he served as an officer in France under Charles Brandon, Duke of Suffolk, and was knighted by the Duke for his gallantry while fighting at the crossing of the Somme.[23] He also made his name in the lists. At Christmas 1524, he excelled at a tourney at Greenwich, and became 'one of the great champions of the tilt-yard and frequently rode in the royal team against foreign challengers'.[24] Yet he remained at a disadvantage after his father's execution and attainder. The court was full of ambitious young men, often well-connected to leading noblemen and ministers. Despite enjoying his father-in-law's patronage, Guildford lacked 'the prestige to advance Dudley to the topmost rungs of Royal service'.[25] Nevertheless, as a young knight Sir John gained the support of Wolsey and Thomas Cromwell, and later of the King.[26] Being a shrewd judge of character, the King 'saw a man after his own heart, a man who embodied all the virtues of medieval chivalry. Guildford's protégé was tall, darkly handsome, full of charm and recklessly brave.'[27] The young knight was soon 'marked out as a commander whom foes respected and soldiers happily followed'.[28] He became 'a favourite companion of Henry in the tilt-yard and in the hunting field; an unquestioning supporter of royal policy who proved his loyalty in combat of arms and (later) in House of Commons debate'.[29]

It was helpful that Sir John's brother, Sir Andrew, was also proving a successful soldier, 'content to follow his elder brother's lead'.[30] Sir John was no 'empty-headed swashbuckler but a strategist and tactician of the front rank'.[31] He inherited his father's incisive intelligence, applying it 'to the achievement of personal wealth and power'.[32] He avowed Protestant sympathies and as a practical royal servant, 'the King's cause was his cause'.[33] Like most men close to the Crown, he benefited from the purchase and sale of property made available after the dissolution of the monasteries. This spurred him on to seek the acquisition of the family's ancient Midlands estates.

Sir John's father's cousin, Edward, 2nd Lord Dudley, died in January 1532. He had already pawned much of his patrimony to enable him to cut an impressive figure at court. Although his son John inherited as the 3rd Lord Dudley, he was a 'simpleton' with a thirst for ready money. If Sir John could raise the wherewithal, Dudley Castle and its surrounding estates could be his. On 3 July 1532, he turned to his wealthy connections, the Earl of Shrewsbury, Lord de la Warr, Lord Maltravers (Arundel's son) and others for finance and purchased his family's properties for £4,200. This did not endear him to the 8th Lord's heirs, who believed that they had been cheated of their inheritance. Despite their appeals to Thomas Cromwell,

Sir John was already too secure in the King's favour.[34] 'As he prospered, relatives and acquaintances swallowed their pride and clamoured for his patronage.'[35] Gradually, he transferred his powerbase from the south-east 'to make Dudley Castle the centre of a much-augmented barony'.[36] He employed Sir William Sharington, one of the most talented designers in England, to rebuild the castle's accommodation as a manor house.

In 1533, with Guildford now being infirm, Sir John replaced him as Master of the Tower Armoury. On Guildford's death in the following year, he inherited his estates in Kent and Sussex despite facing a legal challenge from Guildford's nephew. He was also returned for Guildford's seat in the House of Commons, attending the last few sessions of the momentous 'Reformation' Parliament. He acquired Ely Place, the substantial home of the former bishops of Ely in Holborn, as a London residence for his family. This occupied ten acres of gardens stretching towards Islington. Jane and their children spent most of the winter months there, while she attended court.[37] By this time, their eldest son Henry was about 8. He was followed by Mary, John, Margaret, Ambrose and Catherine. On 24 June 1533, they christened another son, Robert. He was followed in 1534 by Guildford and later by a second Henry and Charles (who died young). Four other children did not survive infancy.

Sir John inspired deep devotion among those with whom he was associated, and there was a genuine warmth between husband, wife and children. 'His sons, when they grew to manhood, supported him loyally.'[38] He paid careful attention to their education and training despite lacking an academic background; he had learned no Latin and spoke indifferent French. Yet he corresponded with theologians like Cranmer and Hooper and was a patron of scholars such as Thomas Wilson, Walter Haddon and John Cheke.[39] Although he was trained as a soldier and courtier, on becoming Lord High Admiral in 1543, he took a close interest in maritime navigation, leading on to mathematics, cosmography and astronomy.[40]

Sir John's lack of scholarship was compensated by his wife's considerable intellect. Jane had been influenced by the brilliant academics of her age. As a child, she had studied at the royal school attended by Henry VIII's daughter, the Princess Mary, and by Catherine Parr, under the great Spanish humanist, Juan Luys Vives. His book, *The Education of a Christian Woman,* became a lasting influence on the devout and learned ladies at court. These also included Margaret

More, Anne Bacon, Mildred Cooke, another brilliant scholar, who later married William Cecil, and Katherine Willoughby, who became the second wife of Charles Brandon, Duke of Suffolk. While Jane encouraged her children in their education, they also enjoyed the traditional pursuits of well-to-do families, including training in the use of arms, horsemanship and the chase.[41] Henry, the eldest, showed aptitude as a soldier, but John was more artistic and scholarly. Ambrose was also serious-minded and puritanical with an interest in theological debate. Catherine was to become the devout and pious wife of the Calvinist Henry Hastings, heir to Francis 2nd Earl of Huntingdon.[42] Robert was tall, handsome and athletic, loving most sports. He had little natural aptitude in the school room, but he shared his father's fascination for mathematics.[43] In 1564, Roger Ascham was still criticising Robert's preference for geometry and his shortcomings in Latin and other languages.[44] Nevertheless, 'it was interest in the new sciences, coupled with a love of adventure, which inspired Robert's generation of young gentlemen to be the patrons and captains of the great era of Elizabethan maritime expansion'.[45] Much later he acted as a patron for academics writing books on navigation.

Although Sir John was appointed Master of the Horse in 1540 for the new Queen, Anne of Cleves, it was renewed warfare in the 1540s that enabled him to prove his worth with the King. Henry was once more embarked on an aggressive foreign policy to undo the alliance between France and Scotland. It was Prince Edward's uncle, Hertford and his close ally, Sir John, who rose to the challenge. In 1542, on the death of his stepfather, Arthur Plantagenet, Sir John inherited as Viscount Lisle. In that autumn, Hertford and Lisle were posted to the Scottish border. In November, with Hertford being nervous at being positioned too far from court, he asked to be released as Lord Warden and Keeper of his Grace's Marches towards Scotland and was succeeded by Lisle.[46] Two months later, Lisle succeeded Hertford as Lord High Admiral. This was a huge strategic step for him. With its increasing firepower, the English navy's original role in transporting troops to different theatres of action was being progressively enhanced, and Henry was lavishing care and pride on it. Despite his long-term interest in navigation, Lisle rapidly needed to overcome his shortcomings in naval tactics when compared to the captains under his command. He worked tirelessly and, under his tenure of office, the Navy Board was founded as 'a Government department to cater for the needs of ships and sailors'.[47]

> He established the first floating academy for English captains under the greatest living expert, Sebastian Cabot [Cabot was the son of the Venetian, John Cabot, who had made his home in England. Both father and son were the most noted explorers of their day]. [Lisle] patronized scientific scholars like John Dee and William Cunningham. He encouraged and backed enterprising captains and it was during his period of supreme power (1549–1553) that the first official English expeditions began to explore the farthest reaches of the Atlantic, the Levant and the coast of Africa. This stage of maritime expansion culminated in the departure of Sir Hugh Willoughby's fleet questing a north-east passage.[48]

It can be no surprise that Lisle's sons shared their father's enthusiasm for overseas adventure and that Ambrose and Robert were to become prime movers in the colonial expansion of Elizabethan England.[49] Lisle's considerable worth was rewarded. In April 1543, he was admitted to the Order of the Garter and was appointed a member of the Privy Council, although his other duties prevented his regular attendance. This was no mean feat for a man whose father had been executed for treason.

Ely Place was not just the Dudley home, it was Lisle's place of business. He used it to preside over sessions of the High Court of Admiralty, 'hearing complaints about piracy, evasions of harbour dues and plundering of wrecks'.[50] In the spring of 1544, he commanded the fleet which carried Hertford on what became known as the first of the 'Rough Wooings' against Scotland. This was a lightning foray, designed to coerce the Scots into agreeing the betrothal of the infant Mary Queen of Scots to Prince Edward. While the expedition was entirely successful in laying Edinburgh and the area surrounding the Firth of Forth to waste, it failed completely to achieve Scottish agreement to the proposed marriage. The outcome was counterproductive. Henry's belligerence only pushed the Scots into the welcoming arms of France with the betrothal of Mary Queen of Scots to the infant French Dauphin.

Yet Prince Edward always hoped that Mary would become his bride, seeing their union as the means of settling England's difficulties on its northern border.

Hertford sent Lisle south with a letter to report the success of the military mission to the English King. Lisle seemingly put pressure on Hertford to be accorded a proper share of the credit for their success. Hertford obliged and was heartfelt in his praise, writing:

> Pleaseth Your Highness to be advertised that, for as much as my Lord Admiral repaireth unto your Majesty, I can do no less than to recommend him unto your Highness as one who has served you hardly, wisely, diligently, painfully, and as obediently as any that I have seen, most (humbly) beseeching your Majesty, that he may perceive by your Highness that we have not forgotten him.[51]

This suggests that Lisle already feared that Hertford might see him as a future rival. His concerns were to prove correct.

While Lisle seems to have been diffident of his own political abilities, there was no doubting his military prowess. After completing his term on the Scottish border, he was recalled to London to prepare for a new campaign against the French. Having transported the royal army of 40,000 men led by Suffolk (Henry's old comrade-in-arms) safely across the Channel, Lisle was appointed second-in-command at the siege of Boulogne. With Hertford still considered the most able English commander, he too was brought from London to oversee Boulogne's capture, leaving Catherine Parr to act as Regent. On 13 September 1544, Henry entered the City in high spirits at the head of his victorious forces. Although Lisle received his share of praise, tragically, his eldest son Henry was killed during preliminary skirmishing. Although English losses were few, the campaign was ruinously expensive, and Boulogne was of little strategic importance. (It was restored to the French six years' later after Lisle became Protector.) Lisle was appointed Governor of Boulogne, tasked with rebuilding and strengthening its fortifications to put it into a state of defence, while retaining his post as Lord High Admiral. He showed his worth, harrying French shipping and harbours. In 1545, with the French dominating the Channel, he warded off a French invasion attempt on England.[52]

It was the marriage of Henry VIII to Catherine Parr at Hampton Court on 12 July 1543 which had really enhanced the Dudley family's standing. Lisle was abroad on naval duties at the time, but Jane attended the wedding in a service that closely followed Catholic dogma. Only the educated classes were permitted to read the Bible and the clergy remained celibate. Yet Catherine established a moderate reforming clique in the King's immediate circle, 'which the forces of reaction were powerless to remove'.[53] To the disappointment of the Catholic ambassadors, it embraced growing Humanist and Evangelical sentiments. Like the Seymours, Lisle and his wife were at its centre as enthusiastic propagandists for the Reformation.[54] Its key members included Hertford, Queen Catherine Parr, Katherine Willoughby (the Dowager Duchess of Suffolk), Anne Stanhope (Countess of Hertford) and Jane Guildford. When the King died three-and-a-half years later, they were 'in an unassailable position ... and ready to lead England farther along the road of Reformation during the reign of Edward VI'.[55] It was their ascendancy that resulted in Hertford and Lisle becoming the leading figures at court in the last months of Henry's reign.

Catherine Parr, aged 31 at her marriage to the ageing King, proved a model wife, providing a home for his two younger children, Elizabeth and Edward, at the royal manor of Ashridge. She gained their genuine affection and the 10-year-old Elizabeth became deeply attached to her stepmother, while also enjoying the company of her half-brother, Edward, with whom she corresponded. Up to this time, she had suffered an upbringing which encompassed the tragedies of the executions of her mother and Catherine Howard, and the death after childbirth of Jane Seymour. It is understandable that this highly strung but intelligent girl suffered bouts of childhood hysteria. The one stabilising influence was her governess, Kat Champernowne of a family of minor gentry, who provided her early education. In 1545, Kat married Sir John Ashley, a cousin of the Boleyns, but remained in Elizabeth's service despite having children of her own.

Although Catherine Parr's household did not always remain under one roof, contact was maintained 'through a continual interchange of letters and gifts'.[56] She maintained permanent establishments at Westminster and Hampton Court, but if plague broke out, Edward was moved to Copthall or to join Elizabeth at Ashridge. Catherine continued to supervise Elizabeth's and Edward's education, providing them with their own households and tutors. These were mainly academics 'from Cambridge, the home of the English Reformation'.[57] They adhered to humanist principles and proved enlightened and sensitive teachers. The two most influential were John Cheke, Edward's second tutor, and his friend Roger Ascham with responsibility for Elizabeth, both graduates of St John's College. Under Catherine's supervision, Cheke ran a small private school for Edward and his companions. He imbued them with an enthusiasm for learning by 'the sweetness and easiness'[58] of his methods, profoundly influencing Edward's religious and political thinking. Edward thrived in the care of Cheke, whose, 'integrity, devotion and outspokenness were in marked contrast to the sycophancy of the courtiers still trying to climb into the King's favour by distracting him from the strenuous but varied routine devised by his tutors.'[59]

Cheke later became a Member of Parliament and Clerk to the Privy Council. He was knighted and was, for a short time, Secretary of State to both Edward and Dorset's daughter, Lady Jane Grey. It was through him that his brother-in-law William Cecil was employed, initially by Hertford soon after he became Protector, as his master of requests. This positioned him to deal with all those seeking Hertford's (later Somerset's) help and influence, a role which could be lucrative. Roger Ascham was a connection of Kat Ashley's husband. He believed that no education 'ought to be learnt with bondage ... Whatsoever the mind doth learn unwillingly, with fear, the same doth quickly forget'.[60] He:

> was the educational genius of the century. Not only was he
> a brilliant teacher, but his cast of mind was enlightened to a
> degree never yet surpassed. He expressed his loathing of the
> brutal severity commonly used by masters. ... He imparted
> a sense of stability to [Elizabeth's] desperate existence,
> and she seized upon the support he gave with a passionate
> tenacity.[61]

Although he supervised Elizabeth's teaching, he was not always in attendance. From 1544 to 1548 her tutor was Ascham's protégé, the loveable William Grindall, who taught her Greek and Latin. When Grindall died of the plague in January 1548, Elizabeth persuaded Catherine Parr to arrange for Ascham to come himself. He stayed for two years, but remained connected to her studies, eulogising over her abilities until his death.[62] He was also in regular attendance on Edward to assist with his writing, which he found 'rather irksome'.[63]

By 1546, Henry VIII had become feverish from his ulcerated legs, and senior courtiers were positioning themselves for the inevitability of a regency when Edward inherited the throne. His accession would make Lisle one of a 'handful of men in the very top echelon of power'.[64] It became important for these powerful men that their children should attend classes arranged for Edward and Elizabeth. Edward already had close companions in Barnaby Fitzpatrick, eldest son of the Lord of Upper Ossery in Ireland, and Henry Sidney, whose father had been a squire to the body of Henry VIII. In about 1545, they were joined by Edward Seymour, Hertford's son; Henry Brandon, who had recently succeeded as 2nd Duke of Suffolk; and Robert Dudley, despite them being a few years older. This brought Robert, who was 12, into close contact with his contemporary, the Princess Elizabeth. Although her academic talent far outstripped his, they became close friends, sharing interests in 'riding, the chase and dancing'.[65]

Robert was soon well-established at court. As he had two surviving elder brothers, he was not involved in political training or in the management of the family's burgeoning estates.[66] With his extrovert temperament, his interest was in emulating his father's successes in the tiltyard and other martial arts, particularly fencing. He also benefited from the schooling provided by royal tutors, particularly William Buckley, with his novel methods of teaching mathematics. Theology was taught exclusively by protestant preachers, including Hugh Latimer, Archbishop Cranmer and Nicholas Ridley.[67] They provided 'a profound and precise grounding in Protestant theology'.[68] When Latimer lashed out at corruption and greed in court life, so conscience-stricken was his audience that he secretly received £500 over two years from men who had defrauded the Government.

Prince Edward, who was pious and zealous beyond his years, cooperated to ensure that his household was a godly one, rereading sermons for discussion with his fellow students. Yet, he also enjoyed a more relaxed and jovial side with sports, recreations and court revels. This brought him into closer contact with Robert. Some of the young Prince's slightly older playfellows induced him to adopt thundering oaths, which they claimed were appropriate to his sovereign dignity. The culprits, when discovered, duly received a 'sharp whipping'.[69]

Lisle had now reached the forefront of public esteem, seen as England's greatest general, a status which will have rankled with Hertford.[70] He held the convoluted title of Lieutenant General of the Army and Armada upon the Sea in Outward Parts against the French. In July 1545, he entertained the King with his household at Portsmouth on board the *Henri Grâce à Dieu*. On Suffolk's death in the next month, he was catapulted into the void left by Henry's lifelong companion, playing cards with the King until well into his sleepless nights. On 29 January 1547, two days before the King's death, Eustace Chapuys, the Imperial Ambassador, wrote: 'Seymour and Dudley will have the management of affairs, because apart from the king's affection for them … there are no other nobles of a fit age and ability for the task.'[71]

Chapter 2

The Seymour brothers' rivalry

Henry VIII died on 28 January 1547. He had lain unconscious for several days beforehand, making it difficult to ascertain his final wishes, and these were interpreted by those surrounding the death bed to their advantage. Henry had nominated his son Edward, then aged 9, to succeed him, followed by his two daughters, Mary and Elizabeth, notwithstanding that each had previously been declared illegitimate by Acts of Parliament. As soon as he expired, Hertford rode through the night with Sir Anthony Browne to Prince Edward's residence at Ashridge. He gave immediate instructions for the Prince and his household to be moved to Enfield, the winter residence of the Princess Elizabeth. Robert Dudley and his colleagues 'were busy for several hours in supervising the packing of chests and carts for the twenty-mile journey'.[1] It was not until their arrival that the royal children were advised by Hertford of their father's death. The demise of such a dominating figure left an enormous chasm in their lives, leaving the whole atmosphere subdued. Edward sobbed with apprehension in his sister's arms, while Hertford and Browne 'knelt in homage' to him.[2]

Hertford had no time to indulge in 'shocked inertia'.[3] Although Henry had placed power in the hands of a 'Committee of Equals', common sense dictated that a powerful individual was needed at the helm. As the King's uncle, Hertford was the logical choice and he assumed the title of Lord Protector. He was 'a dry, sour, opinionated man', but his new status was not questioned by other members of the Council, and Lisle wholeheartedly supported him. Gardiner, who was an articulate and dangerous opponent, strongly resisted his appointment in his efforts to retain Henrician doctrine. His role was now reduced to that of organising the mourning for Henry VIII, and even then only under Cranmer's supervision. There was also a half-hearted objection from Thomas Wriothesley, the Lord Chancellor, another with Catholic affiliations.

To accord with the King's apparent wishes, the new Council granted themselves titles of a higher rank than before. The new Lord Protector became Duke of Somerset, with Lisle being made Earl of Warwick, a title chosen because he was a distant connection of the Beauchamp Earls. The former Earldom had died with Warwick 'the Kingmaker', whose daughter Anne had married Richard III. Wriothesley was bought off with the Earldom of Southampton, and the Protector's ally, Sir William Paget, became a Knight of the Garter, as did Dorset (although he was not made a member of the Council). Sir John, Lord Russell, was granted lands at Woburn in Bedfordshire. The most influential members of the Council were now Somerset, Warwick, Cranmer and Paget. Cranmer was in an unassailable position as the mastermind of the English Reformation. Within a few weeks, Southampton was forced to hand over his role as Lord Chancellor to Somerset, who also claimed the roles of High Steward, Lord Treasurer and Earl Marshal of England.

With Warwick's ambition for land and wealth, he pressed hard for the grant of Warwick Castle, hoping to make it the focal point of his Midland estates. He had never envisaged himself in a position of supreme power and harboured no jealousy over Somerset becoming Protector. From the outset, it is apparent that Somerset felt isolated while trying to establish his authority, and he, not Warwick, should be blamed for 'sowing the seeds of enmity' between them.[4] With his military achievements making him universally popular, Warwick seemed a threatening rival whose authority needed to be curbed. Although he was granted the purely ceremonial office of Lord Great Chamberlain, it rankled with him when forced to resign as Lord High Admiral, so that the role could be granted to Thomas Seymour. It had been lucrative and he had devoted great energy to it. He had no respect for Thomas, who had served under him as Vice Admiral. Thomas had caused 'his superior considerable trouble by inadequate performance of his duties and scandalous patronage of pirates'.[5] He had turned a blind eye to their looting of ships, in return for sharing in the spoils. Nevertheless, Warwick was now left free to attend council meetings, where he could develop his political abilities. His tactic was to encourage his son Robert, whose status was now enhanced as an earl's son, to reinforce the family's friendship and influence with the young King.

Thomas was extremely jealous of his brother's appointment as Lord Protector and was 'a restless ambitious ne'er-do-well'.[6] He was always a thorn in Somerset's side, despite being 'somewhat empty of matter', though 'brilliantly good looking'.[7] 'He had only to enter a room for everyone to stop talking and turn to stare at him.'[8] As the younger uncle of the young King, he went out of his way to charm people of both sexes to advance his career. He had fulfilled diplomatic roles on behalf of the Crown and was indisputably persuasive. In 1539, he escorted Anne of Cleves from Calais to London to meet Henry. Yet he lacked ability and was thoroughly mistrusted by Somerset. Having been nominated to the Regency Council on behalf of Edward VI, Somerset's offer of the role of Lord High Admiral, hitherto held by Warwick, left him at his brother's beck and call to spend long stretches on his naval duties abroad. As a sop, Thomas was created Lord Seymour with the grant of the idyllic Sudeley Castle in Gloucestershire in addition to other valuable estates. This did not prevent him from scheming to unseat his brother, and he was prone to 'outbursts of spiteful bad temper when he did not get what he wanted'.

In accordance with tradition, the first few days of the new reign were spent by the court in the uncomfortable surroundings of the Tower while secure government was established. Its royal suite, which had remained unoccupied since the death of Anne Boleyn, was hastily made ready with furnishings from the Wardrobe Tower. Robert was present when Edward made a well-rehearsed speech for the investiture of new council members with their titles.[9] Two days later, Edward was radiant when he was greeted by the 'people's wild acclaim'[10] as he processed through the streets thronged with cheering Londoners from the Tower to Westminster for his coronation. One commentator exclaimed: 'Your heart would melt to hear him named – the beautifullest creature that liveth under the sun; the wittiest, the most amiable and gentlest thing of all the world.'[11] He had never been in better health. Dorset was given the honour of carrying the Sword of State in front of the King, who was followed by several thousand men-at-arms. Robert also played a prominent role.[12] As an earl's son, he will have been positioned towards the front of the procession. When the King conferred six knighthoods, as was the custom, one of these was granted to Warwick's eldest surviving son John, now Viscount Lisle. During the coronation ceremony conducted by Cranmer at Westminster Abbey, Edward was created Supreme Head of the Church of England, a role which became 'the mainspring of his life'.[13] He was established as an absolute monarch but was expected to defer to the Protector's advice.

After several days of festivities, during which Thomas Seymour particularly excelled himself in the tournaments, normality returned. Somerset saw to it that Edward's household resumed its routine of lessons, games and sermons. Nevertheless, the King was also expected to keep court. He took his meals seated on a cushioned chair of state served by his kneeling comrades, made up of a privileged coterie, shielded from the outside world by the Protector and the Council. Solemn ceremonial was now punctuated with sporting pastimes enjoyed with Robert and others of the King's young companions. They were also involved in entertainments, with costumes being needed for six masques, probably for the Shrovetide revels. 'By 1551, the King's household boasted eighteen trumpeters, two lutenists, one harpist, one rebec player, seven viol players, four sackbut players, one bagpiper, eight minstrels and several singing men.'[14] Edward was learning the lute and virginals himself. He also practised dancing, archery, and took part in real tennis, hunting and running at the ring (a game to practise jousting by charging at a ring suspended on a rope with a lance), but the natural desire to protect him from injury limited his involvement with his 'more expendable companions'.[15] Although he enjoyed playing cards and chess, Ascham discouraged gambling.

Thomas Seymour looked for any means to promote his standing, which his brother seemed to be thwarting. His first ploy was to approach Dorset through an intermediary in London to suggest that he could arrange for Jane Grey to become betrothed to his nephew, the young King, who was a year her junior. With Henry VIII having always hoped to arrange Edward's betrothal to Mary Queen of Scots, no alternatives had been considered, but in July 1548, Mary set out for France as the intended bride of the French Dauphin. This left Edward open to offers, with Somerset hoping that he might arrange his marriage to one of his daughters. Marriage to Edward was not a connection that the Dorsets are likely to have considered for Jane, and there is no doubt that they were flattered and excited at the prospect, which would be extremely advantageous for them. Despite their initial scepticism, when Thomas offered the Dorsets a tempting loan of £2,000, they were won over.[16] They agreed that Jane should move with her attentive tutor, John Aylmer, from their family home at Bradgate Park in Leicestershire to live, from February 1547, as Thomas's ward in his household at the palatial Seymour Place in the Strand. Jane, who was aged 10, was blissfully ignorant of the intrigue. She was easily won over by Thomas and described him as 'a loving and kindly father',[17] although she did not see him frequently. There can be little doubt that separation from the torment of a stringent upbringing at home and from her frivolous younger sisters suited Jane, and she flourished under Aylmer's tutelage in the indulgent environment provided by her guardian.

Thomas's next ploy was to consider his own marriage. He had been romantically linked to Catherine Parr during her widowhood (following the death in 1543 of her second husband, Sir John Nevill, 3rd Lord Latimer) prior to her marriage to Henry VIII. Yet when she became attached to the household of the Princess Mary, she had caught the eye of the ageing King, and saw it as her duty to accept his marriage proposal, rather than the infinitely more glamorous Thomas. Thomas was quickly removed from view with appointments as ambassador and later Marshal of the royal army in the Netherlands. He was abroad when the royal marriage took place, but later held senior military posts in England, including that of Lord Warden of the Cinque Ports. In the meantime, he worked hard to secure a royal marriage for himself, becoming romantically linked to Mary Howard, Duchess of Richmond, the widow of Henry's illegitimate son, Henry Fitzroy. Following Henry VIII's death, he even approached his brother to seek marriage to the Princess Elizabeth, now 14, and later to the Princess Mary, now 32, but Somerset told him in no uncertain terms that 'neither of them was born to be king, nor to marry a king's daughter'.[18] Undaunted, Thomas rekindled his courtship of Catherine Parr, who was living at Chelsea Manor with the Princess Elizabeth, now deeply attached to her stepmother. Catherine was a tall, attractive woman of almost 35, who had been left extremely wealthy under Henry VIII's will. Furthermore, she had always been in love with Thomas. She later wrote to him: 'As truly as God is God, my mind was fully bent the other time I was at liberty, to marry you before any man I know.'[19]

Soon after Jane Grey's arrival at Seymour Place, Catherine and Thomas became lovers, but with Catherine still in mourning they were forced to conduct their relationship in secret. He visited her at dead of night and they were clandestinely married in May 1547. With Catherine retaining her apartments at the royal palaces, the young King, who had been advised of the secret at an early stage, gave it his blessing. He continued to visit them when she was at court, enabling Thomas to gain private access to him to work out the best way to break the news to Somerset.

Somerset was furious when he heard, and the Princess Mary also disapproved of their indecent haste, but Thomas moved into Chelsea Manor, bringing Jane Grey with him. This was a positive development for Jane and her parents, who were admirers of Catherine and could only approve. Although she remained Thomas's ward, she could now spend more time with Catherine, who welcomed her with open arms, while her tutor, John Aylmer, continued to encourage her in her studies.

Thomas's marriage to Catherine met with the strong disapproval of Somerset's second wife, Ann Stanhope, 'a woman for many imperfections intolerable, and for pride monstrous, subtle and violent'.[20] She had already arranged for Somerset's children by his first wife, Catherine Fillol, whom he had divorced in 1535, to be declared illegitimate and she attempted to dominate her husband, undermining his authority. She now claimed precedence at court as the wife of the Protector. Catherine Parr had disapproved of Somerset's appointment as Lord Protector, believing, as King Edward's stepmother, that she should have become Regent herself. As the Queen Dowager, she also claimed seniority, resulting in some unseemly elbowing between the sisters-in-law. She was within her rights, and Thomas showed her great deference at court to demonstrate her superior rank.

Elizabeth remained at Chelsea Manor. She was left short of money, as her £3,000 settlement under the will of Henry VIII was not paid to her during Somerset's Protectorate. She was developing into an attractive young lady and, with her stepmother's love and devotion, was beginning to flourish.[21] Catherine continued to shape the religious thinking of all her charges. She had already published *The Lamentations of a Sinner*, a popular religious pamphlet with a preface by Cecil, who did not spare her blushes with his fulsome praise. It dazzled her charges with her intellect.[22] With the help of Archbishop Cranmer, Edward 'began introducing a series of religious reforms that revolutionized the English church, placing it firmly in the realms of the Protestant movement that was growing on the continent'.[23]

Elizabeth was always reported by Ascham to be a remarkably gifted student. Yet even he saw that the abilities of the precociously talented Jane Grey were superior to those of his own pupil. Jane was soon corresponding with Protestant theologians in Europe. She could speak nine languages and was studying Hebrew. It is reasonable to assume that Elizabeth resented the intensity of her moral outlook and her outspokenness, although all their correspondence suggests that Jane was in awe of her haughty cousin, three years her senior. There can be little doubt that Elizabeth already felt a degree of antagonism before steps were taken to promote Jane ahead of her in the succession.

It is probable that Cranmer and Cheke became concerned at the ambitions of both Somerset and Thomas Seymour. They were worried when Somerset started to adopt the royal 'we' in his correspondence. He was also snubbed by the French King, after referring to him in a letter as 'brother'. They became concerned that Edward was not being involved in the signing of dispatches, which would have enabled them to vet the documentation. Being extraordinarily astute for his years, Edward seems to have mistrusted both his Seymour uncles; he was not taken in by Thomas's attentions and refused to sign a request, drafted by Thomas, to make him the King's personal governor. It may well be that Warwick's contacts at court, particularly Robert, also coloured the King's views against his uncles' ambitions and shortcomings.

To reinforce his own authority, one of Somerset's first steps was to commence another round of 'Rough Wooings' against the Scots. Yet again the objective was to induce the Scottish Government to support the marriage of Mary Queen of Scots to Edward. This would have subsumed the Scots under English control, ending their Auld Alliance with the French. With Mary's mother, Marie of Guise, dominating the Scottish Council as Queen Dowager, she advocated a French marriage for her daughter and was not going to concede her betrothal to Edward without a fight.

In a show of significant strength, Somerset arranged a two-pronged attack into Scotland. While he led a well-equipped force estimated at 16,800 men in the east, Matthew Stuart, 4th Earl of Lennox, now married to Henry VIII's niece, Margaret Douglas, led a second force up the west coast supported by Lord Wharton. Although much of Somerset's army consisted of levies armed with longbows and bills, he had artillery and a nucleus of several hundred German and Spanish mounted mercenaries with arquebusiers (hackbutters), and 6,000 cavalry commanded by Lord Grey de Wilton, the High Marshal of the Army. Although Thomas Seymour should have travelled with the fleet in his capacity as Lord High Admiral he preferred to remain in London. This brought complaints from other members of the Admiralty board that his 'laziness and cupidity amounted to corruption'.[24] With Somerset seeing Warwick as a threat to his position in Government, he was not going to leave him behind, so Warwick was given command of the English infantry for the Scottish campaign. He was supported by Lord Dacre of Gillesland and Somerset himself, who seems to have taken a subordinate role given Warwick's enviable military reputation. Cecil travelled with the army as Provost-Marshal, acting as a judge for the campaign, and seems narrowly to have escaped death from cannon-fire.[25] With the English army marching up Scotland's east coast, it received protection from the English fleet of thirty warships just offshore.

James Hamilton, Earl of Arran, the Scottish Regent, hastily gathered troops to face the English threat. Although he had more than 22,000 men, 10,000 of these were poorly armed Catholic clergy dressed in black, but they were reinforced by pikemen and contingents of highland archers. By repute, many of the Scottish troops were in receipt of English pay, and certainly large numbers made for the English lines when the going became tough. Arran's principal problem was a shortage of cavalry, having only 2,000 lightly equipped horsemen under Lord Home. Although he had heavy artillery, his guns were difficult to manoeuvre, and were rendered useless at an early stage in the battle by archers commanded by Warwick. Arran's infantry, commanded by the Earls of Angus and Huntly, the two most experienced Scottish generals, took up a well-entrenched position at Pinkie Cleugh above the Esk, occupying earthen fortifications, which had been established by the English on an earlier incursion. These were protected by marshland on the Scottish right. Despite the strength of their position, the Scots lacked discipline. In an early skirmish between opposing cavalry forces, Grey's horsemen decimated most of Home's horse, leaving the Scots inadequately provided. When English guns were moved forward to Inveresk to threaten the Scottish right, Arran advanced from his secure position to close in combat before the enemy artillery could be deployed. When 4,000 Irish mercenaries jumped the gun on the Scottish left by moving forward against the English right, they were scattered by a cannonade from the English fleet offshore. Although Angus's pikemen on the Scottish right inflicted early losses on the English cavalry sent to disrupt their advance, their forward momentum was broken by a hail of arrows and shot from arquebusiers. With the English showing better discipline, their cavalry regrouped and renewed their charge to prevent the Scottish centre from supporting Angus. When Sir John Luttrell led the English vanguard of 300 experienced infantrymen against the Scottish centre, the Scots turned and fled, chased all the way back to Edinburgh by marauding cavalry. Luttrell's advance had provided time for Warwick to outflank the Scots and to attack them from the rear. With the Scots being surrounded, many were drowned attempting to swim the Esk, which was in spate. Arran fled back into Edinburgh 'scant with honour'. It is variously estimated that he lost between 6,000 and 10,000 men, while a further 1,500 were taken prisoner. The English claimed to have suffered 200 losses, but it is more likely to have been 500.

Inexplicably, Somerset failed to follow up on his victory. With Edinburgh at his mercy, he contented himself with burning Leith before retiring back across the border. This seems 'a massive blunder'. His objective of persuading Mary Queen of Scots to marry King Edward was lost, as was his ambition to achieve 'peace, unity and quietness'[26] by making Edward the Emperor of a united Great Britain of England, Scotland, Ireland and Wales. Without Edinburgh being taken, the Scottish Government refused to come to terms, and Marie of Guise gained time to bring in French reinforcements. The English force under Wharton was forced back to Carlisle after being defeated in the Western Marches. On 13 December 1548, Luttrell, now the English captain in the east, was pushed back at Broughly Castle. In the following July, French forces besieged Haddington leaving Somerset's German mercenaries in fear of their lives and it fell two months later. With the English being ousted from Scotland, Mary was free to become betrothed to the French Dauphin. Arran was bought off by the French with the Dukedom of Châtelherault.

Although the English army had performed well under Warwick and its other generals, Somerset's failure to grasp the campaign's strategic objective opened him to further criticism on his return to London and it was Warwick who received credit for the victory. Edward wrote: 'Pray thank, in my name, the Earl of Warwick, and all the other noblemen and gentlemen ... God granting me life, I will show myself not unmindful of their service.'[27] In their absence in Scotland, Thomas Seymour had done much to undermine their authority in the Council by criticising Somerset's administrative skills and the financial cost of the Scottish campaign. He tried to persuade the King to give instructions to the Council to transfer the Protectorate to him. After discussing it with Cheke, the King refused.

Thomas also flirted with Elizabeth. In the spring of 1548, he visited her room in the mornings to 'strike her familiarly on the back or on the buttocks'.[28] The pubescent Elizabeth seemed flattered by his interest and may have reciprocated his attentions, but Kat Ashley considered them scandalous, and reported him to Catherine. When tackled about it, Thomas was indignant, claiming that it meant nothing. At first, Catherine dismissed it as innocent fun, even joining in with the tickling on some occasions herself, but after she became pregnant and caught him holding Elizabeth in his arms, she had her removed from the household to live with Kat at the home of Kat's brother-in-law, Sir Anthony Denny, at Cheshunt in Hertfordshire.[29] Ascham went with her. Elizabeth later wrote to Catherine 'replete with sorrow'. Perhaps surprisingly, Jane Grey remained as Thomas's ward, and her parents do not seem to have learned of his inappropriate behaviour. She moved with Thomas and Catherine to Thomas's country estate at Sudeley Castle to await the birth of Catherine's child.

Catherine gave birth to a daughter, Mary, at Sudeley on 30 August 1548, but died from puerperal fever six days later, and Mary lived only two years. Despite Thomas's devastation, he inherited Catherine's very considerable wealth and tried to rekindle his suit for Elizabeth. There can be little doubt that the 14-year-old Elizabeth was rather flattered by the renewed advances of this older, but indisputably attractive man. Even Kat seems to have become wound up in the intrigue. Thomas's main objective was to find a way to supplant his brother as Protector; marriage to Elizabeth would be a significant stepping-stone. He also ingratiated himself with the 10-year-old King by giving him pocket-money and criticising his brother's tight supervision of him. He used his position as Lord High Admiral to promote a rebellion against the Government, for which he claimed to have raised 10,000 men. He seems to have gained the support of Sir William Sharington, Master of the Bristol Mint, and of Dorset, still hoping that Thomas would be able to arrange his daughter's marriage to the King. Sharington embezzled £4,000 of gold from the Mint to strike coinage in support of their cause. They spent this freely and gained backing for the plan from pirates. Nevertheless, with Catherine being dead, Thomas's power was greatly diminished, and support from among the nobility fell away.

On his return from Scotland, Somerset called Thomas to a Council meeting to explain himself. With Thomas no longer having access to the King, he failed to appear. On 16 January 1549, he attempted to kidnap the King at Hampton Court, shooting one of the boy's spaniels, which barked as he was trying to break into the royal apartments. He was incarcerated in the Tower after being arrested carrying a loaded pistol outside the King's bedroom at night. Rumours of his flirtation with Elizabeth implied that she might also be involved in his treasonable plans. She was arrested with Kat Ashley. The Council was convinced of her complicity, particularly as she vehemently defended Thomas and appeared distraught at his arrest.[30] Nevertheless, despite weeks of interrogation she proved 'a master of defiance, logic and shrewdness', providing no evidence of her involvement. Kat revealed all she knew of the flirtation, and Elizabeth had to deny as malicious slander suggestions that she was pregnant by Thomas, even offering to present herself at court to demonstrate that it was untrue.

Although Somerset wanted to protect his brother, Warwick and the Duchess of Somerset lent weight to those who sought Thomas's execution. He was convicted of treason but remained defiant in the hope of a royal reprieve, but Edward approved his death warrant. The loss of his pet dog had irretrievably turned him against his uncle. Thomas showed commendable bravery on the scaffold on 20 March 1549, but there was no outpouring of sympathy, and his enormous inheritance from Catherine Parr was seized by the Crown. Although Dorset avoided being charged, this put paid to any further suggestion that Jane Grey would marry the King.

Thomas Seymour was not the Protector's only casualty. Gardiner's continuing efforts to retain Catholic doctrine irked Protestant members of the Council. He upheld transubstantiation, the Catholic view that the bread and wine became the body and blood of Christ during the sacrament. It was Cecil, newly appointed as Somerset's confidential secretary and right-hand-man, who was tasked with advising Gardiner what he could or could not say in a sermon before the King, after Gardiner's opposition to granting him royal supremacy over the church. Gardiner was incensed at having his views questioned by an upstart Cambridge graduate, who 'showed neither learning, reverence nor respect for his elders and betters'.[31] He complained that Cecil must have exceeded his authority, but Somerset confirmed to him that Cecil was acting as instructed. Gardiner retorted: 'I mislike subjects that rule like kings to the diminishing of the King's authority, and their own estate.'[32] When he ignored Cecil's brief, Somerset sent him to the Tower.

Chapter 3

Somerset's difficulties in Government

Somerset did not find control of Government straightforward, and the public was shocked at him authorising his brother's execution. He failed to act with sensitivity and his attempts to resolve the nation's ills proved 'almost universally unsuccessful'. His efforts with Cranmer to achieve a universal Protestant church were also 'widely resented'.[1] More extreme Protestants, including Warwick, saw the 1549 prayer book as too moderate and ambiguous.

The royal exchequer had been left depleted by Henry's fruitless military involvement on the Continent and Somerset's incursion into Scotland. The young King became irritated that the Protector's efforts to make economies left his royal purse short of money to provide gifts for his staff and courtiers. Meanwhile Somerset was 'daily acquiring more and richer grants of land [and] pulled down two churches in the Strand in order to build his great palace of Somerset House'.[2] Edward was aware that he had purloined the jewels given to Catherine Parr by Henry VIII, which Thomas should have inherited after her death.

Somerset also faced 'unprecedented social and economic turmoil'. A steady population increase was causing deep distress in rural areas. Wealthy landowners were enclosing their estates to provide pasture for increased wool production, thereby removing peasant farmers from their traditional occupations. Rural unemployment and reduced wages were emptying hamlets and villages and causing much social disturbance. A combination of inflation, changing land use and property speculation only increased the problem, causing a steep rise in grain prices.[3] There was also religious conflict, sometimes between papist fathers and heretic sons.[4] 'Students and courtiers, merchants and peasants met in secret groups to study Tyndale's New Testament and other banned books.'[5] This combination of economic uncertainty and religious innovation led to rebellion. It had begun with the Pilgrimage of Grace during the winter of 1536/7 and continued to simmer close to the surface until it broke out again in Norfolk and the west country in 1549, and on several occasions inbetween.[6]

Somerset was persuaded that unrest was caused by greed on the part of wealthy landowners.

> He gave away all his lands round Hampton Court to the farmers and small holders; he set up a private Court of Appeal, so that anyone who had been wronged might approach him personally; he tried to regulate the further enclosure of common land; he instituted schools where there had been chantries and monasteries.[7]

This gained him an epithet as 'The good Duke',[8] but by taking the peasantry's side, he turned the propertied classes led by the Council firmly against him. This only encouraged disorder without relieving distress. Groups of impoverished and unemployed farmworkers started to break down enclosures and plough up pasture. Although the Council asked Somerset to make a show of strength on the landowners' behalf, his calls for the peasantry to return to their homes went unheeded. When he called for the use of the 1549 prayer book and banned the Catholic Mass in churches, almost the whole of southern England was in revolt.[9]

Somerset needed to involve the army but wanted to avoid bloodshed. With the Council opposing him, he did not dare to leave London, where he had control of the young King, and did not want Warwick or other Council members gaining in stature in command of his troops. In the end, he gave command to John Lord Russell, Sir William Lord Herbert, Sir William Lord Grey de Wilton and Northampton, Catherine Parr's brother. Northampton was sent to regain control of Norwich, then the second city in England, which was being held by a rebel army led by Robert Kett. Kett was a landowner of some substance who had attracted several members of the Norfolk gentry to his cause. With Northampton underestimating the rebels' strength and determination, he bungled it and had to hurry back to London after more than a hundred of his men had been slain.

The Protector had no choice but to give command to Warwick but dithered and made several changes to his instructions. When, at last, his orders were clarified, Warwick moved quickly and decisively, but was unwell. He gathered a large body of men able to bear arms. In early August, with his sons Ambrose and Robert (who was now just 16) at his side, he led a large group of Dudley retainers to the Midlands, where he assembled 6,000 foot and 1,500 horse at Warwick Castle. Robert was given command of his own company of foot (no doubt with experienced captains at his side).[10] From here, they marched towards Cambridge to join up with levies from Essex, Suffolk and Cambridgeshire. On 22 August, they arrived at Wymondham in Norfolk to be billeted at the home of Sir John Robsart at Stanfield Hall. It was here that Robert first met Sir John's only daughter Amy, whom he was later to marry. Dressed in 'part armour, plumed helmet and scarlet sash', he must have 'cut a fine figure'.[11]

The East Anglian landowners were seriously rattled. Their granaries had been pillaged for forage and many of their servants and tenants had joined the rebels. Some of them (including two of Robsart's stepsons) had been captured and were being held prisoner at Norwich. The situation was complicated. Much of the rebel discontent arose from rivalries and greedy self-interest between competing landowning families.[12] Many families found their allegiances split. Robsart, who was a principal Norfolk landowner, was married to Elizabeth Appleyard. Through her first husband, Elizabeth was Kett's sister-in-law.

On the following day, Robert said his goodbyes after his brief acquaintance with Amy. The army moved on to Sir Thomas Gresham's estate at Intwood to make preparations to face Kett and his followers at Norwich. Warwick's force has been variously estimated at between 7,500 and 14,000 men with a few pieces of artillery. Although many were 'scantily trained levies, there was a hard corps of veterans and mercenaries'.[13] In addition to Warwick, the army's command included four other peers of the realm, all experienced soldiers, Northampton, Lord Grey of Powis, Lord Willoughby of Parham and Lord Bray. Kett had mustered 12,000 men 'who made up in desperation what they lacked in military experience'.[14] When conciliation failed, Warwick embarked on the unwelcome process of slaughtering his own countrymen, which he was to execute with 'dispatch and efficiency'.[15] After the failure of Northampton's earlier mission, Warwick made a point of giving him a chance to redeem himself by commanding the attack on St Stephen's Gate. After artillery had battered down the portcullis, Northampton headed the successful charge through the breach, making him Warwick's undying friend. Ambrose, who was with him, also acquitted himself with distinction. When St Benedict's Gate was thrown open, Warwick marched his army into the town to establish control. When forty-nine rebel captives were hanged, the citizens in the market square agreed to cooperate. Nevertheless, the rebels remained strategically positioned on high ground outside the gates at Mousehold Hill. They still controlled areas of the town north of the river and in the east, where they managed to capture some of Warwick's artillery after it took a wrong turning, removing several pieces to Mousehold Hill. Hand-to-hand fighting continued without respite for the rest of the day and night, during which the rebels set light to the south-east quarter in a tactic designed to divert troops from the walls. Warwick did not fall for this and, to the citizens' anguish, left the fires raging.

With Norwich being difficult to defend, the City fathers lacked confidence in Warwick's prospects and tried to encourage his departure to avoid further damage. Warwick showed all his leadership skills. He called his captains together and, in front of a large crowd of citizens, made them confirm that they would fight on the King's behalf to the last. This bravado won the citizens' support. When 1,100 German mercenaries arrived as reinforcements, he launched cavalry forays to cut off the rebels' supplies. On 27 August, after leaving his infantry (including Robert) to defend the walls, he launched a massive cavalry offensive at Dussindale. This left 3,500 rebels dead as salutary retribution for Somerset's mistaken policies.

The Norfolk gentry and Norwich citizens rejoiced at Warwick's success, but he called for pardon and mercy to restrain them from further vengeance to sate their sense of outrage. This aligned him with the views of the young King, who had been influenced by Cheke to call for moderation. Cheke wanted to reason with the insurgents rather than to burn them at the stake. His approach so much impressed Somerset that he was appointed to negotiate and calm the rebels' grievances. Meanwhile Robert had time 'to renew and deepen his friendship with Sir John Robsart's daughter'.[16]

Although Warwick's return to London was met with 'the cheers of a relieved populace' and 'the congratulations of his fellow councillors', he received no thanks from the Protector, who failed to honour 'the man who had just saved the country from insurrection'.[17] When Warwick sought offices for Ambrose as reward for his bravery at Norwich, Somerset snubbed him by offering them to Warwick's former steward, now one of Somerset's secretaries. Although the emphatic victory had sown seeds of criticism of the Protector, it was 'merely the precursor to a further round of power broking' within the Council.[18] While no one doubted that Somerset should go, many Council members sought a regency governed by committee as set out in Henry VIII's will. Nevertheless, 'with a child king on the throne, and two bastardized half-sisters next in succession, England needed a strong man to hold the reins of power'.[19] Warwick had not initially envisaged himself as England's political leader, but the need to end class hatred and the breakdown of social order led to his conclusion that Somerset's protectorate should be ended.

Somerset failed to recognise the growing antipathy to his leadership and, with his judgement impaired, retired to his Hampshire estates for several weeks of hunting. Although this 'made the task of palace revolutionaries very much easier',[20] the coup, when it came, was far from straightforward. Although Russell had achieved similar success in quelling the rebels in the west country, it was Warwick who took the credit for restoring peace. He pushed the Council into accelerating the process of religious change and establishing foreign alliances to confirm the Protestant faith. With religious change engulfing the whole of Europe in international conflict, England had 'to decide which alliances she might be obliged in principle or self-interest to enter into'.[21]

Warwick's principal ally to remove Somerset was the devious Southampton who was seeking a Catholic coup with support from Arundel in the Council and Bishop Gardiner in the Tower. They were seeking to appoint the Catholic Princess Mary, now aged 33, as Regent for her half-brother. They needed Warwick to overthrow Somerset, because of his 'obvious stature and the support he commanded', but planned to dispose of him later as an 'accomplice in the Protector's treasons'.[22]

Meanwhile the royal household had been moved to Hampton Court, where Somerset, who maintained an affectionate bond with his nephew, encouraged Edward to become more involved in Government administration. By this time, Cheke had been appointed Provost of King's College, Cambridge, in recompense for his efforts to smooth ruffled feathers in Norfolk. Somerset had tasked William Thomas, one of the clerks of the Council, noted as an advanced Protestant and a very clever man, with providing political training to the King.[23] It was not until Somerset's return to court on 1 October 1549 that the atmosphere deteriorated, setting the stage for a coup.

Somerset soon became aware of the strength and unity of the opposition to him within the Council. When he sought allies to bring troops to Hampton Court to assist him, no one arrived. Londoners supported the Council and rose in arms against the Protector. Somerset told Edward and his household that the Council was planning to do away with the King, just as Richard III had with the princes in the Tower. Although this gained him some local support, Ambrose and Robert, who were at court, were caught between the two factions. With no army appearing from London, Somerset decided to make a run with the King for the relative security of the Tower. On arriving at Kingston bridge, he received news that the Tower was in the Council's hands. He turned back, taking the King and his household to Windsor. This involved a hard ride well into the night only to find 'unmade beds, unfurnished chambers and an empty larder'.[24]

With so many of the King's companions in the Privy Chamber being allied to Council members, pamphlets were smuggled into the castle outlining Somerset's crimes and explaining that the Council's only motive was his removal from power. Somerset replaced them with 500 of his own men, who complained to the King of the Council's disloyalty. Nevertheless, Edward supported the Council. He had developed 'a great rheum' (a cold) after his exertions and complained that he was being held 'in prison'[25] without galleries or gardens to walk in.

Two days were spent in fruitless negotiation, during which more and more Council members, particularly his two principal generals, Herbert and Russell, turned against the Protector. On 10 October, Somerset realised that the game was up, and Paget wrote to Warwick that he would resign the protectorate in return for assurances that he would not face trial for treason. He was escorted to the Tower, where he was received graciously by the Lord Mayor. 'The good Duke' was still popular and Warwick had to play his cards carefully.

After recovering from his cold, the King returned to Hampton Court, where he welcomed Council members, but on hearing of Somerset's imprisonment, called for his life to be protected. With Cecil being Somerset's secretary, he too was arrested and spent eight weeks in the Tower but was released after paying a hefty fine. When Somerset tried to build an alliance with Gardiner, hitherto his enemy, Cecil, on Warwick's behalf, tried to resurrect his career by preparing a case against Gardiner for his offences against the Council and the King. This prosecution lost Gardiner his bishopric. Although he had been assured that he would be released, this did not happen, and he remained in the Tower until Mary's accession.

On 17 October, Edward returned to London attended by his entire retinue, riding through the City to the cheers of its relieved populace. Warwick was one of six nobles appointed to be attendant on him and he became Lord Great Master of the Household 'to give order for the good government of his royal person, and for the honourable education of his highness in these tender years in learning and virtue'.[26] He was reappointed as Lord High Admiral, and became President of the Council, Lord Warden General of the North and Earl Marshal of England.[27]

Chapter 4

Warwick establishes control

Although Warwick now dominated the Council, he was suffering one of his periodic bouts of illness, so meetings were arranged at Ely Place, sometimes in his bedchamber. He set up an oligarchy of four to supervise Government, with Southampton being one of them to maintain a religious balance. Paget, Somerset's erstwhile ally, was given a peerage. Southampton, with assistance from Arundel, now began to put in motion the second part of his plan. With four other Catholics being promoted to the Council, there were rumours that the Reformation would be stopped in its tracks with Protestant leaders being persecuted and the Princess Mary becoming Regent. This would inevitably lead to the restoration of Catholicism and a new alliance with the Papacy. Southampton examined Somerset in the Tower to gather evidence for his attainder. The prospect of an 'impending ruthless political purge'[1] alarmed Archbishop Cranmer and even those politicians inclined to the old religion.

Although Southampton thought he was manipulating Warwick to achieve his Catholic ambitions, it was Warwick who was pulling the strings. After making minor concessions to uphold Catholic days of fasting, he used his friends around the King to obtain royal assent to appoint some new Protestant Council members to counterbalance Southampton's Catholic allies. The denouement came when the Council was meeting round Warwick's bed, with Southampton outlining Somerset's treasonable actions to justify his execution. After silencing him, Warwick placed his hand on a falchion (curved sword) lying on his bed, saying: 'My Lord, you seek [the Protector's] blood. He that seeketh his would have mine also.'[2] The meeting broke up in embarrassment, but Warwick's allies were sufficiently powerful to announce what had happened. At the end of October, a royal proclamation confirmed, on pain of imprisonment, an end to rumours that Somerset's imprisonment would lead to a return to 'the old Romish service, Mass and ceremonies'.[3] Southampton was a broken man. He was quietly dropped from the Council and retired from court due to illness, dying in the following year.

With waverers hurrying to Ely Place to confirm their loyalty to Warwick, he now held complete control. To remove any cause for future conflict, moves to attaint Somerset, who continued to have allies and remained popular, were quashed. On 6 February 1550, after a decent interval, he was released from the Tower and, two days later, was restored to the Council. Warwick's only objective was to keep him away from controlling the King. He needed allies with Protestant leanings. On 5 September 1550, the 29-year-old Cecil, who had spent nearly a year in the wilderness after Somerset's demise, became Warwick's Secretary of State with a place on the Council. To fulfil his new role, he acquired a house at Canon Row in Westminster. He now acted as the conduit for all legislation and religious debate, but carefully disassociated himself from his master's policies, sometimes by feigning illness at crucial times.

Warwick made no immediate attempt to become Protector or to obtain a Dukedom, being content with his role as the Council's president to promote clear-cut plans and provide proficient leadership. By packing the Council with his own supporters, he was able to delegate to it genuine power, and, given his declining health, his absences sometimes made this a necessity. It soon developed into 'the efficient administrative and executive body'[4] once enjoyed by Thomas Cromwell. He had no fear of stamping on civil disorder and he reformed revenue collection methods. This restored order at home and peace abroad.[5] Currency values started to recover, and the Protestant religion settled down to use the book of Common Prayer produced by Cranmer in 1549 (but revised by him in 1552). With former church lands becoming available for sale, landowners took the opportunity to increase their acreages.

Edward adopted the 47-year-old Warwick as a father figure. Having been brought up as a fervent Protestant, perhaps even more so than his mentor, he can only have approved of and even encouraged the Council's policies. Warwick 'never treated [Edward] as a cypher, never used him to bolster his own authority'.[6] With Cheke restored as his tutor, Edward's daily routine was changed to accelerate his 'assumption of sovereignty and to relieve the studious solemnity of his life'.[7] 'Frequently [Warwick] expressed his longing for the day when the young Tudor would assume full kingship and allow Warwick to take his sick and ageing body into weary retirement.'[8] Edward often attended Council meetings and spent long hours closeted with Warwick 'understanding the day-to-day concerns of his ministers'.[9] To counterbalance this workload, Warwick encouraged court entertainments and promoted Edward's interest in the martial arts. As Lord Great Master of the Household, Warwick also enjoyed 'supreme control of the court'.[10] He was well-supported by his family. His son, John, became Master of the Buckhounds and, in 1552, was appointed Master of the Horse. His brother, Sir Andrew, became keeper of the Wardrobe, keeper of the Palace of Westminster and, in 1552, became Chief Gentleman of the Privy Chamber, being granted the Order of the Garter in the following spring. John, Ambrose and Robert were frequent participants in court 'triumphs' – 'chivalrous exercises such as jousts, tilts and barriers, accompanied by spectacular masques, pageants and interludes'.[11]

To cement his rapprochement with Somerset, Warwick even arranged for John to marry Anne Seymour, the deposed Protector's eldest daughter, and their wedding took place at Sheen on 3 June in the presence of the King, who was in excellent health and gave the bride a ring valued at £40. With Robert being 18, he gained his father's approval to marry Amy Robsart and the wedding took place on the following day with both Edward VI and Elizabeth present. Both celebrations were at Somerset's home at Sheen, as Warwick was too unwell to attend. While John's wedding was a lavish affair, accompanied by jousts with dinner and dancing, that of Robert and Amy was less elaborate, but Amy met Warwick's exacting expectations in terms of dowry. As an only child, she was heiress to the manors of Syderstone, Newton and Great Bircham in north-west Norfolk. Warwick added to these by settling on them the reversion of substantial neighbouring lands at Coxford Priory. He also provided them with £50 and Sir John with £20 per annum. In 1552, he added the manors of Hemsby near Yarmouth and later Saxlingham near Holt to their inheritance. They were now prominent Norfolk landowners, with considerable local standing on the back of Warwick's achievement in putting down Kett's rebellion. Cecil later described Robert's union with Amy as 'a carnal marriage, begun for pleasure and ended in lamentation'.[12] With Sir John Robsart being 'a relatively insignificant country squire',[13] the connection has to be viewed as a genuine love match. Warwick generally sought politically helpful alliances for his sons and daughters. His other children all made more glittering connections. He arranged for Ambrose to marry

Anne, daughter of William Whorwood, the Attorney General, for Henry to espouse Margaret, daughter of Thomas Audley, Henry VIII's Lord Chancellor, for Mary to wed Sir Henry Sidney, Edward's close schoolroom friend and for Catherine to marry Henry Hastings, heir to the Earl of Huntingdon, the Plantagenet pretender to the throne.

After his marriage, Robert was soon put to work. He was employed as the royal agent in Norfolk to collect subsidies granted to the King by Parliament or to move prisoners between jails. In 1552, he became Lieutenant for Norfolk and in 1553 was returned as a Member of Parliament. Yet his responsibilities at court also increased. In August 1551, he had become a Gentleman of the Privy Chamber and was present whenever Edward held an audience. With Amy revelling in the luxury and glamour of court life, they enjoyed all the entertainment and 'occupied quarters close to the royal apartments in every house where the court was lodged'.[14] Robert was in constant attendance, keeping watch on servants and 'ensuring the smooth day-to-day running of the household'.[15]

The King showed a natural aptitude for outdoor games. In May 1551, Daniele Barbaro, the Venetian ambassador reported that he:

> is of a good disposition, and the whole realm hopes the best from him, as he is handsome, affable, of becoming stature, seems to be liberal, beginneth to interest himself with public business and, in bodily exercises, literary studies and knowledge of languages, appears to surpass his contemporaries and the standards of his age.[16]

Edward had still hoped to arrange his betrothal to Mary Queen of Scots, and he received her mother, Marie of Guise, in October 1551, as she returned overland to Scotland after visiting her daughter in France. Robert formed part of the retinue, which received her with special honour at Hampton Court, but the Queen Regent put paid to any hopes of the marriage, as Mary was already betrothed to the French Dauphin.

A particular bone of contention for both Warwick and Edward was continuing agitation by the Catholic party, led by Gardiner from the Tower, to allow the Princess Mary to celebrate Mass in private. She was also in close alliance with the meddlesome Duchess of Somerset, who had persuaded Somerset to support her. Soon after his accession,

Edward had promised to 'wink at' the celebration of Mass by his elder sister, of whom he was indisputably fond. Nevertheless, the Council had understood that the concession related to Mary alone and not to her entire household of fifty persons. Since then, Mary's determined adherence to the Catholic faith had become an embarrassment, and the Emperor Charles V even invited her to take refuge with him on the Continent. Warwick encouraged Edward to hold meetings with her aimed at seeking her conversion. She blamed Cecil for the Council's hardened attitude, but Edward had to establish control and called Mary to see him. Having delayed her visit, she burst into tears when they met. Edward did not give in and wrote to explain that exceptions had been made for too long and she should conform to the new religion. Mary became confrontational, riding into London supported by Catholic peers to the cheers of Catholics in the streets. This only hardened Edward's and the Council's views. Neither side would back down. Charles V sent an ultimatum. If Mary were refused the Mass, he would declare war. As alliance with France was not yet formalised, the Council had to be pragmatic. It agreed to her celebrating Mass in private for a further unspecified period. As Edward had not been present, the Council had difficulty in persuading him to confirm his agreement. He dug in his heels, but eventually capitulated after having 'burst out into weeping and sobbing'. He exclaimed: 'Be content … be content … Let me alone.' The Council warned the Imperial ambassador, Jean Scheyfve, that they would later have to insist on the Princess's obedience, but she could continue holding Mass in private for the time being. Edward would take a final decision when older.

By this time, Warwick was operating with 'colourless efficiency', revealing 'neither wit, charm, intellect nor force'.[17] Yet he was careful to act as the 'ideal companion for an intelligent and lively' king.[18] He kept Edward so well briefed that when 'His Majesty entered the Council Chamber, his initiative and grasp of detail amazed and sometimes perturbed his ministers'.[19] Yet Warwick continued to balance this with distractions such as archery, tilting and running at the ring.

With the King showing fanatical Protestant zeal, he encouraged the Council to revive Catholic persecution. Cranmer conducted a purge on the shortcomings of Catholic priests. Many did not reside in their parishes, and some did not know the Lord's Prayer, or who wrote it.[20] Protestant clergy were encouraged to preach against the Virgin Mary

39

and popery.[21] 'Ultra-Protestant' legislation authorised the replacement of altars with tables. More significantly Warwick was empowered to sweep 'up gold and silver altar plate and vestments valuable for their gold and silver thread'.[22] Although this supplemented royal coffers, it also lined his pocket. Robert had responsibility with Sir John Robsart for the 'removal of objects of [Popish] superstition'[23] from churches in Norfolk.

To establish himself in the international arena, Warwick opened negotiations for a new French alliance to be cemented by the betrothal of Edward to Elisabeth de Valois, the daughter of Henry II. With England crucial to the balance of power between France and the Habsburg dominions, his overtures were welcomed by Henry II, who saw an alliance against Charles V as more important than concerns about the spread of heresy.[24] The French King became a Knight of the Garter and Edward was granted the Order of St Michel, the highest order of French chivalry. Jacques d'Albon, Marischal de Saint-André, made a visit to England to receive the Garter on Henry's behalf, during which Edward played to his visitors on the lute. Most importantly, approval was given for his betrothal to Elisabeth de Valois, although she was more than six years younger than him. Charles V warned Scheyfve, the Imperial ambassador, that, in view of England's French alliance, it could no longer expect Imperial support.

Warwick's principal problem was the continuing popularity of Somerset, who was still seen as the 'Good Duke' after having supported the peasantry against landowners. This assured him his position on the Council and left Warwick unable to rely on Somerset's allies for support. With Cecil now firmly allied with Warwick, he tried to infiltrate Somerset's staff. Warwick was impressed at his loyalty. Somerset now realised that he dared not step out of line from Council policy. When asked to seek more tolerant treatment for the Princess Mary, he backed Warwick's stance. Warwick held another meeting with Scheyfve without Edward being there, to tell him that Edward had reached the maturity to take a decision on Mary's continued use of the Mass. The young King made his position perfectly clear: 'It would be against my conscience to allow the Mass, but in other matters I will treat the Lady Mary's Grace as my good sister.'[25]

With Warwick's influence over the young King steadily increasing, on 11 October 1551, at the age of 47, he was raised to a Dukedom, choosing the Northumberland title of the attainted Percy family, which brought with it parts of their huge Northumberland estates and others taken from the bishopric of Durham. Even Somerset encouraged his elevation and participated in the ceremony. John, Viscount Lisle, now took the courtesy title of Earl of Warwick and, as a Duke's younger son, Robert became Lord Robert Dudley. Without giving warning to Somerset, the newly created Northumberland raised the rank of all his principal supporters. Sir William Lord Herbert became Earl of Pembroke, Sir John Lord Russell became Earl of Bedford and William Paulet, the Lord Treasurer, who had become Earl of Wiltshire in 1550, was created Marquess of Winchester. Cheke, Cecil and Henry Sidney were knighted. Dorset became Duke of Suffolk. (Despite his shortcomings, Northumberland had been determined to gain his kinsman's favour. Following the death of Henry VIII's sister, Princess Mary in 1533, Charles Brandon, the 1st Duke of Suffolk, aged 50, had married his wealthy ward, the 14-year-old Katherine Willoughby of Eresby. Although this had raised a few eyebrows, she provided him with two sons, born in 1534 and 1537 respectively, half-brothers of Frances Brandon. On their father's death in 1545, the eldest son, Henry, became the 2nd Duke of Suffolk, but, in 1551, both brothers tragically succumbed to the 'sweating sickness' while at Cambridge. Northumberland now persuaded the King to grant the Dukedom to Frances, as the first Duke's elder daughter, allowing Dorset to become Duke of Suffolk, in right of his wife.)

With Northumberland having failed to steer Somerset towards a more supportive role, his backing of Northumberland's dukedom seems surprising and may have been designed to put him off the scent of some plotting with Gardiner and other Catholics, which has never come to light. He was now Northumberland's leading opponent on the Council, unable to tolerate a position of equality with his colleagues.[26] Having failed to uncover any treasonable wrongdoing, Northumberland resorted to subterfuge, as he was to admit before his own execution. He suborned Sir Thomas Palmer and Sir John Gates to provide false evidence against his rival. (Rumours of this contributed to Northumberland's growing unpopularity and resulted in the execution of Palmer and Gates with their master.) According to Palmer's story, Somerset was attempting to gain Gardiner's liberation from the Tower and was planning to 'raise the people' to support his reinstatement as Protector, despite lacking royal endorsement. Palmer also claimed that he was plotting to invite

Northumberland, Suffolk, Northampton and others to a banquet, where they were to be assassinated. The purported coup was to be led by Sir Ralph Fane, with Sir Thomas Arundel delegated to gain control of the Tower and Sir Miles Partridge to seize the Great Seal and rally the apprentices to establish control of London. Any member of the City militia failing to join the rebels was to be massacred. It was further claimed that he planned to break the French alliance so that the King could marry his daughter, Jane Seymour. His kidnapping of the King and moving him from Hampton Court to Windsor was cited as evidence of his violent and tyrannical intent. His support for the Princess Mary evidenced his wish to return to papacy with the Reformation being overturned. In all, the evidence named thirty-nine conspirators, including the Duchess of Somerset, her family and servants.

On 16 October, Somerset attended a Council meeting, at the end of which Winchester accused him of high treason. He was taken to the Tower, where he was joined by his wife and children. The King accepted the story as entirely plausible and the charges were proclaimed to the judges with witnesses being assembled. Nevertheless, parts of the statements of evidence were at variance and contradictory. These caused a delay of several weeks while inconsistencies were resolved. After Somerset's trial, they were quickly destroyed. Despite the evidence, Somerset, at Northumberland's request, was acquitted of treason, but was immediately convicted of felony for having raised a contingent of armed men without license. 'Somerset was not deluded by this masquerade of leniency.'[27]

Edward was concerned at the prospect of authorising his uncle's death, but Northumberland kept his mind away from it by keeping him well entertained over Christmas, with his range of schoolroom subjects being made less taxing. The court's festivities were overseen by a lord of misrule, with 'costumes, props and ingenious devices'.[28] There was 'spectacular buffoonery',[29] which lasted for twelve days. To humour the citizenry, entertainments were extended into the London streets. Ambrose and Robert played prominent parts in masques and mock tourneys, joining a retinue of young knights and gentlemen, who 'boarded the Royal barges at Greenwich, dressed in gaudy silks as attendants of the lord of misrule, and disembarked at Tower Wharf to caper merrily through the streets, dispensing free wine and largesse.'[30]

With the partying over, Northumberland persuaded Edward to sign the warrant for Somerset's execution, and, on 22 January 1552, the former Protector died with commendable bravery. Edward noted laconically in his diary: 'The Duke of Somerset had his head cut off upon Tower Hill between eight and nine o'clock in the morning.' This does not suggest any great feeling of remorse. Paget, for so long Somerset's ally, was another casualty. He knew too many of Northumberland's secrets and, on 22 April, was accused of embezzlement of crown property. His Garter was rescinded, and he was imprisoned, remaining incarcerated until reinstated in Mary's reign. With Somerset's execution having made him a martyr, Northumberland's security now depended on him being seen to act in the name of the King and on maintaining his absolute confidence. He now faced united opposition from Catholics, the peasantry and his personal enemies, particularly Arundel.

'Edward's relations with the Princess Mary were now too strained for them to see much of each other.'[31] Although Northumberland was nervous of her, he was careful to hedge his bets by remaining in close contact with both Mary and Elizabeth. He had always made a point of demonstrating his friendship with them, and they realised that, as the Dudleys and their allies dominated Government, there was a need to keep on their side. Although Mary had always been attentive to the young King, who found her more sympathique than Elizabeth, he strongly disapproved of her continued adherence to the Catholic Mass, even in private. Northumberland considered it his duty to support him in accelerating 'the pace of Protestant revolution'. Elizabeth was also careful to remain close to Edward and seemed far more amenable in religion than Mary. Nevertheless, he seems to have seen through her displays of fervent Protestantism, which she was to discard on his death, and stories of her flirtation with Thomas Seymour were still circulating. Northumberland provided her with her own establishment at Hatfield House, a royal property which he had purloined for himself. He even provided 'a surveyor to keep her affairs in order – Secretary William Cecil'.[32] (Cecil did not reside at Hatfield, but Elizabeth seems to have sought his advice on property and financial matters.) Although she visited court infrequently, Robert was encouraged to maintain his close friendship with her.

> On 21 January 1551, the 17-year-old Princess 'was most honourably received by the Council … to show the people how much glory belongs to her who has embraced the new religion and is become a very great lady', and on her entry to London she was met by a hundred of the king's horse.[33]

In the spring of 1552, she rode in state with her ladies through the City and was received by the King at St James's, where she maintained apartments. Although she demanded Durham Place as a residence, as promised to her under her father's will, this was resisted by Northumberland, who did not believe that she needed a permanent London home in addition to Hatfield.

With the Dudleys riding high, Northumberland granted his friends and family lucrative positions and accepted large grants of land 'confiscated from ecclesiastical bodies and enemies of the regime'.[34] In early 1552, John was appointed Master of the Horse and Robert took over his former role as Master of the Buckhounds, with responsibility for arranging royal hunting parties. This carried an allowance of £33 6s 8d per annum, which rose to £100 following the grant of other royal perquisites. Although John was now involved in diplomatic missions to France, Robert was occupied in 'ceremonial and court functions',[35] where he had every expectation of preferment from the young King. On 25 February 1553, he was appointed Chief Carver. When Anne of Cleves, who had survived Henry VIII, was required by the Council to relinquish certain manors granted to her for life, Robert paid £400 to acquire the reversion of some of them.

Warwick Castle was now the focal point of Northumberland's dominions with its lands stretching across the Midlands from Worcester to Coventry. Each of his children was catered for: Mary, who had married Sir Henry Sidney, was granted the Guildford family estates at Halden; the Sidney family received Penshurst Place after the attainder of Sir Ralph Fane, who had been an ally of Somerset. The Sidneys also gained some Kentish iron foundries. Henry Dudley was granted lands acquired by his father around London and Middlesex. When Ambrose's first wife, Anne Whorwood, died of the 'sweat' in 1552, he quickly remarried Elizabeth, Baroness Talboys, who owned great estates in Lincolnshire and Yorkshire. Even Lord Dudley's family was not left out of the spoils. In 1553, Dudley Castle, which Northumberland had purchased from him was restored to his eldest son Edward on his inheritance of the barony, and his younger brother, Henry, was employed on diplomatic missions. Both became devoted supporters of their kinsman. The family members' ability to feather their own and their allies' nests was widely frowned upon. If Edward VI were to die and the Catholic Princess Mary were to gain the throne, they had little hope of weathering the storm.

Chapter 5

Efforts to circumvent the succession of the Catholic Mary Tudor

Northumberland was sensitive to criticism and blamed the young King for promulgating the Council's more radical policies. He admitted going to bed 'with a careful heart and a weary body, and yet … no man hath scarcely any good opinion of me'.[1] During the winter of 1552/3 it became clear that his grasp on events was not as firm as in the past. His energies had been severely drained by illness and he lacked the will to carry the burden of state.[2] He was plagued with depression and self-doubt, longing for the time he could hand over full executive powers to the young King. In 1552, the Council agreed 'to advance Edward's majority from his eighteenth [birthday as ordained in his father's will] to his sixteenth birthday'.[3] He tried to end the practice of Council members heaping riches on themselves, which he, more than any, had benefited from. Yet they continued to amass perquisites. He was already tarnished as a ruthless oppressor with his hand in the till and no longer commanded universal support from the great magnates. The Earl of Cumberland, who was married to Eleanor Brandon, turned down his proposal for Cumberland's daughter, Mary, to marry his son, Guildford.

On 2 April 1552, Edward developed a rash with a high fever which lasted for a week, during which he was dangerously ill. Although he believed that he was suffering from smallpox, it is more likely to have been measles. With his robust health, he quickly recovered and was able to attend the Garter ceremony three weeks later, but he was fatigued and convalesced at Greenwich until his strength returned. To reassure the public, he rode at the ring at Black Heath and held a military tattoo. Despite his seeming recovery, his illness, in retrospect, can be seen as the precursor to consumption, which appeared ten months later. The Princess Mary visited him at Greenwich as did Scheyfve, the Imperial ambassador, but the question of Mary's attendance at Mass was not raised and the meetings seem to have been friendly. Later in the year, Scheyfve again visited the King, asking for his support to curb Henry II's hostile activities in the Netherlands. Edward showed considerable diplomacy by leaving the question unanswered, in view of his French alliance. In October he even agreed to stand as godfather to Scheyfve's son but declined to attend the Catholic christening as this would contravene his coronation oath.

In June, Cheke developed a severe and prolonged attack of the sweating sickness. The physicians gave up hope for him, but Edward was determined that he would not die and prayed devotedly until at last, Cheke began to recover. Cheke retired to Cambridge to recuperate but was able to return to join a royal progress around the southern counties being organised by Northumberland. When Edward visited the dockyards at Portsmouth he gave orders for improvements to their fortifications before going on to Southampton. He again seemed fatigued, resulting in the trip being curtailed. After resting at Wilton, where he was entertained with a show of great magnificence by Pembroke, he claimed, on his return to Windsor, that his health was recovered. Although Edward still did not admit to feeling unwell, by October Northumberland was sufficiently alarmed to call an Italian physician and astrologer, Girolamo Cardano, to give advice. Cardano concluded that his face had the mark of death, but dared not reveal his real opinion, simply telling Cheke not to over-fatigue the boy.

Shortly after this, Edward became involved in a controversy over kneeling to receive the sacrament. Cranmer, who was dominating both the Council and the debate on Anglican dogma, believed that kneeling was a matter of reverence and humility. Northumberland believed that the Anglican church should follow the Calvinist practice of standing. He brought John Knox to England to preach before the King. Knox opposed kneeling, which he saw as 'a cringing attitude savouring of idolatry'. Although Northumberland's objective was to discredit Cranmer, the plan backfired. Edward, who had made several changes to the content of the second prayer book of 1552, supported the archbishop. Cranmer was extremely riled by Knox's interference, not least because the prayer book, which had adopted much of the reforming liturgy emanating from the Continent, had already gone to press and any change would result in delay or dissatisfaction. He wrote to the Council, imploring it to ignore Knox's suggestions. After a debate between Cranmer and Knox at Windsor, it was agreed that kneeling should be retained, but wording should be inserted to show that this was in reverence, not in idolatrous adoration. Attempts were made to appease Knox with the bishopric of Rochester, which he declined, and he vented his fury over losing the argument on Northumberland. In a sermon before the King, he described the Protector as 'an ungodly, conjured enemy of God's true religion'. Northumberland would not be drawn and after letting him thunder on, recommended to Cecil that Knox should be appointed as the King's preacher in the North, or be moved back to Scotland.[4] Edward, who had attended the debate, made no mention of it in his journal, in which his last entry was made at the end of November. Perhaps, he was too unwell.

The King was sufficiently restored at the New Year to appoint Cheke to the Council. Cheke had gained Northumberland's respect for his important role in moulding Edward's political understanding. At the beginning of February, Edward invited the Princess Mary, despite their religious differences, to attend a masque at Westminster to be acted by children. Northumberland arranged for her to be accompanied by Jane Guildford and Frances Brandon. He was still careful to remain on good terms and restored her Royal Arms, of which she had been deprived since her mother's divorce.[5] On arrival, the 15-year-old Edward was bedridden and too unwell to receive anyone, causing the masque to be cancelled. Three days later, Mary joined him at his bedside in the presence of other court members. She was 'honourably received and entertained with great magnificence',[6] but was distressed at his deteriorating condition and steered clear of matters of religion, realising that he was dying.

The King's symptoms turned into congestion in the lungs and modern diagnosis implies that this was pulmonary tuberculosis. Until so recently, he had been 'tall and of a healthy constitution for a boy in middle youth',[7] but now his right shoulder was much higher than his left. He suffered a high fever with agonising struggles for breath. Although he fought tenaciously for his life, determined to recover, those around him feared for 'the slight, weak form in the great bed at Westminster'.[8]

Although Robert remained on good terms with the dying King, being granted lands at Rockingham in Northamptonshire and at Eston in Leicestershire, the Dudleys faced the bleak prospect of Mary Tudor becoming Queen in accordance with Henry VIII's final will. In the spring,

Edward started to show some signs of recovery and was able to walk in the palace gardens every day. He moved to Greenwich, but, by the third week of May, was again confined to bed and seemed to be wasting away. He was unable to watch the departure of the expedition, financed by Northumberland, of three ships attempting to find a north-east passage to China, led by Sir Hugh Willoughby and Richard Chancellor. (They encountered terrible storms; the bodies of Willoughby and his crew were found by Russian fishermen in the following spring. Chancellor, whose ship had become separated from the remainder, reached Archangel and began a trade with Russia's northern ports, which lasted 300 years.)

As Edward's condition worsened, he became horrified at the prospect of Mary undoing all his work in advancing the Reformation. Its legislative framework was already in place, and England was primarily Protestant. 'Gone were the Mass, the images in churches, and altars. All services were now conducted in English, and priests were allowed to marry.'[9] Yet the Reformation lacked universal support and could easily be undone by a Catholic monarch. Mary would leave England a prey to Continental Catholic powers seeking her hand in marriage. Northumberland became distraught and quite ineffective. Despite their outward shows of cordiality, there is no doubt that Mary blamed him for influencing the King towards his determinedly Reformist views and for the desecration of Catholic churches. He had no hope of surviving if she became Queen.

There has been much debate whether it was Dudley or the King, who initiated the scheme for Jane Grey to become heir to the throne, notwithstanding that Henry VIII had reinstated both Mary and Elizabeth to the succession in his final will. It is important to understand the succession's legal complexities, which had been exacerbated by Henry's determination to make his own choice, rather than follow the correct dynastic line. Parliament had agreed to this under the Third Act of Succession of 1544, allowing him to nominate his heirs in his 'last will and testament signed with the King's own hand'.[10] When the will was prepared he was too ill to sign it, so it was completed with a metal stamp of his signature inked in afterwards by a clerk. This caused doubts over whether he had been conscious during its preparation, calling its validity into question. Nevertheless, it nominated his three children, Edward, Mary and Elizabeth. While it is understandable that he would want his own progeny to succeed him, he was well-aware that Mary remained irretrievably Catholic. Furthermore, it was contentious as both Mary and Elizabeth had been illegitimated by Acts of Parliament in 1534 and 1536 respectively. Elizabeth was also illegitimate in Catholic eyes as Katherine of Aragon was still rightfully Henry's consort at the time of Elizabeth's birth.

If his own line failed, Henry decreed that the throne should pass to the grandchildren of his favoured Protestant younger sister Mary, who had married his great friend Charles Brandon, Duke of Suffolk. This overlooked the progeny of his Catholic elder sister Margaret, despite her prior dynastic right. To bar Margaret's heirs, Henry had ordained that no one born outside England should inherit the Crown, although, at the time of Margaret's marriage to James IV of Scotland, no such impediment had been put in place. While this barred her granddaughter, the Scottish born Mary Queen of Scots, it did not bar Margaret's daughter, Margaret Douglas, by her second marriage to the Earl of Angus, as she had been born in the north of England. Margaret Douglas had married with Henry's approval, Matthew, 4th Earl of Lennox, and they had an infant son, Henry, Lord Darnley. Nevertheless, she was a steadfast Catholic and had been declared illegitimate by Henry (on entirely spurious grounds) to protect the claims of his own children. In other respects, however, she remained in his favour. She had ridden in the funeral procession of Jane Seymour, had been appointed first lady-in-waiting to both Anne of Cleves and Catherine Howard and had acted as a bridesmaid to Catherine Parr. It was thus her Catholicism that caused Henry to debar her (but did not cause him to debar his daughter Mary).

Henry had also overlooked his nieces Frances Brandon, aged 29, and Eleanor, aged 27, the surviving children of his younger sister Mary, both of whom were Protestant and on good terms with the King. Instead he nominated their progeny. It has been argued that he was looking for a male Protestant heir and hoped that Frances would yet produce one. Nevertheless, it seems more likely that Henry, who was a good judge of character, disapproved of Frances's husband, now Duke of Suffolk, and would not countenance the thought of him becoming King consort. Despite being academically bright and well-educated, Suffolk had shown himself ineffective both as a politician and as a soldier, lacking any modicum of common sense. He was an inveterate gambler, often leaving his family very short of money, and was open to offers of financial perquisites. Despite his close connection to the Crown, Suffolk was not awarded office during Henry's reign and was excluded from the sixteen-man Regency Council for Edward VI. In addition to being married to Frances Brandon, he was the great-grandson of Elizabeth Wydeville, who had espoused his great-grandfather, Sir John Grey, before her marriage to Edward IV. He was thus the son of Henry VIII's half first-cousin.

The outcome of Henry VIII's will was that, after his own progeny, he had nominated Frances's daughter, Jane Grey, to succeed to the throne. Everyone was aware that in dynastic terms this overlooked Mary Queen of Scots, Margaret Douglas, Lord Darnley and Frances Brandon. There was really no logic to it except that, other than his daughter Mary, he wanted to avoid a Catholic succession. To achieve this, it might have been less controversial and more effective to provide legislation which barred Catholics from the throne, as was eventually provided in another era by the Act of Settlement in 1701. With the Council being dominated by Reformers, it should have been able to carry such anti-Catholic legislation through Parliament.

Faced with the same problem, Edward and Northumberland decided to ignore anyone overlooked in Henry VIII's will. This still left the Princess Mary, a Catholic, and the Princess Elizabeth, a Protestant, as next in line. Their remedy was to bar them, because they had been declared illegitimate by Act of Parliament. The half-Spanish Mary was also opposed by the French, with whom England was now in alliance, as they wanted to avoid the development of Spanish influence over English Government.[11] It was also argued that Elizabeth could endanger the Protestant succession by marrying a foreigner.

It has generally been assumed that Northumberland initiated the plan for Jane Grey to succeed Edward and to marry his son, Guildford. This would leave him as the 'eminence grise' behind the throne. Yet all the evidence suggests that he personally favoured Elizabeth, for whom he had provided a household and accommodation at Hatfield. She had the advantage of standing immediately after Mary in the succession in accordance with her father's will, and had demonstrated a Protestant demeanour to the King with her quietness of manner and plainness of dress on her visits to court.[12] She was also popular, and much better known than Jane. There can be little doubt that it was Edward who focused on Jane, nominating her in 'my devise for the succession' in his own handwriting. He had all his father's authoritative persona, was an obsessive Reformer and was determined to secure his country's religious revival.

Edward attracted extraordinary devotion from all those who knew him, and Northumberland was indisputably in awe of him. If Henry VIII were permitted to nominate his successors under his final will and testament, why should Edward VI not do the same? With Jane undertaking classes with him, there can be little doubt that he recognised her as academically brilliant, more so even than Elizabeth. It is also probable that he was aware that she had been considered as his potential consort. He may also have seen the 19-year-old Elizabeth as less compliant and tainted by her perceived involvement with Thomas Seymour in the failed attempt to kidnap him.

If Jane were to be promoted ahead of Elizabeth, Edward knew that only Northumberland commanded the authority to execute such a plan, and the 15-year-old would need to be married. To gain his support, Edward suggested Northumberland's 18-year-old son, Guildford, as her consort. Northumberland would always support a plan which promoted the Dudley dynasty to the Crown. There is no doubt that he gave every encouragement, even if he did not initiate the plan, and he implemented it after Edward's death.

Edward and Northumberland still had to gain support from Frances Brandon and Suffolk. She seems to have overcome her own demotion from the succession by focusing her attention on the interests of her deeply religious and academically talented eldest daughter. Nevertheless, for parents who had been hoping that she would espouse the King, Guildford was 'a devastatingly poor substitute', and they vigorously opposed the marriage. Although Jane's succession only gained the Council's approval after the wedding, the plan must have been floated beforehand. It is inconceivable that Frances would have condoned the marriage without knowing the broader picture. This suggests that Edward's devise existed in draft before Jane's marriage, thereby gaining Frances's approval. Nevertheless, neither Jane nor Guildford seem to have been told that she was heir to the throne. Her succession still faced legal hurdles and there was no value in building expectations in advance.

There was no difficulty in persuading the 'timid and trustful'[13] Suffolk to support his daughter's marriage to Guildford Dudley in expectation of her becoming Queen Regnant. He had been beholden to Northumberland for making him Duke of Suffolk and Jane's accession could only be financially beneficial for him. Frances's 'womanly scruples were of little avail',[14] and she knew that she had no choice but to comply. No one considered the views of Jane and Guildford. Jane did not find him attractive and made no effort to hide her contempt at the prospect of marriage to him.[15] He was considered 'spoilt, conceited and disagreeable'.[16] It took her father's thrashings and her mother's insistence to reduce her to acquiescence.[17] Frances argued that Guildford was 'a comely, virtuous and goodly gentleman'.[18] Nevertheless, he lacked his siblings' charisma. The feeling was mutual. Guildford made 'no secret of his dislike for his bride, nor of the fact that he was marrying her because she was the great-niece of Henry VIII and chosen for him by his father'.[19]

Edward did everything he could to encourage the marriage. He provided the fine bejewelled clothing for the bridal party from the Royal Wardrobe and sent handsome presents to the bride and groom. Jane wore a gown of royal purple, with gold and silver brocade embroidered with diamonds and pearls, a far cry from her normal sombre attire.[20] On 25 May, the whole Dudley family attended the nuptials at Durham Place opposite Charing Cross with its gardens running down to the Thames, followed by 'exceedingly splendid and royal' celebrations designed to impress the populace. Marriages were also arranged for other female claimants to the throne to husbands who enjoyed Northumberland's trust. Jane's sister, Catherine Grey, who was not yet 13, espoused Henry Lord Herbert, Pembroke's son. This was certainly no love match and was declared null and void shortly after the failure of the coup to place Jane on the throne. Yet Pembroke was a capable soldier and, as a key member of the Council, became an important, but short-lived ally of the Protector. Catherine Dudley, Robert's youngest sister, married Henry Hastings, Huntingdon's heir. Northumberland recognised the supreme value of his position as the most senior of the Plantagenet claimants. Every effort was made to make the triple wedding as magnificent as possible, with games and jousts.[21] Even the 8-year-old Mary Grey was betrothed to a distant cousin, Arthur, later Lord Grey de Wilton, although this marriage never took place. Although Edward had promised to attend, he was already too unwell. There were even rumours that he had died. Although he made a supreme effort to appear at a window at Greenwich, he was quickly carried back to his bed and was never again able to leave it.

The only hiccup at the wedding celebration at Durham Place was food-poisoning, which afflicted Guildford and several of the guests. Guildford was suffering for a month afterwards. This may have been the reason that the marriage was not immediately consummated. Jane also seems to have become ill, but perhaps more out of stress. After a high-pitched row between the Duchesses of Northumberland and Suffolk, she received consent to move with her servants, but without her husband, from Durham Place to Chelsea Manor with its happier memories of her time there with Catherine Parr.

On 12 June 1553, Edward called Lord Chief Justice Montague and leading law officers to his sickbed to draw up a new will and to put his 'devise for the succession'[22] into proper legal language. His initial draft left the crown to 'the Lady Jane's heirs male', followed by her sisters' heirs male, but when he realised that he was unlikely to live to see them, he changed it to 'the Lady Jane and her heirs male' (but did not make a similar change to include her sisters). It was a poignant scene:

> Northumberland and a small group of councillors stood beside the bed. The judges knelt. The King spoke with a fervour enhanced by shortness of breath of his concern for the maintenance of the new religion. Everyone waited for Montague's reaction. He knew that what the King was demanding was contrary to the law, but could he say so to the dying boy? Falteringly he tried. The King grew angry. 'I will hear no objections,' he gasped. The judges withdrew in confusion.[23]

When they returned two days later, they told the King that they could not undertake his request. For his will to be enforceable, Parliament would be required to repeal the Act of Succession of Henry VIII. 'Anyone who attempted to alter the succession while it remained unrepealed would be guilty of high treason.'[24] On hearing this, Northumberland:

> entered the Council Chamber, a sight that no one who saw it ever forgot. The well-known suavity of the Duke's manner had totally disappeared. He was trembling with rage. He swore that he would 'fight in his shirt' with any man who refused his demands.[25]

At a further audience, Edward, 'with desperate haughtiness ... asked [the judges] how they dared hesitate to obey his will'.[26] 'I will hear no objections. I command you to draw up the letters patent forthwith.'[27]

They were finally driven 'to do what their professional training had made them declare impossible'.[28] After requesting a pardon for themselves, they undertook to prepare the letters patent to devise the crown to Jane and her heirs male, for subsequent confirmation by Parliament. With the Duchess of Suffolk dynastically standing ahead of her daughter, she was called to see the King at Greenwich, where she renounced her rights in Jane's favour. She had no choice in the matter. Northumberland could be very frightening. When the will was prepared, he ensured that it was endorsed by all the leading members of the Council and other people of influence. Cecil, who had been careful to avoid involvement in its preparation, signed it, but afterwards claimed that this was as a witness; he knew that he was in great peril if he refused. Cranmer and Cheke took a lot of persuasion, but it was the dying King who melted their hearts to gain their support. Northumberland retained the will for safekeeping, and it was not immediately published.

With Edward suffering from ulcers all over him, 'his body dry and burning, his stomach swollen, his fever very high … he would never again leave his bed'.[29] Circulatory problems were causing the top joints of his fingers and toes to become gangrenous and disfigured. The physicians' only objective was to keep him alive for as long as they could. Their stimulants made it 'impossible for him to slip into a merciful unconsciousness'.[30] Speech was an effort. The swallowing of food almost impossible. He longed for oblivion.[31]

> The ensuing days were tense and melancholy for Robert and the other close attendants of the dying King. Edward's long bouts of continuous, convulsive coughing now brought up a sputum, which was 'livid, black, foetid and full of carbon; it smells beyond measure'.[32]

Although he asked to see ambassadors, visitors were kept to a minimum, and those surrounding him were sworn to secrecy over the seriousness of his condition. He died in the arms of Sir Henry Sidney on 6 July 1553.

Jane was not immediately proclaimed Queen. Northumberland's approach was surprisingly indecisive. Although he might have been expected to retain Mary and Elizabeth at court, he failed to do so. It was not until two days before the King's death, that Northumberland at last summoned them, but he had kept them fully informed of the

King's condition. Rumours of his plan to install Jane on the throne seem to have leaked, and fearing a trap, neither of them arrived. Elizabeth pleaded illness and was probably tipped off by Cecil. Although, his wife Mildred Cooke, was a kinsman of the Greys, Cecil could see the legal difficulties of promoting Jane and was at pains not to be implicated. He wanted to see a monarch of the new religion, but his connection to Elizabeth makes it likely that he preferred her claim. Mary set out slowly from Hunsdon, but received warning after reaching Hoddesdon, five miles closer to London. Northumberland sent his sons, John and Robert, with 300–400 mounted guards to provide the appearance of a party to escort Mary to the capital as was the custom. Despite this implying that he planned to place Mary under guard, forcing her to renounce her crown, his actions do not suggest this. He had always treated the princesses with the utmost courtesy. It is much more likely that he was keeping his options open. If Mary had come to London, where he was in military control, he could have brokered a deal with her, supporting her claim on conditions acceptable to the Protestant Council. All he had to do was to tear up Edward's illegal will.[33] If she refused, he could arrest her and install Jane, arguing that Mary and Elizabeth were illegitimate as confirmed by Parliament.

With Mary having been warned, early on 7 July she left Hoddesdon with her suite for Kenninghall in Norfolk, which, following the attainder of the 3rd Duke of Norfolk, had been provided by the Crown for the use of Mary and Elizabeth. Mary believed that Norfolk landowners with their Catholic sympathies would support her. Having seized the initiative, she called for support to establish herself on the throne. If John and Robert pursued her into Norfolk, their role became more sinister, and would no longer be seen as that of an escort. They could not establish the level of support for her, but knew that she enjoyed considerable public sympathy, even among their escort party. John told Robert to ride after the Princess with the bulk of their men. If Mary headed for the coast as was expected, he was 'to raise loyal men from his own Norfolk estates to stop her'.[34] John galloped back to London to report to the Council, intending to return with more troops as reinforcements.

Robert travelled through the night, arriving at Cambridge before dawn. He had lost track of Mary, who had travelled to Sawston Hall further south, where she lodged with John Huddleston, a kinsman of one of her attendants. After gaining intelligence of Mary's whereabouts and gathering local support, Robert rode to Sawston at sunrise, but some of his men deserted en route. On arrival, he found that she had left for Newmarket only an hour earlier. Being tired and frustrated, he unwisely set fire to the property (Mary later rebuilt it). The motive for chasing after her was now plain for all to see. Meanwhile, he received reports that she was gathering support from among the East Anglian gentry wherever she went. He decided to withdraw to Cambridge, always a centre with Reformist leanings, to await John's return. With John arriving later the same day, they set out for Newmarket 'into an enemy country'.[35] The people they passed, who had cheered Mary on, were now 'sullen and uncooperative'.[36] Her flight had become a triumph and she received a civic reception in Bury St Edmunds. Meanwhile, the Dudleys' escort party was evaporating, making further pursuit impossible. They split up to gather more supporters, with Robert heading for his estates in north-west Norfolk. It was imperative that Mary should be apprehended quickly.

On 8 July, two days after the King's death, Northumberland was forced to reveal his hand. He sent his gentle and affectionate daughter, Mary Sidney, to collect Jane, who was still recuperating at Chelsea Manor, and to escort her up-river to Syon House. To their surprise, there was no one there to greet them. Northumberland was advising the Lord Mayor of London of Edward's death and that Jane had succeeded him. He also sent messages to all the great landowners round London seeking levies for the defence of the realm. He reported that Mary had fled abroad to seek foreign support to back her claim, but Mary was safely at Kenninghall surrounded by Catholic allies, 'ready to move onto the offensive'.[37] She had declared herself Queen and wrote to the Council demanding their immediate submission.

It was some time before Northumberland arrived at Syon with four council members. After some further delay, Jane was told of the King's death, and, to her great embarrassment, Northumberland and his colleagues knelt before her. At this point, they were joined by the Duchesses of Suffolk and Northumberland with Elizabeth Brooke, Marchioness of Northampton, closely followed by Jane's father and husband. In the presence of the assembled company, Northumberland advised her that on his death bed, the King had nominated her as his successor. Jane was 'stupefied and troubled'.[38] She fell to the floor 'in an agony of grief and shock'.[39] She cried out: 'The crown is not my right and pleases me not. The Lady Mary is the rightful heir.'[40] It took much argument from Northumberland and her father to persuade her to submit to their will and to behave in a regal manner.

There is no surviving physical description of Jane's features – except that she was less than 5ft tall – and no authenticated portrait, but the French Ambassador saw her as 'virtuous, wise and good looking'.[41] At about 3.00 pm on 10 July, dressed in royal regalia and escorted by her mother and father, Jane was conveyed by barge to the Tower of London to meet the people. She was given no choice, but her path was 'shadowed by uncertainty'.[42] When the proclamation appointing her as Queen was read out, 'no one present showed any sign of rejoicing'.[43] One report said: 'The world is dangerous. The great devil Dudley ruleth.' Even when a crier called out that both the Princess Mary and the Princess Elizabeth were illegitimate, there was no stirring of support for Jane. Both princesses were popular, while she was almost unknown and will have appeared reticent. There was considerable surprise that it was her mother, the Duchess of Suffolk, with a better claim to the throne than herself, who carried her train. Although the proclamation was repeated in other parts of London and throughout the kingdom, the people remained unconvinced. On entering the Tower, she was greeted by Northumberland and the Council, while Guildford watched cap in hand. The three ambassadors present confirmed that the ceremony was conducted with 'accustomed pomp',[44] although they also noted the silence of the crowd.

In addition to Northumberland and Jane's father, the most prominent members of the Council were Northampton; Winchester; Arundel (Suffolk's brother-in-law); Pembroke; John Russell, Earl of Bedford; Francis Talbot, Earl of Shrewsbury; John Bourchier, Earl of Bath; Thomas Radcliffe, Earl of Sussex; Sir William Paget; and Thomas Cranmer, Archbishop of Canterbury. They had all signed the documentation confirming her as Queen. Although Winchester presented Jane with the crown which, very reluctantly, she tried on, she was gathering her wits about her. When it was suggested that Guildford might also be offered a crown, she made it quite clear that this was not her intention, but she would consider a dukedom. This resulted in a show of 'youthful petulance' from Guildford. 'He went off to fetch his mother. The Duchess of Northumberland could at first scarcely believe her ears. She poured out commands and revilings … that would have cowed many people.'[45] Jane was not to be moved. It was simply a marriage of convenience. It is apparent that by now the relationship had been consummated, as the Duchess suggested that Guildford should withdraw Jane's conjugal rights and retire to Syon House! This only strengthened Jane's view that he should not become King and she sent orders through Arundel and Pembroke that 'he was to behave himself to her in a friendly fashion',[46] and to remain with her at the Tower. He did what he was told. She would not be bullied, nor as compliant as Northumberland had hoped.

When a message was received from Mary that the Council should renounce Jane and recognise 'herself as their undoubted liege lady', Council members became 'astonished and troubled',[47] realising that Mary was about to fight for her rights. Northumberland composed a defiant reply, but, by now, very few Councillors remained as his reliable allies. With Arundel being Catholic, he was the first to transfer his allegiance to Mary, notwithstanding that he was Jane's uncle by marriage. Jane played her part in trying to rally the remainder. She issued a warrant to her father's old friend, Northampton:

> You will endeavour yourself in all things to the uttermost
> of your power, not only to defend our just title, but also to
> assist us in our rightful possession of this kingdom, and to
> disturb, repel, and resist the feigned and untrue claim of the
> Lady Mary bastard daughter to our great uncle Henry the
> Eighth of famous memory.[48]

With Northumberland already being branded as a tyrant and attempting to deprive Mary of her birth-right, his supporters started to desert him. Nevertheless, the Dudley family hung together, and Robert laboured hard for their cause. He assembled tenants, neighbours and friends at Syderstone, establishing control as far as Wisbech. On 18 July, he proclaimed Jane as Queen in King's Lynn with support from the mayor and 300 citizens. Elsewhere, Mary was rapidly gaining support and she set up court at the Howard stronghold of Framlingham, south-east of Kenninghall. On 12 July, Norwich proclaimed her as Queen and sent men and weapons to her aid.[49] Northumberland found his calls for levies being ignored, or, worse still, soldiers marched to join up with Mary's growing band of supporters. Although he sent his cousin, Sir Henry Dudley, to France to seek support from Henry II, the Imperial ambassadors cynically considered his plea to be 'the courage of a resolute tyrant'.[50] Although Queen Jane held court in the Tower, it was rapidly becoming a prison.

Northumberland knew that he should remain in London to assure the Council's loyalty, and his initial plan was to send Suffolk with a force to support John and Robert in apprehending Mary. This was vetoed by Jane, who did not want to lose her father's assistance in containing Dudley family ambitions. Furthermore, support for Mary was continuing to grow, and it was well-known that Suffolk was not the best man in a military role. Northumberland realised that he had no choice but to go himself. On 14 July, he set out for East Anglia with an army of 3,000 well-equipped men. He seemed full of confidence, but Jane's cause was already lost. His departure was a fatal mistake and a great relief to his fellow Councillors. On reaching Cambridge, several of his officers deserted. From here he moved to Bury St Edmunds, 24 miles west of Framlingham, where Mary had amassed 20,000 supporters. Growing numbers of towns were proclaiming her accession and 'Royal ships in Yarmouth defected to her'.[51] With Northumberland's confidence ebbing away, he retreated to Cambridge. Worse still, several more Council members in London defected. In addition to Arundel, these included Sussex and Bath, both of whom held Catholic sympathies. On 18 July, a Council meeting led by Pembroke and Arundel at Baynard's Castle in London did a volte face. Acting as their spokesman, Pembroke stood before a crowd of overjoyed Londoners to declare support for Mary and surrender the Tower to her. Cecil supported them against his former mentor and was careful to send messages to Mary to test his standing with her. The bells of the City churches began to peal. Jane and her ineffective father had lost control. The Council's only interest was to seek Mary's mercy for the treason they had committed. They stripped 'the nine-day Queen Jane' of her title and her robes. Jane spoke to her father with great dignity to express her relief:

> I much more willingly put them off than I put them on. Out of obedience to you and my mother, I have grievously sinned and offered violence to myself. Now I do willingly and obeying the motions of my own soul relinquish the crown and endeavour to solve those faults committed by others if, at least, so great faults can be solved, by a willing and ingenuous acknowledgement of them.[52]

Jane's father, who bore a significant share of the blame for Jane's predicament, went out onto Tower Hill to proclaim Mary as Queen.

Jane, Guildford and the Duchess of Northumberland were held as prisoners by the Lieutenant of the Tower. Jane and Guildford were closely confined and kept apart, but Suffolk and his wife were permitted to retire to their home at the Charterhouse at Sheen. Suffolk was not left there for long and was soon under arrest. Despite claiming illness, he was quickly returned to the Tower, leaving Frances Brandon to approach her cousin Mary, with whom she had always been on good terms, to seek mercy for her family. She laid the blame solely at Northumberland's door and complained that Suffolk had been poisoned. Whether true or not, Mary agreed to release Suffolk to house arrest at Sheen. This shows that she too blamed Northumberland for perpetrating the treasonable acts against her. It now seemed possible that Jane would be reprieved, despite her continuing confinement.

When a price was placed on Northumberland's head, the game was up. He received a letter from the Council, signed by Cecil, commanding him to disarm. He immediately proclaimed Mary as Queen in Cambridge, claiming that he was acting in accordance with their wishes. Arundel and Sir William Paget, carrying the Great Seal of England, rode to advise Mary what had happened. Arundel was sent to Cambridge to arrest Northumberland, and on 24 July, brought him under guard to London. The crowds jeered as Northumberland was brought from the City gate to the Tower. He was joined by his brother, his sons, and six principal supporters. Nevertheless, 'instead of facing death like the brave man he was, he grovelled for mercy'.[53] He wrote to Arundel:

> Alas, is my crime so heinous as no redemption but my blood can wash away the spot thereof? … How little profit my dead and dismembered body can bring her, but how great and glorious an honour it will be in all posterity, when the report shall be that so gracious and mighty a queen had granted life to so miserable and penitent an object.[54]

This cut no ice.

Mary set out for London on a wave of popular support. With Elizabeth, quick to realise which way the wind was blowing, she joined her from Hatfield, equally piqued at having been superseded. After meeting at

Naked Haw Hall, in Essex, which was later to be converted by Robert into Wanstead as a home for Lettice Knollys, they entered London, sumptuously arrayed, with a large escort of infantry.[55] Arundel rode before the Queen, 'bearing the sword in his hand'.[56] Cheering crowds lined the streets as they came.

Robert was apprehended at King's Lynn, from where he was taken to Framlingham. Although he also threw himself on the Queen's mercy, he too was moved to the Tower to join his father and brothers in company with Bishop Ridley and Northampton. On arrival, he was held with Guildford in the Bell Tower, while John was in the Beauchamp Tower and Ambrose and Henry in the Coldharbour Tower, but, as more prisoners arrived, they were moved to be together in the Beauchamp Tower. John set to work carving their crest of a bear and ragged staff on its walls by the fireplace, signing it 'IOHN DUDLI', as can still be seen by visitors. This was surrounded with a girdle of leaves and flowers, roses for Ambrose, gilley-flowers for Guildford, oak leaves for Robert (From the Latin 'robur' – oak) and honeysuckle for Henry.[57] (John was undoubtedly a talented sculptor.) Robert left a small carved oak branch, with the initials R.D. By repute, it was Guildford who provided the simple word IANE, suggesting that he had developed some affection for his new bride. Jane was initially lodged in the Lieutenant's house, but later moved to live with the Gentleman Gaoler adjacent to the Beauchamp Tower. Robert was incarcerated for eighteen very uncomfortable months, generally under the threat of execution. Gone was the luxury of court life, but prominent prisoners generally enjoyed 'such indulgences as their rank demanded and their purses could command'.[58] They could order food, books, furniture and even pets, and were attended by servants.

Despite attempts to cast all the blame onto Northumberland, other Council members were soon occupying the remaining prison accommodation. They were joined by leading Protestants and churchmen detained for their religious convictions. Cecil met Mary to convince her of his innocence. Although, he was careful to destroy any incriminating evidence, she probably did not believe him. Nevertheless, he was not imprisoned and did not lose his growing fortune. He received a royal pardon at her coronation but gained no political post during her reign.

Chapter 6

Events leading to Lady Jane Grey's execution

On 18 August 1553, Northumberland, Northampton and John were escorted to Westminster to face trial for high treason. With the newly restored Duke of Norfolk presiding, the outcome was a foregone conclusion. Despite John's 'tender years',[1] all three were found guilty and sentenced to be hanged, drawn and quartered, as was normal practice in treason cases. They were then returned to the Tower. In the final outcome, only Northumberland had to face execution.

Jane showed great remorse, referring to her 'want of prudence, for which I deserve heavy punishment, except for the very great mercy of your majesty'. She blamed Northumberland for her predicament, telling Mary: 'No one can ever say that I sought [the crown] as my own, or that I was pleased with it or ever accepted it ... I was deceived by the Duke and the Council and ill-treated by my husband and his mother.'[2] Mary undoubtedly believed her and wanted to show clemency, but Simon Renard, the Imperial ambassador, counselled her 'not to exercise it so as to prejudice the establishment of her reign'.[3]

Mary's new regime, headed by Northumberland's enemies, Bishop Gardiner, Norfolk and Arundel, was determined to force him into 'humiliation, degradation and recantation'.[4] He was inundated with visits from councillors and priests seeking a public confession that the Protestant faith, which he had stalwartly supported, was 'damnable heresy'.[5] He was offered a pardon if he would recant. Trusting in offers of a reprieve and to save his own skin, he confessed his reconversion to Catholicism. This was all that his enemies wanted and was a huge propaganda coup for Mary. His family was shocked and disappointed, but they stood stalwartly behind him. On 21 August, his sons were summoned to St Peter ad Vincula in the Tower where Bishop Gardiner officiated while Northumberland, Sir Andrew Dudley, Northampton, Sir John Gates and Sir Thomas Palmer, all now condemned men, were forced to take Mass. At the end, Northumberland confessed:

> Truly, I profess here before you all that I have received
> the sacrament according to the true Catholic faith: and
> the plagues that is upon the realm and upon us now is that
> we have erred from the faith these sixteen years. And this
> I protest unto you all from the bottom of my heart.[6]

It was the ultimate humiliation for both Northumberland and his family, but his enemies had no intention of honouring any pledge of a reprieve. Robert was left with a bitter 'loathing for the religion espoused by Mary and Gardiner'.[7] It caused Ambrose and Robert to become 'the main pillars of Elizabeth's Protestant state'.[8] Jane was also horrified. When it was suggested that his objective was to obtain a pardon, she exclaimed: 'Pardon! Woe worth him! He hath brought me and our stock in most miserable calamity! … What man is there, I pray you, though he had been innocent, that would hope of life in this case? Being in the field against the Queen in person as a general?' She knew that Mary would never have pardoned him and was shocked that he would 'risk his immortal soul for the preservation of his earthly body'.[9] She later recorded:

> Like as his life was wicked and full of dissimulation, so was
> his end thereafter. I pray God, I, nor no friend of mine, die
> so. Should I, who (am) young and in my few years, forsake
> my faith for the love of life? Nay, God forbid! Much more
> he should not, whose fatal course, although he had lived his
> just number of years, could not have long continued.[10]

On 22 August, the day after taking Mass, Northumberland was led to his public execution on Tower Hill in front of 50,000 people. Although he avoided the ignominy of being hanged, drawn and quartered, his body was sent for a traitor's burial under the altar at St Peter ad Vincula next to that of Somerset. He was spared the final indignity of having his head displayed on a pole, thanks to the intercession of his old friend, John Cork, Lancaster Herald. Cork went to Richmond Palace for an audience with Mary to beg to be allowed to take the head to give it a decent burial. Mary also offered him the body, enabling the entire corpse to be interred in the Beauchamp Chapel at the parish church in Warwick. 'Queen Mary had no desire to start her reign with a blood bath and, for the moment only Northumberland and [his] two associates, Palmer and Gates, went to the scaffold.'[11]

With Northumberland's assets being attainted, Jane Guildford was denuded of her title and the family's great fortune other than her marriage portion of some land at Halesowen. As a concession, Mary permitted her continued use of a 'house in Chelsea and some treasured keepsakes'.[12] These enabled her to furnish it as befitting a lady of her rank. Everything else reverted to the Crown. An army of royal officials made a detailed inventory of the possessions at the various Dudley properties. She was now aged 45 and devoted herself with great spirit to seeking her sons' freedom, but no member of the royal suite or Council would 'defile themselves by befriending the tainted Dudley family'.[13] No date had been set for John's execution, but with the judicial process begun, all her sons remained very vulnerable.[14] If the Government wanted to make an example, they were obvious targets. This gave them a vested interest in ensuring a smooth transfer of power to Mary and her Catholic advisers.

Mary's honeymoon period with the public did not last long. Her initial welcome soon turned to 'mistrust, hatred and contempt'.[15] She faced immediate opposition to the dismantling of the religious structure established over the previous twenty years. When her chaplain preached at St Paul's Cross, there was a riot. A dagger was hurled at him and he was lucky to escape with his life. The Council was split into factions, particularly when she began to rely on priests and foreigners for advice. 'Parliament, when it met in October, proved uncooperative about repealing old statutes.'[16] Nevertheless, an Act of Repeal was used to dissolve the religious laws established by Edward VI. All religious services were now to be conducted in Latin. Most unwisely, Suffolk abused Mary's clemency by expressing his concern at her changes. If he wanted to protect his daughter in the Tower, he needed to keep his mouth shut.

Elizabeth, who was now 20, made every show of supporting her sister. She attended Mary's coronation at Westminster Abbey wearing a heavy gold coronet and driving in a litter accompanied by Anne of Cleves.[17] With the 38-year-old Mary devoting herself to the service of

God and the restoration of the Catholic faith, opposition only grew. It was rumoured that she was contemplating marriage in hope of providing a Catholic heir. Although she considered her second cousin, the lacklustre Edward Courtenay, Earl of Devon, the Plantagenet pretender to the throne, he was a Protestant. (Courtenay was a great-grandson of Edward IV, through his daughter, Katherine Plantagenet.) In late 1553, news was published that she was negotiating marriage to Philip, heir to the Spanish crown, 'a prince ripe in age and estate, worthy of her pleasant embraces',[18] and eleven years her junior. She was too excited to conceal their betrothal and instructed Bishop Gardiner, now Lord Chancellor, to proclaim it throughout the realm as 'the most splendid royal match since the Norman Conquest'.[19]

A combination of national pride and anti-Catholic hatred caused an outcry. Scurrilous pamphlets were distributed, and Mary was obliged to double the palace guard. 'A dog was thrown in the Presence Chamber at court with shaved head, cropped ears, a halter about its neck and a label saying that all priests and bishops should be hanged.'[20] With Gardiner facing death threats, he was forced to take up residence in the royal household.[21] Steps taken to restore law and order rapidly filled the prisons. Hundreds fled to Germany and Switzerland to avoid charges of heresy and treason and to seek the safety of the more extreme centres of Protestant reform. None of this helped the prisoners in the Tower, and the Queen was advised to take action against rival 'claimants to the throne, in whose interests rebellions might be launched'.[22]

The people most at risk from any purge of royal rivals were the Princess Elizabeth and Jane Grey. Elizabeth was retained at court, but irritated Mary by displaying half-hearted conformity to the restored Catholic faith.[23] Jane's problems were more immediate. On 13 November, she was brought to trial at the Guildhall together with Guildford, Ambrose and Henry Dudley and Archbishop Cranmer. She was dressed entirely in black as a sign of her penitence, carrying a prayer book in her hand. Although Cranmer initially quibbled about pleading guilty, all of them ultimately confessed to high treason and were sentenced to be hanged, drawn and quartered. As was normal practice in treason trials, none of the accused was permitted to speak in their defence and no witnesses were called. They showed no sign of distress before being returned to their quarters in the Tower. It is probable that Mary hoped eventually to release them, as she had already released Suffolk.

Robert had to wait for his trial as his treasons had occurred in Norfolk, and local evidence was needed. On 9 January, a commission of 'oyer and terminer'[24] was held in the Shire house at Norwich. It found that he had:

> possessed and in warlike manner fortified [King's Lynn] and there traitorously published and proclaimed to be Queen of this realm of England one Jane Dudley … and that … with [Northumberland] and … other traitors he continued to levy very cruel war against the said Queen Mary his sovereign and … falsely and treacherously worked for, abetted and encompassed the utter destruction of the said Queen …[25]

On receiving this report, Thomas White, the Lord Mayor of London, assembled a court at Guildhall to hear Robert's plea. This was in the name of 'Robert Dudley', as his courtesy title had disappeared with his father's attainder. The court was to consider evidence, pass judgement and pronounce sentence. On 22 January 1554, he arrived from the Tower on foot, preceded by the Gentleman Gaoler bearing his axe. It was bitterly cold, and the mood of the people was tense. With Spaniards now being frequent visitors to London, few citizens waited in the streets to jeer him as he passed, and there were growing rumours of rebellion in the country. When Robert pleaded guilty, he was sentenced to be hanged, drawn and quartered, as befitted a traitor. Yet again, hope remained that his sentence would not be carried out.

Jane, who remained steadfastly Protestant, continued to be held in the Tower. It was not just Northumberland, whose attempt to recant had gained her disrespect. Dr Thomas Harding, a former chaplain at Bradgate Park, chose Mary's accession as the time to convert to Catholicism. She lamented the 'state of his soul' and wrote severely to reduce him to repentance. She referred to him as 'the deformed imp of the devil … now the unshamefaced paramour of antichrist … O wretched and unhappy man, what art thou but dust and ashes?'[26] This was no shrinking violet!

The shock of Harding's conversion can have been nothing to that of Jane's father accepting Catholic rites. This seems to have been entirely political, as an attempt to protect Jane when condemned to death. Suffolk's former chaplain, John Hooper, had noted him as 'pious, good, and brave, and distinguished in the cause of Christ'.[27] His conversion did not involve any outward display of conformity as required of

Northumberland. His claim to support the Spanish marriage seems to have had the desired effect on Mary, who 'reinstated him by means of a general pardon'.[28] This took the pressure off any decision on the future of Jane and the remaining Dudley sons, so that the conditions of their imprisonment in the Tower were relaxed. Amy was able to visit Robert 'at any convenient time', and it is probable that Jane and Guildford were permitted time together. Robert exercised on the leads of the Beauchamp Tower and was sometimes able to meet other prisoners as a guest at the Lieutenant's table. Northampton, who had been condemned beside Northumberland, was pardoned and permitted to leave the Tower.

Even Elizabeth appeared to conform to the Catholic faith, despite Jane's praise for her 'religious modesty'.[29] She asked Mary to send her 'ornaments for her chapel: copes, chasubles, chalices, crosses, patens and other similar objects'.[30] Yet she let her allies see 'the perfunctory nature of her conversion'.[31] Mary became suspicious of her involvement in 'some great evil'[32] and arranged for her house to be watched. Cecil took Mass at his home, and even Cheke, who was being held in the Tower, 'could not face the fires of martyrdom, and recanted. Miserable and outcast, he retired to the country, where he died – of a broken heart, people said – in 1557.'[33]

Mary's betrothal to Philip of Spain caused great consternation. Parliament refused him the Crown Matrimonial, which would have subsumed England under Spanish rule by allowing him to rule England as King if Mary predeceased him. There were several plots contemplating the murder of the Queen to allow for the succession of Elizabeth, who was to be married to Devon. She was more popular than Jane, who was little known, but the threat of insurgency placed each of them in dire peril. Sir Thomas Wyatt led a rebellion in Kent, with a diversionary revolt in the West Country led by Sir Peter Carew. 'With a treachery and ingratitude equalled only by his incompetence',[34] Suffolk raised a force in the Midlands to support Wyatt. This was extraordinarily unwise, given his daughter's predicament in the Tower at a time when she was hoping for a pardon, but it shows that his new religious views were only skin-deep.

Devon, who had already spent fifteen years in the Tower, generally in solitary confinement, was a nervous participator. When questioned, he revealed all he knew. This implicated Suffolk. Mary tested Suffolk's loyalty by sending instructions to Sheen for him to take command of royal forces levied against Wyatt's Kentish men. By the time her messenger had arrived, Suffolk was already committed to rallying the West Midlands on Wyatt's behalf with help from his younger brothers. Although he undertook to act on Mary's instructions and Frances tried to make him abandon his unwise rebellion, he set off for his Leicestershire estates. This action was to result in Jane's execution.

As soon as Mary learned of Suffolk's deception, she pronounced that he was 'ungrateful for the favour he had received and the pardon he had obtained from his sovereign, after Northumberland's sedition'.[35] She sent Huntingdon to chase him down. Huntingdon was a good choice as he was in conflict with Suffolk over land acquisitions in Leicestershire. Suffolk was still calling for Jane's restoration, even though Wyatt was planning to install Elizabeth on the throne. If Jane were not already doomed, this was the final straw. As always, Suffolk proved incompetent and Huntingdon quickly routed him, taking both his baggage and money. Although Suffolk managed to hide with his brothers at one of his properties, an estate worker seeking a reward for their capture exposed them, and Huntingdon brought them back to London under arrest. Although Suffolk wrote a confession, this no longer survives. It apparently displayed his irritation at arrest, rather than any penitence for his treasonable actions, despite implicating several of his fellow conspirators. It made no mention of Jane whose life was now in jeopardy.

In Kent, Wyatt's rebel army of 3,000 men marched on London. Although the veteran Duke of Norfolk confronted the insurgents, many of his men defected to the rebel cause. The remainder trailed back into London, 'their coats torn, all ruined, without arrows or strings in their bows'.[36] Mary showed 'splendid courage',[37] urging Londoners to take up arms. 'She had thus far retained the love of her people',[38] but her plans to marry Philip of Spain were unpopular.

As Wyatt approached London, shipping was cleared from Tower Wharf, so that guns could be trained across the Thames. Although his men overran Southwark on 3 February 1554, they failed to take London Bridge.[39] This forced them to head west and to cross the Thames at Kingston, from where they advanced through the west of London four days later. Being short of provisions, many crept away after failing to gain Londoners' support. Wyatt reached the City walls at Ludgate, where the outcome hung in the balance for some hours, but he was forced back and surrendered at Temple Bar. With his bedraggled supporters, he was marched to the Tower for distribution within its overcrowded quarters.

Urged on by her Catholic advisers, Mary inflicted savage reprisals on the rebels. Gardiner and his supporters then pushed her into approving the execution of Jane Grey and Guildford Dudley. Their concern was to remove possible rivals for the throne, who might jeopardise her Spanish marriage and incite more rebellion. Jane was probably advised of Mary's decision on 7 February. She behaved with 'great resolution',[40] determined to die steadfast to her faith. With her execution confirmed, Mary offered her one last opportunity to recant to save her immortal soul. She sent Dr John Feckenham, Abbot of Westminster, to debate with her, hoping that she would back down as everyone else seemed to be doing. Feckenham was a staunch Catholic, who had spent much of King Edward's reign in the Tower. On his first visit, he realised he was making no progress, but, out of kindness, asked Mary for more time to win Jane over. Mary agreed to defer the execution date by three days until 12 March. Unlike Northumberland and her father, Jane welcomed death as a means of demonstrating martyrdom for her faith. She was well able to hold her own with Feckenham and was fired up by their debate. Despite being saddened by his failure, Feckenham respected her fortitude. Having developed a mutual understanding, he proved a great comfort to her, undertaking to remain at her side during her execution.

On 12 February, Jane wrote some words to her father in her prayer book:

> The lord comfort your grace that in his word wherein all creatures only are to be comforted and though it has pleased god to take away two of your children yet think not I most humbly beseech your grace that you have lost them but trust that we by losing this mortal life and I for my part as I have honoured your grace in this life will pray for you in another life. Your grace's humble daughter, Jane Dudley.[41]

The Prayer book was then passed by her jailer to Guildford, who also wrote to Suffolk:

> Tarry not for I am even at the point of death: Your loving and obedient son wisheth unto your grace long life in this

world with as much joy and comfort, as did I wished to myself, and in the world to come joy everlasting. Your most humble son to his death, G. Dudley.[42]

Although Guildford requested a final meeting with Jane on the eve of their execution, Jane declined. Her focus was on remaining composed for the ordeal that was to follow.

> She let him answer that if their meeting could have been a means of consolation to their souls, she would have been very glad to see him, but as their meeting would only tend to increase their misery and pain, it was better to put it off for the time being, as they would meet shortly elsewhere and live bound by indissoluble ties.[43]

This does not denote any great earthly feelings for him. She had never wanted to marry him, but their fates were now intertwined.

Guildford was the first to face death. Having embraced his brothers, he was taken to the place of his father's public execution at Tower Hill, outside the Tower. By all accounts he made a brave end, resolute in his faith to the last and refusing the ministrations of a Catholic priest.[44] Jane saw his bleeding carcass from her lodging window as it was returned to the Tower. She cried out: 'Oh Guildford, Guildford', and was overcome by the reality of it all. Her own execution had to be delayed while she recovered her composure. When she was at last taken down, she was met by Sir John Brydges, the Lieutenant of the Tower. He much admired his courageous charge and she gave him her only remaining possession, her small prayer book, in which she had inscribed her messages. Her last entry ended with the words of Ecclesiastes: 'There is a time to be born and a time to die and the day of death is better than the day of our birth.' She did not have to face public execution but was taken to a specially erected scaffold on the green outside St Peter ad Vincula, in full view of the remaining Dudley brothers from the Beauchamp Tower. She walked to her place of execution, 'prayed, spoke to a few bystanders, knelt and submitted her neck to the axe'.[45] She had to be led, as a handkerchief had been placed round her eyes, but died with quiet fortitude from one swing of the axe. There is no memorial erected to her, but she was immediately recognised as a martyr. Such executions left a bitter taste.

Suffolk, who had been arrested two days earlier, was executed on 23 February. Wyatt was hanged, drawn and quartered in April, but most of the remaining rebels were freed in a great show of compassion. They were marched through the London streets in bonds to the tiltyard at Westminster, where they knelt before Mary to receive her pardon. Cecil's ally, Sir Nicholas Throckmorton, was acquitted by a London jury and survived to become one of Elizabeth's foremost advisers.

Gallows were set up all over London for the religious persecution that was to follow. Prisons became so overcrowded that many prisoners were housed in churches, 'forty or more at a time'.[46]

Chapter 7

Surviving Mary Tudor's reign of terror

In the wake of Wyatt's rebellion, Elizabeth was summoned from Ashridge, but feigned illness, causing Mary to place more spies in her household. It is difficult to judge the extent of her complicity, but she was too cunning to be incriminated and Wyatt's later testimony exonerated her. There can be little doubt that Cecil had advised her how to act.

Three councillors arrived to collect Elizabeth for examination at the Tower. Although she had pleaded with Mary to send her elsewhere, Gardiner 'had persuaded the Queen and bullied the Council'.[1] Renard urged Mary not to miss the 'heaven-sent' opportunity to remove her head. 'He had noted her attraction to the people, which he thought might menace the prospects for his master's son, the Prince of Spain.'[2] She moved there by slow stages, 'prostrate with anxiety' and 'all swollen'.[3] On arrival, she travelled through 'a city of horror and desolation, where traitors' heads and quarters spoke their obscene warning from the City gates and twenty gallows stood to recall a day of awful butchery just past'.[4] She reached the Privy Stairs (not Traitors' Gate as is sometimes claimed) on Palm Sunday 1554, terrified to be at the place where her mother had been executed and buried. She made a brief speech to the Lieutenant: 'Oh Lord! I never thought to have come in here as a prisoner; and I pray you all good friends and fellows, bear me witness that I come in no traitor but as true a woman to my Queen's majesty as any is now living: and thereon I will take my death.'[5] A party of 'yeoman-warders broke rank, and, kneeling down, called out: "God save your Grace!"'[6] Without Elizabeth, the Protestant cause would have no plausible figurehead on which to focus attention.

With Wyatt's objective having been to place Elizabeth on the throne, Gardiner was convinced that she must be implicated. Despite her repeated denials of involvement, she and those in her service faced remorseless interrogation, but she was already a master of duplicity and professed her loving allegiance to Mary and adherence to the Roman Catholic faith. Although it appeared that Wyatt had written letters to her on two occasions, she denied receiving them and there was no evidence that she had replied.[7]

Elizabeth was housed in the Bell Tower, next to Robert in the Beauchamp Tower. With the execution of Jane Grey and Guildford Dudley having removed any potential rivalry between the Dudley family and Elizabeth, they were not initially permitted to see each other. She was surrounded by the strictest security, with five guards whenever she stepped out of her room. Her only meetings with Robert would have been as guests at the Lieutenant's table, but he may have smuggled messages of encouragement to her. For several weeks, she remained unwell and, being confined to her rooms, permission was granted for her to walk on the leads and later in the Privy Garden, where they may have been able to meet. Their shared experience in the Tower undoubtedly established a strong bond between them.[8] This was only strengthened by Mary's marriage to Philip of Spain which took place by proxy after Easter, followed, after his arrival, by a ceremony at Winchester Cathedral on 25 July 1554.

With a complete lack of evidence being uncovered, the judges declared that there were insufficient grounds to convict Elizabeth. Mary and Gardiner were left with little choice but to authorise her release after two months in the Tower. Being the focus of every new Protestant uprising, she was in an extremely vulnerable position and was unlikely to be able to talk her way out of involvement for a second time. On 19 May, she was moved under house arrest to Woodstock in Oxfordshire, with country people calling out in sympathy as she travelled. At Woodstock, she was kept out of reach of London for fear of unrest associated with Philip's unwelcome arrival. Kat Ashley was not permitted to stay there, and a troop of soldiers was positioned on a hilltop outside to watch her movements and prevent attempts to free her. To his horror, her custodian, Sir Henry Bedingfield, found several of her allies residing at the Bull public house in Woodstock. He was no match for Elizabeth's incessant requests for concessions.

Jane Guildford pinned her hopes for gaining her sons' release by promoting their potential as soldiers. In the spring of 1554, when Philip's Spanish retinue started to arrive in increasing numbers, she befriended members of the King's Privy Chamber and their ladies. She was permitted to return to court, where she hoped to gain help in her sons' plight. She was soon cultivating the Duchess of Alva, wife of Philip's pre-eminent Spanish General and adviser, and gained the friendships of the Duke of Medinaceli, Principal Gentleman of the Bedchamber, and Don Diego de Mendosa, whose family held several senior Spanish diplomatic roles. She was assisted by her son-in-law, Sir Henry Sidney, who had survived at court following Edward's death, but not with the same goodwill as previously. In March 1554, he joined a diplomatic mission sent to Spain to negotiate Mary's marriage. He must have made a good impression on Philip, who became a godfather to his son, Philip Sidney, born later that same year. Nevertheless, it was an uphill task to persuade Mary to show any mercy to the Dudleys.

At last, Jane Guildford's hard work started to pay off. When John fell ill in the Tower, permission was given for him to visit her daughter, Mary Sidney, at Penshurst, but he died there on 21 October 1554, three days after his release. This was one tragedy too many for Jane, who expired at Chelsea three months later. In the light of this, orders were given for Ambrose, now Earl of Warwick, Robert and Henry to be released, although their attainders were not immediately lifted. Robert was not permitted to inherit his mother's legacy to him of 50 Marks of land at Halesowen, or his inheritance in right of his wife received on the death of Sir John Robsart on 6 June 1554. This left Amy and him in dire financial straits and he had to borrow from friends to pay off his mother's debts. Despite her request for a simple burial in a wooden coffin, the brothers arranged a fitting funeral. This involved a procession of seventy-two torch bearers with two servants carrying branched candlesticks at Chelsea church.

Freedom provided the surviving Dudley brothers with the opportunity to show off their prowess in martial arts. In December 1554, Ambrose and Robert participated in a tournament held to celebrate Anglo-Spanish friendship. They needed Philip's goodwill to assure their welcome at court, and when friends commended them to the Spanish prince, they were permitted to return to London. Robert's kinsmen, Edward, Lord Dudley, and his brother, Sir Henry, had already been re-employed, with Edward appointed as Lieutenant of Hampnes. After a short spell in the Tower, Sir Henry had satisfied his interrogators and was taken into the Queen's service. By the summer of 1554, he was at the French court, where he became involved in a new plot to oust Mary and her Spanish affiliates.

French leaders and English émigrés were involved in a scheme to place Elizabeth on the throne with Devon as her consort with £50,000 from the French Exchequer. A thousand French troops led by Sir Henry were to land on the Isle of Wight in the confident expectation of gathering rebel support on arrival. In return for French involvement, Calais was to be handed over to France. When the plan was betrayed, many English-based conspirators lost their heads at Tower Hill in July 1555, before the rebellion had begun.

Elizabeth and her allies were once more in a most dangerous position. Several of her staff including Kat Ashley, Dee and Giambattista Castiglione, her resident tutor, were brought to the Tower for interrogation. Although Kat hotly denied that Elizabeth had any knowledge of the plot, she was retained in the Tower for three months. Dee, whose principal occupation for Elizabeth was casting her horoscope, revealed no more. There is no firm evidence implicating Robert and his brothers, but there can be little doubt that they were aware of the plot and Robert was keeping Elizabeth informed through his Hatfield contacts. He had several friends among the émigrés in her service and was able to arrange their repatriation after Elizabeth's accession. These included both Sir Henry Dudley and the diplomat, Sir Henry Killigrew. The Dudleys had to be careful. When they were spotted talking to malcontents near St Paul's, they were warned to retire to the country. As Robert commended himself to Philip as a potential military commander, any possible treachery seems to have been ignored.

It was Spanish influence, which did much to protect Elizabeth. This arose initially while she was still at Woodstock. When Mary concluded that she was pregnant, there were Spanish concerns that she could die in childbirth. Philip recognised that if Elizabeth were considered illegitimate, the dynastic heir to the English throne was Mary Queen of Scots, soon to be married to the French Dauphin. If the next Queen Consort of France became Queen Regnant of England, the balance of power in Europe would change to the great detriment of the Spanish Empire. Philip recognised that Spain's future relationship with England depended on alliance with Elizabeth, the next heir under Henry VIII's will. As a member of Philip's suite, Robert was positioned to convey messages to Elizabeth of the Spanish King's warm attitude towards her. Philip urged Mary to show her sisterly friendship and to return her to court. With Elizabeth enjoying Philip's favour, Mary could not arrest her for any part in Sir Henry Dudley's rebellion. She was 'a person of too much wisdom, honour, truth, and respect to duty and honesty to be a party to conspiracy'.[9] Sir Thomas Pope, founder of Trinity College Oxford, was sent to act as her guardian. Elizabeth reported that he was courteous and congenial and wrote platitudes confirming her undying loyalty to Mary. Her biggest concern was to stave off marriage. When Devon died in Padua in September 1556, Philip proposed that she should espouse his ally and military commander the Duke of Savoy. Mary was stubbornly reluctant to agree to this, as it would involve recognising Elizabeth as her heir. Nevertheless, she was so 'intoxicated with love'[10] for Philip that she agreed. Elizabeth was summoned to court, but when pressed to marry the Duke, she refused and was sent back to Hatfield in disgrace.

Left to herself, Mary would not have restored Elizabeth to favour. She saw her cousin and close friend, the Catholic Margaret Lennox, as her rightful heir and provided her with sumptuous apartments at the Palace of Westminster. Margaret had been born in England and had a son, Henry, Lord Darnley. With Elizabeth being illegitimate in Catholic eyes and Mary Queen of Scots debarred as a foreigner, Margaret was next in line dynastically and was certainly very astute. It was the Spanish viewpoint which prevailed. This was a huge disappointment to Margaret, but Philip was wary of her husband, Lennox, who had been brought up in France and retained close French affiliations.

Mary reacted slowly to the request for Elizabeth to be returned to court, but the prospect of childbirth gave her a greater sense of security. Elizabeth was brought back into seclusion at Hampton Court, where, progressively, she was permitted visitors. When Mary took to her bed, to her great embarrassment it turned out to be a phantom pregnancy. Philip only wanted to escape from a wife 'who was too old and worn to heat his blood'.[11] It is apparent, as he confessed in his later years, that he had developed an affection for his pale, red-headed sister-in-law, who was fighting her corner so powerfully and was dutifully attending Mass. He had every intention of making her his bride, if Mary should die without children. At the same time, Elizabeth 'used every art to ingratiate herself with [him]'.[12] After he left for the Continent on 26 April 1555, Mary lived almost in seclusion, and Elizabeth started to be courted as her likely heir.

In September 1555, following the abdication of Charles V, Robert returned to France as a junior member of the entourage to establish control of Philip's dominions in the Netherlands. With Philip becoming King of Spain, all nationalities making up his vast empire were represented. Robert acted as a messenger, carrying reports to English ambassadors elsewhere on the Continent and to diplomats back in England. Although war between France and Spain had been briefly halted by the Truce of Vaucelles, it broke out again the following year. Philip called for English troops to be sent to the Continent to support their Spanish allies. He left nothing to chance and planned a visit to England to commandeer supplies. Robert was chosen to advise Mary, who was overjoyed to hear that Philip was coming. Despite her best efforts, Philip's call for English troops was strongly resisted both in the Council and Parliament. The Dudleys were among several disgraced courtiers, who took this as their opportunity. They offered to raise men on Philip's behalf, if their estates and titles were restored.

Having reached Greenwich on 17 March 1556, Robert set about raising money to fund his forthcoming military involvement. On 30 May, he raised £500 by selling 1,200 acres at Bulcamp in Suffolk, which was a part of Amy's marriage settlement. He also raised a loan on the Halesowen estates, using it to buy out his siblings at a cost of £1,100. He then pledged the entire estate as security for loans of £1,928 6s 8d. Significantly, it was Robert who took the initiative rather than Ambrose or their uncle, Sir Andrew. By this time, Sir Andrew was an invalid, and, although he lived for another three years, his will made at this time described him as 'sick of body'.[13] It might have been expected that Ambrose would take the lead. He did not lack courage and was to prove an effective soldier. Yet Robert was the stronger character with the gifts of the consummate courtier, so that the rest of the family followed in his wake.[14] He was also a lot better looking. When later seeking a husband for Mary Queen of Scots, de Quadra claimed that Elizabeth told William Maitland, the Scottish Secretary of State, that 'she wished to God Lord Warwick had the grace and good looks of Lord Robert, and that each could have one of the brothers'. It was not that Ambrose was 'ugly, either, nor was he ungraceful, but his manner was rather rough, and he was not so gentle as Lord Robert'.[15] Particularly after the death in 1559 of their uncle, Sir Andrew, it was Robert who became the driving force in the family to achieve the restoration of their estates with a mixture of 'persistence, flattery and graciousness'.[16] Mary Sidney also played her part by becoming one of Elizabeth's best loved ladies-in-waiting. Robert befriended prominent members of Philip II's suite, and even the King himself, using a combination of gifts and bribes to servants, which left him heavily in debt. He continued to cultivate Spaniards as allies, retaining them for years to come.[17] Much later, the walls of Kenilworth included portraits of Philip, Alva, the Duke of Feria, Charles V and the Duchess of Parma.

In July 1556, when the English sent a force of 6,000 men under Pembroke to the Netherlands, the Dudley brothers went with it, each having raised small contingents to join the expedition. Robert was designated Master of the Ordnance.[18] At the beginning of August, their force linked up with Philip's main army under the Duke of Savoy, largely consisting of German mercenaries, to cross the border into France. It immediately laid siege to St Quentin on the Somme. When Anne de Montmorency, the Constable of France, brought a French relief column to the town's rescue, it was annihilated by the Spanish allies, who took him prisoner along with many others. When St Quentin capitulated, it was mercilessly looted.

Robert demonstrated 'courage and administrative skill that pleased Philip greatly'.[19] As a reward, on 30 January 1557, the Dudley family's attainders were at last lifted. Robert was given the honour of carrying news of the victory to the Queen at Greenwich and she restored him to the manor of Hemsby. Tragically, Henry Dudley, who was not yet 20, was killed by a cannon ball beneath the walls of St Quentin in Robert's full view. The shock of losing his brother and the atrocities committed by the Spanish army made a lasting impression on him. Ambrose and Robert were now the only survivors of Northumberland's eight sons. Neither of them had produced children of their own. Despite eight years of marriage, Amy Robsart had failed to conceive, and this must have been a great tragedy for the couple.

Inexplicably, with Paris at his mercy, Philip did not press home his advantage. He disbanded most of his army, sending the rest into winter quarters. This bought time for the French to recall the Duke of Guise from Italy to restore their morale and to protect the terrified Parisians. Under his leadership the French, on 1 January 1558, captured Calais, by when Ambrose and Robert were safely back in England. The grateful French King, Henry II, now confirmed his approval for the marriage of Guise's niece, Mary Queen of Scots, to his son and heir, the French Dauphin, Francis. This took place at Notre Dame of 24 April 1558.

England was gripped by religious persecution: 300 Protestant martyrs were burned at the stake and many more were forced to recant in public; 800 wealthier citizens avoided persecution by escaping to the Continent. This only deepened Protestant resolve. Even Catholics abhorred the oppressive regime of a Government being dictated to by Jesuit fanatics. 'The involvement in foreign war, the loss of Calais, the frequent clashes between Spaniards and Englishmen, the failure to deal with the realm's economic problems – all these were bitterly resented.'[20]

Robert was at the forefront of those despising Mary's policies. Instead of trying to capitalise on his faithful service to the Crown, he withdrew to his Norfolk estates for as long as Mary remained Queen. At least his share of the loot from St Quentin enabled him to settle his debts, and he managed to sell his mother's property at Halesowen. This involved some haggling, and he did not receive payment until 1561, but he amassed a profit of £3,000. Although he and Amy could live in some style at Syderstone, it lacked the pasture and woodland acres that he desired. He contemplated purchasing another property, but his ambitions were overtaken by events.

In October 1557, when Mary returned to St James's Palace to attend Parliament, Elizabeth retired to Hatfield. She was short of money to fund her household, but following Robert's return from the Netherlands, he had sold parcels of land with the support of Ambrose – apparently to assist her. Much later, on 16 August 1561 when the scholar and diplomat, Hubert Languet, briefed Augustus, Elector of Saxony, on Robert's prospect of marrying Elizabeth, he reported that her advisers opposed it:

> but she was more attached to him than any of the others because when she was deserted by everybody in the reign of her sister not only did he never lessen in any degree his kindness and humble attention to her, but he even sold his possessions that he might assist her with money, and therefore she thought it just that she should make some return for his good faith and constancy.[21]

Writing in the seventeenth century, Gregorio Leti refers to a gift of £200 sent to Elizabeth by the hand of a lady on Robert's behalf. Admittedly, Leti was a 'romancer', whose comments should be read with caution.

With Mary's health already causing concern, Elizabeth was gaining the attention of all those disillusioned with England's Catholic regime. She now had a constant stream of gentlemen and pages seeking service with her. She had to be extremely careful to whom she spoke and, of necessity, there is great difficulty in unravelling her network of allies, among whom Robert was undoubtedly key. Many of them were living abroad or formed part of Philip's entourage. There is very little information on Robert's relationship with her at this difficult time. He was careful to develop allies among her staff, and if he did send her messages, it was through her comptroller at Hatfield, Sir Thomas Parry. At this time, he counted Cecil as a close associate. John Dee, who had been Robert's teacher, was another, as was Castiglione. Robert was also an old friend of Ascham, who had returned to her service as Latin secretary.

Elizabeth met Cecil only rarely during Mary's reign, although he remained her surveyor to assist with her legal work. He was almost schizophrenic. On the surface he was Mary's loyal subject attending Mass at his home and happy to serve his Catholic monarch. Behind the scenes, he remained a secret critic of her government, and was without a job. With Mary expected to remain as Queen for an indefinite period, he would need to change his spots if he were to resume a political career and to demonstrate his loyalty to the new regime. Perhaps surprisingly, he was chosen to travel to Brussels to greet Cardinal Reginald Pole and to escort him to England. Even more surprisingly, they became friends, and Cecil used Pole's influence to gain restoration to favour, providing him with legal advice and being appointed High Steward of Pole's manor at Wimbledon. When a bill was placed before Parliament seeking to expropriate the land of Protestant exiles, Cecil was determined to prevent it becoming law. Knowing they had a majority in the House of Commons, its opponents locked the doors, forcing the Speaker to call a vote which defeated it.[22]

Mary was running out of time. Men flocked to support Elizabeth, who was recognised as her heir 'by the irresistible right of popular expectation'.[23] On 8 November 1558, Mary's councillors called on her to nominate Elizabeth as her successor. Much to the disappointment of Margaret Lennox, she agreed, but rather pathetically, coupled her recognition with a request for Elizabeth to retain the Catholic religion. Robert's prospects suddenly looked very much brighter. Elizabeth was well prepared. In the previous February, Cecil had taken the opportunity of her visit to Somerset House to hold a secret meeting with her. Nothing was written down, but from now on Cecil was an integral part of her plans for Government. Sir Thomas Parry, her Comptroller at Hatfield, and Cecil were given the task of identifying Council members for when the time came.

Mary died on 17 November. Several members of the Council immediately travelled to Hertfordshire to offer their allegiance to Elizabeth, but Cecil was there ahead of them. Elizabeth told them:

> The law of nature moves me to sorrow for my sister; the burthen that is fallen upon me maketh me amazed; and yet, considering that I am God's creature ordained to obey His appointment, I will yield thereto, desiring from the bottom of my heart that I may have assistance of His grace to be the minister of His heavenly will in this office now committed to me.[24]

Her first reaction was to give thanks to God. She then made a list of people who needed to be told immediately.

From the outset, Elizabeth showed extraordinary political acumen. Never for a moment did she appear to be overawed by the enormity of her new role. She knew that she was born to be England's monarch. She modelled her authority on that of her father and was to share his vanity and a love of beautiful possessions and surroundings. She wished to be adored. Nevertheless, she ate and drank little, seldom dined in public and when she did, often left the table with the meal only half finished. For ordinary drinking she preferred the lightest sort of ale (which was less prone to contamination than water). She maintained an exacting standard of personal cleanliness and expected those around her to do the same. She lived simply and was prepared to work hard.[25] She warned her advisers that she did not want an unwieldy Council nor one 'whose complexion was old fashioned'. She had no intention of alienating those who would now find themselves in retirement and begged those whose services were foregone not to think that this arose from their disabilities, but 'from her conviction that a multitude made for discord and confusion, instead of good counsel'.[26] Maintaining their support was fundamental. Not only was she illegitimate in Catholic eyes, but until Parliament met, also in accordance with English law. If the Pope declared against her, Mary, the Queen Dauphine of France, was poised to claim the English throne.

Most propitiously, Cecil was appointed as her Secretary of State and as a member of her Privy Council. From the outset she told him:

> This judgement I have of you, that you will not be corrupted with any manner of gift, and that you will be faithful to the State, and that without respect of my private will you will give me that counsel that you think best. And if you know anything necessary to be declared to me of secrecy, you shall show it to myself only, and assure yourself I will not fail to keep taciturnity therein, and therefore herewith I charge you.[27]

He repaid her by working assiduously on her government's behalf for the rest of his life. He:

> might sometimes lament that she would not do what he wanted her to do; he had never to complain that she would not give her mind to the matter. The closest bond between Elizabeth and the man who worked hardest for her was that they shared the same consuming interest.[28]

Parry, who joined the Council, was knighted and named Comptroller of the Household, but he did not prove influential and died in 1562. Kat Ashley was made First Lady of the Bedchamber with her husband becoming Keeper of the Queen's jewels. Ambrose was appointed 'chief pantler' to provide food for the coronation, and Master of the Ordnance. Yet it was Robert whom Elizabeth favoured. He arrived, reputedly on a 'milk-white steed', and was appointed Master of the Horse. With Sir Peter Carew, he was sent to advise Philip II on the Continent.

PART 2

ELIZABETH'S FAVOURITE

Chapter 8

Master of the Horse

Robert returned to England to take up his role as Master of the Horse, a position of considerable importance, which he held for almost the rest of his life.

> It entailed the buying, stabling, physicking, training, breeding and making available at all times of the large body of horses required by the Queen and her household – the Queen's riding horses and those of her attendants as well as the pack-horses and mules for her baggage trains when she moved from place to place.[1]

He was also responsible for 'purveyance', which involved demanding a certain number of horses from each district to meet royal requirements.

Robert's role involved arranging hunting parties, all the pageantry involved on state occasions and organising royal progresses. These were a logistical nightmare, with hundreds of men and women of all ranks needing to be housed, fed and watered wherever they went. He also provided 'great horses' for jousts and military needs. He was ideally suited to the task, which had been fulfilled by his brother John for Edward VI, and he lavished great care and attention to it. It was no sinecure; he headed one of the busiest departments of the household, which involved a significant financial outlay.[2] He was a good judge of horse flesh and purchased animals on the Continent to build a breeding program designed to improve the native strain. This became the precursor to the development of the thoroughbred. In May 1581, he received a gift of six Hungarian greys for Her Majesty's coach. Although they were light grey, their manes and tails were dyed 'orange-tawney, according to the manner of their country'. They were used to draw her coach for the opening of Parliament in 1584, with 'bridles studded with pearls' and 'diamond pendants on their foreheads'.[3] There were regulations covering the export of horses from Spain, but Robert concluded that the Spanish authorities might be more receptive if he offered English dogs in exchange. He was soon spending £400 per year on purchasing new horses and harness alone. He hired Neapolitan riding masters, particularly Prospero d'Osma, who for many years ran a successful école de manège at Mile End and provided 'excellent advice on improving pasture, covering mares, rearing foals, breaking colts and counteracting diseases'.[4] In 1564, the new French ambassador, Michel de Castelnau, Sieur de Mauvissière, brought over the Italian, Hercules Trincetta, who Robert wanted to employ. Trincetta 'gave place to no other in the breaking of young horses'.[5] Following the Massacre of St Bartholomew in 1572, Robert was looking for a riding master to teach the art of manège, which 'involved the horses stopping suddenly and wheeling in a small space'.[6] With so many French lords being casualties of the massacre, Robert hoped that he might find a suitable riding master unemployed. In September, he wrote to Francis Walsingham, then ambassador in Paris, authorising him to offer £30 per annum and his keep. Walsingham wrote back that they were demanding £75, so Robert found one in Italy. Elizabeth was always frugal and expected the best results with minimum expenditure. She enforced existing statutes requiring landowners to maintain a specified number of mounts commensurate with their station.

Robert had a good understanding of court ceremonial, being both an exceptional horseman and showman, 'tall, powerful, active and handsome'.[7] With his natural panache, he dressed expensively, often spending £400 at a time on costly materials ordered in European markets.[8] He was a convivial friend, loving good food and enjoying a wager on his sporting contests. His healthy appetite became a standing joke in court circles.[9] Inevitably, he needed to delegate, but he was a 'hands-on' manager, particularly when he felt that his personal touch was called for.[10]

Robert's new role kept him near to court and close to the Queen. It positioned him to restore the Dudleys from the brink of extinction. Elizabeth was captivated by this 25-year-old, with his outrageous sense of fun, his slim athletic physique, dark hair and long slender fingers that matched her own. She referred to him as 'Two Eyes', and he would sign his letters to her as 'ō ō'.[11] They had shared difficult times together in the Tower, but he had not put her life in danger with some hot-headed fanatical scheme to place her on the throne. She would never forget how he had sold property to help her finances when she returned to Hatfield. He was totally devoted to the Crown, just as his father and grandfather had been. With most of her advisers calling on her to make political decisions, he provided a welcome diversion from affairs of state. He encouraged her to enjoy the fresh air, and she rode out with him in the royal parks or to go hunting. She liked 'good gallopers' and frightened even Robert when 'she spareth not to try as fast as they can go'.[12] This 'passion for riding and hunting never abated'. At a hunt at Windsor, the Spanish ambassador recorded: 'The Queen went so hard that she tired everybody out, and as her ladies and courtiers were with her they were all put to shame. There was more work than pleasure in it for them.'[13] Robert greatly enjoyed riding with her and was an invaluable trustworthy companion. 'Every letter [he] wrote to his sovereign bore extravagant protestations of loyalty.'[14] He spent lavishly on costly gifts for her, frequently being left out of pocket.[15] Yet he was married and Elizabeth, initially at least, had no time for dalliance. She was far too occupied with political issues.[16]

Robert was not offered a political role and was not made a member of the Privy Council. This may seem surprising, as Cecil, who was responsible for its make-up, had been a close ally of the Dudleys and remained close to Robert in the final days of Mary's reign. Cecil's objective was to fill the Council with those who would be supportive of a Protestant religious policy, but they needed to be people of standing and political influence. Many of its members had served under Edward VI and even under Henry VIII. They viewed politics very differently from Robert, who was only waiting for the day that he could emulate his father's military achievements. He was a hawkish nationalist and would have loved nothing more than to make his name by returning to the Continent to recover Calais. To face the combined might of Catholic Europe, he needed support from German Protestant princes. He could rely on a few Protestant extremists and allies at home, such as Francis, 2nd Earl of Bedford, who was a member of the Council and had spent part of Mary's reign in exile. Others included his brother-in-law's father Huntingdon, his brother Ambrose, and Pembroke.

Cecil knew that taking an aggressive approach on the Continent would be disastrous. Robert's dogmatic Protestantism made him confrontational; he was not a man to grasp the subtleties of Cecil's objectives. The Royal Exchequer was empty, there was uncertainty whether Elizabeth commanded universal support at home, and she faced the prospect of diplomatic isolation if Spain, France, and the papacy combined to extirpate heresy. It was not just in England that religious beliefs were polarised. Committed Protestants all over Europe had gathered in Geneva, Zurich, Frankfurt and other Protestant centres to develop their extremist views. Those from England returned, fired up with a reforming zeal to challenge the Jesuit doctrines of Mary's Spanish advisers. Cecil sought inclusive government to attract the Howards and other cliques marginalised during the development of the Reformation of Edward's reign. He wanted to cultivate Catholic powers on the Continent, particularly the Spanish, to believe that England was well positioned to maintain the balance of power between French and Spanish rivalry and was not their legitimate prey. With Elizabeth only doubtfully legitimate, he had to prevent the French from seeking to place Mary Queen of Scots, their Queen-Dauphine, on the English throne. At least the English had established the Scottish lords as allies across their northern border. These had turned to Calvinism to combat the threat of being subsumed under French control.

The European superpowers were exhausted by war and needed a period of peace. After the Constable's release in October 1558, the Guise family's hawkish policies were reversed, and Cecil elbowed his way into the negotiations between France and Spain to ensure that they did not combine to launch a Counter-Reformation against England and other parts of Protestant Europe. He realised that England was in no position to recover Calais. He wanted peace at almost any price. Elizabeth, who was no Protestant fanatic, supported Cecil. She was careful to cultivate Philip II as a possible marriage suitor, and to blur the edges of her religious affiliation until firmly secured on her throne.

In the meantime, Elizabeth kept Robert fully occupied in his role and in her company to provide spontaneous light relief from her political workload. Inevitably, this led to rumours and insults at the favour being shown to him. Robert brushed them off, and jealously guarded his standing with her. The Spanish ambassador advised Philip II to revise his list of pensioners to include Cecil, Robert and Bedford.

Chapter 9

Elizabeth establishes herself as Queen

On 23 November 1558, Elizabeth set out from Hatfield with her retinue to claim the English throne. She made a triumphant journey through cheering crowds, for whom 'no music is so sweet as the affability of their prince'.[1] On reaching London 'accompanied by a thousand or more lords, gentry and ladies',[2] she stayed for five days at the Charterhouse in the City. This was the home of Sir Edward, Lord North of Kirtling, a staunch Protestant who had been a member of the Council in the latter part of the reign of Henry VIII and under Edward VI. From here, she processed in state to take possession of the Tower. With her well-known equestrian skills, she appeared to full advantage on her great charger in a dress of violet velvet with a scarf about her neck. Robert rode behind her mounted on a black stallion. His new role assured that he would soon become well-established in the public eye.

For the next few weeks, Elizabeth was closeted with Cecil and her Council establishing the machinery of government. At Christmas, Robert adopted plans for court revels with an anti-Catholic slant. With her love of fine clothes, Elizabeth brought a new splendour and gaiety to the festivities.[3] Gone were the puritanical garments she had donned to visit Edward VI. By out-dancing everyone, she immediately showed 'her genius for creating a *rapport* with her people'.[4] Sir Nicholas Bacon, Cecil's brother-in-law, was able to speak of the nation's good fortune at having 'a princess to whom nothing – what, nothing? No, no worldly thing – was so dear as the hearty love and good will of her subjects'.[5] Christmas was followed three weeks later by her coronation, after Dee had cast her horoscope to establish a propitious date. Robert supervised the arrangements for a spectacular procession and pageants, providing troops to keep the routes clear for the 'smooth transit of thousands of dignitaries' past cheering crowds.[6] The whole event cost £20,000 and was designed by the Council to cement Elizabeth's position on the throne.

She was carried in a litter trimmed to the ground with gold brocade. Robert rode immediately behind, 'leading the fully caparisoned palfrey of honour'.[7] The citizens of London presented a Bible, 'urging her to uphold Protestant truth and tread down superstitious error'.[8] The ceremony took place at Westminster Abbey followed at three o'clock by a feast for 800 guests at Westminster Hall. Arundel, in cloth of silver, and Norfolk, in cloth of gold, rode their horses into the hall to herald the arrival of each course. The Queen was served by Sussex but sat speechless and exhausted after developing a severe cold. She lasted until one o'clock in the morning but might be forgiven for missing the jousting arranged for the next day.

Elizabeth's illness delayed the opening of Parliament from 23 to 25 January. It faced three important issues: England's religious settlement; the restoration of financial stability in the wake of Mary's disastrous foreign policy; and Elizabeth's marriage, which was likely to dictate foreign policy for the future. With religious sentiment being polarised, Cecil adopted a conciliatory approach, while bravely steering England back towards the reforms achieved during the reign of Edward VI.

> The Religious Settlement of 1559 was a determined attempt at religious toleration. It declared that supreme power over the national church was vested in the Crown, but the oath of supremacy was administered only to those in office; refusal to take it meant loss of office, but it was not to be put to old and venerable men. People, who wrote or spoke against the supremacy were liable to the death penalty, but only on the third conviction.[9]

Cecil's approach was unlikely to please extremists, but his objective was to embrace as many as possible by fostering the middle ground and tolerating both Catholic and Puritan services. Nevertheless, it 'stood four-square against the errors of the Church of Rome',[10] placing it in conflict with Continental Catholic powers. Catholics objected to the Crown's claim to supremacy over the church, but it followed Henry VIII's position that his authority 'on earth was next under God'.[11] While Puritans accepted this, they repudiated the Catholic church and objected to the use of church vestments, bellringing and even wedding rings. They considered that ministers should be chosen by their congregations and that bishops should not sit in the House of Lords, thus being reduced to the standing of the rest of the clergy. 'The Puritans were not numerically formidable, but they had an influence out of all proportion to their strength, and their sympathizers were found among the bishops themselves and in the Privy Council.'[12]

Elizabeth was not dogmatically Protestant and did not initially sign herself as Supreme Head of the Church as her father and brother had done. Nevertheless, she 'had not only assented to [the Religious Settlement]; she had been a member of the committee that drew [it] up'.[13] She preferred the 'rather more traditional and ambiguous' Lutheran doctrine embodied in the 1549 prayer book, to the more 'strident and evangelical' views of that of 1552,[14] which Cecil and other members of the Council advocated. While she tolerated Catholicism and, for a period, maintained Mass in her private chapel, as soon as she felt more secure, she publicly adopted Protestant liturgy. At Christmas, she instructed the Bishop celebrating Mass in her chapel not to elevate the host. When he refused, she walked out after the Gospel. 'Two days later she issued a proclamation which permitted certain parts of the service to be said in English.'[15]

> What mattered most was to prevent Catholic bishops and clergy from attempting to stir up trouble before the country became accustomed to her authority … There is no doubt that she believed she was God's lieutenant on earth and that all subjects owed to her unconditional obedience.[16]

It was convenient for her that at Mary's death, five bishoprics were vacant, and five more incumbents died within the year. All were replaced by Protestants.

The Supremacy Bill faced a bumpy ride through Parliament. Conservative bishops and peers argued 'that only the Church could determine matters of belief'.[17] Bedford stood up and asked whether it was true that when a Catholic deputation was sent to Rome during Mary's reign, 'the Roman Cardinals had offered to get them whores?'[18] John White, Bishop of Winchester, and Thomas Watson, Bishop of Lincoln, 'were charged with disobedience to common authority and were sent to the Tower'. Without them being present, the Bill was carried by three votes. London was very quickly restored to the Protestant faith. Within a few days all offenders held in prisons for their religion were released and it was clear that Philip II would 'have no further government' in England.

It was 'Puritanism [that] aroused [Elizabeth's] indignation and abhorrence'.[19] As Bishop White exclaimed: 'The wolves be coming out of Geneva and other places of Germany, and hath sent their books before, full of pestilent doctrines, blasphemy and heresy to infect the people.'[20] She hated John Knox, although they never met, but *The First Blast of the Trumpet against the Monstrous Regiment of Women* was an anathema to her with its criticism of women rulers. Although it was not aimed against her, and Knox wrote 'to convey his unfeigned love and reverence',[21] he told her that she ruled by the will of the people and not by dynastic right. She refused in future to have his name mentioned.

Elizabeth was now surrounded by the 38-year-old Cecil and those other 'brilliant sons of Cambridge with whom [her] education and life had been so intimately linked'.[22] During the first six months of her reign, she reduced the Crown's expenditure to £108,000 from the £267,000 spent during the last six months under Mary. This was largely achieved by ending English hostilities against France on behalf of the Spanish. The Treaty of Cateau-Cambrésis, signed on 2/3 April 1559, confirmed her as the rightful English Queen, but this was bought at a price. Calais was ceded to France and St Quentin restored to French control in exchange for French concessions in Italy. Thomas Gresham was sent to the Netherlands to negotiate repairs to English credit. Debased coinage issued by Mary had seriously interfered with English trade. It was now recalled and reissued in a reliable form.[23]

Elizabeth's marriage became a constant topic of concern. She made great efforts to string Philip II along as a suitor in the hope that he would 'paralyse hostility at Rome' and protect her right to the throne;[24] this did much to prevent her being declared illegitimate. He soon ruled himself out by requiring her to convert to Catholicism and by admitting he would need to spend much time abroad. Nevertheless, Catholic though he was, he was determined to undermine Mary Queen of Scots' claim to the English throne, as an Anglo-French alliance would threaten his means of communication through the Channel. He sent Gómez Suárez de Figueroa y Córdoba, Duke of Feria, as his ambassador to ensure that Elizabeth chose a husband acceptable to the Spanish interest. Philip was confident that Feria, as a Spanish grandee, would be able to influence her. He had been Mary Tudor's principal adviser, but 'was devoid of humour, proud and patronising'.[25] When he explained that she owed her throne to his master's goodwill, Elizabeth made clear that she was no one's puppet and owed her position to the support of the English people. He soon realised that this 25-year-old was a power to be reckoned with. He wrote to Philip: 'She seems to me incomparably more feared than her sister, and gives her orders, and has her way as absolutely her father did. Her present Comptroller, Parry, and Secretary Cecil govern the Kingdom ...' Having heeded the Council's concern at the prospect of a Spanish marriage, she kept Feria's attention with vague promises, until she felt sufficiently secure to tell him that she had decided not to marry for the time being. 'He was exasperated at the cool manner in which he was treated. Instead of being given a room at court and taken into counsel on every question, as he expected, he found himself in embarrassing ignorance of what was going on.'[26]

When it came to diplomacy, Elizabeth adopted indecisiveness as a weapon in a manner that exasperated her advisers but did much to protect her in the early part of her reign. She learned her skills extremely quickly, and her ability to survive unscathed from the rebellions of both Thomas Seymour and Wyatt had already demonstrated that she could look after herself. She refused to invade Scotland to back its rebel cause led by Lord James Stewart, the illegitimate half-brother of Mary Queen of Scots, against the Queen Regent, but provided him with money while hotly denying any involvement to the foreign ambassadors in London, 'at which she was expert to the point of genius'. Her powers of dissimulation were such that the ambassadors had to admit: 'She is the best hand at the game living.'[27] It was these skills that she would use to great effect to defend herself from criticism of her morality.

Initial diplomacy was all about finding Elizabeth a husband. She 'was far and away the best marriage to be had in Europe'.[28] She gave the impression of very great intelligence and her love of music and dancing made her attractive. According to Sir Richard Baker: 'She was of stature indifferent tall, slender and straight.' She had 'delightful hands' with 'fingers of unusual length ... whiter than whitest snow'.[29] She had piercing eyes but seems to have been short-sighted, so that enlarged pupils hid their golden yellow colour, making them appear black. Nevertheless, Feria considered her 'the daughter of the Devil and [one of] the greatest scoundrels and heretics in the land'.[30] He concluded: 'I am afraid that one fine day we shall find this woman married, and I shall be the last person in the place to know anything about it.'[31]

Elizabeth needed to marry and a powerful alliance would be welcome, but the principal concern was for her to produce an heir. Without this, there was every prospect of war, with the French and Spanish fighting it out on English soil. Philip put forward his cousins, Archdukes Ferdinand and Charles, brothers of the Emperor Maximilian. Ferdinand, whose Catholicism was unassailable, was soon withdrawn as Elizabeth was 'not sound in religion', and the Emperor became concerned at the thought of subjecting Charles 'to the danger of forfeiting the eternal salvation of his soul'.[32] Quite apart from the religious complexity, they had never met, and after Henry VIII's disappointment on first seeing Anne of Cleves, and Philip's agony on meeting Mary Tudor, Elizabeth would not trust a portrait and 'would not give the Archduke cause to curse'.[33] Although there were plans to bring Charles to England incognito, the Emperor Maximilian would not hear of it. The Prince of Savoy, another Habsburg connection, was also still being considered. Prince Eric, heir to the Swedish throne, was another to put his name forward, and his ambassador showered lavish presents on members of the court, who accepted his gifts, but laughed 'at his outlandish ways'.[34] Elizabeth, who was a fine exponent of courtly love, enjoyed all the attention and strung everyone along. Nevertheless, she claimed to have no desire for the wedded state: 'In the end, this shall be for me sufficient, that a marble stone shall declare that a Queen, having reigned such a time, lived and died a virgin.'[35] The House of Commons 'did not think that there was anything alarming in the prating about virginity. Let political considerations or passion single out some man, and another protesting spinster would go the way of most flesh.'[36] Even she admitted that 'she was but human and not insensible to human emotions and impulses, and when it became a question of the weal of her kingdom, or it might be for other reasons, her heart and mind might change.'[37] Robert was married, apparently quite happily, and initially did not consider himself as a suitor. This did not stop her enjoying his company. He was very attractive and turned heads. By 18 April 1559, Feria was writing:

> During the last few days Lord Robert has come so much into favour that he does what he likes with affairs and it is even said that her Majesty visits him in his chamber day and night. People talk of this so freely that they go so far as to say that his wife has a malady in one of her breasts and the Queen is only waiting for her to die to marry Lord Robert. I can assure your Majesty that matters have reached such a pass that I have been brought to consider whether it would

not be well to approach Lord Robert on your Majesty's behalf promising your help and favour and coming to terms with him.[38]

Italian observers wrote similar reports. Eleven days later, Feria wrote: 'Sometimes she speaks like a woman who will only accept a great prince, and then they say she is in love with Lord Robert and will never let him leave her.'[39]

Elizabeth showered Robert with gifts. He was granted parcels of land in Kent, Leicestershire and Yorkshire, with the manor on the river at Kew. He also became Constable and Lieutenant of Windsor Castle and Park. On 23 April 1559, he was made a Knight of the Garter along with Thomas Howard, 4th Duke of Norfolk, and Edward Manners, 3rd Earl of Rutland, both allies of Cecil. Yet, Robert was given preferential treatment. He was excused payment of the parliamentary subsidy in 1559, while Norfolk had to pay £160, one of the highest charges in the country. Cecil was concerned that their shared pleasure in music and dancing was encouraging a growing infatuation between them. It seemed that only Amy's life stood between Robert and the Crown.[40] He was now the focus of attention for all those wishing to press suits upon the Queen.[41] As her intermediary, he was inundated with letters and requests, and no doubt benefited financially from having the Queen's ear. He was particularly responsible for the preferment of staunch Protestants to bishoprics and deaneries. These included Thomas Young, Archbishop of York; Edmund Grindal, Bishop of London; Robert Horne, Dean of Durham and later Bishop of Winchester; Edwin Sandys, Bishop of Worcester, and Edmund Scambler, Bishop of Peterborough. Such patronage did little to maintain his rapport with Cecil and senior peers led by Norfolk, who formed an anti-Dudley faction at court.

Elizabeth also tasked Robert with brokering her foreign marriage negotiations. On the face of it, he was ideally placed for this. He had known Elizabeth from childhood and had served under the King of Spain. Nevertheless, her reluctance to commit herself was interpreted as an attempt by him to promote his own suit at the expense of more desirable political attachments. 'The fungus of bitter envy grew naturally and luxuriantly on the tree of Elizabethan court life.'[42] Suits for Elizabeth's hand arrived from many quarters. In October, there were 'ten or twelve [ambassadors] competing for [her] favour and eyeing each other in a far from friendly manner'.[43] Eric of Sweden had been formally rejected in May 1559, but he came back for more and faced four rejections in all, even after threatening to 'hasten to her through the seas, dangers and enemies, confident that she would not chide his faith and zeal'.[44] Having several suitors provided a degree of safeguard from hostility elsewhere, and she strung along the Archduke Charles, who was politically the best match, as an insurance policy.[45]

While the Council expressed particular hopes that she would choose within the realm, Robert was certainly not the preferred candidate. The widowed Arundel, who was Catholic and aged 46, seemed to believe that his standing made him a serious contender, but 'he was not handsome, and rather silly and loutish'.[46] With Elizabeth's enjoyment of the ritual of elaborate courtship, she played him along, spending five days at his home at Arundel in August 1559, until he believed that he had won her favour. He had become an implacable enemy of the Dudleys after imprisonment by Northumberland in the Tower without trial, but Elizabeth never trusted him. In May, while Robert was at Windsor on a hunting expedition, she also flirted with the diplomat, Sir William Pickering, a 'comely' 43-year-old bachelor, 'very much a lady's man, and said to have enjoyed the intimacy of many'.[47] Arundel was upset when she granted Pickering rooms in Whitehall Palace. This enabled her to play them off against each other, and Pickering over-stretched his diplomatic credentials by calling Arundel 'an impudent, discourteous knave'.[48] She told the Council, which had become anxious at her delaying tactics:

> Whenever it might please God to incline her heart to marry, her choice would light upon one who would be as careful for the preservation of the realm as she herself; or if it pleases Him to continue her still in this mind to live unmarried, provision would be made for the succession to the throne.[49]

Robert may not have been too concerned at the threat posed by either Arundel or Pickering but another candidate, the Scottish James Hamilton, Earl of Arran, a confirmed Protestant, was more concerning. He was in line to the Scottish throne after Mary Queen of Scots and his father, Châtelherault, the Scottish Regent. This was not the first time that such a marriage had been considered. Twelve years earlier, Henry VIII had hoped that an English/Scottish alliance could be reinforced by Châtelherault's son marrying his younger daughter, while Prince Edward married Mary Queen of Scots. With these negotiations coming to nothing, Arran spent much of his upbringing in France and distinguished himself against the Spanish at St Quentin. While still in France, rumours of his interest in marrying Elizabeth started to spread, and he was threatened with arrest. In August 1559, Cecil spirited him to London to test whether, once more, he should be considered as Elizabeth's spouse or whether he had potential as a Scottish Regent rather than Lord James Stewart. Cecil, who housed Arran at his home in Canon Row, Westminster, also discussed the possibility of Arran and Elizabeth replacing Mary Queen of Scots, who remained in France, on the Scottish throne.

Robert saw Arran's suit as threatening to his own relationship with Elizabeth and 'at once set about frustrating Cecil's national policy for his personal advantage'.[50] He immediately renewed discussions for the Austrian match of the Archduke Charles. He seems to have hoodwinked his sister, Mary Sidney, into believing that Elizabeth was supportive of the Archduke's suit. Acting on Robert's instruction, she told the new Spanish ambassador, Alvarez de Quadra, Bishop of Aquila, of Elizabeth's interest, but claimed that, as a woman, she would need to be 'teased' into it. It may well be that Elizabeth was in on the act and played along 'with pretended anticipation of the coming of her Imperial lover'.[51] Although de Quadra called for the Archduke Charles to visit, when he raised the proposal with Elizabeth she immediately backed off, but on Mary Sidney's advice he continued to press her. Mary was highly embarrassed, believing that she had been duped by Robert. Both she and Sir Henry were furious with him, but their anger quickly subsided. Nevertheless, de Quadra considered Robert devious. Cecil was also extremely angry at him trying to thwart his objective of keeping the Archduke's suit simmering along, without it coming to fruition. He now concluded that Robert 'was ready to swear allegiance to any cause to serve his purpose of dominating the Queen, a purpose which was ... dangerous to the national welfare'.[52] When de Quadra realised that Robert was using the Archduke as a decoy to thwart Arran's suit, Robert began promoting the match of Eric of Sweden. Meanwhile his enemies whispered that he was planning to poison his wife and to marry Elizabeth himself.[53]

Although Arran was interviewed by Elizabeth in London, he came up short and the marriage proposal came to nothing. It is not clear whether

Robert's intervention played a part in this. Tragically, Arran's family suffered from a strain of inherited insanity. The first reports of him being delusional arose during the siege of Leith in the following year, but, by 1562, he had become completely deranged and had to be locked away. It is quite possible that signs of madness were already manifesting themselves in London, or it may be that Elizabeth was too infatuated with Robert to contemplate Arran. Unfortunately, there is no written explanation available.

To develop his political skills, Robert was elected as a Member of Parliament for Norfolk, where he was gaining local respect, but Cecil blocked him from joining the Council. No one could accuse him of a lack of conscientiousness, but politics required an incisive mind. Nevertheless, his provision of patronage gave him the authority to influence the monarch.[54] This brought him into conflict with Cecil, who found himself increasingly insecure after having his policies countered. Despite being knighted, Cecil was not an aristocrat and his position depended on the Queen's goodwill. He was careful not to display any resentment at the favours she showed to Robert, but preferred to cultivate the 24-year-old Norfolk, Robert's rival.

Robert's forte was in organising court functions. In May 1559, he greeted the French mission, which arrived to ratify the treaty of Cateau-Cambrésis, meeting them at Tower Wharf and escorting them to their lodgings. He arranged 'five days of banquets, processions and entertainments, all of which demanded his presence'.[55] In October he welcomed Duke John of Finland, who arrived at Harwich to promote the suit of his brother, Prince Eric of Sweden. Eric had sent Elizabeth glamourous presents of ermine fur, and both gold and silver money.[56] With the French looking for any means to prevent her from making a Habsburg alliance they promoted Eric, but, to Robert's relief, Elizabeth remained disinterested, although the suit lingered on.

In July 1559, political uncertainty was heightened when Henry II of France was killed in a jousting accident in Paris, resulting in Mary Queen of Scots becoming the French Queen consort. Her ambitious Guise uncles were quick to assume control. This resulted in additional French troops being sent to Scotland to support their sister, Marie of Guise, in her struggle to maintain the Scottish throne for her daughter. The English Government saw their arrival as a prelude to a French incursion into England from the north. The Protestant lords in Scotland asked Elizabeth for assistance to oust them, but she remained lukewarm. She detested the republican sentiments of Calvinist doctrine as espoused by John Knox and needed to maintain peace with France, so dearly won by the treaty of Cateau-Cambrésis. Although Norfolk waited for her instructions at Berwick, she frustrated Cecil by leaving his invasion force inadequately manned and equipped, despite the Scottish lords' good progress against the hard-pressed French. When she at last relented, Norfolk's attack on the French garrison at Leith on 7 May 1560 resulted in him being repulsed with the loss of 1,000 men. This was no disappointment to Robert. It did not help that Scottish prostitutes in Leith, not wanting to lose their French clientele, threw burning coals from the walls onto the attackers!

It was the French who capitulated in Scotland. The rising power of the Huguenots had beset France with its own religious divisions. This allowed Catherine de Medici and her less hawkish allies to challenge the authority of the Guises. Following the death of Marie of Guise, the French sued for peace to prevent their military costs in Scotland bringing 'the ruin and desolation of France'. The Guises turned to Philip II to defend Catholicism in Scotland by mediating on their behalf. With his main interest being to retain England as an ally and to avoid Mary Queen of Scots also becoming the English Queen, it suited him to be pragmatic. Without consulting Mary, French and Spanish representatives met with the Scottish Regent, Châtelherault, and his deputy, Lord James Stewart. It was probably on Robert's instigation that Cecil arrived from London to conduct negotiations on Elizabeth's behalf. The Guises saw the Treaty of Edinburgh, signed on 6 July 1560, as a French sell-out. Elizabeth was recognised as the rightful English Queen and Mary's claim was dropped. French and English troops were to be withdrawn from Scotland. Catholic services in Scotland were banned. Mary had retained her throne, but at a price.[57] Although this one-sided treaty needed the ratification of Mary and Francis II, they never signed it.

Robert was delighted to have Cecil away from London. To the chagrin of Council members, he spent much time closeted with Elizabeth leaning her towards a rapid change in religious policy. Catholic bishops and officials were thrust into prison.[58] When Cecil returned in triumph after his successful negotiations in Edinburgh, he expected some recompense for his efforts, and pensions for the Scottish lords who had supported him. Instead, he was criticised for not achieving the restitution of

Calais or an indemnity to cover England's war expenses.[59] He found Robert in 'close intimacy with the Queen, who appeared to be quite engrossed by his society'.[60] Robert saw to it that neither Cecil nor Norfolk were rewarded by the parsimonious Queen, who had already contributed £241,000 as the military cost of freeing Scotland from French domination.[61] Cecil was left out of pocket by £383 for his travel expenses. He blamed Robert for Elizabeth's meanness and considered resigning. He wrote to Throckmorton in Paris to suggest that he should take over as Secretary, but this did not happen.

Cecil told de Quadra that Elizabeth would be ruined by her continued intimacy with Robert and even insinuated that they were contemplating bringing about Amy Robsart's death by poison, so that they could marry. He did not believe Robert's marriage to Elizabeth would be tolerated by the nation at large and hoped for a foreign alliance as the means of restoring the Exchequer's finances. All the rumours of Amy's planned murder seem to have emanated from Cecil, who was not above promulgating such dirty tricks, and they show his sense of desperation as Robert's romance with Elizabeth unfolded. By telling de Quadra, Cecil could rely on him quickly disseminating the story. If Amy were seriously ill, as it appeared, her demise would happen naturally; Robert had no need to take precipitate action. Her sudden death in suspicious circumstances would be disastrous.

At the end of July the court left Greenwich, moving by easy stages to Windsor where Robert was in daily attendance on Elizabeth. They spent much time riding and hunting together. In Essex, there was even gossip that she was pregnant. Rumours on the Continent reached such a pitch that the Imperial ambassador made enquiries about Elizabeth's virtue. Those who had known her since childhood 'swore by all that is holy that she had most certainly never been forgetful of her honour'.[62] In August, Baron Brenner, the Archduke's representative, reported that Kat Ashley went on her knees to implore Elizabeth to marry, warning her of the disreputable stories circulating about her relationship with Robert, which 'threatened to sully her honour and rouse discontent in her subjects'.[63] Although Elizabeth was alarmed, she had apparently replied:

> She hoped she had given no one just cause to associate her
> name with that of her equerry or of any other man. But in

this world, she had had so much sorrow and so little joy! If she showed herself gracious to her Master of Horse, he deserved it, for his honourable nature and dealing.[64]

'She did not see how anyone could think evil of her conduct: she was always surrounded by her ladies of the bed-chamber and maids-of-honour'.[65] Nevertheless, she admitted that, if she had wanted 'such a dishonourable life', no one could forbid her. Brenner added: 'I rather incline to believe it is but the innocent love which subsists at times between young men and young maidens though it be unseemly for such a Princess.'[66] It seemed clear that she wanted to marry Robert, who no doubt encouraged the romance, but they would need to wait until Amy died.

Chapter 10

Robert's relationship with Amy Robsart and her tragic death

Royal duties, imprisonment and military service abroad had kept Robert and Amy apart for much of the nine years of their marriage. In their early times together, a period of passionate romance when Robert was closely attached to Edward's entourage, Amy had enjoyed the glamour and excitement of court. Nevertheless, she did not return at the beginning of Elizabeth's reign. Several reasons can be put forward: that she was not well, perhaps suffering from breast cancer; that she preferred the countryside; that living in London or at court was too expensive for the couple; or that she wanted to steer clear of the growing relationship between Robert and Elizabeth. There may be some truth in all of these but there is no hint of any estrangement between Robert and Amy. She wanted to avoid being left isolated in Norfolk and spent most of her time on extended visits to friends who lived closer to London, where Robert could visit her as time permitted. She was often at Cumnor Place, at Denchworth near Abingdon, a house rented by the congenial Anthony Forster and his wife from William Owen, the physician to Henry VIII, Edward VI and Mary. Amy occupied permanent quarters there and retained Elizabeth Odingsells, Forster's sister-in-law, as a companion. Robert visited her there as often as he could and regularly sent presents, including gold buttons, haberdashery, Holland cloth, spices, and venison. Sometimes she visited him when the court was at Windsor, staying at lodgings nearby.

As Robert's relationship with Elizabeth developed, Amy's absences in the country became 'convenient'. The Queen was always jealous of those living with her male companions and Robert may have wanted to shelter Amy from court gossip, some of which was 'obscene'.[1] Her affliction was well known in court circles, and it was recognised that she did not have long to live. It is reasonable to assume that she was aware of rumours that Robert was only waiting for her death so that he could marry Elizabeth. Yet Robert still trusted her to continue the administration of their estates, and she was not too sick to travel or to delight in the latest fashions.

As Elizabeth's love-play with Robert developed, so too did concerns about Amy's wellbeing. As has been seen, Cecil started to use this to his advantage, telling the Spanish ambassador that Robert and Elizabeth contemplated doing away with her, so that they could marry. Within days, Amy was dead of a broken neck after being found on a landing at the bottom of two steps of stairs. Cecil only had to ask whether she fell, or was she pushed?

On Sunday 8 September 1560, Amy encouraged her staff to attend the Abingdon fair. Although Elizabeth Odingsells was also invited to go, she did not consider it seemly for her to be seen in a town full of 'servants and ill-bred people'[2] and said she would go on the Monday. The house was empty except for Amy, Elizabeth Odingsells and William Owen's elderly widowed mother, who also occupied quarters there. It was Amy's returning servants who found her body on a landing below a 'pair of stairs',[3] which led from her rooms towards the hall. The immediate question was whether she could have broken her neck by falling down two steps? Was it possible that she had fallen the full length of the stairs and then been repositioned on the higher landing? If her body had been moved, she could not have committed suicide. It seemed surprising that her hooded headdress remained undisturbed.

In 1956, Professor Ian Aird in the *English Historical Review* put forward a plausible theory on what might have happened. He explained that in a half of all cases involving breast cancer, 'secondary deposits' are present in the bones, including the spine, making them very brittle. Bones may collapse, causing a broken neck, even from the slight strain of walking, but this is more likely to occur while stepping downstairs.[4] No modern commentators suspect foul play. Amy had breast cancer and was depressed, perhaps because she had failed to provide Robert with children, perhaps because she had heard of his growing attachment to Elizabeth. The Dudley family did not seem unduly surprised, and the condolences of Huntingdon (his brother-in-law's father) were encapsulated in a letter asking Robert's views on the quality of his venison pies.

On the following morning, one of the servants, named Bowes, was sent to Windsor to advise Robert of Amy's death. As he went, he met Robert's kinsman, Sir Thomas Blount, who happened to be travelling from Windsor to Abingdon on Robert's behalf. The servant then carried on to Windsor. As soon as Robert was told, he realised the implications for his relationship with Elizabeth. There was an inevitable assumption that she had been murdered. Was it possible that the Queen was implicated? Robert immediately sent a mounted messenger after Blount to ensure that he arranged a thorough independent investigation, saying: 'As I have ever loved you, do not dissemble with me … but send me your true conceit and opinion of the matter, whether it happened by evil chance or villainy: and fail not to let me hear continually from you.'[5] He also wrote to Amy's half-brother, John Appleyard in Norfolk, asking him to go to Cumnor Place to assess the matter for himself.

Rather than going straight to the house, Blount put up for the night at a hostelry in Abingdon, hoping to sound out local opinion. Having posed as a traveller he questioned the landlord, who assured him that it seemed to have been an accident. On arriving next day at Cumnor Place he found the coroner already there with his jury. Blount advised him of Robert's wish that he should carry out a full and thorough investigation. He reported back to Robert that the jury was made up of sensible countrymen and Amy's death appeared to be the result of a fall from a pair of stairs. Nevertheless, there were also rumours that Anthony Forster might have been in collusion with Robert to dispose of Amy.

Blount made his own enquiries, talking to Amy's maid, Pinto, who claimed to have heard Amy on several occasions praying to be delivered from her desperation, but she confirmed that she thought Amy's death was mischance, as Amy was too good a woman to commit such a mortal sin as suicide. Blount reported back that the outcome of the inquiries was likely to demonstrate Robert's innocence, but that Amy's mind may have been unbalanced. There can be no doubt that she was lonely and ill. Whether her desperation arose from her affliction, or from rumours of Robert's romance with Elizabeth was not clear. The considerable tittle-tattle deeply distressed Elizabeth, and she sent Robert away to his house at Kew until a verdict could be established. No one under suspicion was permitted in the Queen's presence until cleared. She felt 'undeniable guilt' that she had retained Robert at court 'knowing that this must mean his desertion of an affectionate and faithful young wife'.[6]

103

While awaiting the outcome of the inquest, Elizabeth remained 'pale, listless and irritable, seldom venturing from her private apartments'.[7] The situation could not have suited Cecil better. With Robert being rendered powerless, Cecil was immediately back in favour.[8] He wanted Elizabeth to make a marriage which would achieve a valuable alliance, in addition to the necessity of providing children. He visited his disconsolate rival kicking his heels at Kew and probably brought messages from the Queen. Robert wrote to thank him for his sympathy and to ask when he thought he could return to court. He knew it was inappropriate for him to go to Cumnor Place as he would like to have done. While still at Kew, he sent for his tailor to be measured for mourning clothes.[9]

On 13 or 14 September, Robert received an unofficial communication from the foreman of the coroner's jury to say that there were no indications of foul play. Robert was concerned that this irregular correspondence might indicate that he was trying to tamper with the jury's findings. 'He had to clear his name of every vestige of suspicion'[10] and called for the evidence to be re-examined by a second jury. His future at court and with Elizabeth depended on it. Elizabeth grasped at the indication of Robert's innocence and welcomed him back. This was several days before the official verdict from the coroner's jury of death by misadventure. She then announced that the matter was closed; Robert was restored to favour and she vigorously defended him. Amy's lavish funeral took place at St Mary's Church in Oxford a fortnight after her death. In the meantime, her body had lain at Worcester College for two days. As was the custom for a husband, Robert did not attend, but the service was taken by his chaplain, Dr Babington.

It was only Cecil who continued to insinuate that Amy was pushed, yet rumours of Robert's involvement in her murder, with the Queen's connivance, dogged him for the rest of his life. Cecil did nothing to dampen them, in the hope of preventing their marriage and recovering influence. In Paris, Throckmorton, the English ambassador was dismayed at the prospect of their marriage. He sent his confidential secretary, Jones, to London to explain the damaging impact it would have in France.[11] Jones unguardedly reported to Cecil that Mary Queen of Scots, who considered that the English throne was being kept from her unlawfully, had listened to the scandal with 'vivid enthusiasm' and exclaimed: 'The Queen of England is going to marry the Master of her Horses, who has killed his wife to make room for her!'[12] It is clear that Cecil passed this on to Elizabeth, who in turn, told Robert. Robert tackled Jones to confirm what he had said, furious that Cecil would bandy such stories about. Jones was warned by Sir Henry Killigrew: 'I think verily that my Lord Robert will run away with the hare and have the Queen.'[13] Jones was not to be bridled. When he met with the Queen, 'he threw discretion to the winds' and told her 'the injuries Lord Robert Dudley was working on her name and dignity'.[14] Elizabeth stoutly defended Robert, saying that there was no truth to rumours of his complicity in his wife's murder. The investigation had cleared 'both Lord Robert's honesty and her own honour'.[15] Nevertheless, she looked 'sickly' and Jones concluded: 'Surely the matter of my Lord Robert doth greatly perplex her and [the marriage] is never likely to take place.'[16] Cecil had to warn Throckmorton that 'his blunt expressions of opinion were doing more harm than good with his mistress'.[17]

The rumours continued. On 31 December, Throckmorton wrote to Cecil that 'marriage to Lord Robert in the circumstances would so extinguish the Queen's reputation, she would cease to carry any weight in European diplomacy'.[18] She seemed to see the danger. In Robert's absence, Cecil 'extracted a positive assurance from the Queen direct, that she would not marry [Robert]'.[19] Cecil was convinced that the danger of their marriage had passed. Much later, Robert claimed that 'he had the Queen in a very good tune, till [Cecil] took her aside and dealt with her secretly, and then she was very strange suddenly'.[20]

Chapter 11

The not so virgin Queen

Elizabeth tried to demonstrate her continuing regard for Robert by having letters patent drawn up to offer him an earldom. This was ill-advised because at this time Ambrose, the senior member of the family, had not been restored to the earldom of Warwick. Eventually, she cut the grant in pieces. Robert, who was 'particularly anxious for such a solid sign of favour … was as angry as he dared to be'.[1] It was unfortunate that the whole court knew what she had done. Although he reproached her for her unkindness, she remained unmoved. With the suit of Prince Eric of Sweden still rumbling on, Dymock, a jeweller who undertook work at the Swedish court, wanted to end further rumours that Elizabeth intended to marry Robert. He approached Kat Ashley, with whom he was acquainted, and Kat told him 'solemnly' that the Queen was not entangled with any man living and that she would *not* have Lord Robert. Her husband, who was Keeper of the Queen's Jewels told Dymock that the Queen would rather not marry, and certainly not to Robert. He told him that, although Robert had expected a Christmas gift of £4,000 and a dukedom, he had received only £400 in indifferent land.

Nevertheless, Elizabeth continued to be infatuated by Robert's company. There was no decline in her affection for him. He was still benefiting from providing help to those who sought her assistance and continued to enjoy 'most favoured'[2] status with significant influence, but without any formal political authority. It was probably not until after Amy's death that they seem to have become lovers in the full sense. By April 1561, he was conveniently lodged in apartments next to hers at Greenwich, and they were almost inseparable. While she could claim to be surrounded by her ladies in her own chamber, it is apparent that she visited Robert in his adjacent one. Certainly, Bess of Hardwick, who had been a Lady of the Privy Chamber, later told Mary Queen of Scots, that they had been lovers. Nevertheless, Elizabeth would not

106

agree to marry him. He did not know where he stood with her. She seems to have accepted that their marriage would upset her adoring public, but if she fell pregnant, they could tie the knot very quickly. She assumed, probably correctly, that the prospect of an heir to the throne would overcome all criticisms of her choice of husband. There was no satisfactory form of contraception in Elizabeth's time and church law did not permit copulation without the intention of procreating, although that does not mean that it did not happen! (The missionary position was the only approved sexual act!) If pregnancy should arise, they would probably argue that they were already secretly married, which would be difficult to disprove. Even though marriage might take place after pregnancy, so long as it happened before a child's birth the child would be deemed legitimate. Elizabeth herself was conceived before the marriage of Henry VIII to Anne Boleyn.

Robert could not understand Elizabeth's refusal to marry him, while showing 'an eager, enthralled, enchanted pleasure in talking about marrying him'.[3] He had 'great virility, strength, handsomeness, all those qualities to which Elizabeth was highly susceptible'.[4] He assumed that she held back out of a phobia about marriage, rather than any falling out with him, and she always loved male attention. Her upbringing had been fraught with anxiety. Her parents' marriage had shown her that there was safety in being courted, but risk, if the marriage fell out of love. Her mother had ridden on the crest of a wave until she produced only a daughter. Elizabeth had seen Janc Seymour dying in childbirth and her cousin Catherine Howard being executed after misalliances during her unhappy marriage. Catherine Parr, to whom she was devoted, also died in childbirth, and Elizabeth's relationship with the charming but highly unsatisfactory Thomas Seymour nearly caused her downfall. For Elizabeth, marriage was not an attractive proposition, and by espousing Robert, she would lose the goodwill of her people, which she held more important than anything. It has been suggested that she was frigid, but this seems most unlikely given the undoubted sensuality of her feelings for Robert. There were also rumours on several occasions that she had had a child by him, but it seems nonsensical that she would not make any child legitimate when England needed an heir to the throne.

With both Elizabeth and Robert being aware of the strength of the Council's opposition to their marriage, she continued to sound out foreign powers to establish their approval. Robert approached the French Huguenots, although they were in no position to help him. De Quadra also reported that Robert sought Spanish backing for the marriage in return for Elizabeth's support for an English Counter-Reformation. This extraordinary proposal seems to have had her blessing. In February 1561, Robert asked his brother-in-law, Sir Henry Sidney, to approach de Quadra on their behalf. It has been seen that Sir Henry was well known to the Spanish, having joined the diplomatic mission to Spain in 1554 proposing Mary's marriage to Philip. He seems to have concluded that, if Elizabeth failed to marry and have children, England would inevitably fall prey to Catholic powers.[5] Hume (whose history of Cecil shows that he was no fan of Robert) claims that Robert's instruction to his brother-in-law demonstrates that he 'was without shame, scruple, or conscience … his sole objective was to force or cajole the Queen into marrying him, and he grasped at any aids towards it'.[6] Robert told Sidney that if Spain would support his suit, with armed force if necessary, Elizabeth would restore Catholicism, would extirpate heresy and would regard Philip as the arbiter of English policy at home and abroad.[7] When Sidney made this proposal to de Quadra, he confirmed that once Robert was granted the Crown Matrimonial, 'he would thereafter obey your Majesty [Philip II] as one of your own vassals'.

De Quadra was incredulous at the request, not least because he found it extraordinary that Elizabeth would consider marrying Robert after the scandal of his wife's death. Yet Sidney confirmed that he had made searching enquiries himself and could find nothing to contradict the jury's verdict.[8] He also claimed (quite electrifyingly) that 'the Queen and Robert were lovers, but since their object was marriage, what did this matter?'[9] As de Quadra was well known for his loquacious tongue, Sidney was unlikely to have provided such a juicy piece of scandal unless it were true. Although de Quadra remained sceptical of the veracity of the proposal, he wrote to Philip, that he thought the marriage would be in the Spanish interest. He also said:

> The general opinion, confirmed by certain physicians, is that this woman is unhealthy, and it is believed she will not have children, although there is no lack of people who say she has already had some, but of this I have seen no trace and do not believe it. This being so perhaps some step

may be taken in your Majesty's interests towards declaring, as the Queen's successor after her death, whoever may be most desirable to your Majesty.[10]

Rumours of Elizabeth's infertility abounded, apparently because of reports circulating that she had very few monthly periods. These symptoms, which were repeated independently by Sir James Melville, the Scottish ambassador, would have been well-known in the circle of laundry maids paid to provide such tittle-tattle to interested parties. Elizabeth's doctors did not agree, and on two occasions gave their view that she could expect to conceive, and the menstrual problems appear to have righted themselves at a later stage.[11]

When de Quadra met Elizabeth, he told her that Philip had always held Robert in great affection. As de Quadra was a bishop, she asked to speak to him as her confessor, confirming 'that she was no angel' and could not deny 'having some affection for Lord Robert, for the many good qualities he possessed, but she certainly had not decided to marry him or anyone else'.[12] De Quadra confirmed that Philip would support the marriage, and this seemed to please her. Afterwards, Robert thanked de Quadra profusely, asking him to continue to promote his suit, which would leave Philip in control of British Government policy.

Without de Quadra being the impeccable source for this story, it would be very difficult to believe it. It seems inconceivable that Elizabeth would have been prepared to forgo the Religious Settlement of 1559 that she had worked so hard with Cecil to achieve, or to allow Spanish troops to massacre her subjects. With Robert being so strongly Protestant, it seems unthinkable that he would have deserted all his long-held beliefs to satisfy his hopes of becoming King. It appears much more likely that Elizabeth, with Cecil's connivance, was testing Robert's moral integrity. Was his soaring ambition to marry Elizabeth more important to him than his Puritan rectitude? When he ran with the plan, he probably ended any hopes of Elizabeth marrying him, but this did not end her addiction for him. This was not the only occasion that Elizabeth put Robert's integrity to the test, as will be seen.

Sidney and Pembroke advised Robert to give the Queen an ultimatum. She should marry him before Easter, or else let him go to war in the service of the King of Spain. Robert paid no heed to them, and Cecil ensured that the marriage plan foundered. On hearing of Robert's negotiation, he announced that he had evidence of a Catholic plot to achieve a Counter-Reformation. This brought talks with Spain to an abrupt end. He also asked de Quadra to provide a letter from Philip II recommending Robert's suit, which could be laid before Parliament. De Quadra thought better of it, despite mistrusting Robert. Although he realised that Robert would be doomed, he was not prepared to risk his own standing with Elizabeth.

Despite all this, Robert remained in Elizabeth's company and, for several years, continued his negotiations to gain Spanish backing for the marriage in return for supporting a Counter-Reformation. On 30 June 1561, he gave a water-party for the Queen, to which de Quadra was invited. While the three of them sat in the poop of a barge, watching the festivities, Robert asked de Quadra to marry them then and there. The Queen immediately suggested that de Quadra would not know enough English. De Quadra told them that, if they resurrected the plan to be rid of heretics, he would be pleased to oblige. Although this offer was ignored, the pressure on Elizabeth to marry continued, not least because the widowed Mary Queen of Scots had returned to Scotland.

Despite being fervently Catholic, Mary Queen of Scots was seeking nomination as Elizabeth's heir. Cecil was determined to prevent this, but it did not help his cause that, in the previous year, her rival and the preferred claimant under the will of Henry VIII, the 20-year-old Catherine Grey, had made a complete fool of herself. De Quadra had already described Catherine as:

> a vain, touchy, silly girl, eagerly responsive to attention and very ready to feel herself slighted. Elizabeth was temperamentally averse from this young woman, nor could she forget the fatal fact that Jane Grey, however unwillingly, had been proclaimed Queen in defiance of the rights of the Tudors. As Lady Catherine had a great awareness of her position as one of the heiresses presumptive to the throne, but not a grain of common sense to accompany it, she was bound to fall victim to whatever party, hostile to the Queen, wanted to exploit her.[13]

He also reported that Elizabeth retained her as a Lady of the Presence Chamber and was 'making much of Lady Catherine to keep her quiet'.[14]

Catherine's childhood marriage to Lord Herbert had been annulled immediately after the failure of the plot to place her sister Jane on the throne, and the 13-year-old had returned to live with her mother. Her Protestantism seemed pragmatic, and de Quadra considered her sufficiently flexible to contemplate her return to the Catholic faith, even hinting at her kidnap for marriage to Philip II's son, Don Carlos.[15] During mid-1560, she had clandestinely escaped from court for long enough to marry Somerset's wayward son, Edward, Earl of Hertford. She had not sought Elizabeth's consent, which was a requirement for heirs to the English crown under the Act of Succession of 1536. The only known witness was Edward's sister Jane, who died of consumption shortly after.

By December, Catherine realised that she was pregnant, and the marriage would soon be discovered. Elizabeth, who may have been aware of the elopement, sent Hertford on a grand tour of Europe where he met up with Cecil's son, Thomas, in Paris. To Cecil's chagrin, Thomas seems to have been led badly astray by Hertford, overspending his allowance, gambling, becoming an inordinate lover of unmeet plays and causing his father a concern that he might not 'return with a chaste body'.[16]

Before leaving England, Hertford had handed Catherine a deed of jointure, providing the only known evidence of their nuptials, but she had managed to lose it. In early 1561, she was required by Elizabeth to rejoin the court when at Ipswich but managed to hide her pregnancy until her eighth month. She then approached Bess of Hardwick, who had spent a part of her upbringing with Catherine in the household at Bradgate Park. When Bess berated her and refused to intercede, Catherine sought help from Robert, after arousing him from his sleep in his chamber at dead of night. With Elizabeth in the next room, Robert was terrified of being caught with a pregnant lady in his bedroom. The following morning, he told Elizabeth all he knew. Catherine was thrown into the Tower, where Hertford joined her in separate quarters on his return from the Continent. It was not just her secret marriage, but her pregnancy that angered the Queen, perhaps because Elizabeth had not achieved this with Robert. When cross-examined, neither Catherine nor Hertford would name the priest who had married them, claiming that he had been hauled in off the street. If there were other witnesses, they wisely failed to appear, and there was no documentation to confirm a marriage having taken place. Hertford was fined 15,000 marks by the Court of Star Chamber for seducing a virgin of the royal blood and the marriage was annulled, making them guilty of fornication. On 24 April 1561, Catherine gave birth to a son, and during a seven-year period in the Tower achieved a second son by Hertford, although he too was declared illegitimate to debar him from the throne. Their jailer, Sir Edward Warner, was removed from his post and imprisoned for his leniency. Catherine was so filled with remorse at her predicament that she became unable to eat and died in the Tower on 26 January 1568 at the age of 27.[17]

Elizabeth's affection for Robert remained undiminished; he continued to receive her gifts and his political activities were widened. He was granted a licence to export white cloth, which proved enormously lucrative, and received a pension of £1,000 chargeable on the London customs.[18] In December 1561, the attainder against his father's estates was lifted. Ambrose was restored to Warwick Castle with its surrounding lands and Robert arranged for him to be reinstated to his earldom. Grants of other former Dudley lands in the Midlands came to Robert. He approached Edward, Lord Dudley, with an offer to repurchase Dudley Castle which had been restored to Edward's family by Robert's father. Although Edward politely turned him down, Robert retained his lands nearby, so it was natural, when offered an earldom, that he would choose that of Leicester.

Despite so much royal favour, Robert made no progress with his marriage suit, but continued to parry the efforts of other suitors. His attempts to progress his personal ambitions were mistrusted by other Council members. He was known to be holding secret discussions with foreign powers after developing his own network of agents and contacts on the Continent. His meddling and his close association with Elizabeth had made him extremely unpopular with Norfolk and members of the Council. De Quadra reported:

> The Duke of Norfolk is the chief of Lord Robert's enemies, who are all the principal people in the kingdom ... he said that if Lord Robert did not abandon his present pretentions and presumptions, he would not die in his bed ... I think his hatred of Lord Robert will continue, as the Duke and the rest of them cannot put up with his being king.[19]

When Norfolk complained, he found himself posted to the Borders as Lieutenant of the North. De Quadra again reported that 'there is a plot to kill [Robert], which I quite believe'.[20]

In July 1562 Robert Keyle, the attaché at the Swedish Embassy, had arrived in London to renew the hopes of King Eric. When Keyle attempted to circumvent Robert, Robert tried to have him imprisoned, and Keyle was warned that his life was under threat. Elizabeth gave every impression of being furious with Robert for interfering with her diplomacy and very publicly made clear that she would never marry him. Following this humiliation, Robert contemplated pastures new. Eric had five very attractive sisters. Following the wedding celebrations of the Princess Catalina in 1560, the bridegroom's brother, George Johan Vedentz, had been found undressed in the bedroom of the Princess Cecilia at the castle of Vadstana, resulting in their arrest by Eric. His father, the elderly King Gustav Vasa was furious with his nubile daughter and called for her collection of jewels. He observed: 'We have spent enough money on her magnificence which does not seem to have produced much return in honour.'[21] He ordered that a diamond cross should be removed and given to one of her sisters. King Gustav was also furious with Eric for his indiscreet handling of the affair. Eric magnanimously took his sister's part and, after establishing that there had been no sexual impropriety, arranged for a medal to be struck. This depicted Susannah, the chaste heroine of the Book of Daniel, on one side, and the apparently less chaste, but clearly desirable, Cecilia on the other. Eric gave her a copy of the medal cast in gold, and rimmed with rubies, diamonds and pearls.[22] George Johan was not so lucky and was castrated. When King Gustav died in 1561, Eric became King of Sweden, and was approached by Dymock, the jeweller. Dymock told him that Robert would support Eric's suit to marry Elizabeth, if Robert were rewarded with the hand of Cecilia and a suitable fortune. Nothing came of the proposed bargain, but it seems to have been genuine, as it was raised again in 1577.[23]

De Quadra was also in trouble. Cecil's spy network had recruited Borghese, de Quadra's confidential secretary, as an agent. Borghese revealed de Quadra's secret dealings with disaffected English Catholics. There were plans for the murders of Elizabeth, Cecil and Robert to place either Catherine Grey or Darnley on the English throne.[24] Borghese reported a discussion de Quadra had undertaken on behalf of Margaret Lennox to establish support from English exiles in the Netherlands to install Darnley as King of England. Elizabeth and the Council were indignant to discover what de Quadra had written to Philip concerning her relationship with Robert, particularly a claim that they were secretly married. De Quadra denied this, but at the same time regretted being unable to confirm it. He claimed that Elizabeth had told him of the rumours circulating of her marriage, and Robert had told him she had promised to marry him, 'only not this year'.[25] It is apparent that Elizabeth was giving the impression of being secretly married, lest she had to explain an embarrassing pregnancy.

De Quadra spent his last year in London under virtual house arrest at Durham Place. Cecil accused him of making it a hotbed of conspiracy and of disobeying the law of the land. He changed the keys of his entrance gates to prevent the ambassador from going out. Elizabeth asked him to leave and would not see him. When Philip II refused to settle his debts, he was left bankrupt and heartbroken. Although his futile plotting had provided the pretext for his disgrace, Cecil's real purpose was to show to Robert and discontented Catholics that 'they were leaning on a broken reed when they depended upon Spain to help them against [the Council]'.[26]

In early 1562, Mary Queen of Scots tried to arrange a meeting with Elizabeth to confirm her claim to the English succession after Elizabeth's own progeny. Much to Cecil's concern, Elizabeth agreed to meet her in York. Mary was confident that she could use her personal magnetism to win Elizabeth's backing. With the Treaty of Edinburgh remaining unratified, the Council strongly disapproved of the meeting. Robert was said to support the meeting as, if Mary were recognised as Elizabeth's heir, English Protestants would seek Elizabeth's marriage to him to get her with child. Cecil had two concerns. He did not want a Catholic heir nominated and wanted to avoid promoting Guise prestige in Europe, when England's policy was to support the French Huguenots.

Luck came Cecil's way and the meeting was cancelled. On 1 March 1562, Mary's uncle the Duke of Guise, while travelling with his men from Joinville to Paris, attacked a group of Huguenots holding an unauthorised service in a barn at Vassy in Champagne. This left twenty-three Huguenots dead and more than 100 wounded.[27] Huguenots, led by Louis de Bourbon, Prince of Condé, and Admiral Gaspard de Coligny, Seigneur de Châtillon, took up arms. Although Cecil advocated conciliation, Throckmorton, the English ambassador and Cecil's staunch ally, urged Elizabeth to assist the Huguenots, who were in dire straits. With backing from English Protestant circles, Robert now persuaded Elizabeth to support the Huguenot cause, hoping that the Huguenots would back their marriage. With Robert having 'widespread contacts throughout the Protestant world',[28] he gained an ally in Throckmorton, who made him a godfather to his youngest child. This diminished Throckmorton's former close friendship with Cecil.[29]

Coligny negotiated with the English during June and July, offering to return Calais if they would send an invasion force. As Calais was not in Huguenot hands, they promised Le Havre (known by the English as Newhaven) in the meantime. By October, when the English at last established a garrison of 6,000 men at Le Havre, the Huguenots had been forced back. Although Robert asked to be given command, Elizabeth would not let him leave her side. Ambrose led the English force, while Robert kept closely in touch. He sent a fine horse, and Elizabeth provided a 'token'[30] for Ambrose to wear round his neck.

At this critical moment, Elizabeth, who was at Hampton Court, became dangerously ill with smallpox. It was slow to develop, but she became delirious, hovering 'on the brink of death, too ill to make her wishes known'.[31] In a sudden moment of lucidity, with her councillors assembled round her bed, she nominated Robert as Protector of the Realm, with an income of £20,000 per annum. She went on to confirm 'her trust and love for Lord Robert – love she assured them, which had never involved them in any impropriety'.[32] She was ever the master dissembler and she granted Robert's highly trusted servant, Tamworth, who slept in his bedchamber, a massive pension of £500 per annum. Only he could verify the extent of any intimacy between them.[33] Her reputation depended on his continued loyalty. Her distraught councillors granted everything she asked.[34] They agreed to co-opt the 29-year-old Robert into their number. To avoid any jealousy, Cecil insisted on the 26-year-old Norfolk's appointment at the same time. Robert continued to occupy his Council place with regular attendance for the rest of his life. He never played a dominant role but used his presence to keep himself informed and to maintain his standing 'at the innermost circle of the sphere of power'. This improved his opportunity to sell his support or information and to dispense patronage to gain allies.[35]

Elizabeth's smallpox was treated by a German doctor, Burcot, who wrapped her in a bolt of red cloth and laid her on a mattress before a fire, providing a drink, which she found 'very comfortable'.[36] Although pock marks developed, she was not badly disfigured, and in less than a month was up and about again. Only her favourite maids were permitted in attendance. Mary Sidney, who remained constantly at her bedside, became wretchedly disfigured after contracting the disease. When Sir Henry returned from the Continent, he reported: 'When I left my wife at court to go to Newhaven, she was a full fair lady; in my eyes the fairest. On my return I found her as foul a lady as the smallpox could make her …'[37] She was never prepared to be seen in public again, keeping to her own chamber at court, and retiring to Penshurst to care for her children.

The invasion of France demonstrated that England's Huguenot allies were unreliable and, as always, Elizabeth left her army short of resources. Although 3,000 men were detached from the English garrison to support Condé in defending Rouen and Dieppe, both towns fell to their Catholic besiegers, leaving Ambrose pinned down in Le Havre. With French national pride being shocked by the prospect of losing Calais, Huguenots combined with Catholics against the English invaders. Although Elizabeth instructed Ambrose to defend Le Havre despite his dearth of supplies, he needed a larger military commitment. Nevertheless, he commanded the garrison 'with great bravery and constancy',[38] but Robert could not persuade her to commit more money even to repair the town's defences. She did not criticise Ambrose and, in April 1563, commended the garrison's bravery, making him a Knight of the Garter. In July, Le Havre was struck by the plague and with his men dying in large numbers, Ambrose received Elizabeth's authority to come to terms. He responded that the garrison 'well perceived [the] great care your Majesty have of us all, and that in respect of our lives and safeties, you do not regard the loss of this town'.[39] While parleying with his attackers from the walls he was shot in the leg, a wound which left him on a stick for the rest of his life.

On the garrison's return to Portsmouth in August, it brought the plague with it. Despite it being highly contagious, Robert risked death to visit his brother at Southwick. The Queen was furious and forced him into quarantine. On 1 September, Ambrose was released. He returned to court with his leg strapped up with 'taffety'. Nevertheless, the outbreak spread to London, causing 3,000 deaths in a week. One of these was de Quadra. Even Catherine Grey and Hertford were removed temporarily from the Tower. Catherine was held at the home of her uncle, Lord John Grey at Pirgo in Essex, while Hertford was moved to Middlesex. Robert was again asked to intercede on their behalf, as she was Guildford's sister-in-law.

Fully recovered from smallpox, Elizabeth visited Cambridge in August 1563. Robert went on ahead to inspect the arrangements, both as Master of the Horse and as High Steward of the university. With King's College being 'turned inside out' to accommodate the court, Robert inspected the Provost's lodge, where the Queen was to stay while visiting the chapel, in which a stage had been built. There was a place in the choir for her to 'repose herself',[40] which in the end was not required. As the university's Chancellor, Cecil also arrived early, despite an attack of gout, and was determined that Cambridge should make a good impression. He saw to it that the students were properly and sombrely attired as befitted 'a storehouse of learning and virtue',[41] and he introduced Robert to university members. On the Queen's arrival, she was dressed in black, with her hair in a gold net under a black hat with gold-spangled black feathers.[42] She remained on horseback to hear a long oration in Latin and moved on to another oration before dismounting and entering the chapel, which she much admired. After a Te Deum and sermon, she retired to the Provost's Lodge. The programme continued in a similar vein for five days. Elizabeth listened intently until, on the last evening, she became too tired to sit through a performance of Sophocles's *Ajax*.

In April 1564, the Treaty of Troyes brought lasting peace between France and England. Charles IX was made a Knight of the Garter, and the Queen's cousin, Henry Carey, Lord Hunsdon, was sent to Paris to deliver the insignia. When Hunsdon examined the Garter paraphernalia, he wrote to Robert of his embarrassment at its quality. The Garter itself was much too big for a puny boy and he could not wear it. The chains, which were traditionally returned on the death of a previous recipient, were very worn and inappropriate as a gift for the French King. He complained that there were several rich chains in the treasury and asked Robert to send another as soon as possible. All seems to have been well, as Castelnau was sent to England and was at particular pains to cultivate Robert's friendship.

With Robert's standing growing in France, he considered visiting Paris himself. Hunsdon recommended the horse fair at St Denis, where animals arrived for sale from Flanders, Germany and Denmark. If Robert had been there, he would have spent 'one or two thousand crowns'.[43] Throckmorton sent him a list of suitable clothing and presents to bring. Despite this Elizabeth eventually vetoed the trip, but Robert sent Catherine de Medici a spaniel, a mastiff and some cobs.

Chapter 12

The political background to Elizabeth's European marriage negotiations

It is necessary to pause in the chronology of this narrative to assess the impact of European politics on Elizabeth's marriage negotiations, in which Robert had become intimately involved.

Europe was dominated by two Catholic superpowers, Spain and France. The huge Spanish empire had been ruled by Charles V until his abdication in 1556. His son, Philip II, inherited Spain, the Spanish-American colonies, the Netherlands – encompassing most of present-day Belgium and Holland, and Spain's Italian provinces, Naples and Milan. Charles's brother, Ferdinand I, became the Holy Roman Emperor controlling Hungary, Austria, the Czech Republic and Croatia. Ferdinand had numerous children, including Maximilian II, who succeeded him as Holy Roman Emperor, Ferdinand II and Charles II, who became Archdukes of Austria. Charles V also had an illegitimate son, Don John of Austria, a romantic military commander, who made his name at the Battle of Lepanto in 1571, during which the Turkish fleet was destroyed. France was in some disarray following Henry II's death in a jousting accident in July 1559, followed in December 1560 by the death of his eldest son, Francis II, the husband of Mary Queen of Scots. Although Mary's Guise uncles had assumed control of French Government, their belligerently pro-Catholic policy faced Protestant Huguenot opposition. Progressively, the conciliatory approach of Francis's mother, Catherine de Medici, enabled her to regain control, and she became Regent. Both the superpowers were exhausted by continuous war but realised that their domination of Europe depended on establishing an alliance with England, which was well able to cause its own nuisance with incursions onto the Continent. Nevertheless, England was financially weakened by fighting against the Scots and

Irish and, during Mary's reign, on behalf of the Spanish in Northern France. It was during this conflict that it had lost its last remaining Continental outpost at Calais.

Henry VIII had severed English links with the Papacy to allow him to divorce Katherine of Aragon. The resultant English Reformation had been reinforced by the ardently Protestant protectorate for Edward VI. Although Mary Tudor restored Catholicism while married to Philip of Spain, her brutal policies had made her extremely unpopular. The backlash had provided Elizabeth with overwhelming support to inherit the throne and to revert to Protestantism after her accession. While the Papacy encouraged the superpowers to invade England, this did not appeal to either Spain or France. Although Elizabeth was illegitimate in Catholic eyes, neither of them wanted to promote Mary Queen of Scots, the rightful Catholic claimant, in her place. They were exhausted by war; any military intervention would be prohibitively expensive and was likely to meet with strong English resistance. Spain was facing open hostility from the Dutch in the Netherlands, and the Catholic French Government was embarking on civil war against the Protestant Huguenots. With Mary being Queen Dauphine, and soon to become Queen Consort of France, Philip II had no desire to hand England to the French on a plate. Furthermore, Catherine de Medici, who was in the process of wresting control of the French Regency from Mary's Guise uncles, wanted to avoid enhancing their status by making their niece Queen Regnant of England in addition to Scotland.

The Spanish supported Elizabeth on the English throne but sought a suitable husband for her who would be supportive of Spanish interests against the French. No one was in any doubt that Elizabeth's foremost task was to choose a spouse to provide her with an heir. Philip was now advocating his cousins the Archdukes Ferdinand and Charles, who owed allegiance to neighbouring German Protestant princes, but her Protestantism remained a stumbling block. Ferdinand soon withdrew his suit and died in 1564. The Guise faction in France continued to support Mary Queen of Scots, but they were out of power. She was also banned under the 1536 English Act of Succession, having been born outside England, and under Henry VIII's will. Nevertheless, the English Government recognised the strength of her dynastic claim and insisted on her choosing a spouse acceptable to their interest, notwithstanding that Elizabeth had not recognised her as her heir.

Although Elizabeth was now firmly established on the English throne, marriage considerations within Continental Europe were greatly hampered by her continuing infatuation for Robert. In the early part of the reign, he acted as the liaison for overseas marriage suits and, with her connivance, did his best to scupper those which threatened their relationship. Nevertheless, Cecil's detailed notes are full of the perceived disadvantages of Elizabeth marrying Robert and his preference for foreign princes. Robert's interference particularly upset those of her council who were trying to negotiate politically advantageous suits from abroad. Norfolk told Robert to stop meddling. As we have seen, Elizabeth was eventually persuaded by Cecil not to marry Robert after he had sought Spanish support for their marriage in return for backing another Counter-Reformation. His political shortcomings greatly disappointed her but did not immediately end their intimate relationship.

As will be shown, Elizabeth was placed under a great deal of pressure to agree to a Continental marriage alliance, and by 1563 she had realised that she had to end any hopes of espousing Robert, although he remained the love of her life. The first, most obvious, hint of this was her proposal that he should marry Mary Queen of Scots. This did nothing to encourage her to look elsewhere, and she may well have decided by then that if she could not marry Robert, she would not marry at all. While her obsession for him is generally blamed for her reluctance to marry, she had not become pregnant and may have feared that she was infertile. She had seen Mary Tudor's embarrassment at failing to conceive, so it is a reasonable assumption that she was fearful of finding herself in a similar predicament. When she heard that Mary Queen of Scots had given birth to Prince James on 19 June 1566, she complained, with understandable jealousy: 'Alack, the Queen of Scots is lighter of a bonny son, and I am but of barren stock.'[1] The birth certainly strengthened Mary's position as a claimant to the succession. At about this time, there were two contradictory medical opinions of Elizabeth's fitness for child-bearing. During the negotiations for her to marry Charles IX, one of her physicians told a member of the French embassy: 'If the King marries, I will answer for her having ten children, and no one knows her temperament better than I do.'[2] Nevertheless, Dr Huick, who had been Catherine Parr's physician and had known Elizabeth since she was 15, discouraged the marriage because of 'her nervous resistance', which Camden described as 'I know not what womanish infirmity'.

With the English Council redoubling its efforts to find Elizabeth a suitable Continental spouse, the suit of the Archduke Charles rumbled on. She never quite said: 'No!', but when the Archduke Ferdinand died suddenly in July 1564, Dr Mundt, the English Agent to the house of Austria, proposed an approach to his eldest brother, Maximilian II, the Holy Roman Emperor. This would have been a serious diplomatic coup. Maximilian was the most powerful marriage prospect available. With Elizabeth's connivance, Cecil wrote a carefully worded letter to explain her inclination towards marriage as he saw it. Mundt reported:

> He can with certainty say nothing; than that he perceives that she would rather marry a foreign than a native prince, and that the more distinguished the suitor is by birth, power and personal attractions, the better hope he will have of success. Moreover, he cannot deny that the nobleman who, with them, excites considerable expectation, to wit Lord Robert, is worthy to become the husband of the Queen. The fact of his being her Majesty's subject, however, will prove a serious objection to him in her estimation. Nevertheless, his virtues and his excellent and heroic gifts of mind and body have so endeared him to the Queen, that she could not regard her own brother with greater affection. From which they who do not know the Queen intimately, conjecture that he will be her future husband. He, however, sees and understands that she merely takes delight in his virtues and rare qualities, and that nothing more is discussed in their conversation than that which is most consistent with virtue, and furthest removed from all unworthy sentiments.[3]

This was endorsed by Cecil: 'Written to Mr Mundt by the Queen's command.' No doubt, it was what Elizabeth wanted people to believe.

Robert did not initially accept that the prospect of marriage to Elizabeth was at an end. There was no sudden schism and they remained close friends and allies for the rest of Robert's life, despite each seeking romance elsewhere. Elizabeth's decision was entirely political, and her secret infatuation sometimes bubbled to the surface, but she was now in better control of her emotions. When the able Don Diego de Silva y Guzmán replaced de Quadra as Spanish Ambassador,

Robert sent messages of greeting to him before Elizabeth had time to do the same. De Silva asked Robert to convey a request to the Queen for an audience, which Robert immediately obtained. De Silva soon gained the impression that Robert remained a friend of Spain and the Catholics, while Cecil was their enemy. Robert warned him that there was great enmity between himself and Cecil.[4] It was clear to de Silva that Robert saw Cecil as the barrier to him marrying the Queen but could not make up his mind whether their marriage would go ahead, as opinions were constantly changing.[5] To resurrect his suit, Robert needed Cecil out of the way. He suggested that Cecil should lead a diplomatic mission with Throckmorton to promote her suit with Maximilian. Cecil immediately sent his wife to petition for him to remain at home, as he was 'weak and delicate'. This enabled him to sidle out of it.

Unlike the Spanish, the French had no suitable royal scion of an appropriate age to put forward as Elizabeth's suitor. To bring negotiations with Maximilian to an end, the French bribed Robert to suggest that she should marry Charles IX of France. Robert 'pretended to be strongly in favour of the match'.[6] With Elizabeth's suit for Maximilian or the Archduke Charles being negotiated by Cecil, Norfolk and Sussex, they were furious at Robert's interference. Despite having sought Spanish support to marry her himself, he now argued that Spain was England's great enemy. His inconsistency only confirmed views that he was too unreliable to become Elizabeth's consort, diminishing the last vestiges of support for his suit in the Council. In February 1565, Paul de Foix, the French ambassador, saw Elizabeth in her presence chamber to confirm that Catherine de Medici would be the happiest of mothers if Elizabeth should marry her son. 'She would find in the young King, both bodily and mentally, that which would please her.' As Elizabeth was 30 and Charles IX was 13, this was never going to happen, but it might render Maximilian's suit – upon which Cecil's marriage policy depended – abortive.

Cecil was not too upset at the prospect of a French match, as he hoped that it would provoke the Spanish into greater action to promote Maximilian, but he needed to stop it developing too far. He was fearful that, if it progressed, the Spanish would be able to marry-off one of their nominees to Mary Queen of Scots. He drew up a list of the advantages and disadvantages of a French marriage. With the disadvantages greatly outweighing the advantages, Elizabeth repeated them to the 'ruffled' de

Foix but did not rule it out. Arundel claimed that Cecil did not want Elizabeth to marry, as 'he was ambitious and fond of ruling, and liked everything to pass through his hands, and if the Queen had a husband'[7] he would become subordinate.

Eventually, Elizabeth graciously 'deplored that she was not ten years younger',[8] and politely refused Charles IX, causing the French to think again. In another attempt to stop the Austrian negotiation, they now bribed Eric of Sweden to resurrect his suit, but Elizabeth showed no interest. With her suit to marry Maximilian rumbling on, the Austrian envoy – the Lutheran Adam Swetkowitz (or Zwetkovich), Baron Mitterburg – appeared in London, but was in no hurry to promote the Emperor until his future status in England was clarified. Cecil had jealously guarded the question of religion and made clear that, as a consort, Maximilian would have no authority. Such conditions were unlikely to gain Habsburg support. Although Cecil and Sussex laboured hard to arrange a visit for Maximilian, the Emperor was 'doubtful about the religious conditions and did not want to risk a loss of dignity'.[9]

Although Mitterburg hoped that Robert might be instrumental in helping to modify Cecil's terms, Cecil tried to weaken Robert's standing by telling de Silva that Elizabeth would never marry him. He even persuaded her to confirm this. On 9 October, de Silva reported that Elizabeth had told him in confidence:

> I am insulted both in England and abroad for having shown too much favour to Lord Robert. I am spoken of as if I were an immodest woman. I ought not to wonder at it: I have favoured him because of his excellent disposition and his many merits, but I am young, and he is young and therefore we have both been slandered. God knows they do us grievous wrong, and the time will come when the world will know it also. A thousand eyes see all that I do, and calumny will not fasten on me for ever.[10]

It may have been fortuitous that she was not pregnant.

In his determination to keep Spain and France from joining in alliance against heretic England, Cecil strongly disapproved of Robert's interference in Elizabeth's marriage negotiations, as he wanted a political marriage beneficial to the English interest. The demise of

Huguenot influence in France heralded strongly Catholic French calls for an alliance with Spain to extirpate heresy. Catherine de Medici had already met her daughter, Elisabeth to Valois, now Queen of Spain, at Bayonne to cement closer ties. This posed the real threat of Mary Queen of Scots being promoted as the English Queen. Cecil had always relied on balancing French and Spanish rivalry. If Elizabeth married one of their Continental allies, even one with Protestant sympathies, he hoped that England would be provided with protection.

Such niceties were completely lost on Robert, and Cecil considered him a loose cannon. That is not to suggest that Cecil particularly disliked him, and they always remained on cordial terms, but as has been shown, he saw Robert's approach to European politics as erratic and hawkish. He was always careful not to reveal his personal views, but his detailed notes setting out advantages and disadvantages show his true concerns. While these remained hidden, he manipulated others to take the lead. This was not difficult to achieve given Norfolk's intense dislike of Robert. Norfolk repeatedly told Robert not to interfere with the Government's European marriage negotiations in which he was involved. There was no love lost between them. 'When Norfolk showed himself anxious that the Queen should accept the Archduke Charles, Lord Robert told him that no true Englishman wanted to see the Queen married to a foreigner.'[11] Matters came to a head in March 1565 during a real tennis match between them at Whitehall in Elizabeth's presence. Norfolk was incensed at Robert's impertinence for leaning over to use Elizabeth's napkin to wipe his sweating brow. It was Elizabeth's turn to become indignant when Norfolk threatened Robert with his racquet.

Sussex was another senior peer who detested Robert's meddling. In July 1565, when Robert tried to rekindle his suit to marry Elizabeth, he faced violent opposition from Sussex, who was about to go to the Continent with Norfolk to spearhead negotiations with the Archduke Charles. He considered that Elizabeth's only important task was to marry and have children. He did not realise that it was she who would never agree to the Austrian match, and he blamed Robert for putting personal ambition above the interests of his country.

Chapter 13

Marriage considerations

Following Elizabeth's illness with smallpox in 1562, her succession had become a matter of increased concern. The Protestant faith was at stake. Although Mary Queen of Scots had readied herself for news of Elizabeth's death, no one supported her succession in the English Parliament. Opinion on Elizabeth's likely successor seemed to be divided between Catherine Grey and Henry Hastings, who had now succeeded his father as 3rd Earl of Huntingdon and, following the death of Devon, was the Plantagenet claimant to the English throne. Cecil wanted to follow the will of Henry VIII by backing Catherine, but she had seriously diminished her chances by her own shortcomings and remained under arrest after her ill-advised marriage. With her children being deemed illegitimate, Elizabeth had no respect for her. It was generally assumed that Huntingdon would succeed. He was an ardent Puritan and had married Robert's sister, Catherine Dudley, but they had no children. Although Robert strongly supported his brother-in-law, Elizabeth was wary of him. Despite Robert's best efforts, this had resulted in Huntingdon being excluded from high office and, perhaps as a result, he became impoverished. He was devastated that Elizabeth might consider him untrustworthy and was only looking for some signal cause to confirm his loyalty.

Huntingdon eventually sought permission from the Queen to sell his estates and to equip an army in support of the Huguenots. Given his financial difficulties, this might have seemed foolhardy. Elizabeth had no desire to see good English money being frittered away on some foreign cause and 'refused out of hand' to allow him 'to withdraw himself and his wealth 'in this strange sort'.[1] Eventually her attitude thawed. Perhaps through Robert's and even Cecil's influence, he became an assiduous, if much hated, jailer of Mary Queen of Scots, and later achieved the politically important role of Lord President of the Council of the North.

Despite the lack of English support for Mary Queen of Scots, the choice of her husband was of paramount interest. Although she had hoped to marry Philip II's son, Don Carlos, his mental and physical disabilities made any possibility of this unthinkable, but neither Mary nor the Spanish ambassadors seem to have realised the extent of his incapacity. Although she also considered marriage to the Archduke Charles, she did not consider that the Austrian Tyrol offered sufficient military clout for her to assert her rights and did not want Elizabeth's cast-off. With Catherine de Medici remaining in conflict with Mary's Guise relations, she vetoed Mary's marriage to another of her Valois sons. Cecil made it very clear that he wanted her choice of husband to be approved by the English interest. With Mary increasing her diplomatic pressure for nomination as Elizabeth's heir, she sought a meeting with Elizabeth at York, which Cecil was determined to avoid.

With Elizabeth's marriage also being urgently considered by the Council, the majority seemed to believe that Robert was preferable to no husband at all. Sussex, who had quarrelled with Robert, wrote to Cecil that the most important outcome was to achieve a 'child of the Queen's body'. He continued: 'Therefore, let her choose after her own affection; let her take the man at sight of whom all her senses are aroused by desire.' That was the surest way to bring them a blessed Prince, and he declared: 'Whomsoever she will choose, him will I love and honour, and serve to the uttermost.' The Council sent a delegation hoping 'that it would please your Majesty to dispose yourself to marry, where it shall please you, to whom it shall please you, and as soon as it shall please you'.[2] Elizabeth merely prevaricated. As it was obvious that she wanted to retain Robert without marrying him, the delegation focused on her naming a successor. She told them that 'she was very conscious of her duty to her people but that she would not declare herself yet on the succession issue "because I will not in so deep a matter wade with so shallow wit"'.[3]

Matthew Parker, Archbishop of Canterbury, together with the Bishops of London and Ely, wrote a joint letter to tell her that it was her duty to submit herself to marriage and childbearing as the only means of safeguarding the Protestant succession. Cecil's confidante Sir Thomas Smith, the English ambassador in Paris, produced a series of addresses with characters, who argued the case in favour of childbirth, 'to gain so precious treasure' for 'a little pain in birth of an hour or two, or at most one day'.[4] During a sermon before Elizabeth at Westminster Abbey in January 1563, the Dean of Westminster, Dr Alexander Nowell told her:

> As the marriage of Queen Mary was a terrible plague to all England, so now the want of *your* marriage and issue is likely to prove as great a plague … If your parents had been of your mind, where had you been then? Or what had become of us now?[5]

Cecil even prepared a Bill suggesting that if Elizabeth died without an heir, her divine authority would be transferred to the Council, making England an 'aristocratic republic'.[6] Parliament would then choose her successor, converting England into an elected hereditary monarchy. This, of course, predated the Glorious Revolution by 150 years. Elizabeth would have none of it. She stifled the Bill, preferring to live with uncertainty. If the Bill had been passed, there is considerable doubt who Parliament would have chosen.

It seems that Elizabeth was influenced by the pressure placed on her and knew that a foreign marriage suit was politically desirable. Cecil remained immovable over Robert's hopes and had told her that he would resign if she married him. Despite her popularity, she knew that marriage to Robert would threaten the real possibility of rebellion and assassination. With Robert apparently out of the running, despite his continuing close attendance on her, Elizabeth, with her political hat on, realised that she should extract herself from the relationship. Without discussing it with him in advance, she made the heart-wrenching decision that he should marry Mary Queen of Scots. In March 1563, she mentioned it to Maitland, who was in London to promote Mary's nomination as her heir. Most people saw it as a ploy to delay Mary choosing a husband less wedded to the English interest, but Robert had already failed Elizabeth's test of his integrity by promoting a scheme to revert England to Catholicism.

Marriage between Robert and Mary was not a bad political alliance. He was a suitor entirely acceptable to the English interest, and the marriage was strongly supported by the key members of the Council including Cecil, no doubt because they wanted to end his interference with Elizabeth's European marriage negotiations. Cecil may well have promoted the idea. Not only would it remove Robert from constant contact with Elizabeth, but by placing a staunch English ally in Scotland, the menace of Mary making a French or Spanish marriage would be ended. Robert would be a steadying hand, and it was assumed by everyone that their marriage would result in her being accepted as heir to the English throne. It had long been recognised that Cecil opposed this, but a letter he wrote to Sir Thomas Smith shows that Elizabeth was also in two minds about nominating her, even if married to Robert. He reported: 'I see the Queen's Majesty very desirous to have my Lord of Leicester placed in this high degree to be the Scottish Queen's husband; but when it cometh to the conditions to be demanded [the English succession], I see her then remiss of her earnestness.'[7] In the light of Elizabeth's experience during the reign of Mary Tudor, when her position as de facto heir to the throne placed her at great risk, she remained determined not to nominate a successor who might act as a catalyst for rebellion against her rule. Cecil was always determined to prevent a Catholic succession, even by a monarch married to a Protestant. Nevertheless, he wrote a letter to Maitland wholly supportive of Robert's marriage to Mary, saying that he:

> is a nobleman of birth – yea, noble also in qualities requisite, one void of all evil conditions that sometimes are heritable to princes and in goodness of nature and richness of good gifts comparable to any prince born, and, so it may be said with due reverence and without offence to princes, much better than a great sort now living. He is also an Englishman and so meet a man to carry with him a consent of this nation according to yours, which amongst all other aspects hath not the least interest. He is also dearly and singularly beloved [sic] esteemed of the Queen's majesty, so as she can think no good turn nor fortune greater than may be well bestowed upon him.[8]

Maitland was taken aback at the marriage proposal, particularly when Elizabeth told him that Robert was one 'in whom nature had implanted so many graces, that if she wished to marry, she would prefer him to all the princes in the world'.[9] He responded that:

> it was a great proof of love to his Queen that her Majesty was prepared to give her a thing so dearly prized by herself,

but he did not think that the Queen of Scots would deprive her of the joy and solace of his companionship.[10]

He was right. Mary considered marriage to Elizabeth's cast off and her 'groom' as demeaning unless it was accompanied with recognition as Elizabeth's heir. Furthermore, under no circumstances was Robert prepared to be put out to grass in Scotland, however attractive Mary might be. When he asked Sir James Melville what Mary thought about it, Melville admitted that she was 'cold'. Melville reported:

> Then [Robert] began to purge himself of so proud a pretence as to marry so great a Queen, declaring he did not esteem himself worthy to wipe her shoes; declaring that the invention of the proposition proceeded from Mr. Cecil, his secret enemy. For if I, says he, should have appeared desirous of that marriage, I should have offended both the Queens and lost their favour.[11]

Mary admitted that Robert told her privately that the proposal was a 'mere fetch [contrivance]' on Elizabeth's part.[12] Cecil also became nervous about it. He realised that if Robert were prepared to seek Spanish help to underpin his marriage to Elizabeth in return for supporting a Counter-Reformation, he was even more likely to do the same when married to Mary.

Robert was in an impossible position. It seems that he was still secretly sharing Elizabeth's bed and had no desire to spend the rest of his days isolated in Edinburgh. He believed that Cecil had dreamed up the plan as a means of getting him out of the way. Nevertheless, Thomas Randolph, the English ambassador in Scotland, was incredulous that Robert would forgo such a woman of perfect beauty as Mary. He wrote to Sir Henry Sidney: 'How many countries, realms, cities and towns have been destroyed to satisfy the lusts of men for such women.' Robert had spurned a kingdom and the chance to lie with her 'in his naked arms'.[13]

Robert desperately looked for a face-saving solution without offending Elizabeth, to enable him to re-establish his suit with her. He adopted a progressively more anti-Catholic stance to make himself less appealing to Mary, becoming one of their bitterest enemies. By 1564, he was firmly espousing the Puritan beliefs of his upbringing. Nevertheless, rumours about his private life made his cultivated strains of Puritan devotion appear hypocritical, particularly when the Earl of Leicester's Men were performing some bawdy play. Furthermore, he was not averse to continuing his support for Catholics or Catholic causes that were useful to him.[14]

When Cecil realised that Robert was unwilling to marry Mary, they hatched a plot to send Elizabeth's Tudor cousin, Henry, Lord Darnley, to Scotland. He was a tall and athletic sportsman and a virtuoso on the lute, but seemed insufferably spoilt, bisexual and devoid of common sense. Neither of them had a good opinion of him. He was described by the Cardinal of Lorraine as a 'gentil huteaudeau' [agreeable nincompoop]. Despite this, he was male; he had been born in England and was dynastically third in line to the English throne after Mary and his mother, Margaret Lennox. Margaret had been scheming for him to marry Mary since her own failure to gain nomination as Mary Tudor's heir. Their combined dynastic credentials seemed to make them unassailable. Unfortunately, Margaret had made unguarded comments that, once married, they should immediately claim the English throne; these were overheard by spies in her household.

It may seem surprising that Cecil and Robert suddenly supported Darnley's suit. They had had ample opportunity at the English court to see his shortcomings for themselves. Cecil concluded that, if Mary 'take fantasy to this new guest, then shall they be sure of mischief'.[15] His objective was to put paid to both their ambitions to be nominated as Elizabeth's heir in one go. He gambled that if Darnley should marry Mary, he would destroy her credibility. 'He probably considered the suit as another temporary diversion to delay her more serious opportunities, never expecting that Mary would tolerate his bisexual and boorish character for long.'[16] What Cecil failed to appreciate was that their marriage would seriously jeopardise the status of the Protestant members of Mary's Scottish Government, with whom he was closely allied.

Darnley was a loose cannon. He had ambitions to obtain the English and Scottish thrones for himself. He portrayed himself to Continental superpowers as a more ardent Catholic than Mary, who was continuing to demonstrate toleration to her Reformist subjects. His arrival on the Scottish scene caused a 'volte face' in Continental opinion over Mary's suitability to remain the Catholic pretender to succeed Elizabeth. Darnley had been cultivating Spanish support. It was now the Spanish rather than the French who backed their marriage and their claim to the English throne. De Silva in London reported:

> Considering the Queen of Scots' good claims to the Crown of England, to which Darnley also pretends … the marriage is one that is favourable to our interests and should be supported to the full extent of our powers … if they will govern themselves not to be precipitate but will await a juncture when any attempt to upset their plans would be fruitless, I will then assist and aid them in the aim they have in view.[17]

From the distance of Scotland, Mary was unaware of Darnley's shortcomings and was attracted by his close dynastic claim to the English throne. To give the marriage suit any chance of gaining Scottish approval, Darnley's father, Lennox, needed to have the attainder over his Scottish estates lifted after his part in supporting the English during the Rough Wooings. It so happened that Elizabeth had written to Mary in June 1563 asking her to restore Lennox to his Scottish titles and estates. For more than a year Mary had ignored this request, but when she realised that it might provide an opportunity for her to meet Darnley, Lennox was invited to Scotland, where he was favourably received in September 1564. Mary quickly restored him to his honours and dignity without the prior approval of the Scottish Government. He now sought consent for Darnley to join him on the pretext that it would enable him to be enfeoffed into the Lennox estates as part of their restitution.

As Lennox had travelled north, Sir James Melville, the Scottish ambassador, had come south for further discussions on Robert's possible marriage to the Scottish Queen and the related question of her succession to the English throne. He came with secret instructions to Margaret Lennox to obtain a passport for Darnley to visit Mary in Scotland. Melville arrived in time to see Robert's investiture as Baron of Denbigh and Earl of Leicester, which took place on 29 September 1564. (The Lordship of Denbigh came with sizeable estates in North Wales and the office of Chief Forester of Snowdon.) These titles had been designed to promote his cause with the Scottish Queen. Melville noticed that, during the ceremony, Elizabeth could not resist tickling Robert's neck. The lanky Darnley carried the sword of state at the ceremony and when Elizabeth saw him, she turned to Melville, telling him: 'Yet, ye like better yonder long lad!' Melville was taken aback that Elizabeth seemed to be aware of his secret mission to gain a passport for Darnley to visit Scotland. He recovered himself sufficiently to assure her that no woman would prefer a 'lady-faced boy'[18] to so fine a man as Robert.

At the festivities after Robert's investiture, the French Ambassador, Paul de Foix, proposed that Robert should be offered the Order of St Michel, France's highest order of chivalry, to promote his cause with Mary Queen of Scots. This was an embarrassment for Robert, who was still cultivating the Spanish, and did not want anything done to promote him with the Scottish Queen. To enable him to accept it with 'some decency', Throckmorton suggested that the Queen might ask for another Cross of the Order to be granted to Norfolk. 'When Cecil learned this, he was obliged to remonstrate with the Queen, and point out how undesirable it was in the present state of affairs to place two of her most powerful nobles under an obligation from France.'[19] Cecil was still trying to hold together the suit for Elizabeth to marry Maximilian, which Robert, to protect his own position with Elizabeth, wanted to prevent. Nevertheless, seven years later in 1571, the French investiture went ahead, with the chains of office being handed over at St Mary's Church, Warwick, by Charles IX's deputies, despite Norfolk's great reluctance to be reconciled with Robert.

After the ceremony to make Robert Earl of Leicester, Melville met with Elizabeth in her bedchamber, where Cecil was talking to Robert at the opposite end of the room. She opened a little cabinet and produced some miniatures wrapped in paper. On one of these was written, 'My Lord's Picture'. When Melville persuaded her to unwrap it, he saw that it was Robert's portrait. He suggested that it should be sent to Mary, but Elizabeth said she could not spare it as it was the only version she had. Melville looked over at Robert and retorted: 'Your Majesty has the original.' He then pointed to an enormous ruby, which was also in the cabinet. and suggested sending this to Mary as a token. Elizabeth replied that if Mary agreed to 'be ruled by her, then in time she would inherit everything Elizabeth possessed'.[20] It seemed to Melville that Elizabeth was having cold feet about losing Robert. She later suggested nonsensically that Mary should move to London and that they should live in a ménage à trois as an extended royal family, but Mary saw this as unworkable.[21] She needed a husband with her in Scotland to maintain control of her kingdom.

Despite his differences with Robert, Cecil realised that Mary Queen of Scots needed a husband. As Robert was not going to marry her, they combined to persuade Elizabeth to grant Darnley a passport to join his father. It was assumed that he would not proceed to marriage without obtaining Elizabeth's assent. Neither Cecil nor Elizabeth believed that Mary would tolerate him for long, but after his arrival in Edinburgh in February 1565, she became infatuated with 'a fantasy of a man', with its inevitable consequences. Although Elizabeth ordered Darnley back to England, it was already too late. Even when she told Mary that she would consider her nomination as her heir if she married Robert, Mary was already passionately committed to Darnley. Despite Elizabeth placing Margaret Lennox in the Tower and attainting the Lennoxes' substantial Yorkshire estates, Darnley and Mary ignored her. Cecil had only to sit back and watch as the 'mischief' in Scotland unfolded.

The prospect of Mary's marriage to Darnley was perhaps a relief to Elizabeth as she could rekindle her relationship with Robert. In May, he suffered a riding accident while hunting with her at Windsor. Although no bones were broken, he retired to bed severely bruised. When de Silva called, he had to wait as the Queen had come to talk to him before dinner. When the ambassador was at last able to see him, he was with Maitland, Cecil and Throckmorton, who was to be sent north to replace Randolph as Scottish ambassador. When they were at last alone, de Silva told Robert that the Spanish were in support of his marriage to Elizabeth. Although Robert was grateful, he confirmed that she wanted a great prince, but with Mary Queen of Scots marrying Darnley, she might think differently. Although de Silva had been irritated by Robert showing favour to the French, he offered to speak to the Queen on his behalf. He later reported that the Queen thanked him for his kind words, which seemed to show that the 'affair [with Robert] is not off'.[22]

Following Mary's marriage to Darnley, which took place on 29 July 1565, events in Scotland did not run smoothly. As Governor of Berwick, Bedford called for extra men to protect England's northern border and to provide support for Lord James Stewart, now Earl of Moray, leading a group of Protestant Scottish Lords who had opposed the marriage. Cecil and Robert, with most of their Council colleagues, backed Moray, but Elizabeth wanted to avoid being seen to support a rebellion against an anointed monarch. She was supported by Norfolk and Sussex, but they seem to have been trying to avoid an anti-Catholic policy developing, which might strengthen Robert's hand. With Moray denuded of English military support in his 'Chaseabout Raid', he had to escape to England, leaving Scotland at the mercy of increasingly pro-Catholic policies.

Darnley's strongly Catholic stance played havoc with Mary's previous policy of religious toleration. After the well-documented murders of Riccio and of Darnley himself, and Mary's unwise marriage to the Earl of Bothwell (generally known to have arranged Darnley's murder), the Scottish lords took up arms against her. She found herself imprisoned, probably unjustifiably, by nobles of all religious persuasions who had united against her rule in support of a regency for her new-born son, Prince James. Elizabeth was extremely shocked at their treatment of their anointed Queen, despite her tarnished reputation. It was Robert's ally, Throckmorton, who was sent to negotiate with the Scottish Government to defend Mary's interests. Nevertheless, the French were now turned against her, and even Spain's new-found loyalty temporarily evaporated.

Although Mary's and Darnley's marriage had ended any vestige of English support for their combined claim to the English Crown, Catherine Grey's position in the Tower was not made any easier by a book called *A Declaration of the Succession of the Crown Imperial of England* written by John Hales, Clerk of the Chancery Exchequer. Hales's objective was to clarify the succession to avoid any future argument. He concluded that Catherine was the most suitable claimant and it was essential that her marriage should be validated to demonstrate her sons' legitimacy, enabling the Crown to block Mary Queen of Scots' claim. He failed to appreciate that Elizabeth did not want any heir nominated, but if she had to do so, would choose the apparently innocent Mary, or her son James, over the fornicating Catherine. As always, she argued that the nomination of any claimant would make him or her a focus for rebellion against her rule, just as she had been during the reign of Mary Tudor. Furthermore, she had not forgotten that it was Catherine's sister, Jane, who had attempted to usurp her own claim. Huntingdon wrote furiously to Robert about 'a foolish book, foolishly written'.[23] Robert seems to have calmed matters but Hales was lucky only to face six months' imprisonment.

Chapter 14

Patronage and trading projects

To judge Robert as a failed suitor for the hand of Elizabeth with a less than astute grasp of politics and (as will be seen) an imperfect military record, would be to do him great injustice. In many respects he was the most important figure in Elizabethan England. He was the prime mover in the Elizabethan renaissance, through which Protestant influence established a new interest in English history as a backdrop for 'present problems and for justification of existing regimes'.[1] It was no coincidence that Continental ambassadors saw him as their first port of call on arrival in England. For anyone who had a new project seeking the Queen's assistance, it was often he who saw its potential and put his hand in his pocket. He was the most influential entrepreneur in the land with an extraordinary breadth of vision.

Robert had an unparalleled range of interests. He deserves particular recognition for his influence as Chancellor of Oxford University. It was he who arranged for its incorporation by Act of Parliament, confirming all privileges previously bestowed. This obviated the need for a new Charter at the accession of each sovereign. He also overhauled its income from leases, which were now granted for shorter periods of twenty-one years, greatly reducing the impact of inflation.[2] Before taking office he had streamlined the university's domestic government, vesting power in its senior officials. Some of these were his protégés, often European Protestant émigrés, who now made their homes in England. As Chancellor he had used his patronage to appoint them as heads of colleges. This enabled him to lean the university towards Protestantism. In 1581, he enforced an oath on all undergraduates over 16 years old requiring them to acknowledge the Royal Supremacy and the Thirty-Nine Articles of Religion, which had become established as Church of England doctrine in 1563.[3] This made Oxford exclusively Anglican. Although 'Cambridge had adopted a vigorous Reformed element since the time of Erasmus ... Oxford

135

had been the stronghold of Catholicism, and [his] interference in this direction brought him a fresh accession of unpopularity'.[4] He caused further disagreement by criticising undergraduate behaviour, 'looseness of apparel and absence from lectures'.[5]

In August 1566, the Queen visited Oxford University during her summer progress. With Robert as its Chancellor, he acted as her host. A fortnight before her visit, he moved to Kenilworth, from where he could supervise everything. He invited his nephew, Philip Sidney, a 12-year-old schoolboy at Shrewsbury, to attend the festivities. Robert was extremely fond of Philip, who enjoyed 'a lovely and familiar gravity', and was showing every sign of becoming the paragon for which he was later recognised. With his father, Sir Henry, being in Ireland, Philip was in the charge of the invaluable family steward, Mr Marshall, who brought him from Shrewsbury to Kenilworth. With the Sidneys being lamentably impoverished, Philip's clothing was not suitable for a royal occasion. Marshall had done his best by converting an old black velvet cloak into a pair of trunk hose, but these were not fit for purpose. Robert instructed his London tailor to kit Philip out with a new wardrobe, including a crimson satin doublet, a green taffeta doublet, a canvas doublet striped blue, and a range of other garments and shoes to make him presentable.

The Queen reached Woodstock in the third week of August, accompanied by de Silva. Robert soon appeared, but as she was undergoing medical treatment for what seems to have been migraine, she was unable to hunt with him.[6] Instead, Robert took de Silva out in Woodstock Chase. As they talked, the ambassador concluded that Robert had still not abandoned his pretensions to marry the Queen.

Robert returned to Oxford two days before the court's arrival to finalise arrangements. He was attended by Ambrose and Huntingdon. They met Cecil at Christchurch, where they sheltered from a storm at the Master's Lodge. On Elizabeth's arrival on 31 August the day was clear. Her coach was decorated with vermilion and gold leaf and she showed no effects of her malady. After a greeting, she attended a specially composed Te Deum in Christchurch Cathedral sung to the music of cornets. She listened to a speech of welcome from the outstanding historian, Edmund Campion, who provided words of praise for Robert as Chancellor. Campion later gave a dissertation to the Queen on the influence of the moon over the tides. His 'brilliancy of expression and his unusual charm of manner marked him out'.[7]

When the Queen later returned to Woodstock, she asked de Silva for his impressions of the day. De Silva admitted that they were excellent, but that the academics had plenty of time to prepare and would have done less well ex tempore. The Queen immediately called for scholars to come to Woodstock to debate in Latin, impromptu. Campion was among them and said afterwards that the 'sudden great pomp in which the Queen came forth to hear him', was daunting until he reminded himself 'that she was but a woman and he a man, which was the better sex!' He considered 'all the splendour which glittered in his eyes was but transitory vanity and had no substance in it'.[8] He again spoke brilliantly, and the Queen asked Robert to provide financial support for him. When Robert asked him his ambitions, Campion replied that 'he would ask nothing; the Chancellor's friendship was more than any gift'.[9] Robert's assistance resulted in Campion's *History of Ireland* being dedicated to him (see Aftermath). Campion's thanks were genuine, but he was a closet Catholic, who soon fled to Douai, only to return as a leader of the Jesuit cause.

Philip Sidney duly went to university at Oxford, where Robert sought a special dispensation from Archbishop Parker to allow him to eat meat during Lent. In May 1572, he was sent abroad and Robert wrote to ask Walsingham in Paris to keep a watching eye on him. He wrote: 'He is young and raw, and no doubt shall find those countries and the demeanour of the people somewhat strange to him.'[10] Walsingham attached him to his embassy, where he liaised with Protestant Princes seeking a means to combat the Spanish. He then set out on his grand tour of Europe, during which he did much to further Robert's interests. He wrote:

> There be nothing of which I am so desirous … as to have continual and certain knowledge what your pleasure is by which I may govern my little actions. I cannot be without some grief, that neither since I came into Germany I could by any means understand it. Wherefore, I have most humbly to beseech your lordship that if in any of my proceedings I have erred you will vouchsafe to impute it to the not knowing your Lordship's and their [the Council's] pleasure, by whose commandment I am likewise to be directed.[11]

It was through Philip's diplomacy that Robert developed a close link with William of Orange and his allies.

Another of Robert's interests was in architecture. The Elizabethan era was a period of extraordinary productivity, when great properties were established that no longer required fortification. Cecil built three Renaissance mansions and wealthy families like the Earl and Countess [better known as Bess of Hardwick] of Shrewsbury created a galaxy of spectacular homes. In June 1563, Elizabeth granted Kenilworth to Robert, a castle with curtain walls surrounded by a lake. It had previously been acquired by Robert's father from the Duchy of Lancaster but had reverted to the Crown on his attainder. For some time, Robert had sought a suitable centrepiece for his Midlands estates. Kenilworth, which dated from the twelfth century, with additions made by John of Gaunt, was in a poor state of preservation, but Robert took advantage of the military features of this mediaeval stronghold to create 'a magnificent pleasure house where Elizabeth and her court could be brought to take their ease and to be diverted with a great variety of entertainments'.[12] He 'converted the old south causeway into a tiltyard overlooked by viewing galleries'.[13] He changed the access so that the castle was approached across a wooden bridge, 600ft long, to an entrance in Mortimer's Tower. To the left of the bridge he created a pool, which was later the scene of water pageants. He did much to restore John of Gaunt's great hall, but also added a magnificent tower of his own.

We are indebted to Robert Laneham, one of Robert's protégés, for the vivid description he made of Kenilworth and its entertainments in 1575. Laneham spoke several languages and Robert had gained him the post of Keeper of the Council Chamber door, responsible for preventing ambassadors from spying on its proceedings. His 'enthusiastic gratitude was expressed in his account of himself, his office and the great doings at Kenilworth'.[14]

> On the north side of the castle, between the twelfth century keep and the outer wall, [Robert] created a pleasure garden. At its eastern end stood the Swan Tower, overlooking the mere. All along, just inside the castle wall, he had reared a terrace, ten or twelve feet broad; on this, against the wall, was a marvellous aviary protected by a gilded mesh; inside, nesting holes for the birds were hollowed out of the wall itself. Along the terrace stood obelisks surmounted by spheres, and white bears mounted on curious bases.

Below the terrace lay the pleasure ground, with paths sanded 'not light not too soft … but smooth and firm, pleasant to walk on as a sea-shore when the water has avoided'. Here on the grass was a magnificent fountain 'of rich and hard white marble', whose jets, falling into an octagonal basin, maintained there 'two feet of the fresh falling water'. The apple, pear and cherry trees in fruit, the beds of flowers, the breeze on the terrace, where one could pick 'delicious strawberries' and eat them from the stem, the sight and sound of the water, the fluttering and warbling in the aviary, all seemed to Laneham to form a terrestrial paradise, which glorified the great Earl, who had called it into being.[15]

Robert set about the renovation work with a will, spending £60,000 – despite his careful eye on the cost of each item of expenditure. Unlike many of his contemporaries, he was not concerned with achieving symmetry, but wanted the castellated harmony of a design set within its own landscape; on one side, a lake stocked with fish and on the other, a park containing 'shaded bowers, arbours, seats and walks',[16] brimming with red deer. It was designed to captivate the Queen and to impress her court and foreign visitors with legendary entertainments. It was this approach that led to the eighteenth-century development of the English country garden by such names as 'Capability' Brown. Laneham eulogised over:

the rare beauty of building … all of the hard quarry stone, every room so spacious, so well belighted and so high-roofed within … by day time on every side so glittering of glass, a' night by continual brightness of candle, fire and torchlight, transparent through the lightsome windows.[17]

With Robert being a patron of the arts, Kenilworth, with its hall of 45ft by 90ft, became the setting for his magnificent picture and literary collection.

Against the darkness of wood panelling the furniture displayed a fairy-like beauty, for some of it was upholstered in coloured lamé; there were chairs covered in 'purple-silver', in 'peach-silver' and in 'crimson-silver'. The great beds, their curtains of satin or velvet, crimson, green or blue, were embroidered all over with twinkling gold or silver, their posts were carved with the Earl's armorial bearings, their counterpanes of satin to match the curtains bore in the centre the bear and ragged staff, worked in gold or silver thread.[18]

In 1565, Elizabeth paid a brief visit during its construction. Leicester had written to Anthony Forster, his Steward of the Household, to make provision for everything 'against my chiefest day'. He needed to procure tapestries for the dining chamber complaining: 'I cannot have such hangings as I have looked for [from Flanders]', but heard there were some 'very good' available in London. 'In any case, deal with Mr Spinola ... he is able to get such stuff better cheap than any man, and I am sure will do his best for me.'[19]

It was not just Kenilworth. He also wanted to make Denbigh the focal point for his estates in North Wales. He was unimpressed when Denbigh's burgesses elected their own candidate to Parliament in April 1572, rather than his nominee as a Lord of the Manor should expect. He demanded that the election be cancelled so that they could demonstrate the regard in which he was held, but to his fury they persisted with their own man. Nevertheless, he made important repairs to its castle and provided land to build a shire hall. On 1 September 1578, he appealed to the church for funds to build a cathedral. It was not large, but its unostentatious design reflected, for the first time, the simple non-ritualistic liturgy of Puritan dogma. Funds were raised only slowly, and it remained incomplete at his death. Although further money was provided later, it was never finished. He also established magnificent houses in London. As will be seen, after his reconciliation with Elizabeth in 1565, he was granted the lease of Durham Place, previously occupied by de Quadra. It had been used for the reception following the marriage of his brother, Guildford, to Jane Grey. His lease expired in 1568, and he lighted on Paget Place, also in the Strand opposite St Clement Danes. It was in the occupation of the Spanish Ambassador, de Espés, who was considerably inconvenienced when required to move. He was offered the much less imposing Winchester House on the south side of the river in Southwark, the property of the Bishop of Winchester. Neither the Bishop, who 'raised some difficulties', nor de Espés cared for this new arrangement, which had been foisted onto them. The lease had to be settled by an order from the Council. Robert not only instructed the Bishop to give up possession, but arranged the rental charge, which both parties accepted.

Paget Place was one of a line of mansions in the Strand. It stood behind a gatehouse opening into the forecourt of a house surrounding four sides of an inner court. Its south front faced onto an oblong formal garden leading down to the river stairs. This southern block housed a great hall, terminating at its eastern end in a battlemented tower. Robert occupied the great chamber and withdrawing chamber above. He renamed the premises Leicester House and occupied it until his death, making it 'the centre of his social and political existence'.[20] It was the very height of luxury. He provided accommodation for other members of his family, including Ambrose, who did not have a London residence of his own. In 1575, he added a little banqueting house in the garden by the river, with the state room on its second floor. Cecil provided the stone for its walls.[21]

In 1577, Robert purchased Naked Haw Hall six miles out of London in Essex, with the neighbouring manor of Stonehall as a country retreat for Lettice Knollys.[22] This unfortunately named property, built by Richard, 1st Lord Rich, during the 1550s in what had been one of Henry VIII's hunting parks, contained a hall, a great chamber, a chapel, twenty bedrooms and stabling for fifty-eight horses.[23] Robert arranged for it to be significantly expanded and it was renamed Wanstead Hall [the White House]. Like all Robert's residences, it was palatially decorated and the walls were covered with portraits, which included Henry VIII, Elizabeth, Mary Tudor, and an assortment of European heads of state including two of Anjou. He nominated rooms for his principal guests including a Queen's chamber for when she visited, with its bed hung with cloth of tinsel. Robert's own chamber contained a bed with 'gilded posts, curtains of yellow damask and a quilt of straw-coloured taffeta'.[24] He had wardrobes of rich clothing and hats. In addition to other chambers, there was a long gallery, a withdrawing chamber, and a hot house for taking baths. The purchase and cost of extending Wanstead placed an enormous burden on Robert's overstretched finances and by 1580 he was obliged to take out a mortgage on the property to raise £4,000.

In 1585, Elizabeth appointed Robert as Chief Justice Itinerant of all the forests 'this side of the Trent', with the role of ranger of 500 acres of virgin woodland surrounding a stone-built lodge with mullioned windows at Cornbury in Oxfordshire. This looked out onto 'parkland scattered with trees that gradually thickened into deep woods'.[25] When she also granted him the manor of Langley, he acquired the surroundings woodlands and the forest of Wychwood.

Robert loved beautiful possessions and display, indulging himself with more than he could afford.[26] All his houses were filled with magnificent and costly items, often adorned with the Dudley crest of a bear and ragged staff. He was especially fond of Turkey carpets, sometimes hung at windows or as a covering for tables; he was an early user of oriental carpets as floor coverings. His possessions included venetian glass, silver-gilt tableware and an array of portraits of members of his family and of Elizabeth. A tapestry made for the banqueting house at Leicester House still survives in the Victoria and Albert museum.[27] It housed sculptures of both Robert and the Queen until the late 1580s, but they seem to have disappeared, perhaps a result of Lettice's influence.

Robert also patronised artists including the miniaturist, Nicholas Hilliard. When Elizabeth granted a lease of premises to Hilliard in 1582, the letters patent remained uncompleted in the offices of the Chancellor of the Exchequer, Sir Walter Mildmay. Robert wrote to Mildmay to expedite the documentation and within three months, Hilliard had moved in. He executed a miniature of Lettice Knollys shortly after her marriage to Robert in watercolour on vellum. This is set in an emerald and diamond frame. One of Hilliard's two daughters was named Lettice in her honour.[28] He also painted a miniature of Penelope Devereux and made a small full-length portrait of Robert in 1588.

More significant was Robert's patronage of famous poets, writers and playwrights, who 'habitually assembled'[29] with great thinkers at his houses. The most famous of these was Philip Sidney. In February 1577, Philip's elder sister, Ambrosia (named after Ambrose), had died, and Elizabeth wrote a most sympathetic letter to Sir Henry and Mary Sidney offering, if it would suit them, to take their younger daughter Mary, who was then 14, into a position at court. This offer was gratefully accepted. She shared all her brother's charm and good looks and, within a year, had become betrothed to Henry Herbert, who had succeeded his father as Earl of Pembroke in 1570. He was then aged 42 and was widowed but was a glittering prospect for the 15-year-old. The Sidneys were delighted and ascribed the connection to Robert's influence. Their daughter now lived in great style between Pembroke's London residence at Baynard's

Castle in the City, and his country seat at Wilton in Wiltshire. Mary provided Pembroke with two very able sons and made Wilton, where Robert visited her, into 'a paradise for her relations'.[30] In 1580, Sir Henry was so captivated that Elizabeth had to remind him to return to Ireland. Philip found refuge at this beautiful house, surrounded by its serene woods, soaking up the society of his most dearly loved sister, writing *The Countess of Pembroke's Arcadia* as a romance to amuse her. He explained:

> You desired me to do it, and your desire to my heart is an absolute commandment. Now it is done, only for you, only to you … Your dear self can best witness the manner, being done in loose sheets of paper, most of it in your presence.[31]

It is perhaps his most brilliant work, full of reference to contemporary fashion.

In 1577, Timothy Kendall dedicated a collection of verses, *Flowers of Epigrams,* to Robert, saying: 'Your courteous nature doth minister encouragement to presume.'[32] Two years later, Robert's protégé, the poet Edmund Spenser, was employed at Leicester House as his secretary and messenger. While there, Spenser wrote his first major work, *The Shepherd's Calendar.* He seems to have been on good enough terms with his employers to allude to the passionate nature of their romance. He also played a minor part in an inner circle that included Elizabeth's former tutor, Dee, and Philip Sidney, who read, wrote and discussed poetry. Robert often used their output as a means of disseminating his political and religious thinking. It was they who carried the standard for reformed religion into Europe and encouraged Elizabethan imperialism 'through the development of the navy and mercantile enterprise into lands beyond the seas'.[33] Such appeals to nationalism were causes and policies which Robert was promoting in the Council.

Spenser was first introduced to Elizabeth in July 1578 on a visit among Cambridge University members to Audley End. It was unfortunate that he presented political ideas to the Queen with which she did not always agree. His *Mother Hubbard's Tale* was an allegorical fable in opposition to her marriage to the Duke of Anjou. She was very unamused to find Anjou's representative, Jean de Simier, Baron de St Marc, of whom she was extremely fond, being 'lampooned as a gibbering ape and Cecil represented as a half-crazed chicken thief'.[34] Robert had to dismiss Spenser but gained for him a position as secretary to the new Lord Deputy of Ireland, Arthur, Lord Grey de Wilton. It was during Spenser's period in Ireland that he worked on *The Faerie Queen* begun at Leicester House. This is an intricate allegorical work, in which Elizabeth is represented as Gloriana, the Fairy Queen, and Robert as King Arthur. Spenser's career in Ireland proved a prosperous one, but it was not the one he had wanted, and it may well have limited his poetic output.

Robert's many interests resulted in him establishing vast libraries of books at Leicester House and Wanstead. At Leicester House, these were bound in crimson velvet and stamped with Leicester's crest in gold. By the time of his death, there were several hundred volumes, some in Latin and Italian. These included a book of Common Prayer and a Bible covered with yellow leather.[35] At Wanstead, the books were beautifully bound in blue, 'with the bear and ragged staff deeply stamped in gold in the centre of their covers'.[36]

With his natural flare for pageantry, Robert became the theatrical impresario of the age. As the leading patron of pre-Shakespearian drama, in 1559 he formed his own troupe of players, later known as the Earl of Leicester's Men, who opened the eyes of the English public to the stage. Perhaps to curb their sharp wit, the permitted number of players in a household was restricted, and they could not go on tour unless attached as servants to a nobleman. Robert's actors sought to be employed on their existing wages as 'household servants and daily waiters'[37] and to be acknowledged by him in that capacity. He seems to have footed bills for their props and transportation.

Theatrical performances were not just the province of professional actors. There was a strong tradition at the universities and at the Inns of Court. When the Inner Temple wanted help to establish their ownership of Lyon's Inn, Robert gained the Queen's help to provide it for them. This resulted in his arms being hung in their hall and rules being laid down that no member was to act in any suit against him. He was also made master of their revels at Christmas, often attended by the Queen. Themes and characters were drawn from mythology or history to provide comment on the prevailing issues of the day.[38] One such was a gruesome and tedious allegorical play, *Ferrex and Porrex,* by Elizabeth's cousin Sir Thomas Sackville, which propounded the analogy that her failure to provide an heir would lead to civil war.[39] In March 1565, Robert brought some Gray's Inn players to a tourney at Whitehall organised for the Queen. Their play involved a dialogue between Juno and Diana, with Juno advocating marriage, and Diana chastity. Jupiter's verdict was in favour of matrimony. The Queen turned to de Silva and said: 'This is all against me!'[40] He considered it a very English custom to make oblique criticism to the monarch's face; this would not be attempted in Spain! On Twelfth Night 1567, the gentlemen of the Inner Temple performed *The Tragedy of Tancred and Gismunda*. Act IV had been written by a tall good-looking 26-year-old lawyer, Christopher Hatton. Two years earlier, he had been noticed by the Queen for his graceful dancing. He was already a Gentleman Pensioner, a position for which 'his personal devotion to the Queen made him eminently suitable'.[41]

It was Robert who predated Shakespeare in linking ribald comedy with the elegant classical tradition of the universities and the Inns of Court:

> [The Earl of Leicester's Men] gave the stage a measure of respectability. They extended the range of drama: buffoonery and bombast were contributed by the wandering players, subtlety and grace by the lawyers. They created a wider audience for serious plays. And this they were able to do because their patron had a passion for the drama in all its aspects.[42]

At last, in 1574, Robert received a royal patent for his players 'to perform throughout the realm, without hindrance from local authorities, any play which had been approved by Elizabeth's Master of the Revels'.[43] By performing in different parts of the country, they were kept fully employed, despite a degree of Puritan objection to theatricals, which 'might attract prostitutes and confidence tricksters'. In 1585, his actors accompanied him to the Netherlands. Their broader exposure made them less dependent on noble patronage and greatly widened their general appeal. Choir boys from St Paul's and the Chapel Royal frequently appeared in court masques, pageants and plays.[44] He thought nothing of the expense of hiring a choir to entertain the Duke of Anjou for dinner at Leicester House.

Robert's theatricals were a prelude, a decade later, to the building of London's first permanent theatre by James Burbage, who initially had been one of The Earl of Leicester's Men. 'The Theatre' had to be built outside the city walls at Shoreditch to appease the sensibilities of London's Puritan burghers. When the Queen's company of players was formed in 1583, Robert released some of his best performers to join her group, but it was The Earl of Leicester's Men, who remained more prestigious. He had attracted the best available talent and after his death in 1588 they continued to perform, but eventually, 'its leading members joined the Lord Chamberlain's company, for which Shakespeare wrote most of his masterpieces'.[45] These included Will Kempe, the great clown of his generation, for whom Shakespeare wrote many parts. Although Shakespeare's first production on the London stage took place in 1591, three years after Robert's death, it was Robert's activities in the immediately preceding period that fostered the 'great explosion of literary and dramatic talent'.[46]

Writers also acknowledged their debt to Robert. One was the chronicler John Stow who, in 1562, had obtained a copy of *The Tree of Commonwealth,* written in the Tower by Robert's grandfather, Edmund Dudley. He provided Robert with a copy at 'his request and earnest persuasion'. Robert then financed Stow's writing of the *Chronicles of England,* which researched the 'famous antiquities' of its past. Stow confirmed Robert's 'great love ... to the old records of deeds done by famous and noble worthies'.[47] Robert urged him to 'trace the ancient lineage of the house of Tudor and extol the Protestant imperial ideal'.[48] Another, historian, Richard Grafton included accounts of Robert's ancestors in his *Abridgement of the Chronicles of England,* also dedicated to Robert. Shakespeare based many of his plays on Ralph Holinshed's *The Chronicles of England, Scotland and Ireland.* Holinshed's dedication to Robert refers to 'the incomparable valour' of his father Northumberland in the service of Henry VIII and Edward VI. Arthur Golding had dedicated the first volume of his 1564 translation of Ovid's *Metamorphoses* to Robert. This was followed in 1587 by a second volume, in which the dedication again emphasised Robert's interest in translations as a means of enhancing the English language. In 1566, Thomas Nuce dedicated his Latin play *Octavia* to him, 'for his favourable and gracious humanity to scholars'.[49]

Robert's patronage covered a wide range of other interests. He supported treatises on 'chess, military strategy, the rearing of horses, politics and philosophy, translators of works in Latin, Greek, French and

Italian, and musicians'.[50] With his interest in navigation, he supported William Cunningham's *The Cosmographical Glass, Containing the Pleasant Principles of Cosmography, Geography, Hydrography and Navigation*, written in 1559 and dedicated to him. In 1570, John Montgomery addressed a treatise *On the Maintenance of the Navy* to him. This included advice on ship design and navigational aids. Robert also supported the pioneering of new surgical techniques based on scientific study to overcome quacks and charlatans and those wedded to astrology and ancient books.[51]

Robert was one of 'the foremost supporters of commercial, exploratory and privateering ventures'.[52] These included mining calamine [zinc carbonate] in Somerset, copper in Ireland, iron in the Forest of Dean and in Northumberland, often with co-financing from Cecil and Pembroke. He also invested in mining first grade copper ore at Borrowdale in Cumbria. These projects led to the formation of the first English joint stock companies, the Mines Royal Charter Company and the Mineral and Battery Company founded in 1568, although their ventures lost money.

In 1576, Robert and Ambrose each invested £50 in Frobisher's first voyage in search of the North-West Passage to the Pacific. In 1562, along with a syndicate of London merchants, Robert backed the first voyage of Hawkins to the Americas. This shipped African slaves to the West Indies in return for hides, pearls, ginger and sugar, proving highly profitable. On a second voyage in 1564, Robert and Pembroke chartered the *Jesus of Lubeck* as Hawkins's flagship. Any Spanish colonists reluctant to trade with him were forced into it at gunpoint, ensuring that the trip was a financial success. One of Hawkins's captains was Francis Drake; it was Robert who provided much of the funding for Drake's circumnavigation starting in 1577. A map of the route of this voyage was retained at Leicester House. Drake was entertained there, and they became partners in many ventures. In 1581, Robert bought a fine armed merchantman, renamed *The Galleon Leicester* for an abortive trip to the Spice Islands, intending to take up concessions acquired by Drake. It later sailed as a privateer under Drake's command. Other trading ventures included the Barbary Company founded in 1585 to acquire Moroccan saltpetre, in which Robert invested £3,000. When this proved too pricey for the English market, it was shipped to Mexico to be bartered for metals. Robert also had ships trading on the North African coast, but piracy made this particularly difficult.[53] Pioneers looked to the merchant communities in Bristol and London for financial backing, and Robert often funded expeditions under the auspices of the Merchant Venturers and Muscovy Company. When ventures seemed particularly risky, they generally turned to Robert, Pembroke, Hatton and others to attract investors willing to take a bigger gamble; this made Robert their 'figurehead'. The Queen had to be more circumspect; she would not be associated with piratical ventures.

Many of Robert's protégés became his agents, enhancing his prestige both at home and abroad and providing him with intelligence as spies. One of these was Killigrew, who later became Cecil's brother-in-law. It was important to have friends in distant places, and Robert received helpful foreign intelligence for the Council through his own contacts. Numerous young men travelling in different spheres were anxious to assist him in the hope of more permanent employment. He developed a close friendship with the third son of the Elector Palatine, Duke John Casimir. Casimir had ambitions to marry Elizabeth and had sought help in 1564 from the Scottish diplomat, Sir James Melville, to advance his suit. Melville decline the embassage, because he understood that Elizabeth was incapable of bearing children, a rumour which Robert may well have promoted.[54]

Robert's charitable benefactions generally supported Puritan causes with help for distressed protégés and 'poor, friendless suitors' willing to be 'the unfeigned professors ... of God's glory'.[55] It resulted in two Calvinist works being dedicated to him. More permanently, he educated two scholars at University College, Oxford, and gained great local prestige by founding Lord Leycester Hospital, Warwick, to house twelve poor brethren with a hall, a master's lodge, St John's Chapel adjacent to the West Gate, and a number of half-timbered buildings incorporating four sides of a quadrangle, which formerly housed the town guilds.[56] This was endowed to provide it with £200 per annum. In 1585, he changed this public charity to provide a means of supporting his own retainers, particularly dependents born in Warwickshire and Gloucestershire, who might have been wounded in the Netherlands campaign. Other charitable giving included one to 'work an honourable and charitable deed to help to reform [Chester's] decay'.

Financing his enormous investment interests, benefactions and extravagance was a huge drain. Much of his Norfolk estate had reverted to the Robsart family on Amy's death.[57] That was not to suggest that he was short of income and he benefited hugely from royal favour, sometimes gained by pleading poverty. It was said: 'He makes gainful to himself every falling-out with her Majesty ... [and] was never reconciled to [her] under £5,000.'[58] He made the most of estates being lavished on him. He swapped land holdings to consolidate them into four main areas, in the Midlands near Kenilworth, in North Wales around Denbigh, in Essex around Wanstead and in Kent. Other sizeable estates included Cornbury in Oxfordshire, Middlefoy in Somerset and the wardship of the Old Palace at Maidstone, with other lordships of manors in many parts of England and Wales. Like most great landowners, he was generally an absentee, delegating management responsibility to stewards.

There were always pressures to increase income by land reclamation and enclosure. When time-honoured customs were broken, landlords became unpopular. Robert's estates round Denbigh, acquired in 1563, had suffered from years of neglect and he appointed a commission to report on more efficient management.[59] This involved him in recovering barony lands after what he claimed was tenant encroachment and a failure to enforce rental increases. He argued that forests in Anglesey were part of his estates because a stag being hunted by a king in years past had swum the Menai Straits. The freeholders – from whom Robert was now demanding increased rents – took him to court, but the members of the jury were wearing Robert's livery with the silver bear and ragged staff on their sleeves and gave their verdict in his favour. The resultant local rioting called for 'brutal efficiency' from Robert's agents. He had the advantage that his brother-in-law, Sir Henry Sidney, by now President of the Council of Wales, took Robert's side.[60] The freeholders also had a powerful ally in Sir Richard Bulkeley who, as a boy, had been a member of Elizabeth's household before her accession and remained on affectionate and trusted terms with her. He was a dignified local figure, honest and independent with estates in Cheshire and at Beaumaris, where he lived. He came to London to explain the predicament and Elizabeth granted a charter confirming the freeholders 'in the quiet possession of their lands'.[61] This made Bulkeley Robert's lifelong enemy, but Elizabeth always protected her former retainer. Despite this reverse, Robert increased his income from lands in North Wales to £1,500 per annum. He was not alone in having difficulties with tenants. Ambrose faced a riot in Hertfordshire after enclosing common land. This required Hatton to come to his support.[62]

Robert received income from offices held from the Crown. He was the Constable of Windsor Castle and Keeper of its Park, Steward of Warwick, Chancellor of Oxford University, High Steward of Cambridge University, Chamberlain of the County Palatine of Chester, Warden of the New Forest, Steward of Snowdon Forest, and Ranger of Wychwood Forest. In addition to annual fees, he could sell minor offices and receive 'considerations' for the placements of contracts. He held several stewardships from ecclesiastical bodies that brought in fees for administrative work which he sub-contracted. He received a consideration for nominating candidates for membership to the Inner Temple and was also permitted to erect buildings with gardens on their land, which he used for entertainment. He was the most honoured member of their exclusive club.

With Robert's access to the Queen, suitors who arrived seeking an audience seldom came empty-handed and provided gifts or money. He also benefited from trade concessions and the rights to farm import duties. In 1564, he sold his licence for transporting finished cloths to a consortium of Merchant Venturers for £6,267. He subcontracted his rights to farm the duties on sweet wines, oils, currants, silks and velvets, receiving £2,500 annually for the sweet wines' concession alone. In 1566, he was granted a twenty-year licence to export timber from Shropshire.

Despite his huge income, Robert spent massively to maintain his interests and lifestyle. His extravagance always left him short of ready money. During 1558 and 1559, his personal expenditure, when he was acutely impoverished, was £2,589, much of it spent on clothing and gifts for the Queen. In January 1565, he wrote to his Netherlands agent, Baroncelli, seeking two bodices worked in gold and silver for the Queen, and 'two white mares in good condition' for her.[63] At New Year 1572, he presented her with a gold bracelet set with emeralds, diamonds and pearls, which opened to reveal a tiny timepiece. This is one of the earliest recorded wrist-watches.[64] He provided her with lavish presents each year. Her fondness for emeralds was well-known; on New Year's Day 1576, Robert presented her with a gold cross containing five great emeralds, with three pearls hanging from it.[65]

It was not just gifts for the Queen. On 16 May 1566, Robert gave 3¼ yards of crimson satin to the Mayor of Abingdon for a doublet, and

7 yards of black satin to make doublets for two of the Mayor's brethren. Such munificence left him heavily in debt. Between December 1559 and April 1561, he repaid £3,726 to William Byrd, a London Mercer. On 17 December 1576, he had to repay the balance of a debt of £15,000 lent to him by Elizabeth. He prepared a bond to borrow £10,000 from Ambrose, Huntingdon and Pembroke, assigning to them the income from his Denbigh estates. In the end, he raised £16,000 by mortgaging these estates to a consortium of London merchants. These were huge sums of money, and at his death his debts exceeded the value of his chattels by £20,000.[66]

Chapter 15

Flirtation with Lettice Knollys designed to provoke Elizabeth

It was only after the marriage of Mary Queen of Scots to Darnley in July 1565 that Elizabeth's close relationship with Robert seemed to become more fragile. De Silva noted: 'Lord Robert seems lately to be rather more alone than usual, and the Queen appears to display a certain coolness towards him.'[1] It has been suggested that she blamed Robert for failing to support her proposal for him to marry Mary, but it has been shown that she also pulled back from the plan. In August, Cecil wrote to Sir Thomas Smith in Paris: 'The Queen's Majesty is fallen into some misliking of my Lord of Leicester, and he therewith much dismayed.'[2] Elizabeth had been extremely distressed by the death of Kat Ashley, which occurred in the same month. Kat had been her foster-mother and was her only real mentor, so she felt the loss keenly. She suddenly seemed to be much attracted by Thomas Heneage, who had been a Gentleman of the Privy Chamber since 1560 and a close friend of Robert. He was 'a thorough courtier, yet he was kind and eminently good hearted'.[3] He was married and, despite her attentions, showed little more than 'reverence' to the Queen, but held posts of increasing importance until his death, becoming Vice Chamberlain and a member of the Council. Although de Silva did not expect the affair to become serious, it was the first time since Sir William Pickering in 1559 that Elizabeth had shown an interest in anyone other than Robert. Robert was thoroughly piqued, complaining to her of his rival's insolence, but rumours that he was ready to duel with Heneage were dismissed by Robert. Robert absented himself for three days, until Heneage left court allowing him to enjoy 'an exquisitely delightful reconciliation' with Elizabeth.[4]

Heneage was soon recalled and patched up his former friendship with Robert. Sidney confided to de Silva that it did not seem that Elizabeth intended to marry, and Robert 'had lost hope of his business'.[5] This left England in 'a most troublous state ... If the Queen were to die, there would not be found three persons in one opinion as to who was to succeed.'[6] De Silva wrote to Philip II:

> I do not think that anything is more enjoyable to this Queen than treating of marriage, though she herself assures me that nothing annoys her more. She is vain and would like all the world to be running after her, but it will probably end by her remaining as she is, unless she marries Lord Robert who is still doing his best to win her.[7]

With the growing realisation that Elizabeth was unlikely to marry unless she were persuaded to espouse Robert, Throckmorton offered to try to assist him. He suggested that Robert should pretend 'to fall in love himself with one of the ladies in the palace and watch how the Queen took it'.[8] The lady chosen for this subterfuge was Lettice Knollys, the wife of Walter Devereux, Viscount Hereford (created Earl of Essex in 1572). She may have been chosen because she was six months pregnant and unlikely to be receptive to any amorous attention. Nevertheless, in other respects she would be perceived as a threat. She was famously beautiful with great 'sexual magnetism' and was ten years younger than the Queen. Perhaps more importantly, she was the daughter of Elizabeth's cousin, Catherine Carey, and a granddaughter of Mary Boleyn. Catherine had been Elizabeth's most favoured lady-in-waiting and was married to Sir Francis Knollys, one of Elizabeth's most trusted advisers and an ally of Robert. Portraits demonstrate that she showed an uncanny likeness to Henry VIII, and it can be assumed that Henry was her father, conceived during his relationship with Mary Boleyn. If so, Lettice was also Elizabeth's niece, a matter that both would have known. Certainly Elizabeth always favoured Catherine, making grants to her for clothing from the Wardrobe.

Elizabeth was understandably jealous at Robert's attention to Lettice, who was no doubt flattered. 'He deepened the impression of a romance by a request that he might be temporarily released from his attendance at court "to stay at his own place as other men did".'[9] 'The Queen was in a great temper and upbraided him … [for] his flirting with the Viscountess in very bitter words.'[10] As was Robert's usual practice:

> he went down to his apartments and stayed there for three or four days until the Queen sent for him, the Earl of Sussex and Cecil having tried to smooth the business over, although

they are no friends of Lord Robert in their hearts. The result of the tiff was that both the Queen and Robert shed tears, and he has returned to his former favour.[11]

Although it is clear that Robert found Lettice very attractive, it was, at this time, nothing more than a harmless flirtation. There is no mention of Elizabeth showing any hostility to her close relation, but it was probably the cause of future animosity between Robert and Hereford.[12]

Such was the reconciliation between Elizabeth and Robert that, at the end of 1565, she granted him the use of Durham Place, previously occupied by de Quadra. She also appointed him as Chamberlain of the County Palatine of Chester. This made him the Crown's representative within its jurisdiction with almost royal status.[13] In 1578, he felt obliged to write to reproach the Mayor and Justices of Chester that prisoners in their jails had died of starvation. This was a neglect of their legal obligation to provide relief to those in their custody.

With Robert restored to Elizabeth's favour, the hopes for Maximilian's suit waned. It was the less attractive proposition of the Archduke Charles, which remained on the table. Significantly, Elizabeth appointed Robert and Throckmorton to handle the negotiations. Cecil immediately revived the prospect of Eric of Sweden, who again sent valuable presents of sable and plate. Eric's suit was spearheaded by none other than the Princess Cecilia. She had always been anxious to visit the Queen of England and had agreed to marry Christopher II, Margrave of Baden-Rodemachern, only on condition that he would bring her on a visit. Their journey was hampered by Sweden's war with Denmark, but after an eleven-month journey fraught with adventure, she arrived with her husband in England, heavily pregnant. This was the first visit of a member of a European reigning house during Elizabeth's reign and, although she was at Windsor, she prepared a welcome on a grand scale. With her long pale hair loose under a crown and in a black velvet dress with a mantle of cloth of silver, Cecilia caused a sensation. With Bedford being absent in the north, Elizabeth housed her with her entourage at Bedford House in the Strand. Cecil arrived to greet her with his wife, bringing with them Lady Sussex and Lady Bacon.

Within two days, Cecilia was delivered of a prince, and Elizabeth spent a day with her and agreed to stand godmother at the baptism held on 11 November 1565 in the Chapel Royal at Whitehall Palace. This was a magical ceremony overseen by the Archbishop of Canterbury and the Bishops of London, Salisbury and Rochester, with the Queen in attendance. The Queen deputed Catherine Carey, Countess of Nottingham (a niece of her namesake married to Sir Francis Knollys), to carry the child to the font where he was baptised as Edward Fortunatus. Catherine needed assistance from Thomas Butler, 10th Earl of Ormonde (of whom more later), to bear the weight of the child's jewelled mantle.

On the same day, Robert's brother – the twice-widowed Ambrose – married Ann Russell, Bedford's daughter. Given his past differences with Robert, Bedford had been nervous of the match, but Robert assured him of his friendship – confirmed by his backing of his brother's suit – and was able to confirm the Queen's support. It seemed that no one could act without Robert's intervention. Not only was it a very happy marriage, but Ann Russell proved 'mild natured, honest and sweet', becoming one of the closest female companions to the exacting Queen. Robert was given the opportunity as Master of the Horse to demonstrate his skills in presenting pageantry. With Bedford stationed in Berwick, he did not attend the wedding, but Elizabeth and Robert managed everything. The events surrounding both it and the christening of Prince Edward of Baden were 'celebrated by tournaments of extraordinary magnificence lasting two days'.[14] They ended with a great dinner hosted by Robert at Durham Place.[15] Robert's standing continued to grow. Hume has commented: 'Probably Elizabeth's marriage with her favourite was never nearer than at this juncture, when she was carrying on a serious negotiation with the Austrian and was still making an appearance of dallying with de Foix.'[16] De Foix arranged for Catherine de Medici and Charles IX to send a cordial invitation for Robert to visit France, which he understood that Robert would enjoy. Nevertheless, when it arrived, Robert's position at court was assured, and Elizabeth did not want him to be away. With typical teasing she claimed that she could hardly send 'a groom, a horsekeeper' to wait upon so great a King. Then she continued: 'I cannot live without seeing you every day. … You are like my little dog. As soon as he is seen anywhere, people know that I am coming, and when you are seen, they say I am not far off.'[17] Robert no doubt had to bite his lip. Even de Silva and de Foix urged Elizabeth, if she married any subject, to marry Robert.[18] As they found him thoroughly meddlesome in the suits they were promoting, this shows their sense of desperation to avoid a rival European marriage. Elizabeth told de Foix that:

> if she did marry, she was determined not to give up any power, property or revenue to her husband; the mere marriage would make him but too powerful. But, she exclaimed, 'If I think of marrying, it is as if someone were tearing the heart out of my body … nothing but the welfare of my people would compel me to it!'[19]

When Robert gave her an ultimatum to make up her mind by Christmas, she promised to let him know by Candlemas (2 February 1566). De Foix understood that she had already promised to marry him before witnesses, but he reported: 'If she thinks fit to disengage herself, no one will call her to account or give testimony against her.'[20] The ambassadors were certain that 'Cecil … would resist to the last the marriage of the Queen with [Robert], under the patronage of France or Spain.'[21] Candlemas came and went without any word of marriage. When de Foix was replaced as French ambassador by M. de la Forêt, the French continued to support Robert's suit in an attempt to thwart the Austrian match.

Despite Robert's personal influence with the Queen, he was careful not to encroach on the political life that she shared with Cecil. Robert was famous for his gently spoken easiness and knowing when to 'put his passion in his pocket'. He very rarely overstepped the mark. The entrance to the Queen's Privy Chamber, which led to the Presence Chamber, was guarded by Black Rod, a man named Bowyer. When Robert's protégé was forbidden entry, Robert appeared to tell Bowyer he was a knave. Although he stormed into the Queen, Bowyer got there first and, on his knees, asked simply whether Robert were King or Elizabeth Queen? The Queen was furious at Robert's presumption and told him: 'I will have here but one mistress and no master. And look that no ill happen to him, lest it be severely required at your hands.' Robert was suitably chastened and 'his feigned humility was long after one of his best virtues!'[22]

In March 1566, Robert's sister Catherine Huntingdon had become unwell and he left court to visit her at Ashby-de-la-Zouche. She does not appear to have been dangerously ill, and it has been suggested that he departed from Elizabeth in pique caused by the attention she was showing to Thomas ('Black Tom') Butler, 10th Earl of Ormonde, of an

Anglo-Norman family living in Ireland, who had been brought up in the court of Henry VIII. Ormonde had returned to Ireland during the reign of Mary to challenge the authority of the FitzGerald Earls of Desmond, who were opposing English rule. In 1565, in an effort to curb intermittent warfare between the Butler and FitzGerald clans, Sir Henry Sidney, then Lord Deputy, sent the principals to London to explain their differences. Elizabeth favoured Black Tom. 'His good looks, his Irish charm and his responsive gallantry, as well as his strong English sympathies, made him an attractive companion.'[23] De Silva could see that Robert resented the favour being shown to Ormonde by Elizabeth. Although it was a passing fancy, Elizabeth's flirtation had not gone unnoticed. Two months later, Dr Thomas Young, the Archbishop of York, admonished her for showing favour to Ormonde. He seems to have been out of date and she considered it preposterous, until Robert magnanimously intervened to calm her down. Robert's absence to see his sister had done the trick. Elizabeth wrote to recall him. When he asked for a fifteen-day extension, she demanded his immediate return, and he duly obeyed.

On 12 April, there was an extraordinary occurrence. Robert was escorted by 700 footmen of his own and of the Queen's to the City home of Edward de Vere, 17th Earl of Oxford next to St Swithin's Church. As Oxford was only 16, he was quite probably not there. The Queen also set out accompanied by two ladies from Greenwich but was rowed against the tide by a single pair of oars and could only land where there were stairs. On arrival much later than expected at Three Cranes Wharf, a blue-painted coach carried her to Oxford's house. By this time, Robert had left. Nevertheless, he remained at a place she would need to pass on returning to the wharf. 'When she saw him, she came out of her coach into the high-way and she embraced the Earl and kissed him three times.'[24] They then climbed into the coach, crossed London Bridge and went on to Greenwich by road. The escort of 700 footmen gives the appearance of a secret marriage assignation, but Elizabeth dragged her feet and the moment was lost.

By 29 April, Cecilia had outstayed her welcome. Her household had caused considerable damage at Bedford's house, 'breaking and spoiling windows and everything'.[25] Bedford asked them to leave. The Queen, who had entertained them generously, felt obliged to settle their household expenses. Cecilia and the Margrave considered it an impertinence that shopkeepers should ask for their purchases to be paid for. Although the Margrave tried to creep back to the Continent, he was apprehended at Rochester and imprisoned for debt. When he threatened to shoot his way out, the Mayor asked the Queen either to insist that he obeyed English laws, or that the town should be relieved of such an awkward prisoner. Again the Queen paid his debts, but it did not stop the Margrave sending a servant to London to ask Robert, 'as an addition to your previous kindness',[26] to provide an English horse for his journey in exchange for a German one. Although this seems to indicate the success of Robert's breeding programme, he does not appear to have obliged.

Before Cecilia's departure, her ship was boarded by her creditors, who threatened to impound twelve chests belonging to her ladies-of-honour. One of her ladies, Helena von Snakenborg, remained behind. She was 'fair haired and exquisitely pretty, and at her arrival fourteen years old'. She was soon 'a favourite with everyone from the Queen downwards'.[27] With Northampton's wife having died in 1565, he wanted to marry Helena, who wrote to her mother elated at the prospect. Although Cecilia initially gave her consent, she withdrew it in exasperation at her treatment by her English creditors. Helena had no intention of having her prospects blighted. She was made a gentlewoman of the Privy Chamber by Elizabeth and enjoyed life at the English court until old enough to marry the 58-year-old Northampton in 1571, when she was 19. His 'bliss' lasted only six months as it 'sweetly ended his life',[28] but she remained one of Elizabeth's intimate friends until the Queen's death. In 1576, she remarried Sir Thomas Gorges, by whom she had seven children. Gorges later became noteworthy for arresting Mary Queen of Scots prior to her trial at Fotheringhay.

Nothing came of Eric's suit, except that it again delayed Robert's marriage hopes. De Foix reported to Catherine de Medici: 'The friendship and favour of the Queen towards the Earl of Leicester increases daily.'[29] Cecil had told de Foix of Robert's belief that his hopes of marrying Elizabeth were better than those of anyone else, and he should 'relinquish any plan he might be considering of marrying the Queen to a foreigner',[30] Robert even undertook to see that Cecil was promoted, if he would support him. With Cecil sharing Elizabeth's intellectual industry and consuming interest in politics and retaining her deepest respect, this might have seemed demeaning. In typically modest fashion, he simply thanked Robert for his good opinion and friendship.[31]

At Norfolk's instigation, the Council reopened negotiations with the Archduke Charles, and Norfolk warned Robert that he would be held responsible if there were any delay. Robert responded that he would support the Austrian match, 'if it could be so arranged that the Queen would not think he had relinquished his pursuit of her for lack of inclination. This "would cause her woman-like to undo him".'[32] This implies that they were still sleeping together. It was at about this time that one of Cecil's many private notes about Robert's suit included as a disadvantage: 'It will be thought that the slanderous speeches of the Queen and the Earl [being in bed together] have been true.'[33] Cecil gave no hint of his personal assessment of this possibility. Elizabeth Jenkins suggests: 'She clung [to Robert] as a man clings to a spar to save himself from the horrors of drowning; when her mother no longer charmed her father, the King had cut her head off.'[34] Elizabeth later told de Silva that Robert had unselfishly urged her to marry for her own sake, for the benefit of the realm, and to deliver him from the blame of impeding her marriage negotiations.[35] She confessed that if he were 'a King's son, she would marry him tomorrow'.[36] In June, de Silva went to see the Queen at Whitehall; on the grand staircase he met Robert, who told him that, if the Queen would not marry one of her own subjects, he hoped she would marry the Archduke. When they reached the Presence Chamber, they went in together to find Ormonde already there. De Silva noted: 'Certainly he and [Robert] did not look very amiably at each other.'[37]

On 6 August 1566, Robert confessed to de la Forêt, 'smiling and sighing at the same time, that he does not know what to hope and fear'. He confided: 'I have known her since she was 8 years old, better than any man in the world. From that time, she has invariably declared she would remain unmarried.' He explained that if she were to marry an Englishman, it would be him, and Ormonde's position was not to be taken seriously. 'At least the Queen has done me the honour to tell me so, several times, when we were alone, and I am as high in her favour as ever.'[38] It was probably about now that Robert had realised that his suit would never succeed. Cecil recorded: 'The Queen had shown him such affection that he had been led to hope she would marry him, but he would try to bring the matter to a head; if he could not gain her promise, he would cease his habits of intimacy with her.'[39]

Chapter 16

Robert survives political attempts to undermine his standing

Despite conflict abroad, Elizabeth's control of Government had heralded a new stability at home. Although her court was divided into competing factions, she tried to ensure that its members maintained a veil of civility. Membership of her Council remained remarkably static, and Elizabeth's strong personal friendships with councillors and members of her court were repaid with great loyalty. Some of them had come to accept the reality that she would never marry. Although this diminished Robert's prospects, Cecil realised that their deep friendship was unshaken and he continued to have 'favour sufficient'.[1]

While Cecil remained circumspect in dealing with Robert, this was not true of Norfolk and Sussex, heading a list of detractors who regularly clashed with him. Robert's enemies also included William, 1st Lord Howard of Effingham, (whose daughter, Douglas, was soon to become Robert's mistress) and Henry Carey, Lord Hunsdon. (Effingham's second son, Charles, later 1st Earl of Nottingham, had recently married Hunsdon's daughter, Catherine Carey.) Cecil was not above giving them encouragement in the background. The rival groups became distinguished by the wearing of coloured favours, yellow for the Howard/Radcliffe group and purple for Robert's supporters, resulting in occasional brawls. Even Elizabeth could see Robert's arrogance and publicly warned him not to assume that she had no affection for others.

Robert and Norfolk realised that they needed to cool their differences and in early 1567 both left court. Norfolk was absent until September, and Throckmorton advised Robert to stay away to avoid the accusation of interference in the Austrian marriage negotiations. It seems likely that before he went, Elizabeth took the difficult decision to make clear to him that she would never marry him, and they probably ceased to sleep together. In January 1567, de Silva wrote:

> The Earl of Leicester has not been in very high favour with the Queen just now, I was walking out of her chamber when she called me back and said she would be glad if I would show some love and friendship to Lord Robert as I was wont to do.[2]

De Silva was astonished at this 'wistful' plea and assured the Queen that he had no lack of goodwill for Lord Robert (which may not have been true). Nevertheless, the Queen seems to have been trying to provide Robert with a shoulder to lean on at a devastating time for him. He stayed away until late March but admitted to Cecil that he would have preferred to absent himself for longer. His cousin, John Dudley, did not agree, warning him: 'If you come not hastily, no good will grow, as I find Her Majesty so mislikes your absence, she is not disposed to hear of anything that may do you good.'[3] When Robert returned, he was deeply upset to find himself branded as a scapegoat for the failure of her marriage negotiations. He had also lost much of his influence. Although Elizabeth consulted him and valued his opinions, decisions now were always her own. A month later, he again sought leave of absence to visit his Norfolk estates. While in Norwich, he received a letter from the Queen very critical of his perceived faults. He now only wanted to find 'a cave in a corner of oblivion or a sepulchre for perpetual rest'.[4]

It was during Robert's absence that the horrific news was received, on 11 February, of the murder of Darnley at Kirk o' Field, in what seemed to be a conspiracy by many of the Scottish lords to be rid of him. It is very likely that Cecil knew of the plan beforehand and most deviously fanned rumours that Mary Queen of Scots was implicated, when nothing was further from the truth. To give this story some credibility, he encouraged the Scottish lords to entice Mary to marry the Earl of Bothwell, who had organised the murder, thus portraying it as a crime of passion. This achieved Cecil's objective of tarnishing her name and making her unacceptable for nomination as Elizabeth's heir. Robert was not involved in the deception but realised that the hopes of Catherine Grey were significantly enhanced. He quickly sent Ambrose to meet Hertford 'to offer his services in the matter of the succession', while he, as the more able tactician, visited Hertford's mother, the formidable Duchess of Somerset. By this time, Catherine was under the guardianship of Sir Owen Hopton at Cockfield Hall in Suffolk and could not immediately be contacted. Within a year she had died of starvation, when her grief at her predicament apparently made her unable to eat. With her two sons being deemed illegitimate and her sister, Mary, mentally sub-normal, the English succession was in the lap of the Gods.

With Robert away from court and his ally Throckmorton being sent as ambassador to Scotland, his enemies jumped on any means to discredit him. They unearthed Amy Robsart's disreputable half-brother, John Appleyard, who had already benefited from considerable rewards out of his kinship to Robert, including roles under Sidney in Ireland, as a privateer on the Norfolk coast and as the Gentleman Porter at Berwick. Robert had even entered into a bond of £400 to cover his debts, but Appleyard could not be satisfied and claimed to hold unpublished details of Amy's death which reflected against Robert. As he had come to Abingdon at Robert's request shortly after Amy's death, it was reasonable to assume that he knew what had happened. Understandably, Norfolk decided to sound him out. A go-between offered Appleyard £1,000 with more to follow if he would provide information implicating Robert in his wife's death. William Hogan, Appleyard's brother-in-law and one of Robert's servants, became suspicious of him. He warned Robert, who sent Thomas Blount to examine him. Under interrogation, Appleyard admitted the fabrication, claiming that it had been instigated by Norfolk, Suffolk and Heneage. Robert took no further action but dismissed Appleyard after giving him a dressing down.[5]

A year later, on 8 May 1567, the Council was examining a man named Trendle, who averred that Appleyard was again claiming to have 'covered [up] the murder of his sister' to protect Robert. Appleyard was summoned, together with both Blount and Hogan, resulting in the whole of the previous investigation being revealed. Appleyard was thrown in the Fleet prison with instructions to produce any relevant evidence that he might hold of Amy's death. He was also given a copy of the coroner's original verdict. Having seen the evidence that Amy's death had arisen from 'misfortune', he withdrew his allegations. When he was examined in the Star Chamber, he admitted having accused Robert out of 'malice'. He was probably sent to the pillory and was very soon trying to sell his post at Berwick. In 1570, he was sentenced to life imprisonment at

Norwich Castle after taking part in the Northern Rising on Norfolk's behalf. Robert again came to his rescue. After four years, he was released on compassionate grounds, spending his remaining days in the care of Robert's friend, George Gardiner, Dean of Norwich.[6]

Sussex also caused problems. At the end of 1565, he had returned from Ireland where he had faced a seemingly impossible situation as Lord Lieutenant. Elizabeth had left him lamentably short of resources to put down rebellions in Ulster. In January 1566, he was replaced by Sir Henry Sidney, who criticised his ineptitude, and succeeded where Sussex had failed to push the Ulster rebels back into the hills. Robert missed no opportunity to accuse Sussex at a Council meeting of having caused the rebellions, bringing them nearly to blows. The Chancellor, Sir Nicholas Bacon, and other Councillors had to separate them. Sussex retaliated by seeking Sidney's post as Lord President of the Marches of Wales. Sidney, who was heavily dependent on the income from this sinecure, was anxious to retain it, having installed a deputy to perform such duties as were required. With Sussex continuing to petition the Queen, she had to intervene. In April 1567, she agreed to grant the presidency to him if he would be reconciled to Robert, and 'on condition that he gives his word not to complain further on this matter, nor of Lord Robert; and so it was agreed'.[7] Although she forced them to ride back to London and dine together, Sussex was moved out of the way on a further embassy to Vienna.[8] He was never appointed to the Welsh role, which Sidney retained for the rest of his life.

Although de Silva did all he could to kindle animosity between Robert and his enemies, Robert was restored to the Queen's favour, and the Appleyard affair forced the Norfolk faction to make their peace with him. Although Norfolk remained at Kenninghall, by 24 May 1567 Robert had reported to de Silva that they were completely reconciled. De Silva did not expect this to last for long. It did not help Robert that Elizabeth was still using him as a shield to withstand Cecil's continuing pressure on her to make a Continental marriage. Cecil's negotiations with the Archduke Charles had become an obsession, and Robert realised that he could not resist the weight of English opinion in the Archduke's favour. Nevertheless, he knew that Elizabeth would never agree, however strongly he might urge her. This would leave him to shoulder the blame.[9]

As a forerunner to events of the next century, Parliament clashed with the Crown 'amid scenes of unprecedented uproar',[10] in a determination to force the Queen to settle the marriage question. Its members 'charged that they would not vote any money without a promise from the Queen to marry at the first possible moment'.[11] Elizabeth was equally determined that her marriage was not a matter for Parliament and replied: 'Do whatever you wish. As for me I shall do no other than pleases me. Your bills can have no force without my assent and authority.'[12] It also demanded to know who the Queen would nominate as her heir. With Robert caught in the middle, Elizabeth lashed out, calling Norfolk a traitor, while Pembroke had 'all the empty braggadocio of a swaggering soldier'. She accused Northampton of a domestic life that was a disgrace and wondered at his gall in lecturing her on marriage. Yet she also blamed Robert for abandoning her when the whole world was against her. When he responded that he would die at her feet if that would serve her cause, she retorted: 'What has that to do with the matter?' She banned everyone, including Robert, from her presence until further notice.[13]

Elizabeth had to answer Parliament. On 5 November 1566, she made a celebrated speech to placate its members, reducing her monetary demands for her military needs, but without answering their questions:

> I will marry as soon as I can conveniently … and I hope to have children, otherwise I would never marry … Your petition is to deal in the limitation of the succession. At this present it is not convenient; nor never shall be without some peril unto you and certain danger unto me.[14]

This did not silence them. She knew that none of her choice of husbands would please everyone and nominating a successor would lead to conflict. Her marriage to a Habsburg suitor would leave the French with little choice but to support Mary Queen of Scots' succession as the rightful English Queen. Tarnished though Mary was, this would endanger the Protestant settlement in Scotland. Hoping to shatter the fragile negotiations with the Archduke Charles, de Foix reported that Elizabeth and Robert were sleeping together.[15] In this, he was probably out of date. Yet Robert was back in some semblance of favour.

Elizabeth countered the French threat by showing Mary every possible sympathy for her predicament at being imprisoned without trial at the island fortress of Lochleven. On 6 August, Robert wrote to Throckmorton of the Queen's anxiety at her sister Queen's position.

Throckmorton was 'to use all means to let the Queen of Scots know the Queen's great grief for her … The Queen takes the doings of the Lords to heart as a precedent most perilous to any Prince.'[16] Throckmorton was probably well aware that it was in the English Government's interest to keep her incarcerated.

By now Bertrand de Salignac de la Mothe Fénélon had replaced de Foix as the French Ambassador in London. He told Catherine de Medici that Norfolk and Arundel had spoken severely to Robert about his relationship with Elizabeth. They may have been aware by then that Elizabeth had ended her liaison with him. He reported:

> If [Robert] could tell them that she wished to marry him, then they would support his suit. If he could not make that claim, then they must tell him that his conduct towards her was very improper. They charged him with being in her bedchamber before she was out of bed and was handing her the shift that she meant to put on. They further instanced his kissing her without being invited thereto. If he were not troth-plight to her, then such conduct was injurious to her honour.[17]

If he could not 'claim the privileges of a betrothed lover, these doings must cease'.[18] Robert was no longer in a position to persuade Elizabeth to defend him.

In the spring of 1567, Sussex arrived in Vienna to continue negotiations with the Archduke and to confer the Garter on him. In the autumn, Elizabeth came clean and rejected him on the grounds of religion, bringing the pretence of a marriage to an end. Sussex was convinced that Robert had scuppered the negotiations, but he remained unfailingly loyal to Elizabeth. The ending of the suit heralded 'a distinct turn for the worse in Anglo-Spanish relations'.[19] Dr John Man, the provocative Dean of Gloucester was sent as the English Ambassador to Madrid. He proved 'an outspoken, intemperate Protestant', referring to the Pope as 'a canting little monk'.[20] In April 1568, his expulsion from Philip's court resulted in his recall. He was not replaced. At the same time, de Silva left England and, in retaliation, Philip II replaced him with Antonio Guerau de Espés del Valle, 'a fanatic whose desire for prompt action against the heretics was equalled only by his short-sightedness'.[21] On arrival in December 1568, he believed that if everyone exerted themselves, Elizabeth could be replaced by Mary Queen of Scots and Catholicism restored in short order.[22] Although he curried favour with Robert, Robert quickly realised that he was dangerous.

England was lucky that both France and Spain had their hands full elsewhere. France was distracted by its wars of religion with the Huguenots. Spain faced nationalist fervour leading to Protestant outrages in the Netherlands against its officials. Philip II sent Fernando Álvarez de Toledo, Duke of Alva, to Brussels with 10,000 men, but rapidly increased them to 50,000, the largest standing army in Europe. Despite heroic resistance, the Dutch revolt was quickly stamped out, but the presence of this massive hardened force threatened the 'political and financial independence of the Netherland states'.[23] Their leader, Prince William of Orange, fled to Germany.[24] Alva's 'Council of Blood' arranged 1,800 executions. Europe was aghast at the savage and cruel reduction of all the major cities of the Netherlands, during which torture was inflicted on their citizens. England had to rethink its foreign policy, linking up with those opposing Spain. The immense Spanish presence across the Channel threatened an invasion to place Mary Queen of Scots, who was being held at Bolton, on the English throne and to restore her in Scotland. A sound merchant navy was needed to act as the foundation for England's defence.[25] Robert was fully occupied in preparing the country 'for a more aggressive role in world trade'.[26]

After the Le Havre debacle, there was no strong call for English intervention on behalf of the Netherlanders, and the Spanish presence was too daunting. Robert was critical of William of Orange for deserting the Netherlanders' cause and remained the most hawkish of Elizabeth's advisers. De Silva reported that he was leaning Pembroke, the acknowledged soldier on the Council, to his way of thinking. Robert's political judgement was beginning to mature and even Cecil sometimes found himself on the wrong side of his arguments in Council meetings. He 'wrote letters to and received news from all the principal capitals of Europe', obtaining 'regular bulletins from Ireland and Wales'. 'Even [his] political opponents, who rejected his views and questioned his motives, never dismissed him as an ill-informed dilettante.'[27] It was just that he immersed himself too deeply in affairs of state.

The most immediate issue was to deal with Mary Queen of Scots. Little had been done to oppose the Scottish Lords, who had forced her abdication.

Moray had been able to shut out the French by becoming Regent for an anti-Catholic Government on behalf of the infant James VI. Although Mary managed to escape from Lochleven, she was quickly defeated by Moray's forces and, in May 1568, threw herself on Elizabeth's mercy after escaping with eighteen companions to England. While she was in the north with its Catholic affiliations, there was considerable local sympathy for her. Elizabeth had to rely on her personal charisma to maintain authority. She was now extremely popular, even with Catholics. She had:

> avoided ruinous wars on the Continent; adopted a tolerant religious policy; avoided marriage to a potentially hostile foreign husband; maintained a firm administration that, so long as she lived, banish the spectre of civil war; and become 'a dazzling symbol of her government's success'.[28]

She regularly travelled through the country, where her people fêted her wherever she went. There was really no appetite, even in the Catholic north, to replace her with Mary.

Nevertheless, Mary's arrival in England was a political embarrassment. Elizabeth very quickly saw the advantage for her own security of her being maintained under tight supervision. She had no appetite for restoring her to her throne, even under conditions that would make her dependent on English Government support. Meanwhile Mary, who was still being held at Bolton Castle in north Yorkshire, was writing to de Espés: 'Tell your Master if he will help me, I shall be Queen of England in three months, and Mass shall be said all over the Kingdom!'[29] With the power and recognised cruelty of the Spanish forces a few hours away across the North Sea, the threat was very real. An unknown writer sent a letter to Robert:

> begging and imploring him to use his influence with Queen Elizabeth, whom he reproached bitterly for exposing England to the nightmare horrors of invasion and civil war, for the sake of sparing 'one horrible woman, who carries God's curse with her wherever she goes.[30]

Despite Elizabeth's genuine sympathy for Mary, she needed to keep her incarcerated. To appease Continental sensibilities, there had to be an investigation into the events surrounding Darnley's murder. Cecil warned Moray that he would need to provide evidence to justify Mary's detention. Elizabeth's concern was to avoid the precedent of having to find Mary, as a Tudor Queen, guilty of murdering her husband.

A conference was arranged in York with Norfolk, Sussex and the experienced Sir Ralph Sadler as commissioners. When Moray and his colleagues produced letters in Mary's hand as evidence of her involvement in her husband's murder, the commissioners quickly realised that they were obviously fabricated and sought advice from London on how to act. Either they had to declare that the evidence was false, and Mary would be returned to her throne, or that it was true, and Mary would be implicated in murder. Neither of these were solutions that Elizabeth wanted. Cecil, who was in his element, moved the proceedings to London. His plan was to obfuscate. The Scottish evidence was 'huddled up', and Elizabeth pronounced that there was nothing to imply any wrongdoing by her sister queen. Nevertheless, while Moray and his colleagues were free to return to Scotland to resume control of Government, Elizabeth agreed to maintain Mary under house arrest with all the trappings of royalty at remote locations in England. She was moved further south under the charge of the eminently trustworthy and wealthy Earl and Countess of Shrewsbury to live at their various homes. Initially she was moved to the semi-derelict Tutbury Castle in Staffordshire. It was fortified, but cold and draughty and had to be hurriedly furnished to make it even reasonably habitable. Mary became ill there, but was now the object of every Catholic plot to replace Elizabeth.

Chapter 17

The Northern Rising

In the aftermath of the Conference at York, with the proceedings having ended, Maitland, Mary's former Secretary of State, made an approach to Norfolk. Maitland was a 'chameleon-like' character, almost certainly responsible for providing the falsified evidence on behalf of the Scottish lords to incriminate Mary in the murder of her husband. Yet he had married her confidante and senior Marie (lady-in-waiting), Mary Fleming, and wanted to ameliorate the Scottish Queen's plight. He now suggested to Norfolk that he should consider marrying Mary and that Norfolk's daughter Margaret Howard should marry James, the infant King of Scotland. The convoluted plan involved: obtaining Mary's divorce from Bothwell, who was imprisoned in Denmark; restoring her to the Scottish throne, where she would be neutralised politically by vesting her authority in her husband; ending further recrimination about Darnley's murder; her approval of the Treaty of Edinburgh to accept that Elizabeth was the rightful English Queen; a general acceptance of religious toleration in both Scotland and England; an embargo on her making foreign alliances; and Elizabeth accepting her as her successor, in the absence of legitimate progeny of her own.

The plan contained a lot of common sense, and both Norfolk and Mary were receptive, but agreed to shelve it while the Conference in London ran its course. From now on, Mary considered herself betrothed to Norfolk. He was always likely to attract Catholic support despite maintaining a half-hearted Protestant affiliation, and powerful Catholic interests in the north were ready to take up arms on his behalf. Their marriage would resolve the English succession, and it gained fairly general support among Council members. Cecil gave the impression of being supportive but was always careful not to divulge his feelings too openly. At heart, he strongly opposed the marriage in his determination to prevent a Catholic becoming the English Monarch. Robert concluded that if Mary married Norfolk and the succession was resolved, it could reopen the door for him to marry Elizabeth. Moray was approached to seek Scottish support and, having assumed that it had Elizabeth's blessing, sounded out his Scottish colleagues. There were also snags: the Government had to trust Mary not to call in foreign troops to promote a Counter-Reformation; Norfolk's political abilities were doubted; Moray and his fellow Scottish Lords would need to accept that Norfolk would become the senior Government figure in Scotland; and someone would have to sound out Elizabeth, who would be unimpressed to find negotiations taking place behind her back while she was at Greenwich. The concerns were justified. Mary made clear to de Espés that she would have preferred a Spanish husband and would hold her religious policy at the disposal of the Spanish King.

Norfolk persuaded Robert, Pembroke and Throckmorton to widen the circle of those in the know, allowing de Espés to hear about it. It became a plan, not just to support Norfolk in marrying Mary Queen of Scots, but to bring down Cecil, whose anti-Spanish foreign policy was facing concerted criticism. There was now fairly general objection to him sending financial support to Protestant rebels in both France and the Netherlands. In November 1568, storms in the Channel and an attack by French pirates had forced a convoy of Spanish ships onto the English coast, some of which put into Plymouth and some to Southampton. They were carrying about £85,000 in gold to pay Alva's troops in the Netherlands. Cecil seized the treasure, seeing it as a heaven-sent opportunity to replenish England's depleted exchequer. De Espés was furious and Alva retaliated by impounding the goods and ships of English merchants on the Continent and by closing the markets in the Netherlands to the London mercantile community. 'The diplomatic row came at a bad time for the capital',[1] which was in the grip of an exceptionally hard winter. The Government had never been so unpopular and several Council members tried to distance themselves from Cecil's policies, which had seriously damaged trade and seemed to be carrying England to the brink of war with Spain. They objected to his lack of consultation and to his opposition to the marriage of Norfolk to Mary Queen of Scots.

With encouragement from his ageing Catholic father-in-law, Arundel, and from de Espés, Norfolk started to recruit support for Cecil's overthrow and to promote the marriage. Although the conspirators tried to recruit Robert, who was certainly supportive of some check being placed on Cecil, he stopped short of his removal and imprisonment in the Tower. Robert was not initially aware of the full extent of the plans. They wanted: to purge the Council of 'heretics'; to launch a Counter-Reformation with Spanish (and perhaps French) assistance; and to achieve Mary's speedy restoration to the Scottish throne without conditions. They were supported by several northern Catholic magnates led by Thomas Percy, 7th Earl of Northumberland, and Charles Neville, 12th Earl of Westmoreland.

The plan for Cecil's overthrow was abruptly ended by the Queen. On hearing about it, she summoned a Council meeting to confront the conspirators, but many of them (including Robert) excused themselves. On 22 February 1569 at a meeting in her Privy Chamber, she took Robert to task for his non-attendance. Acting as the conspirators' spokesman, he now outlined to her the low popular esteem of her Government, which was adopting policies likely to have the direst consequences. When he blamed Cecil, Elizabeth reacted with 'theatrical' rage. Although Norfolk might have been expected to support him, Robert was left to shoulder the royal invective on his own. From now on, he refused to support attacks on Cecil, realising that the conspirators were taking advantage of his intimacy with the Queen to use him as their front man. Without his support, the attacks on Cecil died a natural death.

By the spring of 1569, it seems likely that Robert, through his network of spies, had become aware of the full extent of Norfolk's and Arundel's scheming. Certainly, he became lukewarm about Mary Queen of Scots' marriage. Elizabeth, who had heard rumours of the plan, did not want to broach the matter herself, preferring the conspirators to have the courage to tell her, or to drop it completely. This would enable her to assess their level of support. Although Sussex supported the marriage, he was unaware of the conspirators' treasonable intent to replace Elizabeth on the English throne. He strongly advocated telling her what he knew, and both Robert and Cecil – who knew how she would react – wanted it done without delay. Although Norfolk suggested sending a 'posse of peers' to Greenwich to present her with a fait accompli, Robert strongly advised against it, knowing that she would hate to be cornered. Although Norfolk had plenty of opportunities to advise her, he lost his nerve. Meanwhile, the court moved to Titchfield, the home of the Earl of Southampton in Hampshire. After discussing his predicament with

Pembroke, Robert decided to reveal to the Queen the full extent of the plot, in so far as he knew it, before his earlier involvement came to light. Claiming to be sick (real or imagined), he asked her to visit his chamber. On her arrival, he poured out the details, telling her that 'his loyalty and devotion forbade him to keep them secret any longer'.[2] The Queen could only see the marriage as threatening. It would force her to nominate Mary as her heir, which would be dangerous and act as a catalyst for a Catholic rebellion against her rule (as proved to be the case). She spoke to Norfolk 'with great sharpness'[3] for acting behind her back, but he denied any wish to marry the Queen of Scots and crept away from court to Kenninghall without Elizabeth's consent. She thought she had done enough to end any further contemplation of the marriage.

In September, de Espés, who was proving inept in his assessment of what was going on, claimed that the Queen's views on the marriage varied from day to day, but Alva was reporting to Philip II that Robert and Cecil were now entirely governing the Queen. Elizabeth then received a warning from Moray in Scotland that Norfolk was still planning a full-scale rebellion. His revelation was in part prompted by an attempt on his life by two of Norfolk's supporters. Northumberland and Westmoreland were now readying themselves to march south to join with Norfolk's own troops from East Anglia and a contingent to be sent by Alva from the Netherlands.

Elizabeth convinced herself that she was at great risk and took every step to counter the perceived threat, but there was no widespread support from English Catholics. When she recalled Norfolk to London, he feigned illness. Although he tried to send a message to Alva, he found the ports closed. On 11 October 1569, he was arrested and sent to the Tower. By this time, Mary was comfortably settled at Wingfield Manor in Derbyshire under the guardianship of the Shrewsburys. Elizabeth told Huntingdon that, if he wanted employment to support a Protestant cause, he should move Mary from the unfortified Wingfield back to the much more spartan Tutbury Castle. Huntingdon acted with dispatch and, despite a violent outcry from Mary, he had, within a week, separated her from half her retinue and returned her to Tutbury, which he garrisoned with 500 men. 'Shrewsbury was castigated [by Elizabeth] for treating Mary with "too much affection" and for having failed her "in my hour of need".[4] Mary disliked Huntingdon intensely, not least because, as a rival claimant to the English Crown, he seemed to be a threat.

Although the rebels' objective was to take Tutbury, Norfolk, who was in the Tower, lost his nerve. He sent a message to Northumberland and Westmoreland not to set out, but they had gone too far and the Northern Rising was on the move with 6,000 men and 1,000 horse. On 14 November, they entered Durham Cathedral, where they restored the Mass and trampled the English translation of the Bible underfoot. Although Alva sent money with Philip's blessing, he would not risk landing Spanish troops on English soil until he was assured of Mary's release. By 23 November, the rebels had reached Tadcaster, fifty miles from Tutbury. Huntingdon feared that he could not hold out for more than a few days. On hearing of the rescue attempt, Elizabeth quickly arranged Mary's removal south to Coventry.

The rebels failed to gather the Catholic backing that they were expecting, and the Yorkshire gentry were demanding to be paid and refused to move south from York. Acting on Elizabeth's behalf, Sir George Bowes, Lieutenant of the North, made a stand at Barnard Castle. With help from his brother, Sir Robert, he held the castle for eleven days, buying 'time for levies to be raised from further south and for Sussex to arrive with reinforcements'.[5] Everywhere further south held firmly for Elizabeth regardless of religious persuasion. When Sussex arrived and was reinforced by troops under Ambrose and Hunsdon, the rebels were pushed back north, forcing Northumberland and Westmoreland across the Scottish border.

As soon as Ambrose was discharged from his military assignment, he joined Robert at Kenilworth. According to de Espés, Robert had worried that the Northern Rising would lead to civil war and was planning to fortify the place. Robert had arrived there with Julio Spinelli, an Italian who had gained engineering experience in the Netherlands. When Robert's fears proved unfounded, he arranged a reunion of his siblings, including Mary Sidney and Catherine Huntingdon, but reported to Elizabeth that her 'Ursa Major and Minor' (Robert and Ambrose) would soon be restored to her service.

This was the only rebellion of Elizabeth's reign, but she was unnerved. She was determined to make an example of the prisoners, insisting on 600 being hanged, with their leaders being tried for treason so that their lands could be forfeited.

In 'a pathetic revelation of papal impotence', Pope Pius V used this as an excuse to excommunicate Elizabeth, despite opposition from Philip II, Alva, and Catherine de Medici, who all feared further reprisals against the English Catholics. The French refused to publish the Papal Bull, *Regnans in Excelsis,* which, in Catholic eyes, deprived Elizabeth of the throne and released her subjects from allegiance to her.[6]

As he had disapproved of Mary's marriage to Bothwell, 'the Pope was careful to point out that the purpose of the bull was to protect the spiritual welfare of the English, not to back her claim to the English throne'.[7] Nevertheless, his action was unwise. Elizabeth's religious settlement of 1559 had been extremely tolerant and the provisions of the Act of Uniformity, which required adherence to the 1559 Prayer Book, had been 'irregularly and slackly enforced'.[8] The Papal Bull rudely shattered this laissez faire attitude. With Catholicism now being associated with foreign aggression, severe anti-Catholic legislation became inevitable.

It was Robert who emerged as the recognised leader of the English religious radicals. In 1572, the Swiss theologian, Heinrich Bullinger, published *A Confutation of the Pope's Bull ... against Elizabeth.* This was dedicated to Robert. Bullinger showed that Elizabeth's struggle against papacy was not just an English problem: 'The matter doth implyingly concern the whole state of Christ's Church, which the Romish Antichrist laboureth to draw away from the obedience and love of her true husband, Christ, to the adulterous embracing of Satan.'[9] This was a view shared by Robert, Walsingham, Sidney, William of Orange and all Protestant champions.

Devout English Catholics were placed in 'an agonising position'.[10] It now appeared that their role was to overturn the Government of 'the pretended Queen of England'.[11] The French ignored the bull. In January 1572, they developed a plan for Elizabeth to marry Charles IX's youngest brother, Francis de Valois, Duke of Alençon, notwithstanding that he was twenty-two years her junior. Elizabeth seemed receptive, even though he was by repute 'short, puny and pitted with smallpox',[12] marvellously ugly and with a curvature of the spine. Elizabeth named him her 'frog', or more politely as 'Monsieur'. Robert claimed that Cecil opposed the plan, but this was not the case and it was Robert who inevitably saw Monsieur as a threat, despite his support for the French alliance. He sent a message to Edward, Lord Clinton, newly created Earl of Lincoln,

(*Above left*) 1. Henry VIII.

His death in 1547 left a huge vacuum for his children and his will greatly complicated his succession.

Holbein the Younger, Hans (1497/ 8–1543)/Belvoir Castle, Leicestershire/ Bridgeman Images

(*Above right*) 2. Edward VI (oil on panel c. 1546).

Edward was determined, with help from Northumberland, to maintain the English Reformation by appointing his cousin, Jane Grey, to succeed him, despite the people's desire for the dynastic heir, his sister Mary.

Scrots, Guillaume (fl. 1537–53) (attr. to)/ Royal Collection Trust © Her Majesty Queen Elizabeth II, 2019/ Bridgeman Images

(*Right*) 3. Mary I (oil on panel, 1554).

When the Duke of Northumberland attempted to place Jane Grey on the English throne, Mary raised the Catholic shires and marched in triumph to be crowned Queen in London.

Mor, Anthonis van Dashorst (Antonio Moro) (c. 1519–1576/77)/Prado, Madrid/Bridgeman Images

(*Above left*) 4. Queen Catherine Parr (oil on panel c. 1545).

Catherine proved a model step-mother for Prince Edward and Princess Elizabeth providing them with a caring environment and an Evangelical (Protestant) education.

Master John (fl. 1544)/National Portrait Gallery, London/Bridgeman Images

(*Above right*) 5. Sir Edward Seymour, Earl of Hertford, Duke of Somerset (panel).

Seymour had achieved great success as a military general, but he proved ineffective as Protector for his nephew, Edward VI, and was replaced by the Duke of Northumberland.

Holbein the Younger, Hans (1497/8–1543)/The Trustees of the Weston Park Foundation, UK/Bridgeman Images

(*Right*) 6. Thomas Seymour, Lord Seymour of Sudeley (oil on panel).

Being jealous of his brother's appointment as Protector, he was determined to outdo him. Being extremely attractive, he married the widowed Catherine Parr, but following her death his attempt to gain control of Edward VI resulted in his execution.

English School (sixteenth century)/National Portrait Gallery, London/Bridgeman Images

(*Above left*) 7. John Dudley, Earl of Warwick, Duke of Northumberland (oil on panel).

He made his name as a brilliant general and replaced Somerset as Protector for Edward VI. He was the father of Lord Robert and was central to the plan to ensure a Protestant succession by promoting Jane Grey to become Queen ahead of the Catholic Mary.

Artist Belcamp, Jan van (1605)/Sackville Collection, Knole

(*Above right*) 8. William Cecil, Lord Burghley (oil).

He was Elizabeth's principal political adviser, determined to see her make a political marriage, rather than choose Lord Robert, who Cecil did not trust.

Sixteenth century after work by an unknown artist/Lebrecht History/Bridgeman Images

(*Right*) 9. Amy Robsart, first wife of Lord Robert (oil on canvas).

She was childless and suffered from breast cancer. She died in mysterious circumstances after a fall down two steps.

English School (sixteenth century)/private collection/Bridgeman images

10. Elizabeth I (oil on canvas).

The sieve she is carrying demonstrated her virginity, but her relationship with Lord Robert ended Cecil's hopes that she might make a political marriage to protect England from Continental aggression.

Massys or Metsys, the Younger, Quentin (c. 1543–89)/Pinacteca Nazionale, Siena, Tuscany/ Bridgeman Images

11. Lettice Knollys, Countess of Essex and Countess of Leicester (oil on canvas).

Much to Elizabeth's chagrin, Lettice was involved in a passionate affair with Lord Robert, whom she later married following the death of her first husband, the Earl of Essex.

Gower, George / ©Reproduced by permission of the Marquess of Bath, Longleat House, Warminster, Wiltshire

(*Above left*) 12. Ambrose Dudley, Earl of Warwick (oil on panel).

Lord Robert's elder surviving brother, who loyally supported his more charismatic younger sibling. He suffered from a wound to his leg sustained at Le Havre (Newhaven) in 1563.

English School (sixteenth century)/ photo © Philip Mould Ltd, London / Bridgeman Images

(*Above right*) 13. Thomas Howard, 4th Duke of Norfolk.

Lord Robert's nemesis, but 'he was a weak man, cursed with the dignity of England's sole Dukedom'. He lost his head after conspiring to marry Mary Queen of Scots in an attempt to place her on the English throne.

English School (sixteenth century)/His Grace the Duke of Norfolk, Arundel Castle/Bridgeman Images

(*Right*) 14. Sir Robert Dudley (oil on panel, 1590s).

Illegitimate son of Lord Robert by Douglas Sheffield née Howard, who became an expert navigator and explorer. He was unsuccessful in trying to prove his legitimacy to gain the Leicester and Warwick titles.

Artist unknown/©National Portrait Gallery, London

(*Above left*) 15. Robert Devereux, 2nd Earl of Essex (oil on panel).

The son of Lettice Knollys, who succeeded Lord Robert, his step father, in Elizabeth's affections and strongly supported him during his campaign in the Low Countries. He later married Frances Walsingham, the widow of Sir Philip Sidney.

Gheeraerts, Marcus, the Younger (c. 1561–1635)/ Private Collection/Photo © Philip Mould Ltd, London/Bridgeman Images

(*Above right*) 16. Penelope Devereux, Lady Rich (oil on canvas).

The daughter of Lettice Knollys, who might have married Sir Philip Sidney, but for the need for her to make a more financially rewarding but loveless match to Robert, Lord Rich. She later married Charles Blount, Lord Mountjoy, who became Earl of Devonshire, in recognition of his success in settling Ireland.

English School (sixteenth century)/Lambeth Palace, London/Bridgeman Images

(*Right*) 17. Frances Walsingham, Lady Sidney and later Countess of Essex (oil on canvas).

The daughter of Sir Francis Walsingham, who married Sir Philip Sidney and nursed him until his death after being wounded at Zutphem. She later married the 2nd Earl of Essex.

Peake, Robert, the Elder, 1594/Photograph courtesy of Sotheby's

(*Above left*) 18. Sir Henry Sidney, KG (oil on canvas, 1573).

Brother-in-law of Lord Robert and Lord Deputy in Ireland. He proved very helpful to Lord Robert in his efforts to gain Spanish support for his marriage to Elizabeth.

Bronckhorst, Arnold (fl. 1565–83)/Petworth House West Sussex/National Trust Photographic Library/ Bridgeman Images

(*Above right*) 19. Lady Mary Sidney (née Dudley) (oil on panel).

Sister of Lord Robert and married to Sir Henry Sidney. She was the mother of Sir Philip Sidney and a favoured lady-in-waiting to Elizabeth.

Eworth, Hans (fl. 1520–74) (circle of)/Petworth House, West Sussex/ National Trust Photographic Library/ Bridgeman Images

(*Right*) 20. Sir Philip Sidney (oil on canvas, c. 1576).

The son of Sir Henry and Lady Mary Sidney and heir to Lord Robert until his untimely death at the battle of Zutphen. He was perhaps the most gifted diplomat, soldier and poet of his era.

Unknown artist (sixteenth century)/National Portrait Gallery, London/De Agostini Picture Library/ Bridgeman Images who was the English ambassador in Paris, to establish Alençon's credentials. Walsingham supported Alençon's suit in the hope of achieving a French alliance and Elizabeth enjoyed the romance of it all. He concluded that it did not need to be taken too seriously but was to find himself mistaken. The marriage proposal, whether realistic or not, had the effect of paralyzing French backing for Mary Queen of Scots.[13] Nevertheless, she had supporters in Scotland, and in January 1570, Moray was assassinated by her Marian allies. With the Protestant Government in Scotland remaining in the ascendancy, Elizabeth arranged reprisals on their behalf. Nevertheless, with Norfolk having remained in the Tower throughout the unrest, there was no evidence that he had instigated the plot against Moray. In August 1570, he was released under surveillance in the hope that he was 'being given enough rope to hang himself'.

This still left the problem of how to deal with Mary. Elizabeth was in a dilemma but still saw her as a catalyst for rebellion. Her famous description of Mary as:

> The daughter of Debate that eke discord doth sow,
> Shall reap no gain where former rule hath taught still peace to grow.

Robert wrote to Sussex, with whom he was temporarily back on cordial terms, that the issue was whether to restore her to her Scottish throne with limited authority, or to back the Scottish Government and retain her in England. He feared that the latter course would lead to war with her Continental allies. Cecil, who had done much to colour adverse opinion against her, always wanted her dead. Robert later changed his tune and supported Cecil in seeking her execution.

Norfolk was like a dog with a bone. He continued to make plans to free Mary, selling silver and jewellery to muster a force and to support her Marian allies in Scotland. He asked Philip II to provide a force of 20,000 infantry, 3,000 cavalry and 6,000 hackbutters with equipment to land at Harwich or Portsmouth ready to march on London to assassinate Elizabeth. (Such invasion plans became known by the Spanish as 'the Enterprise of England'.) He used the services of an Italian banker, Roberto Ridolfi, who had transferred funds to support the Northern Rising and provided a mechanism to communicate with both Mary and the Spanish. Alva had no faith in Norfolk's plan, recognising that an invasion would meet strong English resistance. He would only send troops once Elizabeth were dead. He had little respect Ridolfi, whom he considered a chatterbox, although Ridolfi was little more than a go-between. Unfortunately for Norfolk, Walsingham – who was positioned in Paris as Cecil's master spy – blackmailed Ridolfi into becoming a double agent, allowing all the correspondence passing through his hands to be intercepted. Norfolk was now implicated in a treasonable plot against the English Crown and, on 4 August 1571, was placed under house arrest. When Robert's wayward brother-in-law, Appleyard, and two other East Anglian Catholics, made a hair-brained attempt to rescue him, Norfolk, on 7 September, was restored to the Tower. Robert wrote to Arundel to advise him of Norfolk's second arrest, and even Arundel professed himself to be profoundly shocked. Although he asked Robert to help, Norfolk was too far gone in crime. His fellow peers, including Robert, found him guilty on 16 January 1572. Ridolfi, who by this time was in Paris, was permitted to disappear quietly back to Florence where he became a senator and eventually died of natural causes in 1612.

Having to deal with both Norfolk and Mary placed Elizabeth under great stress. Acute pains caused a shortness of breath and she thought she was dying, perhaps of poison. Robert and Cecil spent three nights sitting up with her until she felt better, but she still looked unwell. Her illness caused great anxiety among her senior advisers. If Elizabeth were to die, Mary Queen of Scots was likely to become Queen, however horrific the prospect of a Catholic monarch might be. With Elizabeth being 40, there were widespread rumours that she did not have long to live. She had become heavily reliant on Dee, who continued to provide her with horoscopes. He used globes to foretell the future, a large 'chrystalline' one and a smaller 'magic' one of a dark and livid colour. In March 1575, Elizabeth visited him unexpectedly at Richmond with the Privy Council and other lords and ladies. On arrival they learned that he had just attended his wife's burial. Elizabeth refused to come in, but Dee brought out his magic globe, and 'to her great contentment and delight',[14] was able to see some of its properties, which indicated the love in which she was held by the English people.

With the prospects for Mary Queen of Scots brightening, she did not need to involve herself in plots for Elizabeth's assassination. She could sit back and wait. Robert was concerned at reports that she considered him an enemy. He wrote to Shrewsbury to establish the cause for this, as he believed that he had a reputation for kindness. With his instincts for self-preservation, he retained 'a show of courteous and even kindly communication with the Queen of Scots'.[15] He certainly did not want to be considered her enemy if Elizabeth should die. He was not alone. Shrewsbury told Mary that he was obliged to act as her keeper as long as Elizabeth was his master, but if she died, he would place the crown on Mary's head. Hatton advised that if Elizabeth died, he would bring Mary the news. Darnley's mother, Margaret Lennox, had roundly criticised Mary for the death of her son, but with the prospect of her becoming the English Queen, she too effected a reconciliation and entered into a rapprochement with her daughter-in-law. Needless to say, when Elizabeth heard rumours of this, she tackled Margaret, who thought it wiser to deny it. Cecil and Walsingham realised that they would irretrievably be doomed.

In February 1572, following the death of the aged Winchester, Cecil was appointed Lord Treasurer and was created Lord Burghley. This role was initially offered to Robert, but he recognised that it required more learning than he could muster, and Cecil was far more suitable. He stood at Cecil's right hand as he received his peerage. In April 1572, Robert deputised for the Queen when Cecil was also created a Knight of the Garter. Robert had rather hoped to be made Great Master of the Household, a role previously held by Pembroke, but for this he would have to wait.

By this time, Throckmorton had died, and Robert was looking for a new ally. This came in the form of Cecil's spymaster, Walsingham, who was brought back from Paris. As strong advocates of a French alliance to counter the Spanish threat, they worked hard together to achieve the Treaty of Blois signed in April 1572. The chief French negotiator, Francis, Duke of Montmorency, arrived in England with a train of forty diplomats and was sumptuously entertained by Robert. Both countries agreed not to interfere in Scotland, and Mary was not even mentioned. At last, the threat of French intervention there was laid to rest.

Elizabeth remained most reluctant to sign Norfolk's death warrant; twice she had been persuaded by the Council, and twice she recalled it. She could not withstand the clamour for long; Norfolk was executed on 2 June. It was the first execution of her reign. Mary had been more circumspect, and there was nothing in her carefully worded correspondence to implicate her in treasonable action. To Burghley's great disappointment, Elizabeth refused to condemn her. Despite strident calls for her execution from both houses of Parliament, she remained under the charge of the Shrewsburys in Derbyshire.

Matters were again thrown into turmoil in August, when news arrived of the Massacre of St Bartholomew in Paris, in which numerous senior Huguenots were killed. On hearing the news, Elizabeth appeared in black before the French Ambassador, and Burghley once more championed a policy of rapprochement with Spain.[16] The prospect of a Counter-Reformation in France jeopardised the Anglo/ French accord. Elizabeth was again pressurised to approve Mary's execution. Hoping to avoid having Mary's blood on her hands, she sent Killigrew to Edinburgh on a mission known only to Burghley and Robert. The purpose was to persuade the new regent, John Erskine, 1st Earl of Mar, and the much more astute James Douglas, 4th Earl of Morton to agree Mary's return to Scotland. She was to be held there securely, but with security of her life. Morton immediately saw through Elizabeth's objective and insisted that on arrival, she should be executed in front of 2,000 English troops. Killigrew had no authority to agree, and Mar, who was unwell, was so horrified that he died shortly after. Any further thought of repatriating Mary was forgotten, but Elizabeth remained under stress with another sharp attack of pain accompanied by a rash. There were fears of another outbreak of smallpox, and Robert again sat up with her until she recovered. He proved a good nurse! Burghley now needed to find another means to justify Mary's execution.

In December 1573, Walsingham replaced Burghley – who was suffering from bouts of gout and had had a seizure – as Secretary of State. With Walsingham being an ally of Robert, Robert's position on the Council was strengthened. Christopher Hatton was another friend, who had much in common with him. He was a successful courtier, who excelled in the tiltyard and at court entertainments. He was a Gentleman of the Privy Chamber and Captain of the Guard, who had been considerably enriched by the Queen. He had 'height, gracefulness, ready speech and sound intelligence'.[17] He was also captivated by Elizabeth, claiming: 'She fished for men's souls with so sweet a bait, no man could escape her net-work.'[18] Yet he never achieved the special status in which Robert had been held, and there was no rivalry between them.

Despite these changes among Elizabeth's senior advisers, the two most influential, Robert and Burghley, remained in place. Although in the past both had come under attack, they were now firmly established with Elizabeth's support. They had often clashed, but there was an 'unconscious realization that they needed each other'.[19] They found themselves working in a close harmonious partnership, in which Robert wrote the letters to keep Walsingham in touch with the court.[20]

Chapter 18

Romance with Douglas Sheffield

There was considerable court gossip that Robert, as a red-blooded male, enjoyed liaisons with ladies of the court. That much of it was 'slanderous was of little consequence. [He] was the sort of charming, handsome extrovert of whom any scandal is readily believed.'[1] He had to be extremely circumspect. He had already incurred Elizabeth's wrath by flirting with Lettice Knollys in 1565, and as long as he hoped to marry Elizabeth, he had to maintain his courtship with her. He was not prepared to embark on any relationships which might threaten his position or lead him into marriage. His liaisons no doubt took place at times when he was not enjoying the Queen's favour, but he needed to maintain the utmost secrecy, not only to keep matters from the Queen, but to maintain his aura of Puritan respectability.

Robert had always owed his political authority to his close relationship with Elizabeth. If he could not marry her, he still aspired to be among her closest advisers. It was the fear of losing his status on the Council rather than the loss of their amorous relationship that concerned him most, and he needed to retain her ear. She had never been wholly under his influence, but always yearned for his company. As his eye started to stray, Elizabeth looked to the likes of Christopher Hatton for romantic amusement, but no one ever displaced Robert. Although she relied on Burghley in political matters, Robert developed into a political force in his own right, able to offer advice independent of her Treasurer. He remained the person she looked to for moral support, well after any romance between them had become a formality.

> The cares and fears, the burdens of her state, oppressed and ailing as she often was, and always preoccupied with some political and social problem of overwhelming importance, made the soothing, reassuring quality of [Robert's] support invaluable to her comfort.[2]

During 1568, Robert accompanied the Queen to stay at Belvoir Castle as the guest of Edward Manners, 3rd Earl of Rutland. Other guests included the wealthy John, 2nd Lord Sheffield, and his wife, Douglas Howard, daughter of Howard of Effingham. Douglas was now aged 22 with two young children. She was 'feather-headed and dazzling, "a star of the court for beauty and richness of apparel"',[3] bearing a strong resemblance to her reckless cousin, Queen Catherine Howard. Robert was soon attracted to her, and according to a later history of the Sheffield family, 'he found her an easy purchase'.[4] After the death of Sheffield on 10 February 1569, she came to court as a Lady of the Bedchamber and began a passionate affair with Robert. It is a mark of Robert's ability to keep it under wraps that the relationship only came to light in 1578 or 1579, when it was over.

Evidence of a purported marriage between Robert and Douglas became the subject of a court case in 1604, when Robert's son by Douglas, Robert Sheffield, tried to demonstrate that he was the legitimate heir to the Leicester and Warwick titles. Although the issue before the court was to establish whether Robert had married Douglas, the action failed on a technicality because Sheffield had 'gone the wrong way about bringing the case',[5] and the evidence for the marriage was never tested. As Sheffield was refused permission to bring forward his action for a second time, it has been implied that there was a cover-up. The defendants were the Sidney family, who were at the time closely allied to the new English King, James I. Even though the evidence for the marriage never came to court, a considerable dossier was assembled both to confirm and refute the marriage. This remains with the court papers.

A second source of evidence of the status of Robert's relationship with Douglas is a letter written in Robert's hand to an unnamed lady, although there is really no dispute that this was Douglas Howard. The letter is undated so it is difficult to assess when it was written, but it was certainly after her husband's death and before she had conceived a child (so before December 1573). The letter makes it apparent that Douglas has been putting Robert under pressure to make an honest woman of her, but he is writing frankly to explain that he is not able to do so, as it would result in his 'utter overthrow' by the Queen. He explains that he has 'long both loved and liked you and found always that faithful and earnest affection at your hands again that bound me greatly to you'. He reminds her that 'after your widowhood on the first occasion of my coming to you', he had explained that he could not marry her and had assumed she accepted the position. When she had continued to press him, they had fallen out, but subsequently made up 'and had renewed their loving intercourse'.[6] He now explained:

> You must think it is some marvelous cause, and toucheth my present state very near, that forceth me thus to be cause almost of the ruin of my own house … my brother you see long married and not like to have children, it resteth so now in myself; and yet … if I should marry I am sure never to have [the Queen's] favour that I had rather never have wife than lose … yet is there nothing in the world next that favour that I would not give to be in hope of leaving some children behind me, being now the last of our house. But yet, the cause being as it is, I must content myself …[7]

Robert is advising her that in the circumstances, for reasons of respectability, she should accept one of the other noble suitors for her hand. He would understand that she might feel an obligation to do so but admits that he still loves her as he has always done.

There is no doubt that the affair continued. According to Shrewsbury's son, the 20-year-old Gilbert Talbot, by May 1573 Douglas was still pursuing Robert, as was her 'sister Frances Howard' (possibly her sister-in-law Frances Gouldwell, the wife of her brother Sir Francis Howard of Lingfield). This caused 'great wars' between the two ladies, 'and the Queen thinketh not well of them, and not the better of him'.[8] Although there is no record of any outbreak of royal anger at the affair, the Queen probably turned a blind eye and did not see Douglas as a threat. She was far more concerned in 1577, when the affair with Douglas came to an end and she realised that Robert was contemplating marriage to her cousin and perceived rival, Lettice Knollys.

In August 1574, Douglas gave birth to a son, who was named Robert Sheffield, but Robert acknowledged paternity of his 'base son'.[9] Ambrose and Sir Henry Lee stood as godfathers, and Robert was always very fond of him, 'caring much for his well-being and education'.[10] Under his will, published on his death in 1588, Robert treated Sheffield as his 'virtual heir'. Nevertheless, he continued to refer to him as his 'base son',[11] even after his child by Lettice Knollys died in 1584. He always 'vehemently denied'[12] having married Douglas, and she never protested at his later marriage to Lettice. It is noteworthy that at this time, bigamy was not a felony; 'it was a misdemeanour dealt with in the ecclesiastical courts; though it was thought reprehensible, it did not carry the modern stigma of a crime punishable with a sentence in gaol.'[13]

On 28 November 1579, after her affair with Robert had ended, Douglas married Sir Edward Stafford. This was a tacit admission that she had not previously been espoused to Robert. Nevertheless, Elizabeth arranged for Douglas to be interviewed to establish if she had entered into any contract with Robert, which might invalidate his subsequent marriage to Lettice. Sir Edward Stafford was asked to talk to Douglas but could find no evidence of an earlier contract. This was not enough for Elizabeth, who believed that Douglas might be concealing something. Sussex was asked to interview her in Elizabeth's presence. As Douglas was his wife's kinswoman, it was hoped that she might reveal something to him. She broke into hysterical weeping, exclaiming: 'She had trusted the said Earl too much to have anything to show to constrain him to marry her.'[14] Sussex had to admit to Elizabeth that he could establish no more. It was clear that Robert had been free to marry Lettice. Elizabeth accepted this and restored him to favour, but Lettice remained out in the cold.

There is another, less plausible, story of Robert's affair with Douglas, designed to blacken his name. This is recorded in *Leicester's Commonwealth* written in 1584. It asserts that while her first husband, Sheffield, was still alive, Robert 'fell in love with Lady Sheffield', and arranged for her husband to 'die quickly with an extreme rheum in his head (as it was given out), but as others say of an artificial catarrh that stopped his breath'.[15] This conflicts with the letter in Robert's hand, mentioned above, which makes clear that their affair only began 'after your widowhood'. There is also a story that Douglas retained a letter from Robert (perhaps the letter mentioned above) about her person but mislaid it. She asked all her women if they had seen it, but it was found and read by one of Sheffield's sisters, who brought its contents to light. The story goes on to suggest that it was shown to Sheffield, who immediately sought a separation from his wayward wife. As the letter in Robert's hand confirms that Sheffield was dead before the affair began, this again seems a complete fabrication. It is even suggested that Douglas deliberately mislaid the letter so that her predicament should be known, but, if so, it seems extraordinary that the story did not come to light until much later.

In 1604, Robert Sheffield, who was now calling himself Robert Dudley, began his case in the Court of Star Chamber to prove his legitimacy. By this time he had married Alice, daughter of Sir Thomas Leigh of Stoneleigh in Warwickshire. Leigh had encouraged him to establish his claim to enable his daughter to become Countess of Leicester and of Warwick.[16] Robert Jr seems to have been assisted by a noted swindler, Robert Drury. According to Stafford, young Robert 'terrified' his mother into giving evidence to confirm that she had married his father. In her written deposition to the court, Douglas claimed to have established an understanding with Robert that he would marry her if she became pregnant. She then claimed that she had signed a betrothal at a house in Canon Row in Westminster in 1571 and had married him at Esher in May 1573 which was, in fact, six months before she became pregnant. She swore that she was married by a clergyman who provided a licence but was unable to remember his name and could not provide the documentation.

There is no reference to a marriage in any church records of the time, but she claimed to have been given away by Sir Edward Horsey, who had died in 1583. Horsey was 'a close supporter of [Robert] and had served as a soldier, pirate and Captain of the Isle of Wight'.[17] Although she claimed that she was married with a diamond ring, which Pembroke had provided, she was unable to produce the ring or to provide any of the numerous letters in which she claimed that Robert referred to her as his wife.[18] Although she averred that ten witnesses were present, most of whom were servants, including Dr Giulio Borgherini (Dr Julio), Robert's Italian physician, none of them were alive in 1604. She provided two witnesses who claimed to have been present at her child's birth, which she said took place two days after the marriage, but Robert Sheffield was not born until August 1574, fifteen months after the marriage date she had given. One of these witnesses was a Mrs Erisa, who was with her during her lying in, and the other was a servant, Magdalen Frodsham. Drury, who was gathering the evidence, confirmed having instructed Mrs Erisa what she should say. He reported: 'She is very forward to depose, for a further consideration.'[19] Although Magdalen Frodsham claimed to have been present at the marriage ceremony, Mrs Erisa said that Magdalen had not entered Douglas's service until after the child's birth. To explain why Douglas had married Stafford, if she were already married to Robert, she claimed that Robert had threatened to poison her, and she sought Stafford's protection. She claimed that when Robert ended their affair, he had offered her £700 per annum to persuade her to disavow it. Although initially she had passionately rejected his offer, after some reflection she had accepted it. (Evidence of this annuity seems the only matter that may be truthful.) Douglas's deposition conflicts with her earlier evidence established by Stafford and Sussex when she was interviewed in front of the Queen. Although Stafford died during the proceedings at the Star Chamber, he provided written evidence of the earlier interviews to the court. In light of this, Douglas's later deposition does not appear credible.

Notwithstanding the accumulation of evidence for the Court of Star Chamber, it was later called into question. Early in the nineteenth century the lineal descendant of the Sidney family, Sir John Shelley-Sidney, inherited Penshurst and claimed the baronies of Lisle and Dudley. The only bar to this was Robert Sheffield's possible legitimacy. The Committee of Privileges of the House of Lords held that Shelley-Sidney had failed to demonstrate that the evidence of the Esher wedding was invalid (which the original court case had not had to do). Even so, it is difficult to conclude that Robert married Douglas Howard, or that he would cause his only surviving son – of whom he was very fond – to be treated as illegitimate, if this were not the case.

Young Robert proved extremely able. He was brought up by his father's kinsman, John Dudley of Stoke Newington. Many of Robert's able protégés acted as his tutors and he visited him when he could. The young man enjoyed long visits to Robert's friends, 'to acquire the etiquette and social graces which could only be learned in a noble household'. In 1587 he entered Christ Church, Oxford, under the supervision of the outstanding Thomas Challoner, becoming a brilliant 'sailor, soldier, explorer, scholar, mathematician, engineer, shipbuilder and author'.[20]

Chapter 19

Religious confrontation

By the mid-1570s, numerous Catholic priests were being smuggled into England. These were trained under the auspices of the English Jesuit Cardinal William Allen at seminaries at Douai, Reims and Rome. It is estimated that, by 1580, more than 100 were established in manor houses to spread their faith and to stiffen the resistance of Catholic gentry. In 1580, Pope Gregory XIII had published an Explanation providing a concession to the papal bull excommunicating Elizabeth ten years earlier. This confirmed that the bull was still binding, 'but Catholics might obey her so long as her Government remained in being, and while no directive had been received that they were to overthrow her'.[1] To counter this, the Council issued a question: 'If an invasion, sponsored by the Pope, were directed against Queen Elizabeth, would you fight on her side?'[2] There was only one acceptable answer and that was: 'Yes!' Penalties for non-attendance at Protestant services were raised to £20 per month, and celebrating Mass was subject to a fine of 200 marks (£133) and a year's imprisonment. It now became treasonable to attempt to convert subjects to Catholicism.

In May 1581, seminary priests were joined by Jesuits led by Robert Parsons and Robert's former protégé, Edmund Campion. At the same time, Catholic adventurers, led by the Papal emissary Nicholas Sanders, landed in Munster in Ireland, where, with the blessing of Pope Gregory XIII, they fomented trouble against their English landlords.[3] Although this expedition was repelled, Elizabeth remained vulnerable. Campion was arrested in July and was taken to the Tower. He was lodged in a cell known as Little Ease, where he could neither stand nor lie down. After forty-eight hours he was released for interview at Leicester House by Bedford and two secretaries in the presence of Robert and the Queen. The objective was to make him acknowledge Elizabeth as his sovereign. Although he accepted her as his lawful Queen, he refused to answer whether he would fight for her against a papal invasion. He claimed that, as a Jesuit, his position was entirely spiritual. Elizabeth explained that her security required her to impose 'observance on the religion of the state',[4] but could not persuade him to attend a Church of England service. He was returned to the Tower, where Robert did much to ensure his humane treatment, providing a bed and other necessaries, but could not protect him from the rack during an attempt to establish those who had sheltered him. Along with fourteen other seminary priests, he was found guilty of treason for his Catholicism. He was brought to the gallows, where Hunsdon and Sir Francis Knollys, who supervised the proceedings, let him hang until death so that quartering was performed on his lifeless body.

The Elizabethan Church of England also faced pressure from non-conformists, who questioned its dogma and criticised the toleration being shown for Catholic worship. Among these, 'Puritans were those Anglicans who objected to some aspects of official liturgical practice, such as the use of vestments and the 1559 Prayer Book, and who refused to conform in such matters.'[5] In the 1570s and 1580s, a smaller group emerged from among them, who adopted Calvinist doctrine and called themselves Presbyterians in line with the Scottish Kirk. They wanted to do away with Episcopal government, through which the church was administered on the Crown's behalf. This placed them in conflict with Elizabeth and, coincidentally, with James VI in Scotland.

Perhaps incongruously, given his pleasure-loving lifestyle, Robert always saw himself as a leading Puritan, taking on the mantle donned by his father. His siblings followed his lead and looked up to him. His brother-in-law Huntingdon, always a devout Puritan himself and impeccably loyal to Elizabeth, considered Robert 'the most highly placed and influential member of the family'.[6] Robert's enemies saw his Puritanism as hypocritical and 'a matter of political convenience'.[7] Nevertheless, his beliefs were heartfelt and from the start of Elizabeth's reign he had used his influence to support international Protestantism. In 1568, the French ambassador reported that he was 'totally of the Calvinist religion'.[8]

Robert was not someone who would sacrifice his political standing for the sake of his faith, but nor were any of his politically prominent colleagues. Elizabeth, Cecil and Huntingdon all received Mass during Mary's reign. Bedford, who was staunchly Puritan, served with the Dudleys under Philip II at St Quentin. Robert took the decision to support a Spanish Counter-Reformation in return for support for his marriage to Elizabeth. This step may well have undone any hopes he had of marrying her, but it was a political ploy which he did not confuse with his Puritan beliefs.

Robert's patronage of Puritan preachers and radical clergy, often working outside the orbit of the episcopal church, was of inestimable value to their cause, and his benefaction grew as his wealth and power increased. To provide them with greater financial security, Robert endowed lands in Warwickshire into a trust fund for their benefit. As his land ownership expanded, so did his influence and the number of benefices in his giving.[9] Many works of Protestant devotion were dedicated to him, and he employed returning exiles as his chaplains, helping several 'sound' men to preferment in the Church of England. William Whittingham, a leader of the exiled community in Geneva, returned in 1561 to Leicestershire, where Huntingdon supported him as an itinerant preacher. In 1563, he acted as Ambrose's chaplain in Le Havre. Robert and Ambrose later gained the Deanery of Durham for him. With Huntingdon's help, he was ultimately appointed as Master of Wigston's Hospital, Leicester.

Robert did much to oppose unsympathetic bishops.[10] Independent lay patronage left them 'powerless to control recalcitrant clergy [who had gained] the backing of great noblemen'.[11] Very often, itinerant preachers were paid by benefactors to provide instruction in private houses, public buildings, or churches, 'entirely outside episcopal control'.[12] This alarmed bishops, who deplored the breakdown of their traditional authority. Perhaps their biggest threat was in Northampton, where Percival Wiburn was supported by local gentry to set up a Presbyterian model of church government espousing Calvinist doctrine. 'Clergy and magistrates jointly ruled a society of enforced morality where the citizens were compelled to attend worship, hear sermons and receive regular instruction in the scriptures.'[13] When the Bishop of Peterborough, Edmund Scambler, intervened, Wiburn turned to Robert for support. Although Scambler personally owed much to Robert, he strongly resented interference in diocesan affairs. While Robert continued to defend Wiburn, Scambler saw him as confrontational in every aspect of Northampton's daily life and threatened to revoke his preaching licence. In 1572, Wiburn was forced to leave Northampton, but with local support, continued his activities in nearby villages.

Robert did not always get his own way. In 1565, Thomas Sampson, who had become Dean of Christ Church, Oxford, was deprived of his post by Elizabeth on the grounds of his Puritan beliefs. Not even Robert (who was temporarily out of favour with her) could gain his reinstatement, but he persuaded the Bishop of London to allow Sampson to preach at Paul's Cross. When Thomas Lever, who had been his father's protégé, returned from the Continent in 1559, Robert arranged his appointment as rector and archdeacon of Coventry. In January 1563, Lever was appointed Master of Sherburn School in Durham. After becoming a canon at Durham Cathedral, he championed diocesan clergy to take a Puritan line against 'popish' practices such as the wearing of a surplice. When dismissed by the bishop, even Robert could not save him. Nevertheless, Lever retained his archdeaconry at Coventry, filling it with non-conformist ministers. Although he was cited for breaches of discipline, Robert worked hard to protect him, but he remained mired in controversy until his death in 1577.

Perhaps the most celebrated and learned of the Puritan leaders enjoying Robert's patronage was Thomas Cartwright, a lecturer and preacher at Cambridge University.[14] He challenged the establishment with 'a clear, logical exposition of scripture … [leading to] widespread non-conformity at Cambridge',[15] while Oxford retained its establishment leanings. To clamp down on him, the Cambridge authorities expropriated his professorship and fellowship in 1571. In 1573, a warrant was issued for his arrest after he openly supported John Field (another of Robert's protégés), who had attacked the Elizabethan church settlement and refused to conform. Cartwright escaped to the Continent, spending eleven-and-a-half years visiting Reformed churches and writing religious works, which Elizabeth and her bishops considered seditious. She had no time for religious zealots and felt threatened by ecclesiastical indiscipline.[16] Nevertheless, Robert always stood by him.[17] He eventually joined with Burghley to beg the Queen for Cartwright's repatriation. When she refused, Cartwright, then aged 50, returned without consent in 1585, only to be imprisoned.

At last, Robert began to feel isolated in his support for firebrand non-conformists and he pulled back. He recognised that there was more discord between Protestant and Puritan, than between Protestant and Catholic. A majority of the Council, including Robert, Burghley, Walsingham and Sir Francis Knollys, began to see Presbyterianism as disruptive, setting non-conformists on a collision course with the establishment. With Elizabeth determined to retain a diocesan structure to support her position as head of the Church of England, Robert saw the urgent need for reconciliation to prevent a disintegration into rival camps.[18] The Council now encouraged different branches of the Protestant faith to work within the aegis of the Church of England. To settle the controversy over vestments, Robert initiated discussions with the Strasburg leader John Sturm and German Protestant princes.

A good example of Robert's more conciliatory approach was in his attitude to Thomas Wood. In 1576, Wood, a local farmer in Leicestershire, who had served under Ambrose at Le Havre, began to participate in weekly 'prophesying' meetings despite not being ordained. Although 'prophesyings' by groups of local ministers had innocently exhorted large numbers to religious study with 'exercises of interpretation of the scriptures', they threatened to become rallying calls for dissent from Anglican dogma. Elizabeth wanted them suppressed. Robert recognised the danger and to the great shock of the Puritan movement, began to support Elizabeth.[19] This resulted in Wood openly criticising Robert's private life until Ambrose had to defend his brother. Robert also wrote a letter, which extended to 3,000 words. He claimed: 'There is no man I know in this realm, of one calling of another, that hath shown a better mind to the furthering of true religion, than I have done, even from the first day of her Majesty's reign to this.' He continued:

> I will not justify myself for being a sinner of flesh and blood as others be. And besides, I stand on the top of a hill, where I know the smallest slip seemeth a fall. But I will not excuse myself. I may fall many ways and have more witnesses thereof than many others who perhaps be no saints neither, yet their faults less noted, though some ways greater than mine.[20]

Although Archbishop Matthew Parker had banned prophesyings in 1574, they had continued to flourish, and the next Archbishop of Canterbury, the Puritan Edmund Grindal defended them. Elizabeth banned Grindal from court and sought to deprive him of office. It was only when the Council, with Robert's encouragement, unanimously defended him that he was permitted to remain as Archbishop, but without any authority, until his death on 6 July 1583. It was an important confrontation as it raised the question of whether the Queen or the Archbishop were the final authority in the Church of England. This was a matter on which Elizabeth would not back down.

Elizabeth was supported by Hatton, who was progressively growing in influence on ecclesiastical matters. It was on his advice that Elizabeth appointed John Whitgift, now aged 53, as Archbishop of Canterbury to replace Grindal. Hatton had never been an ally of religious radicals and had faced an assassination attempt from a fanatical Puritan in 1573.[21] Nevertheless, he remained in awe of Robert. As late as 30 January 1584, Walsingham and Hatton agreed to defer a decision on how to deal with a suspect Roman Catholic priest until Robert could be present on the following day.[22] While Robert 'and the majority of the council had worked for ecclesiastical unity',[23] Whitgift wanted church uniformity and set out to dismantle the broadly-based Calvinist church set up by his predecessors. This 'unyielding prelate strove to restore the dignity and power of all grades of the ordained clergy and ruthlessly stamped out non-conformity'.[24] To achieve this, he needed Elizabeth's and Hatton's support. Hatton gave him warning when he faced opposition in the Commons but assured him of backing at court.[25]

Whitgift was acting with royal authority when he 'required all clergy to subscribe to certain articles concerning belief and practice'.[26] When some refused, he asked Hatton to intercede to prevent tacit support for them from other members of the Council. He complained: 'Unless such contentious persons were some way animated and backed, they would not stand out as they do.'[27] When Cartwright's supporters tried to gain his release, Whitgift refused him a preaching licence. Nevertheless, Robert employed him as a chaplain and appointed him as Master of Leycester Hospital at Warwick with a supplemental annuity of £50. Cartwright irritated the church hierarchy by preaching to packed congregations in the surrounding area. When, after four years, his appointment was terminated, he was jailed. He later travelled to the Netherlands as chaplain to Robert's expeditionary force. On Robert's death, Ambrose continued to provide protection for him but when Ambrose also died, he was again arrested and faced the loss of his income.[28]

With Robert having urged his Puritan friends to work within 'the prevailing pattern of church leadership', he now 'found himself caught up in the crossfire between entrenched episcopal and non-conformist positions'.[29] Although radicals wanted him to stand up to Whitgift and the Queen, the Archbishop asked him to provide practical support for 'that lawfully constituted church authority to which he had given verbal allegiance'.[30] In December 1584, Robert played the role of conciliator, summoning representatives of both viewpoints to Lambeth. The disputants argued before Robert, Burghley, Walsingham and Lord Grey of Pirgo, but failed to resolve their differences. In March 1585, Robert made a blistering attack on Whitgift's policies in the House of Lords. With the country poised for war against Catholics on the Continent, Robert's supporters believed that Whitgift was attacking the wrong enemy. Cecil complained:

> I desire the peace of the Church. I desire concord and unity in the exercise of our religion. But I conclude that … this kind of proceeding is too much savouring of the Roman Inquisition and is rather a device to seek offenders than to reform any.[31]

The Archbishop's intransigence had lost Robert his former control of church policy through Government and prevented him from nominating his own appointees to benefices.[32] Nevertheless, Whitgift retained the Queen's support; in 1586, his appointment to the Council further damaged Robert's authority.

Robert also found himself competing with Sir Walter Raleigh, who had engaged Elizabeth's fancy. In 1582, Raleigh had arrived at court bringing dispatches from Lord Grey de Wilton in Ireland. He was 'dark handsome, lively and extraordinarily intelligent … His charm, his brilliance, his magnetism exercised an engrossing influence over her'.[33] Thanks to her generosity, Raleigh was 'able to indulge his taste in rich clothes, such as the Queen loved to see him wear'.[34] It was Robert who 'clipped Raleigh's wings by bringing forward his stepson, the Earl of Essex'.[35] With his own prestige waning, and Elizabeth pursuing policies which he considered disastrous, he might have withdrawn from public life. Instead he plunged his efforts into taking a more aggressive approach to international foreign policy.

Chapter 20

Royal visits to Dudley homes

In 1572, the Queen paid a visit to Warwick, which Robert always considered his parental home. She was the guest of Ambrose and his wife Ann Russell, who had become the Queen's close companion, and Robert accompanied her. This was a house party that involved the whole town. It took some time for the royal coach to make its way through the thronging crowd up Castle Hill to the gates. Ambrose and his wife were not living in the castle, but the Queen stayed with them for two days at 'Mr Fisher's house'. The climax of the party was a firework display reflected in the river. This was enhanced by cannon brought by Ambrose, as Master of the Ordnance, at his own expense from the Tower. From here she left Warwick by the north gate for a private visit with Robert to Kenilworth, six miles away. She remained in 'blissful retreat' until the Saturday, when she returned to surprise Lady Warwick at supper. She sat down to join everyone, but as usual ate little and, having left the table, went out into the gallery. Here she encountered Mr Fisher, who was prevented by gout from going down on his knees, but he enjoyed a conversation with her.

Elizabeth now returned for a public visit to Kenilworth, where she received the news of the Massacre of St Bartholomew. Her party went on to Berkeley Castle. Henry, Lord Berkeley, who occupied the property, was not present, as his ownership was disputed by the Dudleys, but Robert took Elizabeth hunting in the chase, where they slaughtered twenty-seven stags, and had a 'wonderful day'. Berkeley was furious at the decimation of his stock and blamed Robert for his arrogance, but the Queen took Robert's side.

In July 1575, Robert arranged another visit for Elizabeth and her court to Kenilworth. This was without doubt the most glittering spectacle of her reign. It was memorable for its incredible extravagance and range of entertainments. She had been staying at her home at Grafton in Oxfordshire after making some structural improvements and Robert paid her a visit. He wrote to Burghley, who was to join them at Kenilworth, that she was very pleased with the result. Her only problem had been a shortage of light ale, which she preferred drinking to water that might be contaminated. Even Robert considered the local ale too heady, but eventually a source of light ale was found that met with her approval. She never took strong drink and always added water to wine.

On 9 July, Robert rode out from Kenilworth to greet the royal party at Long Itchington, where he had erected an enormous pavilion for a sumptuous dinner.[1] The party consisted of thirty guests with their servants. These included Sir Henry and Mary Sidney, their son Philip, Burghley, and Lettice Knollys. It is apparent that Douglas Sheffield, whose son was now born, stayed away. The weather was heavenly, hot with a few refreshing showers. When they reached Kenilworth at eight o'clock in the evening, the whole castle was lit by thousands of twinkling candles and torches, 'looking like a fairy palace rising from the lake'.

> On the bridge, seven pairs of columns were adorned with votive offerings: wheat, grapes, branches laden with fruit, cages of birds, platters of fish protected by fresh grass; the sixth pair were in the form of two ragged staves, from whose branches hung glittering armour; the last pair were two bay trees, hung on all sides with lutes, viols, flutes, recorders and harps.[2]

As the visitors approached the Castle gates, 'a salute of cannon greeted the Queen's entry, and at that moment the clock on Caesar's Tower, with its blue dial and gold figures, was stopped; time was to stand still for these enchanted days'.[3] There now:

> appeared a floating island on the large pool there, bright blazing with torches, in which were clad in silks the Lady of the Lake and two nymphs waiting on her, who made a speech to the Queen in metre of the antiquity and owners of the castle …[4]

For the next eighteen days:

> actuality and myth completely overlapped. When Elizabeth went hunting, a savage man and satyrs appeared to recite

flattering verses. Returning on another day to the castle she was 'surprised' by Triton who emerged from the lake, dripping weeds and water, to make another oration. Even at her departing she found Sylvanus running at her stirrup and urging her to stay for ever. There were masques and pageants in plenty, banqueting and bear-baiting. There was a rustic wedding and games arranged for the townsfolk in the tiltyard. There were mummers and a troupe of actors from Coventry who came to present traditional plays. There were tumblers and jugglers, and firework displays.[5]

All the entertainments were accompanied by exquisite music and dancing, with people from the locality invited to watch the spectacle. It can be surmised that the 11-year-old William Shakespeare, living five miles away at Stratford, was in the audience. Much of the analogy in *A Midsummer Night's Dream* seems reminiscent of the Kenilworth entertainment. Killigrew had discovered an Italian maker of fireworks, who sent Robert a programme for a 'pyrotechnical display'[6] that would take two months to prepare. These were Shakepeare's 'stars that shot madly from their courses'. The plan had:

> provided for live dogs, cats and birds to be thrown out of the body of a flaming, flying dragon; but as detailed accounts of the fireworks seen at Kenilworth make no mention of this feature, it may be assumed that it was cancelled.[7]

On the first evening, there were 'serpents of fire in the meads', and on another there was a display in the Castle courtyard of:

> a fountain throwing water, wine and fire for seven or eight hours continuously, and 'three wonderful wheels of scented fire of different colours', a combination of colour, light and scent, the three ideals of Elizabethan pleasure.[8]
>
> There were picnics and minstrelsy on the lake. And everywhere 'magic' surprises – bushes that burst into song, pillars that grew fruit and gushed wine, trees decked with costly gifts. To achieve this effect, [Robert] and an army of servants bustled behind the scenes, ready to change the

programme at a moment's notice in accordance with the whim of the Queen or the weather.[9]

Robert Laneham explained the luxury provided:

> Delicates that any way might serve or delight; as of wine, spice, dainty viands, plate, music, ornaments of house, rich arras and silk (to say nothing of meaner things), the Mass of provision was heaped so huge, which the bounty in spending did after betray. The conceit [was] so deep in casting the [plate] at first: such a wisdom and cunning in acquiring things so rich, so rare, and in such abundance: by so immense and profuse a charge of expense, which, by so honourable service, and exquisite order, courtesy of officers, and humanity of all, were after so bountifully bestowed and spent. What may this express, what may this set out on us, but only a magnific mind, a singular wisdom, a princely purse, and an heroic heart?[10]

Elizabeth lacked her father's gastronomic appetite, and it is recorded that she ate 'smally or nothing', doing 'scant justice to the food and drink',[11] but none of the allegory was lost on her. As always, this concealed personal messages. Marriage was the constant theme. The Queen should marry or should release her suitors from their bondage. This should not be seen 'as a last desperate gamble for the Queen's hand'.[12] Robert's affections had strayed, and his courtship was no more than formal. He now wanted lawful progeny, but he wanted Elizabeth to release him. This theme of Robert's love for Elizabeth continues, not just in Shakespeare, but in John Lyly's *Endymion*. In this, the shepherd (Robert) falls in love with the unattainable Cynthia (the Moon) representing Elizabeth, with Tellus (the Earth), being seen as Douglas Howard, and Floscula (the little flower) as Lettice Knollys.[13]

The allegory may have been overplayed. On the twelfth day of the visit, there had been plans for the royal party to travel three miles to Widgen Hall to dine in a pavilion, but the Queen did not attend, or see 'a ready device', which had been prepared of 'goddesses and nymphs'. Plans had to be changed and the poet, George Gascoyne, who was responsible for the libretto of the revels, was given orders to come up with a 'pièce d'occasion' at short notice.[14] It records that Sylvanus, the man in the woods, meets the Queen on her return from hunting, after hearing nothing but lamentations that she plans to leave, and he begs her to remain so that he can be restored to his former happiness. She seems to have accepted this apology for some offence, the cause of which may have been Robert's friendship with Lettice.

Another problem arose when Robert called on neighbouring gentry to appear wearing his Dudley livery with the blue coat and silver badge of the bear and ragged staff, which the players wore as a privilege. Edward Arden of Park Hall, who had been High Sheriff of Warwickshire, indignantly refused. He also added offensive comments on Robert's private access to the Countess of Essex, dubbing him a 'whore-master'.[15] The Catholic Arden later suffered death for treason, after which some of his lands passed to Robert. It was not safe to criticise Robert and Lettice. Elizabeth's later visit to Robert, when Lettice was the hostess, must have caused an 'electric atmosphere'.[16]

Chapter 21

Marriage to Lettice Knollys

At the end of 1575, Espés reported a frisson of great enmity between Robert and Essex. He went on to claim that while Essex was in Ireland, his wife Lettice had had two children by Robert – which was of course a complete fabrication, despite its mention in *Leicester's Commonwealth* published eight years later.[1] Since 1573, Essex had been engaged on a project to colonise the Great Ards in Ulster, partially financed by Elizabeth, while Lettice remained in England. Despite her now being aged 32, her auburn tresses made her stunningly attractive, just as she had been during Robert's initial flirtation with her ten years' earlier.

Lettice does not seem to have enjoyed domestic harmony with Essex, despite four stunningly beautiful children, and her husband's departure abroad may have been a relief. With Essex in Ireland, she was invited with other local dignitaries to Robert's splendid occasion at Kenilworth in 1575, and Elizabeth afterwards came with the court to Chartley, the Essexes' principal residence. The Kenilworth game book shows that Lettice received a gift of bucks in 1573, when Essex had first gone to Ireland, and again in 1574 and 1575.[2] She also visited to go hunting in 1576.[3] According to Camden, it was during Essex's visit to England from November 1575 to July 1576 that Lettice's relationship with Robert was being talked about, causing Essex to threaten Robert.

Essex's Irish project was under great financial pressure and he had been forced to sell large parts of his English estates to settle his debts. He now needed Council funding for it to continue. Robert seemed keen to ensure that he was safely restored to Ireland, where he was granted what Camden described as 'the empty title of Earl Marshal'.[4] Despite the failure of Essex's earlier Irish project, Robert pressurised Sidney, now back in Ireland as Lord Deputy, to be more effusive in seeking his reappointment.[5] Sidney was suddenly fulsome with praise, describing him as 'so noble and worthy a personage' and 'complete a gentleman'.[6]

This advice encouraged Elizabeth to authorise Essex's return. Two months later, on 22 September, Essex died of dysentery.[7] There were immediate rumours that he had been poisoned. Although Sidney ordered a post-mortem, Essex's secretary confirmed that there was no evidence of foul play. Camden has recorded: 'The suspicion of poisoning was more readily believed "because [Robert] so quickly afterwards abandoned Douglas Sheffield by whom he had a son".'[8]

There seems little doubt that Robert was already enjoying an adulterous affair with Lettice.[9] In Essex's absence, she had attended court in London, occupying Durham Place with her sons, Robert and Walter, and her daughters, Penelope and Dorothy.[10] It may be significant that she was not made an executrix of Essex's will, despite having managed his estates while he was in Ireland.[11] The will seemed more concerned about the care of his children than his wife. His 13-year-old son Robert, who inherited Chartley, was left in the care of Burghley and Sussex. The younger children were to be sent 'for maintenance' to live with the Huntingdons, who were living at King's Manor, York, where Huntingdon was based as president of the Council of the North. Although Robert's sister Catherine had no children of her own, the couple were much respected as devout Puritans and oversaw the education of several children of noble families with great care. Although young Walter seems to have moved there immediately, Penelope and Dorothy remained with Lettice until the New Year of 1578 before moving to York. Under the will, Lettice was not left a jointure over Chartley, their principal home, and after some argument with the trustees, was forced to move out, even though young Robert was living with Burghley.[12] With Essex's activities in Ireland on the Queen's behalf having left his estates heavily encumbered, Lettice persuaded Burghley to grant her a life interest in the lesser property of Benington. Although Elizabeth offered Lettice condolences at her loss, she provided no practical help.[13]

Lettice spent time during 1577 with her friends the Digbys at Coleshill, who had children of a similar age to Penelope and Dorothy. Perhaps conveniently, Coleshill was ten miles from Kenilworth where Lettice made several visits for buck hunting parties, sometimes with Penelope and the Digbys. In mid-1577, Robert decided to take the waters of St Anne's spring at Buxton. As he was overweight and suffering from intermittent bouts of malaria, his need for a cure seems to have been genuine enough. Nevertheless, he may have deemed it wise to remain away from the limelight at Court. It was also convenient, in July, to have an excuse to visit Kenilworth. Camden claims that Robert 'more openly made love to Lettice', whom he had used 'as his good liking before, for satisfying his own lust'[14] during her husband's lifetime. They were now firmly established as lovers and by the second half of 1577, were secretly contemplating marriage. According to *Leicester's Commonwealth*, while Robert followed the court on its progress, Lettice was sent 'up and down the country from house to house by privy ways, thereby to avoid the sight and knowledge of the Queen's Majesty'.[15]

Although Lettice complained to Burghley at her 'slender allowance', she was able to attend court during the Christmas season of 1577. On Shrove Tuesday 1578, the Queen made a payment to the Countess of Essex's players 'for presenting a play before her Majesty'.[16] On the same evening, 'the Earl of Leicester's players had also made their "repair to the court with their whole company and furniture to present a play before her Majesty"'.[17] By then, when not in London, Lettice was residing at her father's home at Grey's Court near Henley.

The hot springs at Buxton had, since Roman times, been famous for their miraculous cures and restorative powers, particularly for gout and female 'irregularities'. They were much frequented by Elizabeth's courtiers, and Cecil visited as speedily and often as his 'old creased body would allow',[18] meeting Mary Queen of Scots there in 1575. Even Elizabeth contemplated a visit in July and August 1575, but when she learned that she might meet Mary she changed her mind. On his visit in 1577, Robert was accompanied by Ambrose and later joined by Pembroke. Shrewsbury, who owned the spa, had been sent a comic menu by Elizabeth to keep Robert to his diet; he was to be allowed two ounces of meat, washed down with the twentieth part of a pint of wine and as much of 'St Ann's sacred water as he listeth to drink'.[19] On feast days, this should be augmented with the shoulder of a wren at dinner and with the leg at supper! Ambrose, being even stouter, was to follow the same diet, except that the wren's leg was to be omitted![20] By chance they also met Mary, but meetings with her were handled formally as Walsingham's spy network extended to Buxton, and even Burghley and Robert needed to be circumspect. By this time, Robert had become florid and was beginning to bald, but neither his physical nor mental activity was impaired and 'his mature handsomeness'[21] remained fascinating to

200

women. He claimed that he questioned Mary on her rumoured betrothal to Don John of Austria, but she revealed nothing.

Robert had a second purpose for coming to Buxton. The ever-ambitious Bess of Hardwick had a daughter, Elizabeth, by her earlier marriage to Sir William Cavendish. She had hatched a plan with her old friend, the equally ambitious Margaret Lennox, for Elizabeth Cavendish to marry Margaret's second son Charles Stuart, Darnley's brother. The couple were introduced at Chatsworth, and being left to their own devices, Charles 'entangled himself so that he could have none other'.[22] A marriage was hastily arranged, but with Charles being of Tudor blood they overlooked the requirement that this needed royal assent. Elizabeth was furious and consigned Margaret Lennox for a period to the Tower. Arbella Stuart was born in due course and, after the tragic deaths of both of her parents, was brought up by Bess in the company of Mary Queen of Scots. Robert, who had always maintained a close friendship with Margaret Lennox, was secretly invited to progress Arbella's claim to the English throne as a more acceptable candidate than either Mary or her son James, both of whom had been born in Scotland. He immediately proposed that Arbella should marry his illegitimate son, Robert Sheffield. Arbella's claim was unlikely to gain Elizabeth's support and certainly did not gain that of Mary, who wrote to Castelnau that she had fallen out with Bess over the preposterous plan. In 1579, when Lettice provided Robert with a legitimate heir, the 'Noble Imp' replaced Robert Sheffield as Arbella's prospective spouse. If Robert could not marry the English Queen, he would cover every option to ensure that his progeny might marry her prospective heirs.

Lettice did not accompany Robert to Buxton. As part of the cure, men were expected to keep chaste from all women. Elizabeth was probably aware of Robert's growing infatuation and that his relationship with Douglas had run its course. She remained bitter at his flirtations and again decided to test his moral integrity. What would happen if she could promote him in marriage to a European Royal Princess? Would his drive for self-advancement override his passion for her wayward kinswoman? It just so happened that the Princess Cecilia had been recently widowed. At the end of 1577, Elizabeth persuaded Robert to write to the ebullient Princess, despite an absence for twelve years, to offer his hand in marriage. Elizabeth also wrote to support his suit. Robert could not resist such a prospect. On receiving his letter, Cecilia sought advice from her brother Karl, who had succeeded Eric as the Swedish King. In January 1578, Karl replied: 'We have received our beloved sister's letter and perceived from that, what the Queen of England has desired of our beloved sister on the Earl of Leicester's part, in which matter our beloved sister has asked our counsel and advice.'[23] He explained that after Cecilia's previous visit to England, he would not have thought she would want to go there again! She declined the proposal, even though it would have meant her seeing Helena von Snakenborg, the widowed Marchioness of Northampton. Robert's suit was firmly rejected and he reverted to the welcoming arms of Lettice, who seems to have been in ignorance of this lapse in his attention. If she had known, there would certainly have been fireworks!

In early 1578, Robert acquired Wanstead to provide Lettice with a home outside London. In May, Elizabeth, who was not – officially at least – aware of the relationship, paid a visit to Wanstead. Lettice kept well out of the way; Robert was again at Buxton and did not return to court until July, so asked Philip Sidney to entertain Elizabeth on his behalf. Philip wrote a masque to be played out of doors called *The Lady of the May,* which compared Elizabeth to the beauty of the May flowers. He ended it: 'I will wish you good night, praying to god … that hitherto it has excellently done, so hence forward the flourishing May may long remain in you and with you.'[24] He was now 23 and had already begun to show 'promise of remarkable genius as soldier, courtier, diplomat and poet'.[25] Robert did much to forward his career. 'He had become his uncle's principal personal representative abroad.'[26] Soon after this, he toured the major Protestant states in Europe canvassing a new alliance in the face of mounting Catholic and Ottoman Muslim pressure. Essex had been anxious for Philip to marry his daughter Penelope, but when it was first mooted she was only 12. This would have forged a link with Sir Henry Sidney, with whom Essex had been so closely associated in Ireland.

Elizabeth was concerned at Robert's absence at Buxton and fretted that he had not taken his physician, Dr Julio, with him. He was suffering from a swelling in his leg, but, on 24 June, he reported to Walsingham that he was finding the waters beneficial. He told Hatton, probably untruthfully, that he lamented that her 'eyes' had not been at Wanstead to welcome the Queen. Had he known of her coming in time, he would have bolted away from the sacred spring, but 'St Ann would have had a short farewell'.[27]

It seems that Lettice had become pregnant and in the spring, she and Robert had entered into a secret betrothal or marriage ceremony at Kenilworth, although no details of it are known. Robert's visit to Buxton may have been a convenient excuse for his absence from court, rather than to provide a cure. Hatton reported that Elizabeth was brooding about a marriage, which she considered to be injurious to her.[28] It is not clear that Hatton was aware of Robert's relationship with Lettice, but he took Robert's side, saying: 'I defend that no man can tie himself to such inconvenience as not to marry ... except by mutual consent on both parts.' He warned Robert: 'I think you shall hear more of the matter.'[29] He also reported that Elizabeth was impatient for Robert's return to court. Life in the household had become drab, and there was a shortage of good horses. On 9 July, Robert told Hatton:

> I hope ere long to be to be with you, to enjoy the blessed sight [Elizabeth] I have long been kept away from. A few of these days seem many years, and I think I shall feel a worse grief ere I go so far for a remedy again. I thank God I have found great ease by this bath.[30]

He caught up with the Queen's summer progress at Audley End on the borders of Essex and Cambridge. With Burghley being Chancellor of Cambridge University, he had arranged a visit of the Vice Chancellor and the Masters of the colleges to greet the Queen. They provided her with a Latin oration, the gift of a Greek New Testament and a pair of scented gloves, which she much admired. Robert's protégé, the young Edmund Spenser, was among the Cambridge undergraduates who attended her.

Elizabeth's progresses always provided a means for her to be seen by the people, strengthening loyalty and affection, and there is no doubt that she enjoyed being in the countryside travelling from place to place. On 1 September, she stayed for two days with Sir Roger, 2nd Lord North, a close friend of Robert, at Kirtling. North had arranged for his home to be 'nobly stocked' for the occasion with every sort of meat and poultry, including 'geese, capons, swans, mallards, cranes, snipe, plovers, pheasants, quails, curlews', with 'beer, ale, claret and sack'.[31] Fish included 'sturgeon, crayfish, crabs, oysters, turbots and anchovies'. Robert had sent his own cooks (who were paid £4) to Kirtling, and the Earl of Leicester's Men received forty shillings for a theatrical performance. Robert then took leave of the royal party, retiring to Wanstead for a second secret marriage ceremony to Lettice. North had been made aware of the marriage plan, as Robert had told him:

> There was nothing in this life he more desired than to be joined with some godly gentlewoman, with whom he might lead his life to the glory of God, the comfort of his soul, and to the faithful service of her Majesty, for whose sake he had hitherto forborne marriage, which long held him doubtful.[32]

Despite their first secret marriage Lettice still lacked security and her father, Sir Francis Knollys, who was Robert's ally on the Council, insisted on him coming to a settlement with Douglas under which she received £700 per annum and agreed to give up custody of their son. Robert assisted her in finding a new husband, the recently widowed Edward Stafford. His mother was Mistress of the Robes and his deceased wife was a kinswoman of Amy Robsart. Sir Francis, who knew Robert only too well, also insisted on a second marriage ceremony between Robert and Lettice to be conducted before accountable witnesses. This took place at Wanstead on 21 September 1578 with Lettice, in view of her apparent pregnancy, in a loose-fitting gown. It was attended by Ambrose, Pembroke, Richard Knollys, the bride's brother, and North; Sir Francis gave his daughter away and the ceremony was conducted by Robert's chaplain, Humphrey Tyndall. Three years later, Tyndall was required by Sir Francis to make a sworn deposition that he had performed the rites and to provide proof of his ordination by the Bishop of Peterborough six years earlier.

Two days after this second marriage ceremony, Elizabeth, who had reached the last stage of her progress, arrived for a second time at Wanstead, by when all trace of the marriage celebration had disappeared, although Lettice was almost certainly present. Robert 'feasted the company with a lavishness that was the theme of admiration',[33] before Elizabeth's return to London. Even now she was not told, although if Hatton's earlier comment is to be believed, she may have had wind of it. Robert still did not dare to risk the loss of his status, which remained dependent on his special relationship with the Queen and even Sir Francis could not persuade him to announce the marriage publicly. He did not feel indispensable.

It is extremely difficult to establish when Elizabeth came to learn of the marriage, as the various records provide conflicting stories. There is no doubt that she was desolate at the perceived slight of losing Robert, particularly in a passionate marriage to her pregnant kinswoman. She will undoubtedly have acted petulantly on learning of his breach of faith. It is thus surprising that there is no record of any reaction among ambassadors' correspondence. The historian Derek Wilson has argued that Robert made his peace with her on 28 April 1578 before his secret first marriage to Lettice, and while he was still untangling his relationship with Douglas. This may explain the complete absence of a public scene. The horrors of Elizabeth's upbringing had forced her to place enormous reliance on the loyalty of a few trusted friends and she had now lost her mainstay. She expected Robert's single-minded devotion and he had deserted her. It was not until 4 July 1579 that there is a letter, written by Mary Queen of Scots, which mentions Elizabeth's anger at Robert's marriage. From now on, Elizabeth's objective was to keep Robert and Lettice separated when she could, and romance with her 'frog' was partly pursued out of pique.

In 1615, Camden published a document which claimed that in July 1579, Simier told her of Robert's marriage, hoping to advance his negotiation for her to marry Anjou. The story claims that she 'wept and fumed', threatening to send Robert to the Tower. If she had already been aware of it for fifteen months, this seems an overreaction, but as has been seen, Elizabeth was an adept actor. The story goes on to say that she turned to Sussex, now Lord Chamberlain, and to Burghley for advice. Sussex spoke to her bluntly and honestly. If she sent Robert to the Tower, she would lose her dignity. A man should not be 'molested for lawful marriage'. He detested Robert, but it was more important that she should maintain her self-control. In all probability, she had known of the romance all along and now listened to Sussex's realistic advice. We know that Robert continued to attend Council meetings, even daring to oppose her marriage to Anjou in her presence, despite being secretly married himself.[34]

Whichever way it came to light, Lettice had to face the full force of Elizabeth's wrath. She remained defiant and was not one to seek her cousin's forgiveness. She was not ashamed of what she had done and was determined to brazen it out. There was a dramatic confrontation between them in the Queen's private apartments at Whitehall. By refusing to bow down, Lettice succeeded in antagonising Elizabeth even further. 'However much she had loved Lettice's mother, the days when Elizabeth shared the same warm feeling for her daughter were over.'[35] Mary Sidney found herself caught in the middle. She had always been on friendly terms with Lettice, but now remained at Penshurst while waiting for matters to calm down. The clandestine marriage had tested their friendship to the limit, and the relationship between the sisters-in-law seems never fully to have recovered.

Robert also became extremely sensitive to his worsening relationship with Burghley, although this had nothing to do with his marriage. Burghley, as Chairman of a committee of the Mint, had issued orders without acquainting Robert or receiving his countersignature as a member of the committee. Robert believed that he had been deliberately slighted. He felt Burghley's antagonism keenly and sought help from his friends to achieve a reconciliation.[36] He later wrote to Burghley at the injustice of the Queen's displeasure with Lettice and threatened to retire to a residence he had acquired in Germany. He hoped for Burghley's help, and Burghley may have played his part in trying to reconcile the Queen to Lettice, but to no avail.[37] Nevertheless, Elizabeth's affection for Robert was deep-rooted, and his influence started to revive. By late 1579, he was restored to the heart of her circle and she dined with him on at least two occasions. 'The long-standing affection between Elizabeth and himself had life in it still, and the old habits of tenderness asserted themselves on any occasion of illness.'[38] In October 1584, he suffered a recurrence of his malaria. She sent frequent requests for bulletins on his well-being, and he took 'the opportunity to express his ardent gratitude and devotion'.[39] Castelnau believed that his great loyalty placed him in higher favour than he had been four years previously. Nevertheless, it never reached its former unassailable strength and he was no longer positioned to counter the threat posed by Anjou.[40]

With Robert spending more time at Court, Lettice spent much of the first year of their marriage at her father's home, Grey's Court. If she were pregnant at the time of her two marriages, as seems likely, the child did not survive. Nevertheless, at the end of 1579, she was safely delivered of a son, Robert, who immediately took the title of Lord Denbigh and was known as 'the Noble Imp'. His father now had the legitimate heir he craved. The Noble Imp was raised in the utmost splendour, having a cradle draped with crimson velvet and a fine little chair upholstered in green. He seems to have been a bit unruly and managed to deface a portrait of 'a gentlewoman in yellow satin',[41] no doubt to the chagrin of his parents. Several portraits were painted of him, one entirely naked to show off the perfection of his body. Most tragically, he fell suddenly ill at Wanstead in July 1584. Robert hurried back from court, which was on progress at Nonsuch, arriving at Wanstead the day before the child's death on 19 July. Robert and Lettice were completely distraught; he had been the focus of all their plans. There is no clear evidence of the cause, but it seems to have been some childhood malady. There is a malicious story that a little suit of armour preserved at Warwick Castle with one thigh-piece rather longer than the other had belonged to him. This implies he might have been deformed, but it has been demonstrated that the armour was not manufactured until around 1625.[42] The death was all the more poignant because, in September 1582, Lettice had been expecting another child, but nothing more is heard of it and the pregnancy seems to have ended in miscarriage. With Robert being 52 and Lettice 41, they must have realised they were unlikely to have other children. Their hopes now rested with Robert Sheffield and Lettice's son, Robert Devereux, 2nd Earl of Essex.

As was the norm, Robert and Lettice did not attend the Noble Imp's funeral and burial in the Beauchamp Chapel at Warwick, but they created a magnificent effigy to his memory. They needed to get away from Wanstead; they spent a few days at Theobalds, Burghley's new house in Hertfordshire, although Burghley was not there. Theobalds had been transformed from a small home into a redbrick palace enclosing three courts, the inner one surrounded by the principal rooms. The hall could be converted into a great chamber for the Queen's visits, with a gallery on the third floor for her use. At the north-west end there was a bedroom in a tower for 'the Queen's Majesty', with several adjoining rooms. A Tower on the south side housed a chamber reserved for Robert.

Robert was pathetically grateful to Burghley. Although he and Lettice were distraught, the loss of their son drove them together. As Robert said in his will, Lettice was 'a faithful, loving and very obedient, careful wife'.[43] Hatton had to explain to Elizabeth the reason for Robert's sudden departure from court. She immediately sent Sir Henry Killigrew with a message of sympathy, but Robert's grief did not soften her heart towards Lettice. Robert wrote to Davison, the Queen's secretary, to thank him for his letter of sympathy, which 'found me from the court, whence I have been absent these fifteen days to comfort my sorrowful wife for the loss of my only little son, whom God has lately taken from us.'[44] For a period, he excused himself from attendance at Council meetings unless specifically needed.[45]

The couple 'spent most of the rest of 1584 in company with their friends and family',[46] much of it at Grey's Court. Robert paid another visit to Buxton, something he always found beneficial. On his return, he spent the night with Catherine Huntingdon at Leicester. After hunting en route, he was able to provide the Mayor and brethren with six bucks and largesse for the town's charities. They returned the compliment with a hogshead of claret and two fat oxen. As he began to overcome his sadness, he seems to have lost at dice, and gave money to the poor and the household servants for their hospitality.[47] Although he was soon called upon to return to court, Lettice continued to be treated vindictively and despite his frequent pleadings, remained banished and out of favour.[48] Although her life revolved round Wanstead and Leicester House, she seems to have moved out when the Queen visited for occasional meetings with the Council. Mary Sidney found the situation too painful. She relinquished her apartments at court provided by the Queen and retired to Penshurst, but Robert was expected to remain.

It was to stem his loss of influence that Robert now advanced Lettice's son, the young Essex, to royal favour. He had been made Burghley's ward following his father's death. He was 13 at the time of Robert's marriage to Lettice, 'athletic, vigorous and flamboyant'.[49] Burghley saw to it that he attended Cambridge, but at the age of 19 he moved to live at Lamphey, his property in Wales, spending his time 'largely in idleness'[50] according to Sir Henry Wotton. Lettice was not going to put up with this and roused him out of his country existence. She asserted her authority to bring him back to London to attend court under the auspices of his stepfather. He was attractive and became an immediate hit with a charisma that he knew how to use to good effect.[51] Yet he was prone to petulance if crossed and found himself having to compete with a coterie of young favourites, including Raleigh, whom he despised.

Although Elizabeth could not be seen to grow old among her new favourites, Robert 'continued to be [her] closest adviser and to convey messages to and from the Council',[52] even though he may have advocated policies, of which she did not approve. Their friendship 'had weathered the storm that threatened it with shipwreck … [She] had still her fondness for his society … and she stimulated and enchained him still.'[53] Their relationship had been punctuated by quarrels and disagreements, causing 'open and great disgraces from her majesty's mouth',[54] but these could not destroy their mutual affection. His role now was to provide devotion, not love.

Despite her antagonism for their mother, Elizabeth showed great concern for the welfare of Penelope and Dorothy Devereux. In January 1581, Penelope, who was just 18, was escorted to court from York by Lady Huntingdon. 'Beautiful, vivacious and intelligent, [she] was an instant hit … in the same way that Lettice had once been.'[55] She rapidly gained the admiration of Philip Sidney, seeming to fulfil the wishes of her father as expressed in his will. Unfortunately, Huntingdon, realising the family's financial predicament, sought a connection for her with deeper pockets. Robert, 3rd Lord Rich – three years older than Penelope and with an income of £5,000 per annum from his Essex estates – was 'a vociferous puritan' and one of the most eligible bachelors available. In other respects, 'he was an unsavoury character with a reputation as a bully'.[56] Without consulting either Lettice or Penelope, Huntingdon wrote to Walsingham, asking him to seek Elizabeth's approval for their marriage, which she duly granted. Penelope made her feelings abundantly clear. She bravely defied convention by fighting against it but was powerless to prevent it from taking place on 1 November 1581. Her second husband, Charles Blount, Lord Mountjoy, later recorded: 'A lady of great birth and virtue, being in the power of her friends, was by them married against her will unto one against whom she did protest at the very solemnity and ever after.'[57]

Although Penelope remained in the Queen's service, she spent most of her time with her mother to avoid Rich's attentions, which she found detestable. Sidney realised that he had let Penelope slip through his fingers. Within a year of her marriage he made her the inspiration for his poem *Astrophil and Stella,* about an unconsummated love affair; although written in 1582, it was not published until after his death. He referred to her as 'the richest [pun intended] gem of love and life', using the words:

> … Yet could not, by rising morn foresee
> How fair a day was near. Oh, punished eyes!

With Penelope no longer available, Robert was attracted by the possibility of establishing another link between the Dudley and Devereux families. In January 1582, he made a will to make provision for his young son. This will also named his stepdaughter Dorothy, then aged 17, as a suitable spouse for Philip Sidney, his nephew. By then Sidney, who had recently been knighted, had eyes elsewhere. In March 1583, he became betrothed to Walsingham's daughter Frances. She may not have had the glamour of Penelope, but was dark-haired and beautiful, and it was a match of 'mutual affection'.[58] Neither family had much money and Sir Henry Sidney told Walsingham that he was looking to him to 'move the Queen to certain suits',[59] which might compensate for his son failing to make a more lucrative connection. This did not prevent Sir Henry from strongly approving of the match. He wrote of 'the joyful love and great liking between our most dear and sweet children, whom God bless'.[60] It was not mentioned to the Queen in advance and, with Philip occupying a prominent position at court, she was displeased at their reticence. Walsingham was incensed and wrote to Hatton that he had not discussed it as:

> I am not a person of that state, but that it may be thought a presumption for me to trouble her Majesty with a private matter between a free gentleman of equal calling with my daughter. ... Let her understand, first that the match is for concluded, secondly how just cause I shall have to find myself aggrieved if that her Majesty shall show her mislike thereof.[61]

The wedding took place in September 1583, and the Queen became godmother to their first child. Robert was delighted.

It was now obvious, even to Elizabeth's councillors, that the Stuart line would provide the next occupant of the English throne. Although Elizabeth refused to acknowledge this, her councillors started to take the Stuarts into account in planning both the nation's future and their own.[62] Robert made a point of maintaining a close relationship with all the potential Stuart candidates. He asked Castelnau to establish him in better standing with Mary Queen of Scots. The ambassador reported to Henry III that he and his wife had dined with Robert and Lettice at Leicester House, which they took as a 'particular mark of attention'.[63]

Robert apparently expressed a wish to Castelnau that their wives should become intimate friends. Castelnau advised Mary that the best way to retain Robert as an ally was by establishing contact with Lettice. Elizabeth seems to have become aware of these overtures. When Robert visited Buxton again in June 1584, Mary was not permitted to attend at the same time. She wrote to Castelnau seeking royal consent to visit the spa as soon as Robert had left and asked him to assess the extent of Robert's support for his brother-in-law Huntingdon's claims to the English Crown. Castelnau reported back that Robert:

> would be the first to combat him, and in the event of the
> death of his Queen, he, with all his relations and friends,
> would willingly render some important service; he told me
> I might acquaint your Majesty with this. But was on no
> account to let anyone else hear of it.[64]

It has already been seen that Robert had made plans for his son to marry Arbella Stuart, but he hatched another connection. Robert was 'even more anxious to be on thoroughly good terms with James'.[65] The attractive Dorothy Devereux remained available. Mendosa heard rumours that, in concert with Walsingham, Robert had proposed to James that if he married Dorothy and would assure them that he would not change his religion, 'they would have him declared by the judges to be the heir to the Crown of England'.[66] Elizabeth seems also to have heard these stories and asked James's representative in London to establish if there was any truth in them. Although they were denied, she blamed Lettice and became:

> so excited about it as to say that she would rather allow the
> King to take her crown away than see him married to the
> daughter of such a she-wolf, and, if she could find no other
> way to repress her ambition and that of the traitor Leicester,
> she would proclaim her for the bad woman that she was,
> and prove that her husband was a cuckold.[67]

Having watched her sister's predicament, Dorothy was not impressed with yet another proposal for an arranged marriage. In July 1583, she eloped with Sir Thomas Perrot, who had frequently participated in tournaments at court. They were married at Broxbourne, Hertfordshire, with five or six witnesses and two men guarding the church door with swords and daggers under their cloaks, while pursuers galloped to the porch in a failed attempt to prevent the ceremony. Even Lettice did not approve, and Elizabeth banished Dorothy from court. Perrot spent a period in the Fleet prison along with the chaplain who had performed the ceremony. Burghley had to intervene to gain their release and he helped the couple in their subsequent financial difficulties. These forced them to retire to Carew Castle in Pembrokeshire, the Perrot family estate.[68]

Remaining on good terms with James was a particular concern for Robert because, in August 1584, Davison, while ambassador in Edinburgh, heard rumours that Robert had 'disparaged the awkward intelligence of the young King'.[69] Davison warned Robert, who dismissed it as a calumny because 'no man of his training and experience would be guilty of such offences'.[70] In July 1585, he wrote to James's Secretary of State, Sir John Maitland of Thirlestane (later Lord Thirlestane), to propose that they should become friends:

> as men that do serve two Princes so near in blood and so
> near in friendship as my mistress and your master be. And
> for my own part … I cannot like to live a stranger with such
> a person but to offer any kindness or acquaintance I may
> devise …[71]

As Elizabeth had recently referred to James as 'that false Scots urchin' after his approval of the execution of Regent Morton, Robert was clearly seeking to cover all the options for the inheritance of the English Crown, if Elizabeth should die.

Elizabeth's continuing anger with Lettice undoubtedly sounded the death-knell on any hope of reconciliation. 'Lettice too was angry and vowed not to cower away and hide as if overridden by guilt.'[72] According to the unreliable *Leicester's Commonwealth,* Lettice's sister Anne:

> added fuel to the fire by saying that 'she nothing doubted
> but that one day she should see her sister, upon whom the
> Queen now railed so much, to sit in her place and throne,
> being much worthier of the same for her qualities and rare
> virtues than was the other.'[73]

It would seem that Elizabeth was not made aware of this. Lettice did not often appear in public, but when she did, she did not move quietly. The Spanish ambassador reported:

> She now demeaned herself like a Princess, vied in dress with the Queen till her Majesty, after sundry admonitions, told her that as but one sun lightened the east, she would have but one Queen of England, boxed her ears and forbade her the court.[74]

While this may seem unlikely, he continued:

> She rides through Cheapside drawn by four milk-white steeds with four footmen in black velvet jackets and silver bears on their backs and breasts, two knights and thirty gentlemen before her, and coaches of gentlewomen, pages and servants behind her, so that it might be supposed to be the Queen or some foreign prince or ambassador.[75]

She also travelled on the Thames in her husband's barge, and despite being barred from court visited many members of society at their homes.

While Robert was serving the Queen, Lettice held court at Leicester House, making it 'the established home of the greatest noble in the land'.[76] It became the scene of regular entertainments performed by the Earl of Leicester's men. She also spent time at Wanstead, employing 150 staff between the two properties. Although Kenilworth was fully maintained, after their marriage Lettice is only recorded to have visited it once, in 1585.[77] An inventory of its contents made in 1578 includes a portrait of her, described as the Countess of Essex.[78] It is known that she continued to use her Essex title until 1584, perhaps to avoid drawing attention to her marriage to Robert.[79] Leicester House was filled with portraits, of Robert and Lettice, of Penelope Rich, of Dorothy Perrot, of Sir Francis Knollys, of other members of the Knollys family, of Philip Sidney and even of Douglas Stafford. One of them was the double portrait of Penelope and Dorothy that now hangs at Longleat.[80]

PART 3

POLITICAL ADVISER AND MILITARY COMMANDER

Chapter 22

Negotiations for Elizabeth to marry the Duke of Anjou

Although the Massacre of St Bartholomew had seemed to sound the death knell for negotiations of a marriage between Elizabeth and Alençon, maintaining the French alliance suited everyone. Elizabeth had said nothing while her 'romance' with Robert wound down, but the suit with Alençon had drifted on in indecisive fashion until 1576, when it appeared to peter out. Although Walsingham recognised that the marriage was unpopular with her Protestant allies, it opened the door for an understanding with France. The paramount objective was to maintain peace between France and Spain to prevent unrest in the Netherlands becoming a major war. War might allow one or other of them to establish absolute control to the great danger of heretic England.

Following the death of Charles IX in 1574, Alençon's remaining elder brother, Henry, became King Henry III, leaving Alençon as heir to the French throne. In September 1575, he fled from the French court after falling out with Henry and their mother, Catherine de Medici. He joined up with the Huguenot rebels led by the Prince of Condé in the south. When, in February 1576, they also joined forces with Henry, King of Navarre, Henry III was forced into signing the very one-sided Edict of Beaulieu. Under its terms, Alençon was created Duke of Anjou, Touraine and Berry, and from then on was generally referred to as Duke of Anjou. Although he remained Catholic, his new Protestant alliance made him much more acceptable as a potential spouse for Elizabeth, but she was 43 with no realistic expectation of having children.

With the European situation changing from week to week, the uncertainty made Elizabeth extremely edgy and indecisive. Only Robert and Hatton were able to broach affairs of state with her and Robert had now become the Council's most influential member. In August 1577,

Walsingham sought his help to persuade Elizabeth to send aid to her Protestant allies in the Netherlands. While Walsingham and Robert were united in their desire to defend Protestantism whatever the risk for England, Elizabeth and Burghley were fearful of the consequences. Walsingham wanted to send Robert's friend Duke Casimir with a mercenary army to assist the Dutch. Although Elizabeth showed her usual reluctance to become involved, she recognised the imperative of saving the Dutch rebels from defeat.

'The Spanish onslaught in the Netherlands was being so courageously and doggedly resisted that the defence was no longer assumed to be hopeless.'[1] The French concluded that if they provided the Dutch with modest support, they might gain 'the whole terrain as a sphere of influence, a prospect which alarmed the English almost as much as that of a complete Spanish domination'.[2] In late 1577, Anjou blundered into the conflict, seeing himself as a champion of the rebels. This greatly irritated Henry III, particularly when Anjou saw an opening for himself as the Netherlands' Protector. From an English viewpoint, this presented the danger of a Franco-Spanish conflict, which might leave one of them in control. The English objective was to allow the rebellion to drift on inconclusively. Although Robert, Walsingham and Burghley argued over how to deal with Anjou's interference and the extent of any support to be given to the Dutch rebels, the issue was to establish whether he was acting on his own, or on behalf of France. If he were alone, his involvement was far less dangerous. Walsingham travelled to the Netherlands with Lord Cobham to assess whether Anjou could be manoeuvred to support the English in their balancing act. In 1578, Elizabeth took the initiative and, without consulting her advisers, sent an envoy to Paris to resuscitate her marriage suit with her 'frog'. It can be no coincidence that the man sent to promote a suit, of which Robert strongly disapproved, was Edward Stafford, soon to be married to Douglas Sheffield. Elizabeth wanted to stop short of her negotiation with Anjou ending in marriage, but the courtship needed to be taken sufficiently seriously to confirm his alliance with the English. This meant keeping all her advisers in the dark. Both Elizabeth and Anjou 'applied themselves vigorously to its restoration to full health'.[3] Robert was extremely nervous of Elizabeth's initiative realising, correctly, that the prospect for England of having a French King would be devastatingly unpopular. Burghley's backing for it seems to have been entirely political in his efforts to thwart Robert and deprive him of French support. Walsingham reported to William Davison: 'The affair of Monsieur takes greater foot than was looked for. She thinks it the best means to provide for her safety that can be offered … though otherwise not greatly to her liking.'[4] Elizabeth played her role with complete conviction, giving Anjou the impression that she was an eager participant and the Crown was within his grasp. This left Robert, without realising it, to play the part of her jilted lover.

In August 1578, while Elizabeth was on her summer progress at Long Melford Hall in Suffolk, she was joined by a French diplomat (apparently named de Bocqueville), who arrived to begin the courtship on Anjou's behalf.[5] Meanwhile Anjou, with Elizabeth's encouragement, 'cavorted ineffectually' in the Netherlands.[6] Robert remained in the dark and complained to Walsingham:

> It may be that I do not give you light enough on our doings, so much as you would wish, but I assure you, you have as much as I can learn … For the matter now in hand of her marriage, no man can tell what to say, as yet she has imparted to no man, at least not with me, nor for aught I can learn with any other.[7]

Elizabeth set up a four-man committee to provide advice. Of these, Robert and Walsingham strenuously opposed the match, while Burghley and Sussex supported it. No one was expecting an heir to result, but her doctors confirmed her ability to bear children, despite her being aged 46. Robert strongly opposed Anjou's Catholicism, despite him being sympathetic to the Netherlands rebels. Fearing that Robert could prove a stumbling block to the marriage, Henry III wrote to assure him on his honour that his position would not be injured by it. He would become Anjou's trusted guide.[8] In January 1579, Anjou sent his close friend, Jean de Simier, an 'accomplished ladies' man',[9] to conduct his wooing. Simier played his game with great charm, realising that Elizabeth had an obsessive fondness for flattery. He became her 'monkey' and she had eyes for no one else, flaunting her affection for him before the court. For six months, he occupied the place that had been held by Robert twenty years before. 'He gained access to her private apartments at all hours, showered her with flattery and love tokens and 'stole' items such as handkerchiefs and nightcaps for his master to keep among his dearest treasures.'[10]

Robert and Hatton became increasingly perturbed at Simier's success and were determined to prevent the marriage. A member of the guard at Greenwich Palace even fired on Simier in an assassination attempt as he travelled in the Queen's barge with the Queen, Robert and Hatton.[11] Robert spread rumours that Simier had 'crept into the Queen's mind and had insisted her to the love of [Monsieur]' with 'amorous potions and unlawful arts'.[12] Elizabeth loved all the attention and was determined to show the 'unfaithful' Robert that he was not indispensable. She forced him to go through all the diplomatic motions of entertaining Simier.[13] Castelnau reported: 'She is gayer and more beautiful than she has been these fifteen years. Not a woman or physician who knows her but says there is no lady in the realm more fit for bearing children than she is.'[14] Although Robert fought to prevent it, in July 1579 a passport was granted for Anjou to visit London. While Simier seemed able to tangle Elizabeth irretrievably in his web, she adeptly frustrated him by finding some way to escape the cords closing round her. Nevertheless, Robert was genuinely alarmed, retiring in feigned illness to Wanstead, where Elizabeth visited him for two days. Anjou arrived in England in August, spending ten days secretly with Elizabeth, who handled the negotiations herself, leaving her advisers in the dark. He may have been puny and pock-marked, but he enchanted Elizabeth – hitherto an admirer of handsome men – with his brilliant conversation, wit and fascinating manners. She 'told him that he had been represented to her as hideous, hunch-backed and deformed. But she found the reverse and most handsome in her eyes.'[15] To make the best possible impression at court, she ordered new suits for her courtiers, but her councillors 'shut their eyes'[16] and avoided being present. When Robert left, his loyal sister Mary Sidney went with him. Her son Philip, now an experienced diplomat in his own right, wrote Elizabeth a long letter opposing the marriage, only to receive 'a severe scolding'.[17]

Robert and Philip were right. Protestant England would not tolerate Anjou as Elizabeth's consort. John Stubbs, a country gentleman trained in the law, published a pamphlet entitled: *The Discovery of a Gaping Gulf whereinto England is like to be swallowed by another French marriage, if the Lord forbid not the banns by letting her Majesty see the sin and punishment thereof.* This was written in outrageous language accusing the Valois house of being rotten with disease and endangering Elizabeth with the prospect of childbearing. Stubbs, together with his printer and publisher, were arrested and condemned to lose their right hands, but the printer was pardoned. When Stubbs's right hand was severed, he lifted his hat with his left and cried: 'God save the Queen!',[18] before swooning.

On Anjou's departure from Elizabeth at Canterbury, 'she took leave of him in an access of sensibility and grief', but did not miss the opportunity to show him the dockyards at Chatham, 'where the sight of the ships under construction made the Frenchman gasp'.[19] A parting gift of a cord for Robert's cap, containing precious stones worth 3,000 crowns, did nothing to sway him.[20] In October, Elizabeth called for a vote on the marriage in the Council, but many, both inside and outside politics, were impatient at its futility.[21] When the majority opposed the match, as she surely knew they would, she flew into every appearance of a rage. As always, she was a brilliant dissembler. 'The national temper was now opposed to Burghley's subtle diplomacy and in favour of positive measures: a definite commitment to the Huguenot cause; a policy of non-appeasement towards Spain; and rigorous reprisals against Catholic fifth columnists.'[22]

The feelings of the people found vent in a popular song:

> The King of France shall not advance
> His ships on English sand,
> Nor shall his brother Francis [Anjou] have
> The ruling of the land.
> Therefor, good Francis, rule at home,
> Resist not our desire,
> For here is nothing else for thee
> But only sword and fire.[23]

Robert was now the leader of those who favoured a more adventurous foreign policy as an implacable enemy of tyranny and popery. This would lead England inevitably into conflict with Spain. Although negotiations with Anjou continued for another two years, it had become a 'political courtship',[24] at which Elizabeth was extremely adept.

Chapter 23

A more aggressive approach to international diplomacy

Although in years past, the English had gone in large numbers to the support of William of Orange in the Netherlands in a religious war against the Spanish, Elizabeth had always shied away from providing a formal English presence. Robert's principal agent in the Netherlands, Thomas Wilson, had arrived there as Elizabeth's representative in 1574. Wilson did much to prevent England coming to any accommodation with Spain and, in 1579, was rewarded with a position on the Council.[1] In January 1575, the Dutch had offered Elizabeth the crown of Holland and Zeeland, hoping to gain her wholehearted support for their cause, but her usual prevarication about supporting rebels against a divinely anointed King lost her her credibility. After much negotiation, she refused the offer, while continuing to turn a blind eye to private English participation. In the summer of 1576, Philip's Spanish garrisons went on the rampage over arrears of pay, causing both Protestant and Catholic Netherlanders to unite against them. They formed an elected assembly, the States General, which was confirmed by the Pacification of Ghent signed between them that November. Philip's reaction was to appoint as regent his illegitimate half-brother, Don John of Austria, the hero of the Battle of Lepanto against the Turks in 1571.

With Robert and Walsingham dictating policy, Elizabeth secretly sent the rebels £20,000 and promised a loan of £100,000. Robert sent an envoy, Sir Edward Horsey, officially to offer Elizabeth as a mediator with the Spanish, but really to 'gauge Don John's strength and intentions'.[2] At the same time, Wilson tried to arrange for Robert to meet William of Orange to propose that he should lead an English force to support the Dutch (although Elizabeth may not have known of this). Although Robert had not seen military service for twenty years, he was determined to demonstrate

221

to Elizabeth and his Puritan supporters that, even at 43, he was willing to back up his policy with action. Although the States General rejected Elizabeth's offer of mediation, they were supportive of Robert bringing an army. Despite this, Don John won the diplomatic battle by offering terms acceptable to the States and they wrote to decline offers of military aid.[3]

In May 1577, Robert was invited to stand as godfather to William of Orange's daughter. With Philip Sidney on a diplomatic mission in Germany, Robert asked him to make a diversion to act as his proxy. Sidney met William at Gertruinenberg, after which they maintained a 'lively correspondence'.[4] He was impressed at the depth of William's faith, which permeated all his decisions. It was even rumoured that Sidney would marry Maria of Nassau, his daughter by an earlier marriage.

No sooner had Sidney returned to England than Don John took to the offensive, seizing the fort of Namur and rallying Spanish subjects to challenge William's supporters. This was a tactical blunder as the Netherlanders reunited against him and reopened negotiations with the English. Charles-Philippe de Croy, Marquis of Havrech, led a Dutch delegation to England in late summer. He invited Elizabeth to send Robert with an English army, fully expecting her to provide a sufficient force to protect her favourite. While Robert was entertaining Havrech and making preparations, Don John developed a fever and died on 1 October 1578. Both Walsingham and Robert considered this miraculous.[5]

In March 1578, a new Spanish ambassador, Bernardino de Mendosa, had been accredited in London. He was the first envoy since the departure of de Espés six years before, tarnished by his involvement in the so-called Ridolfi plot, but Mendosa also remained hostile to Elizabeth. He reported:

> The bulk of the business depends upon the Queen, [Robert], Walsingham and [Burghley], the latter of whom, though he takes part in the resolution of them by virtue of his office, absents himself on many occasions, as he is opposed to the Queen helping the rebels [in the Netherlands] so effectively and thus weakening her own position. He does not wish to break with Leicester and Walsingham on the matter … they being well supported … Leicester … is so highly favoured by the Queen … that he centres in his hands and those of his friends most of the business of the country and his creatures hold most of the ports on the coast.[6]

Mendosa was partially right; Burghley was suffering from gout and was unwell. During his absences, he had been left completely unaware of the venture to send Sir Francis Drake to the Pacific coast of South America on the *Golden Hind*, even though the voyage was financed by the Queen, Robert, Hatton, Clinton, Walsingham, Hawkins and Winter. Plans were finalised while Burghley was taking the waters at Buxton. Nevertheless, Mendosa had misjudged the extent of Robert's authority. Robert was having to resort to calling Elizabeth to his feigned sickbed to hold a meaningful conversation with her, but even then he did not always gain her support and often felt the sharp edge of her tongue. The root cause of her frostiness was his infidelity.

Robert never faltered from his objective of making England an ally of the Dutch Protestants. He wanted to be appointed the leader of a military expedition to drive the Spanish out of the Netherlands. It was of huge strategic and religious importance for England to retain its mercantile and religious allegiance with them. By 1577, he was receiving advice from Davison in Antwerp; Davison had replaced Wilson and was already much in favour with Elizabeth. In October, Robert complained 'to Davison that the solemn burghers of Brussels had undermined the cordial agreement that he had reached with Havrech'.[7] This Flemish change of heart had been caused by the arrival of Alexander Farnese, Duke of Parma, in Flanders to lead a renewed Spanish effort to establish control. Parma very quickly subsumed Catholic Flanders, including Brussels and Bruges, and was preparing to focus on the ports of Zeeland and Holland and on the United Provinces. This reawakened the States to their need for English support, and Robert was much encouraged when Davison told him that his name was held in great respect. Nevertheless, Elizabeth had again changed her mind, fearful that English aggression would lead to a Spanish invasion across the Channel. She concluded that it was safer secretly to finance a mercenary army under Casimir, rather than overtly to send an English force. Casimir arrived in England in early 1578 to discuss the financing arrangements. Robert took him under his wing, and, to promote his own standing, took him to Oxford, where he was Chancellor of the University. Robert assumed that Elizabeth's only issue was how to find the money quickly enough. He suggested either that she should borrow from her 'merchants in Hamburg or Frankfort', or recall the sum already advanced to the Netherland states.[8]

Elizabeth remained non-committal. She mistrusted the Dutch, and the expense of providing support was crippling. They were demanding peace conditions from the Spanish that Philip would consider preposterous.[9] She continued to fear that English involvement might provoke the Spanish King into suspending his campaign there to launch a war to crush England. Much of her popularity had depended on her maintaining solvency without having to ask:

> parliament for heavy assistance … Peace, with its inseparable concomitant, economic stability, was the basis of her extraordinary success and the unique hold it gave her on the people's affection. The States now wanted her to cancel the policy of nearly thirty years, which had brought such great and growing rewards, and, by declaring war on Spain on their behalf, pour out men and treasure until she or Spain fell back exhausted or bled white.[10]

Nevertheless, if the Dutch collapsed she knew that England would be Philip II's next objective.[11] By March 1578, she had again lost her nerve. To Robert's great personal disappointment, he had to tell Davison that she was not going to support the Dutch even with German mercenaries, despite him having 'done [his] best and bettermost to get it forward'. He went on: 'I have almost neither face nor countenance to write to the Prince, his expectation being so greatly deceived.' He was extremely depressed, and with the complexity of his private life arising at the same time, it is little wonder that he sought the restorative waters at Buxton to regain his wellbeing.

With the Spanish pushing northwards, Robert received a letter while at Buxton from Casimir, who was desperate for English support. He wrote to Hatton advocating that Sidney should meet Casimir but wanted Hatton's advice on whether Elizabeth would send Sidney officially, or whether he should go privately. In early 1579, Casimir made a second three-week visit to England, during which Robert spent much time with him. Mendosa reported that when the Queen had attended the Council she had twice called for Robert, only to learn that he was occupied with Casimir. When Robert at last appeared, she told him: 'You have quite forgotten us all, and business too, apparently, since we cannot get you here for the discussion of it!' Mendosa claimed that Sussex and Burghley were not displeased at Elizabeth's criticism.[12] Elizabeth secretly advanced £50,000 to finance Casimir, but faced with the might of the Spanish army under Parma, he achieved nothing. William of Orange now hoped that Robert could persuade Elizabeth to declare herself unequivocally as a Dutch ally.[13] He invited Robert to make a short visit to provide advice, not wanting his influence to be absent from the English Council for any longer than necessary. He proposed that Robert should bring a deputy. Davison had suggested either Ambrose or Sidney, both of whom would be acceptable. All this appealed greatly to Robert's growing self-esteem.

In 1580 two further factors accelerated the prospect of conflict with Spain. The Duke of Alva overran Portugal, and Drake returned from his circumnavigation on the *Golden Hind*. In 1573, Alva had been brought back from the Netherlands by Philip II after his repressive policies seemed to have failed. In 1578, at the age of 73, he was employed to promote Philip's claim through his mother, Isabella, to the Portuguese throne. With no legitimate male heir, the Portuguese crown had been claimed by Don António, Prior of Crato, a bastard grandson of Manuel I. In June 1580, Alva marched into Portugal with 20,000 men, entering Lisbon after defeating Don António's forces at the Battle of Alcântara. Philip II now appointed Alva as the first Viceroy of Portugal. Portugal not only provided the Spanish empire with the entire Iberian Peninsula, but a large military and mercantile fleet and a colonial empire that rivalled that of Spain.[14] Meanwhile the *Golden Hind* arrived in Plymouth laden with Peruvian silver and Indonesian spices. 'Francis Drake had rifled Philip's supposedly secure treasure houses, sailed across ... the Pacific Ocean – and traded in his supposedly reserved markets. He returned with breathtaking wealth.'[15] He did not initially receive the greeting that he had expected. Having arrived in London, he found the Queen obsessed with the consequence of war with Spain. He was summoned to a Council meeting, where only Burghley, Sussex and Sir James Croft (a Spanish agent – as will be seen) were present, but with Wilson as secretary. They called for the treasure to be brought to the Tower, so that an inventory could be made prior to its restitution. 'When the order was taken to [Robert], Walsingham and Hatton, they refused to sign, and exerted their influence with the Queen to get it suspended.'[16] It had not taken much persuasion for the Queen's greed to overcome her sensibilities. 'After paying himself and his crew and making lavish presents to the Queen and chosen courtiers, [Drake] was able to pay his backers [including Robert] £47 for every £1 invested.'[17] Mendosa protested at Drake's piracy in the strongest possible terms, but Drake was extremely popular. With the *Golden Hind* being placed on public display at Deptford, on 15 April 1581 he entertained Elizabeth on board with 'a dinner of such lavishness as had not been known since the days of Henry VIII.'[18] He presented her with a silver casket, and a frog made of diamonds. She arranged to knight him on deck and even persuaded Anjou's representative, Nicholas Clausse de Marchaumont, a Catholic bishop, to perform the ceremony. Drake was later elected to the Inner Temple. To add salt to the Spanish wound, Don António was welcomed to England, where he was installed at Baynard's Castle, Pembroke's London home.[19] Robert spent much time with both Drake and Don António, helping Drake to plan an expedition to seize the Azores in Don António's name. Eventually prudence prevailed, and Burghley swayed 'the majority of the Council and the Queen against the enterprise'.[20]

Philip II was stung into action. He launched a military attack into southern Ireland in support of Irish rebels. He backed the Guises to send the Catholic Esmé Stuart into Scotland to ingratiate himself with the adolescent James VI. This included a plan for the Guises to lead the Enterprise of England by invading through Scotland. At Jesuit insistence, the invasion force was to consist of Spanish troops to support Mary's return to the Scottish throne and to claim the English one. With Parma having overrun Flanders, the sphere of influence of William of Orange was restricted to Holland, Zeeland and the United Provinces. England was now threatened on three sides.

Despite the Dutch rebels' desperation, Elizabeth continued her refusal to provide direct aid, but professed her reliance on Anjou. Much to Robert's surprise, Anjou appeared on an unexpected visit to England in June 1581 anxious to gain Elizabeth's confirmation that she would marry him. Although Robert had cultivated a close friendship with Marchaumont and had approached Anjou's commissioners, he was unable to establish why he would visit at this time. Anjou admitted to Elizabeth that Henry III no longer supported his Netherlands policy, leaving him completely dependent on English aid. This suited her objective of avoiding direct English involvement. By reposing every confidence in his military competence and providing £50,000 to establish him as the Netherlands' regent, she could divert him from his marriage suit. She could also maintain the Netherlands rebellion without overt

English involvement, retaining the option for a protective alliance with France if the Spanish should threaten invasion.[21]

Although Sussex continued to support the Anjou marriage, his only objective was to thwart Robert. When Sussex was granted a licence to breed horses, Robert took it as a personal affront. In July, while in the Queen's presence at Greenwich, they 'almost came to blows in the council chamber', calling each other 'traitor'.[22] This resulted in Elizabeth confining them to their chambers.[23]

By July, Anjou was back in France, but in November he returned to England, and for a few dangerous moments, it seemed to Robert as if his marriage to Elizabeth would become a reality. She had already admitted to Stafford in Paris that the match was extremely unpopular but continued with her game (although it did not seem like a game). She walked with Anjou in the gallery at Greenwich, where she kissed him. She said to the French ambassador: 'You may tell his Majesty that the Prince will be my husband.' She drew a ring from her finger and put it on Anjou's.[24] Robert now feared that it was irrevocable. It is claimed that he asked her bluntly 'whether she were maid or a woman', and she laughed and said: 'A maid!'[25] Elizabeth Jenkins argues that this demonstrates that Robert had never deflowered her. If he had, the question would have been superfluous. It seems more likely that he was asking if she was claiming to Anjou that she was a virgin.

Elizabeth now had to begin the process of extricating herself from the web she had woven. She argued that as Anjou had now taken up arms against Spain, their marriage would 'bring us and our realm into war, which in no respect our realm and subjects can accept'.[26] She saved Anjou's face by offering to conclude an offensive and defensive alliance with him and allowing his credit in the European money markets to be enhanced. She made marriage to Anjou conditional on terms that Henry III was likely to refuse, and she could always raise the bar higher if he agreed to them.[27] It took three months. Anjou blamed Simier for having antagonised Robert by telling Elizabeth of his marriage to Lettice. Simier could not understand why Robert had been restored to favour. Elizabeth told Mendosa that she could not dismiss Robert because, on her instruction, his men manned all the ports. Mendosa accepted this explanation, although it was certainly within her power to recall them. The truth was very simple: despite Elizabeth's ardent wooing, it was all an elaborate game. She did not want to marry, and certainly would not choose Anjou, but she had achieved the substance of an alliance with France.[28] Had she married him, there can be little doubt that Robert would have raised his standard in revolt.[29]

Anjou's departure was one of 'indescribable absurdity',[30] full of tears, recriminations, broken vows and protestations. He did not formally relinquish his position as Elizabeth's lover, but everyone knew that the romance was over. On 7 February 1582, he was escorted to Flushing by Robert (who travelled sorely against his will) with Hunsdon, Sidney, Willoughby, Howard of Effingham, Norreys and 100 gentlemen in fifteen large ships. His task was to counter Spanish power. He was without French support but enjoyed an English alliance and £50,000 provided by Elizabeth, which she paid to the States General. It was a diplomatic triumph for her. She had wriggled out of marrying him and England had not, officially at least, been dragged into the Netherlands conflict.

On arrival at Flushing, Anjou was met by William of Orange and a host of local dignitaries. They were unimpressed with him, and it was Robert whom William considered more useful to his interests. This was their first meeting and they spent many hours together, often with Sidney present.[31] On 19 February 1583, William and Robert escorted Anjou to Antwerp where William presented Robert with a most handsome gilt cup covered in jewels as a gift for Elizabeth. She was soon greatly concerned at the warm relationship developing between them. She had hoped to use Anjou's presence 'to resist the inevitability of [Robert's] Netherlands policy',[32] and quickly ordered Robert's return. So long as the fiction of Anjou's rule there could be maintained, Elizabeth could retain Robert at home, but Henry III quickly repudiated his brother's actions. In January 1583, her 'frog' left the Netherlands, completely discredited after trying to wrest control of Antwerp from his Flemish allies and died eighteen months later on 10 June 1584. With Elizabeth having shown her hand in antagonism towards the Spanish, she was now left without a French alliance.

The death of Anjou caused the French another much greater concern. It made the Huguenot Henry of Navarre the heir to the French throne to succeed the childless Henry III. The ultra-Catholic Guise faction at the French court entered into a 'Holy League' with Spain to guard against a Protestant succession in France. This freed Philip II from French interference in the Netherlands, allowing Parma's strength in the south to become seemingly irresistible. Although the United Provinces again looked to William of Orange as their saviour, on 10 July 1584 he was assassinated in Delft by a Catholic fanatic. There were fears that Elizabeth would be next.[33] Robert readied himself to take up William's cause. 'In May 1584, he wrote urging Elizabeth to forswear foreign alliances and rely on "the mighty and assured strength you have at home".'[34] Many feared that a 'Protestant-Catholic Armageddon was almost upon them'.[35]

By this time, Sussex was ill (Mendosa claimed he was consumptive) and he died on 9 June 1583, 'implacable to the last in his hatred of Robert'.[36] His dying words to Hatton were: 'Beware of the gipsy, he will be too hard for you all. You do not know the beast as we do.'[37] Elizabeth arranged his burial in St Edward's Chapel at Westminster Abbey.

> His chivalry and integrity, his brusque honesty and protective tenderness had been Elizabeth's assets ever since she came to the throne twenty-five years before … He had seen her through a policy of caution, economy, vigilance, self-dedication and single-minded passion, come to a state of hived-up riches and power, and a place in the people's hearts which even her father had not surpassed.[38]

His death had lost her the voice of caution that had been ever-present at her ear. It left the door open for Robert's pursuit of a more aggressive foreign policy that Sussex had so much feared. Nevertheless, Robert was considered two-faced and remained unpopular.

The Holy League began to infiltrate both England and Scotland with plotting in support of Mary Queen of Scots. In July 1582, Mendosa had claimed to Philip II that he had recruited Norfolk's brother, Lord Henry Howard, and Sir James Croft, the Comptroller of the Household, as agents for the Spanish cause. Walsingham immediately blackmailed Howard into silence and Robert seems to have threatened Croft, whom he strongly disliked, to prevent further information being divulged. To deal with the threat posed by Mary in England, Walsingham had employed two moles: Charles Paget in Archbishop Bethune's office in Paris, and Louis Feron, a clerk in the French Embassy in London. As soon as Paget received Mary's correspondence, he divulged its content to both Elizabeth and James VI.

By late 1583, Esmé Stuart in Scotland had successfully ingratiated himself with the young James VI and had been created Duke of Lennox (he was a kinsman of the Lennox Stuarts and was granted the Lennox title despite the claims of Arbella's father, Charles, who also used the title of Earl of Lennox). Nevertheless, when Philip II dragged his feet over providing military support for Esmé, Walsingham's spy network had time to uncover his plotting to place Mary on the Scottish and English thrones. This resulted in Esmé being expelled from Scotland and the Guise-led Enterprise of England having to be abandoned. This did not prevent Mary from continuing to harbour romantic notions of rescue. Feron reported that the Catholic Francis Throckmorton (a nephew of Sir Nicholas) was carrying her correspondence to both Paris and Madrid. Throckmorton was arrested and, before his execution, was tortured to reveal the extent of the plot to rescue her. It became clear that Mendosa was masterminding the invasion plan and Mary was conversant with its details. Mendosa had undertaken to contact justices of the peace with Catholic sympathies with a view to levying English Catholic support for invading forces. By this time, the Catholic hierarchy in England had been so infiltrated by Walsingham's double agents that Cardinal Allen at Douai believed that papist support against Elizabeth was much greater than it was. The revelations of Throckmorton's Catholic plotting also intensified 'the severity and cruelty with which missionary priests were treated' after arrest.[39] When Mendosa was hauled up before the Council, he was given fifteen days to leave. The French ambassador, Castelnau, was also thoroughly implicated, but Walsingham preferred to use blackmail to force him to divulge the full extent of Mary's correspondence. Thoroughly disgraced, he was replaced in September 1585 by Guillaume de l'Aubéspine, Baron de Châteauneuf. Although Mary was aware of the planning, her letters were carefully worded and Elizabeth did not feel that she had sufficient evidence to implicate her.

Walsingham and Robert now argued that Elizabeth could not assure her personal safety and the security of her Crown, unless Mary were dead.[40] Although James VI was safely back in Protestant hands, there was still strong support for Mary in Scotland, and it would be difficult to resist her claim for either Crown if Elizabeth should die childless. Elizabeth was in no doubt of the danger. In March, she had told Parliament: 'I know no creature that breathes whose life standeth hourly in more peril for religion than mine own.'[41] Nevertheless, she refused 'an armed bodyguard, declaring she had sooner be dead than in such captivity'.[42] Her instinct was to go freely among her people.

Chapter 24

Leicester's Commonwealth

It was becoming clear to English Catholics living on the Continent that they needed to undermine anti-papist propaganda in Britain. Their objective was to turn 'popular anger away from the Queen of Scots and her supporters ... directing it upon Dudley and his faction'.[1] A group of unidentified Catholics collaborated to write an attack on Elizabeth's Protestant Government, recognising that the pen was mightier than the sword![2] The objective was to gain acceptance of Mary Queen of Scots as Elizabeth's heir.

On 29 September 1584, Walsingham reported that the Lord Mayor of London had received a printed document which libelled Robert. He described it as 'the most maliciously written thing that ever was penned since the beginning of the world'.[3] He claimed that he had been warned by his agents three years earlier of the existence of such a document, with an intention to provide a similar one about Elizabeth. From the outset he believed that it emanated from English Catholics living in Paris, but it was thought to have been printed in Antwerp or Paris during the summer of 1584. To limit its circulation, he instructed the Lord Mayor to send him his copy so that it was kept securely out of view. Nevertheless, other printed versions in England needed to be hunted down.

With Robert being a leading Puritan and the wealthiest and best known of Elizabeth's advisers, he was an obvious target. He was probably singled out because he was 'the firmest and most influential advocate of the Protestant faith'.[4] His Puritanism was considered hypocritical when compared with his indisputably blemished private life, and the treatise provides a vitriolic personal attack on his perceived shortcomings. With his control of patronage having given him an 'unassailable position in the royal household', enabling him to filter access to the monarch, he is portrayed as an over-mighty subject aiming at supreme power. This criticism wasn't new. He had been the subject of hostile comment and even assassination attempts throughout the reign. Nevertheless, the document has had a profound impact on the way he has been viewed by historians. 'Camden was just one of many who contributed to his blackened reputation.'[5] Robert was not alone in facing hostility; Elizabeth was hardly ever free from plots (or perceived plots) against her rule. Cecil, Bacon, Walsingham, Hatton and others had all faced threats.[6] Furthermore, 'calumny was an established weapon in the armoury of religious and political pamphleteers'.[7]

The work's first edition was given an innocent sounding title:

> *The Copy of a Letter written by a Master of Arts of Cambridge to his friend in London, concerning some talk passed of late between two worshipful and grave men about the present state, and some proceedings of the Earl of Leicester and his friends in England.*[8]

It followed the pattern of many religious tracts by conducting a debate between three disputants: a Cambridge teacher, a London gentleman, and a Catholic lawyer, 'loyal educated subjects who do not support religious extremists',[9] giving all the superficial appearance of a debate on Christian dogma. They argue that extreme Puritans are just as potent enemies of the state as papists. It is 'the great falcons for the field',[10] the court favourites, who promote discord for their own end and prevent harmony. It advocates religious toleration, entirely in accordance with establishment policy as propounded by John Whitgift, the new Archbishop of Canterbury.[11] This opens the way for a vituperative attack on Robert.

Within a year there were French and Latin versions circulating on the Continent, with titles clearly indicating the pamphlet's true intent. One is called: *A discourse on the abominable life, plots, treasons, murders, falsehoods, poisonings, lusts, incitements and evil stratagems employed by the Earl of Leicester.*[12] Another is: *Calvinist Blossoms plucked from the life of Robert Dudley, Earl of Leicester.* As there was an unfounded rumour that the author was the Jesuit Robert Parsons, and it had a green cover, it was also sometimes known as *Father Parsons' Greencoat,* but is now better known as *Leicester's Commonwealth.*[13] The authorities were fairly successful in stifling printed copies arriving in England and it did not cause a huge stir, but it circulated quickly among the Catholic community, who made manuscript copies before passing it on to others. This meant that there were more manuscript versions available than printed ones.

Thomas Lupton, a popular Puritan propagandist, wrote a short tract praising Robert, entitled *A Virtuous Life*, and there were several other efforts to support him.[14] Although they were sent to Robert, he saw no pressing need to defend himself or to publish them. Sidney wrote a rebuttal refuting all the libellous accusations, and belittling the authors' reputed sources as unrealistic, but it was not printed in his lifetime. He asked why they had kept their views hidden for the sake of secrecy, but now suddenly put them into print. He argued that it was 'so full of horrible villainies as no good heart will think possible to enter into any creature, much less to be likely in so noble and well known a man as he is.'[15] On 16 February 1585, James VI issued a repudiation from Holyrood as 'a libel devised and set out by some seditious person of purpose to obscure with lewd lies the honour of our trusted cousin the Earl of Leicester'.[16] Robert had by now cultivated a warm relationship with the Scottish King as a potential heir to the English throne, so James's defence was heartfelt. Reference to Robert as 'cousin' related to the marriage of Guildford Dudley to Jane Grey. With the document being widely circulated in Paris, it became a considerable embarrassment to Sir Edward Stafford (now married to Douglas Howard), the English ambassador. Charles Paget, who may not, by then, have been converted into Walsingham's agent, wrote to Mary Queen of Scots that Robert assumed she was privy to its publication and had plans to persecute her. This seems unlikely as there is no evidence of Robert making any personal effort to suppress or refute it.

Notwithstanding that the document is patently unreliable, it was clearly written by people with a good knowledge of the court and the events of Robert's life. Its principal thrust is to accuse him of trying to remove all the rightful Tudor claimants of the English throne so that, when Elizabeth stood alone, he could assassinate her to promote the Plantagenet claim of his brother-in-law, Huntingdon. 'Yet it is not unlikely but that he will play the bear when he cometh to dividing the prey and will snatch the best parts for himself.'[17] Robert and Huntingdon 'needed only to persuade Elizabeth to dispose of her prisoner Mary, and then the Queen herself would be at their mercy.'[18] For anyone knowing Robert, this was an outrageously far-fetched distortion and not worthy of attention. Whatever his relationship with Elizabeth, 'hatred and distain played no part in it'.[19] Nevertheless, the story plays on the awesome prospect of what would happen on Elizabeth's death if the management of the succession were left in the hands of Robert and his cronies. Its moral is that safety lies in support for the Stuart claim.

In other respects, the book has huge attraction. It is full of racy gossip and scandal written in a vivid style. This has allowed it greatly to influence our understanding of historical events, with its content being taken as fact without any test of its sources. It makes the conflicting suggestions that Amy Robsart was poisoned; that her neck was found broken on the stairs without her hood having being disturbed; that she was first buried at Cumnor before being exhumed for burial at Oxford (which is definitively untrue); that Robert had thwarted every noble match proposed to the Queen, telling envoys that he was already betrothed to her; that Throckmorton (his close ally Sir Nicholas) was poisoned by a salad at Leicester House after reporting that Mary Queen of Scots had referred to Robert as Elizabeth's groom; that Robert had procured the deaths of Essex, Margaret Lennox and Sussex by poison; that Dr Julio administered poison with a delayed effect, and with differing side effects to suit the circumstances (as Dr Julio was Italian and Italians were considered experts in the use of poison, this was a plausible dart to aim); that Robert had made three unsuccessful attempts to murder Simier; that he had conspired with Ambrose to prevent the Anjou match by force if necessary; that an abortion was performed on Lettice by Dr Julio before Essex's death; that he first married Lettice at Kenilworth, before their official marriage at Wanstead (which is probably true); that Lettice raged for many months at Elizabeth's anger at her marriage to Robert; that Douglas and Lettice were known as 'his Old and New testaments'; that he kept 'a void place for a new subcontract with any other when occasion shall require' (which is very unlikely given Lettice's hold over him); that Robert's enormous power and wealth had been established through 'the gracious and sweet dispositions of her Majesty ... he is better furnished at this day than ever any subject of our land' (which his need for extensive borrowings shows is not true); that he had committed high treason by attempting to place Huntingdon on the throne (which is certainly untrue); that he had conspired to achieve supreme power by supporting the claims of Arbella Stuart to the throne; that he had disrupted good order as Chancellor of Oxford University (which is the opposite of the truth); that he is guilty of private infamy as a murderer, a lecher 'of omnivorous appetite',[20] whose failing powers were revived by Italian preparations. It claims:

> No man's wife can be free from him whom his fiery lust liketh to abuse … kinswoman, ally, friend's wife or daughter, or whatsoever female sort besides doth please his eye … must yield to his desire … There are not (by report) two noblewomen about her Majesty … whom he hath not solicited by potent ways; neither contented with this place of honour, he hath descended to seek pasture among the waiting gentlewomen of her Majesty's Great Chamber … if three hundred pounds for the night will make up the sum … even in the laundry itself, or other place of baser quality.[21]

He is seen as a covetous tyrant and 'an atheist who [has] exploited both Catholics and Protestants to serve his turn', an implacable enemy of Archbishop Grindal and Sir John Throckmorton. Although Grindal certainly suffered a rift with Elizabeth, it was Robert who defended him, but *Leicester's Commonwealth* implies that Robert hounded Grindal to death. There is also a claim that Robert brought Sir John Throckmorton (a Catholic brother of Sir Nicholas) 'pitifully to his grave before his time by continual vexations'.[22] Yet, Dr A.L. Rowse confirms that Sir John was:

> a disagreeable man, a harsh landlord, an indifferent Royal servant, a papist, and something of a rogue. In 1576 he fell foul of the Council, was stripped of his offices and was confined for a spell in the Fleet prison. He died soon after.[23]

There is no indication that Robert was particularly responsible for his comeuppance, and he appears to have received only his just rewards.

Leicester's Commonwealth concludes with 'a heap of enormities: theft; simony [the buying and selling of ecclesiastical benefices]; embezzlement; treachery; treason of all kinds; private malice; covetousness; niggardliness; attempts to throttle free speech in Parliament; and encouragement to all honest men to put him down'.[24] It provides the first clearly expressed, but highly doubtful, evidence that he had murdered Amy Robsart, despite the coroner's verdict of accidental death. It claims that while he was conducting his liaison with Lettice before their marriage, she followed the court 'by privy ways', moving from house to house out of sight of the Queen. As a punishment for his lascivious way of life, it says that 'he had developed abscesses on his stomach – 'a broken belly on both sides of his bowels whereby misery and putrefaction is threatened to him daily'.[25] It claims that the Noble Imp had falling sickness (epilepsy – which is a fabrication) 'as a consequence of the parents' sins'.[26]

Perhaps more potently, *Leicester's Commonwealth* also criticises Robert's Dudley ancestry, with both his father and grandfather having died on the scaffold. It claims:

> He has nothing of his own, either from his ancestors or himself, to stay upon in men's hearts or conceits; he hath not ancient nobility as others of our realm have, whereby men's affections are greatly moved. As for valour: 'He hath as much as hath a mouse.'[27]

It was this criticism that so greatly incensed Philip Sidney, and the implication that his grandfather, Northumberland, was not a gentleman born. Sidney considered it an honour, through his mother, to be a Dudley. He assumed that the libellers' motive was to 'backbite boldly so that, though the bite were healed, so the scar would remain'.[28] He offered to challenge the author in single combat anywhere in Europe. His motive for defending his uncle from anonymous libellers has been questioned, but there was huge importance being attached to *Leicester's Commonwealth* by Robert's enemies.

The Queen avoids criticism, but the document claims she is '"of no strong or robustious constitution" but harassed by Robert until she acceded to his demands however unreasonable … and in actual danger from his resentment because she thwarted his ambition by refusing to marry him'.[29] The authors call on her to act against Robert. Far from this, she provided a signed report to disassociate herself from its findings, 'of which most malicious and wicked imputations her Majesty in her own clear knowledge doth declare and testify his innocency to all the world'.[30] She saw the implied criticism of her government as highly damaging. Copies of her report were distributed through the Lord Mayor in London and in the northern counties. The Privy Council also closed ranks behind Robert, denouncing the document as having 'proceeded of the fullness of malice'.[31] They ridiculed it: 'As though her Majesty should ... want either good will, ability or courage (if she knew these enormities were true) to call any subject of hers whatsoever and to render sharp account of them, according to the forces and effects of her laws!'[32]

If the authors' aim was to 'spread discord throughout the realm and within the government', causing Elizabeth 'to remove [Robert] from his pedestal',[33] they were disappointed. There is no evidence that it 'had any great impact upon public opinion at the time'.[34] She was far more loyal than her father, and it never crossed her mind. In 1584, Robert was officially designated to the important role of Lord Steward of the Household, the central position at court. This has to be seen as an attempt by Elizabeth to demonstrate her contempt for *Leicester's Commonwealth*. She had considered relieving Robert from his role as Master of the Horse in view of the workload involved in both appointments, but this would have sent out the wrong message and Robert strongly objected to losing a position that kept him in close contact with her. This remained particularly important, given Lettice's continued banishment from court.

The only person found guilty was Ralph Emerson, who was caught circulating the pamphlet. He and a Jesuit, John Weston, brought copies from France provided by Robert Parsons, who seems to have been a distributor, but not an author. The Bishop of Hereford's son, Sylvanus Scory – a notorious papist – was arrested but later freed by Walsingham. He admitted having heard of the book but claimed never to have seen it. Other names mentioned were generally within the circle of Mary Queen of Scots' supporters in Paris, but there was insufficient evidence to accuse anyone.

It was not until 1641 that the book was republished as *Leicester's Commonwealth*. By then, Thomas Wentworth, Earl of Strafford, was facing impeachment by Parliament after acting as a hatchet man for Charles I. His power and unpopularity bore similarities to Robert's status as an 'over-mighty subject'. The Regicides grasped on this earlier tale to justify Strafford's execution, from which Charles I was in no position to defend him.[35]

Chapter 25

Governor of the Netherlands

In 1585, Elizabeth was again asked by a commission of the Netherlands States to accept the Dutch Crown, but she refused, as to do so would be seen as a declaration of war on Spain. Nevertheless, she agreed to send an English force with both money and men, while expecting repayment when the war was over. As a pledge, she was to hold one town in each province.[1] Although she wanted her assistance provided secretly, the Council told her that this would deprive her aid of its effect. In August, she realised that she had no further option but to send English troops. There were several contributory factors: the assassination of William of Orange; the refusal by Henry III to provide French support for the rebels; and Parma's conquest of the south.[2] She agreed to send 4,000 (later increased to 6,000) foot and 1,000 horse and to provide a loan of £125,000 for their maintenance. She retained Brill and Flushing in English control as pledges against repayment.[3] It was later agreed that Burghley's eldest son, Sir Thomas Cecil, would become governor of Brill, and Sidney would take charge of the garrison at Flushing.

With Robert spending the summer recuperating at Kenilworth and Buxton, it was Walsingham, who argued the case for intervention, but Robert confirmed his willingness to lead the expeditionary force and saw his appointment as a means of making a name for himself. Elizabeth continued to vacillate on whether to give him the command, as she wanted him beside her. He had not been involved in military conflict since fighting for the King of Spain in 1557, and his understanding of military strategy was outmoded. He undoubtedly overestimated his own abilities – and was overweight, but both Walsingham and Burghley agreed on his suitability, particularly as he would be prepared to spend his own money in support of the venture. He would also have experienced lieutenants such as Sir John Norreys and the Welsh veteran Sir Roger Williams beside him. Although Burghley had always been ambivalent about taking a hawkish stand, even he was supportive, but wanted expenditure kept within reasonable bounds. Walsingham saw it as the opportunity he had been waiting for to pitch a Protestant alliance into conflict against Spain's Catholic aggression. Elizabeth vacillated. After signing the covenant to provide aid, she stayed its dispatch. 'The danger of provoking a declaration of war from Spain was so great that it threw [her] into almost unbearable agitation.'[4] When Robert returned to court in September, he found her 'on the verge of nervous collapse'.[5] He sat up with her through several sleepless nights, while she complained that she did not want him to go. By now he was finding her appeals to him tedious and frustrating. He wrote to Walsingham:

> I find her Majesty very desirous to stay me. She makes the cause only the doubtfulness of her own self, by reason of her oft disease taking her of late and this last night worst of all. She used very pitiful words to me for fear that she shall not live and would not have me from her. You can consider what manner of persuasion this must be to me from her … I would not say much for any matter but did comfort her as well as I could, only I did let her know how far I had gone in preparation. I do think for all this that if she be well tonight, she will let me go, for she would not have me speak of it to the contrary to anybody … pray you send my wife word in the morning that I cannot come before Thursday to London.[6]

By 24 September, Elizabeth had accepted that Robert would lead the expedition as requested by the States General, but could not bring herself to sign the order. On her instruction, Robert had retired to Leicester House to write to 200 friends and dependents to muster at the end of October with men and harness. He raised a loan from his bankers and took Ambrose to requisition armour at the Tower of London.[7] Two days later, she again called everything off. He received a message from Walsingham telling him that he would need to speak to her. Although his official response to the Queen, written at 2.00 am, submitted to her will, his private message to Walsingham complained at the irreparable damage of any delay to England's standing in the Netherlands. The Dutch had implored him to make haste, and he had told them that he would ready himself to set out within fifteen days.[8] It seems that Elizabeth's hesitation at this late stage was in part caused by her concern that Lettice would accompany him. Although initially Lettice had planned to go, this was scotched by the Queen. As far as is known, Lettice made no further attempt to do so, even though other wives, including Frances Sidney, accompanied their husbands. Robert was fed up and retired to Wanstead, asking for Sidney to come to him. Later the same day, Walsingham was able to confirm that Elizabeth had withdrawn her objections and the expedition was on again.

Robert did not receive official orders until December, and they were not what he had hoped for. Elizabeth remained nervous. This was not a plan for a Protestant war of liberation. Everything about it was penny-pinching:

> The Lieutenant General was to fight a purely defensive campaign and not to 'hazard a battle without great advantage'. English captains must not be allowed to misappropriate funds. [He] must ensure that the Dutch contributions to the war effort were efficiently collected …
> As [security] for her expenditure Elizabeth … claimed Flushing, Brill and Rammakens [which Robert was to garrison and administer]. He was to act in a purely advisory capacity towards the States General.[9]

She was not attempting to take away these territories from the King of Spain, their lawful sovereign, but was seeking only to secure a degree of civil and religious freedom for the Dutch. The Swedish King considered it 'uncommonly brave of her to risk the crown on her head; no one else in Europe was going to do such a thing'.[10] Elizabeth's policy, which she applied consistently, was to maintain the Spanish in control of the Netherlands as a means of keeping out the French, but she would support the local nobility and local liberties so they were strong enough to prevent the Netherlands being used as a base for a Spanish invasion of England.

Robert was nervous at having limitations imposed on him and wrote to Burghley while still in England to express his doubts and fears at Elizabeth's apparent ambivalence. He hoped that he could rely on Burghley's 'particular good will and regard for [him]',[11] to ensure that she followed through with her commitment, which he duly did. Nevertheless, shortly before Robert's departure Burghley remonstrated over a personal slight against him reported by his tiresome sister-in-law, Lady Russell (née Elizabeth Cooke). She had told him that Robert had made derogatory remarks about him. Robert knew that Burghley was sensitive to personal criticism. He replied that there was no truth in Lady Russell's assertions: 'Your own wisdom will easily discharge me, being so well acquainted with the devices and practices of these days, which men go about rather to sow discord betwixt such as we are, than to do good offices.'[12] He did not need to be side-tracked by having to deal with such issues.

On 8 December 1585, having left Lettice to manage his vast estates, Robert set out for Harwich with a personal retinue of ninety-nine gentlemen and yeoman officers with their servants, including chaplains, cooks, musicians and a troupe of actors. They comprised the cream of the English force, who had answered his call to arms. The bulk of the army of 1,000 cavalry and 6,000 foot sailed from the Thames. Essex, who was ready to taste military action for the first time, accompanied him. When he started to recruit men, he incurred the wrath of his grandfather, Sir Francis Knollys, for running up huge debts. Knollys wrote hoping that 'youthful wilfulness and wasteful youth do not consume you before experienced wisdom shall have reformed you'.[13]

Robert did not know the terrain he was fighting over, and it 'was partially submerged by tidal waters and intersected by dykes, [which] had hitherto proved one of the best defences of the country.'[14] Manoeuvring to every objective was made difficult by intersecting waterways. He was up against Parma, the most brilliant military general of his age, who had used his eight years of experience in the Netherlands to make a minute study of the local landscape. Parma had successfully subdued the southern part of the country and was threatening Antwerp.

Robert's impossible situation caused him to become hopelessly overtaxed. For someone with a reputation for mildness, he became easily irritated, prone to bouts of bad temper and unable to accept criticism. In November 1583, his old friend, John Aylmer, had written:

> I have ever observed in you such a mild, courteous and amiable nature, that you never kept as graven in marble, but written in sand, the greatest displeasure that ever you

conceived against any man. I fear not, therefore, my good Lord, in this strait that I am in to appeal from this Lord of Leicester ... unto mine old Lord of Leicester, who in his virtue of mildness and of softness ... hath carried away the praise of all men.[15]

It was the fall of Antwerp that finally triggered Robert's departure. He had recently fallen from his horse and told Burghley that he could not pull his boot on. On leaving Harwich, he instructed Admiral Stephen Borough to head for Brill. Borough remonstrated that the harbour at Brill was unsuited to so large a fleet, that Flushing was a better anchorage and he had insufficient pilots for a landing at Brill. Robert fumed that he should get more pilots, and instructions were sent to the Thames fleet to make for Brill. Eventually, Borough's experience and the pilots' advice won the day and the fleet made for Flushing, although the confusion meant that some of the Thames vessels, laden with horses and provisions, landed at Brill.

On arrival, Robert's troops received an ecstatic and unified reception from the Netherlanders, with banquets, church bells, cannon and fireworks. People in the streets shouted: 'God save Queen Elizabeth.'[16] Robert was received by Sidney, who had set out three weeks earlier, and over the next two-and-a-half weeks, made a triumphant progress passing through Middelburg, Dordrecht, Rotterdam and Delft to the Hague, with each town competing to provide ever more magnificent displays of welcome.[17] At Delft, the citizenry spent £5,000 on their greeting. Masques and plays hinted at Elizabeth's sovereignty and Robert's princely standing.

Robert plunged himself into his task with great vigour, 'because he believed that the security of the United Provinces was inextricably bound up with the safety of England'.[18] Nevertheless, it is hard to imagine a project facing so many pitfalls. He had to deal with Elizabeth who, in typical fashion, was hopelessly ambivalent about any decision to support the expedition or to provide Robert with authority to act decisively. He led a combined English and Dutch army, 'whose interests differed, and who needed a general of clear vision and iron will to hold them together'.[19] The United Provinces were united in name only and failed to agree a clear plan of action or to take decisive military decisions.

Although they expected him to lead them, they proved unreliable and failed to provide the money to fulfil their part of the bargain.

> There were the zealous Reformers, particularly strong among the urban working class and led by firebrand Calvinist ministers, many of whom had fled from the south and had all the enthusiasm of religious exiles; there were the burgher oligarchies of the towns of Holland whose guiding principle was the maintenance of trade and municipal prosperity; there was the small, but by no means irrelevant Catholic minority, quite capable of betraying a walled city to besiegers; and the noble class, the traditional leaders of Netherlands society, whose members shared a common concern for national and territorial integrity but could not agree on how to achieve it.[20]

Each of these groups was represented in the States General, which was split into political factions unable to agree whether to support French, English or Prince Maurice of Nassau. Burghley despaired of them, complaining that if they could not trust each other, it was difficult to see how anyone else could trust them.

The campaign was already wreaking havoc with Elizabeth's carefully husbanded exchequer. She began preliminary discussions with Parma over the possibility of coming to a settlement. It soon became clear that Philip II would never countenance religious toleration, despite the economic consequences for himself, and his campaign of persecution was based entirely on religious fanaticism. Nevertheless, Elizabeth argued that it was one faith and one Jesus Christ, hoping that if a return to Catholicism were conceded, she could gain fiscal and civil liberties for the seventeen states in revolt and arrange the removal of the Spanish army of occupation. As eleven of these were already Catholic, she did not believe that a settlement should be foregone simply to satisfy the religious sensibilities of the remaining six. Although this sounds like a sell-out of the Dutch Protestants, she was adhering to the political principle of the day of 'cuius regio eius religio – it was the business of the Prince to determine the faith of his subjects'.[21] Any acceptance of Catholic observances, however, completely contravened the wishes of the United Provinces, 'whose inhabitants were prepared to die rather than concede their right to worship in the way they considered the only true one'.[22]

When the Dutch heard rumours of Elizabeth's negotiations, Robert and his colleagues on the ground believed that they were about to desert their English allies. Robert soon realised that the Netherlands were in great confusion:

> the common people without obedience; the soldiers in misery and disorder for want of pay; the governors weary and tired for lack of good assistance and due obedience; the provinces themselves staggering in their union; and every town near [the Spanish] ready to seek new means for their safety, such was their fear of the enemy, triumphant with continual victories and especially now with the recovery of Antwerp; so little was their hope of their own ability to resist and so many were the enemy's deep and secret practices, even in the very bowels of them.[23]

Despite their lack of cohesion, the Dutch were determined to extract every last penny out of their English allies. If they could persuade them to take political control in a gesture of defiance against Spain, Elizabeth would be forced to commit all her material resources behind them. It might also weld them into a unified group with Spain as the common enemy. Elizabeth had already turned down the crown on two occasions, realising that its acceptance would be dynamite.

Robert was instructed to sow seeds that she might accept the crown if the provinces worked in unity together and raised 'liberal taxations' for their own defence. He was to create a new assembly with authority to act without every important decision having to be referred back to provincial governments.[24] He received rather different advice from the Dutch treaty commissioners. They expected him to take the offensive both by sea and land, and to 'keep his court' at Middelburg. He was also to promote the 'reformed evangelical religion' and to bar papists from important offices.[25]

On New Year's Day 1586, a delegation approached Robert with an offer to appoint him as supreme Governor of the United Provinces. This would give him control of Government in all matters civil as well as military.[26] He knew he needed the Queen's approval and, after giving a noncommittal answer, sent a message to England to seek her advice. The idea of it greatly appealed to his inflated ego, allowing him to tour the United Provinces of Holland and Zeeland in royal state. Nevertheless, for someone who claimed to know Elizabeth's mind better than anyone, and knew she had turned down the Crown, he was treading on very dangerous ground with her. On 14 and 15 January, he wrote to Burghley and Walsingham to explain that the Dutch remained insistent on him becoming Governor, and common sense dictated acceptance, even though Elizabeth might disapprove. He argued that the so-called United Provinces needed a powerful figurehead to prevent further quarrelling and make them work together. The timing was critical, as no money had been sent to pay troops from either England or the United Provinces, and Parma was progressively gaining control of towns, some of which were coming to terms with his agents. The letters arrived safely in England, but, with the wind continually in the north and east, no ships could leave for the Dutch coast and Robert waited in vain for a reply. On 22 January, he again wrote to Walsingham urging the Queen not to delay as the enemy was temporarily perplexed.[27] On 25 January, the Dutch persuaded him to wait no longer, and 'in a burst of splendour' he was invested with the 'highest and supreme commandment' within the United Provinces. He sent Davison to explain and to excuse his action to the Queen, but Davison was held up by adverse winds and did not arrive until 5 February.

Robert's decision was most unwise. Unfortunately, Elizabeth heard the news, not from Davison, but in a letter received from the Hague by one of her ladies. Quite maliciously, this reported that Lettice was about to arrive 'with such a train of ladies and gentlewomen, and such rich coaches, litters and side saddles as her majesty had none such [to] establish a court of ladies as should far pass her majesty's court'.[28] Although there was no truth in this, it was in direct contravention of her instruction before Robert had left England, and the letter from the Hague seemed entirely plausible. As late as 24 March, Sidney had heard rumours of Lettice's planned arrival and hoped to stay her from coming. Elizabeth was apoplectic, telling Lettice that there were to be no English courts except her own. It took her months to view Robert's position as Governor dispassionately. She believed she had been deceived and that all her advisers were aware of what he had done but lacked the courage to tell her. She sent a letter to him without a greeting:

> How contemptuously we conceive ourself to have been used by you, you shall by this bearer understand, whom we have expressly sent unto you to charge you withal. We could never have imagined had we not seen it fall out in experience that a man raised up by ourself and extraordinarily favoured by us above any other subject of this land, would have in so contemptible a sort broken our commandment, in a cause that so greatly toucheth us in honour; whereof, although you have showed yourself to make but little accompt, in most undutiful sort, you may not therefore think that we have so little care of the reparation thereof as we mind to pass so great a wrong in silence unredressed: and, therefore, our express pleasure and commandment is, that all delays and excuses laid apart, you do presently, upon the duty of your allegiance, obey and fulfil whatever the bearer hereof shall direct you to do in our name: whereof fail you not, as you will answer the contrary at your uttermost peril.[29]

The bearer was to be Heneage, probably chosen because he had been Robert's rival at court.

It was only now that Davison reached London, having gone first to Walsingham and being shocked to find him so downcast. When Elizabeth received him in the inner drawing room at Greenwich, her anger was 'at white heat throughout the interview'.[30] She 'harangued him' over 'Robert's ingratitude and disobedience'.[31] He provided Robert's explanations, 'but could not slake her consuming indignation'.[32] Taking control of the Netherlands to conduct an aggressive campaign was the one thing Elizabeth had wanted to avoid. She saw his action as treachery, insolence, self-seeking and maddening idiocy.[33] Davison could not persuade her to change the letter she had written three days before. He persisted by seeking a further meeting and was granted two more interviews. Although supported by all her principal advisers, he made very little progress, but eventually persuaded her to modify her instructions to Heneage and to study Robert's account of his negotiations with the States General.

When Burghley heard that Robert was required to make a public renunciation of the governorship at the place he had received it, he remonstrated that the effect would be disastrous, and it would be a lesser evil to allow him to retain it in a personal capacity. When Elizabeth refused to listen, he obliged her to compromise by threatening to resign. A formula was eventually found to enable her to accept Robert as governor, as he had accepted it from the people of the United Provinces and had not usurped it from his monarch. Any attempt by the States to provide the English Crown with sovereignty was utterly repudiated. In all matters affecting the Crown, Robert remained Elizabeth's Lieutenant General, and he was careful to demonstrate his subordinate position on public and ceremonial occasions.[34] At the St George's Day Feast at Utrecht, a chair of state was set aside for the absent Queen, while Robert sat on a stool at the end of the high table. During the banquet, food and drink were proffered to the vacant chair.

Ambrose wrote to Robert to support his acceptance of the governorship but warned him that Elizabeth's 'malice is unquenchable'. He assured him: 'You were never so honoured and loved in your life amongst all good people as you are at this day, only for dealing so nobly and wisely in this action as you have done, so that, whatever cometh of it, you have done your part.'[35] As a further mark of her disapproval, Elizabeth deliberately held back delivery of the funds necessary to pay the army. Robert was full of 'abject self-commiseration'. He asked to return home to resume his duties as Master of the Horse.[36] He should have stood up to her, but instead wrote a long minute, blaming Davison for encouraging him to accept the governorship without her consent, which Davison hotly denied. Elizabeth did not blame Davison and he was appointed to the Council in July, later becoming Elizabeth's secretary. In March, Robert sent Sir Thomas Shirley and Thomas Vavasour to London to explain his position. Shirley adopted the tactic of telling Elizabeth that Robert was unwell, and she immediately sent her physician, Dr Goodrowse to administer to him. By the end of the month, Raleigh was able to report that Robert was once again her 'Sweet Robin'.[37] On 1 April, Elizabeth wrote to him that despite the provocation caused by the inappropriate and inexcusable steps he had taken:

> Your grieved and wounded mind hath more need of comfort
> than reproof ... [having] no other meaning and intent than

to advance our service, [so] we think meet to forebear to dwell upon a matter wherein we ourselves do find so little comfort.[38]

By the end of July, the old familiar tone had returned. She wrote:

Now will I end, that do imagine I talk still with you, and, loathly say: 'Farewell ō ō, though ever I pray God bless you from all harm and save you from all foes, with my million and legion thanks for all your pains and cares. As you know, ever the same. E.R.[39]

Robert's principal concern was a shortage of money. Elizabeth was reluctant to provide more, even to pay her troops. She had a point to make and Robert had been cavalier about accounting for his expenditure. She had agreed to send £160,000 per annum – half her normal annual outgoings – and large instalments had already been sent, but she had received no accounts to justify how they had been used. There can be little doubt that costs had been underestimated. The treasurer told Walsingham that disbursements had grown above the rate agreed at the army's departure and Robert had increased officers' pay, including his own, from £6 to £10 13s 4d per day. Burghley made clear that until expenditure was explained, no further money would be forthcoming. There were several areas of confusion. Before Robert's arrival, there had been 7,000 English troops in Holland in the pay of the Dutch, but these were now transferred without explanation to the English payroll. Money to pay troops was delivered to their captains. They drew pay for their full muster, even if some had disappeared by desertion or death. Elizabeth wanted soldiers to be paid individually, but it was claimed that this would be difficult to enforce. This left soldiers' pay months in arrears. This was not unusual; the Dutch thought they were doing well if they paid their men for six months out of twelve. The suffering was dreadful; they lacked clothing and the officers cheated them of food. They made their 'resentment known by indiscipline, desertion and pillaging of the local citizenry'.[40] Robert considered both Elizabeth and the States General 'slow and niggardly' in contributing to costs. He complained vociferously to the Council in London that 'any men sent as we are and in action for the realm ... [should] be so carelessly and overwillingly overthrown for ordinary wants'.[41] He criticised the treasurer for failing to deliver proper accounts as requested and considered him incompetent. (The treasurer's name is unclear. One source says that he was an uncle of Norreys, but this is unlikely.) Robert was left to bemoan lost opportunities. With soldiers at the point of mutiny, he met £11,000 of military expenses out of his own pocket. This simply encouraged the Dutch to delay further contributions. He realised that his authority with the States General had been undermined by Elizabeth dissociating herself from his office of Supreme Governor, which was 'completely hollow'. This had 'cracked his credit'.[42]

In all the difficult circumstances, Robert's shortcomings as a commander have been overplayed but there is no doubting his inability to delegate and work with others. He failed to recognise the abilities of his subordinates or to cooperate with them. The experience of Sir John Norreys should have made him invaluable. He had fought with William of Orange and was remarkably able. Robert fell foul of him at once, likening him to the Earl of Sussex: 'He will so dissemble, so crouch, so cunningly carry his doings as no man living would imagine there were half the malice of vindictive mind that doth plainly in his deeds prove to be.'[43] Unfortunately for Robert, Norreys had the Queen's ear, and she valued him highly. Robert recognised that such men were too powerful to challenge and later came to respect his abilities.

Robert was also vindictive in dealing with the Commissioners of the States General. He complained that it was 'a monstrous government where so many heads do rule', branding them as 'churls and tinkers' who refused to meet their financial obligations. In Holland, it was the towns that controlled the purse strings. They appealed behind his back to Elizabeth, thereby undermining his authority.[44] He found himself needing to depend on every level within the United Provinces to support the military struggle. His natural allies and advisers were the Calvinists, who sought the exclusion of all those not 'zealous in the Reformed faith'. They wanted a national government formed to dominate the town oligarchies. As a Calvinist stronghold, Utrecht became Robert's powerbase, and other Calvinist centres also backed him. These were opposed by 'libertinists' (men who were anti-confessional, secularist and latitudinarian) from their main centre in Leyden. With Holland and Zeeland deriving their wealth from trade, much of it with Spain, they opposed extremist policies. The Calvinists criticised them on both moral and tactical grounds for conducting trade with the enemy, arguing that an embargo would cripple the Spanish, while the libertinists claimed that income from trade deals helped to finance the war effort and the Spanish could easily source goods elsewhere. In April 1586, when Robert embargoed all commerce with Spain, merchants made vociferous complaints and ignored his ban. He set up an audit office to seek out smugglers and imprisoned his former ally, Paul Buis, the foremost of the libertinists and Deputy of Utrecht.[45] With a coterie of powerful enemies now lined up against him, both Burghley and Walsingham concluded that Elizabeth should sue openly for peace, but they wanted the negotiations placed in Robert's hands.

Despite its shortage of funds, the English army rapidly gained Parma's respect and enjoyed striking initial success. By sending English forces into Zeeland and Holland, Robert prevented Parma from overrunning the north after the fall of Antwerp. By garrisoning Brill and Flushing, he prevented his access to a deep-water harbour, thus disabling the use of his fleet to provision his men. Parma showed his respect for the English by carefully counting their numbers in garrisons at each town. Norreys and Count Hohenlohe forced their way with a strong detachment into Grave, which was being heavily besieged by the Spanish. This well-fortified citadel on the Maas defended one of the principal routes into the United Provinces. It was cut off by a series of forts built by the Spanish along the riverbank. On 6 April 1586, English and Dutch troops showed great bravery in routing a much larger enemy force, leaving 500 Spanish dead. Parma's fortifications were dismantled, and Grave was reinforced with fresh troops provisioned for nine months.[46] Despite this boost to morale, Parma reacted quickly. He forced Robert to divide his forces by sending military detachments in different directions. In May, he suddenly drew together his entire army of 12,000 foot and 4,000 cavalry with artillery to renew his assault on Grave, which had been infiltrated with his agents. When Baron Hemart, the Governor, confirmed to Robert that Grave was fully equipped to continue its resistance, Robert focused on diversionary attacks at Nijmegen and other neighbouring forts. With Parma's artillery battering Grave's walls, his agents unnerved its defenders and Hemart surrendered. This caused a huge loss of heart among both soldiers and civilians. Robert accused Hemart of treachery, but he was of a well-connected noble house. Not even William of Orange had dared to challenge such Dutch aristocrats. Hemart was condemned and, despite Norreys's pleas for clemency, Robert approved his execution on 18 June.

Parma was expected to head north, which would have enabled Robert to undertake a flanking attack as he moved, but instead he consolidated his position round Grave. He deployed his troops and artillery to play 'on the timidity of the burgher-dominated towns', resulting in Venlo and Nuys falling in swift succession. With Robert forced into a campaign of siege warfare for which he was ill-equipped, he appealed urgently for sappers and engineers, apparently to little effect. The English had their own successes. In July, Sidney led an attack on Axel. 'At dead of night, he swam the moat with forty men, scaled the wall, and opened the gate to his forces.'[47] This resulted in the capitulation of four other nearby cities. He then breached the dykes to make the surrounding country impassable. People realised that if the English army were properly provisioned, it could challenge the Spanish on equal terms.

Sidney's success strengthened Elizabeth's resolve. On 9 July, Walsingham reported to Robert that she now considered 'the only salve to cure this sore is to make herself proprietary of that country and to put such an army into the same as may be able to make head to the enemy's.' Nevertheless, increasing costs caused her to 'repent that she ever entered into the action'.[48] On 19 July, she wrote to Robert and 'in a burst of tenderness thanked him warmly for what he had done'.[49] She understood the problems, saying: 'It frets me not a little that the poor soldiers that hourly venture life should want their due, that well deserve rather reward.'[50] At last, in August, she sent more money and men, but could not resist taunting Robert to spend his time more constructively and stop his grumbling and accusations.[51]

Elizabeth's optimism was not shared by the Dutch, and the English no longer commanded their respect. When Killigrew was sent to garrison Deventer, the burghers refused his troops entry. They feared that an English presence would commit them to an uncomfortably stiff resistance. Killigrew adopted subterfuge. He kept its council occupied in protracted discussions while sending Edward Stanley into the town with his men disguised as citizens. When Robert sent Sir William Pelham to make a final demand for the garrison's installation, the burghers made ready to resist. At 7.00 am the following morning, Pelham burst into the council chamber while Stanley assembled his men in the marketplace. When one of the councillors tried to raise the alarm, Pelham unleashed his fury at their betrayal. He disbanded the guard on the gates, imprisoned the councillors and appointed new officers to establish English control.

In August, Parma advanced northwards along the line of the Rhine and the Ijssel, hoping to neutralise Overijssel and Groningen, where support for the United Provinces was less secure. He then planned to turn westward into United Provinces' heartland. He began by besieging Rheinsberg; the town's Dutch commander, Sir Martin Schenck, had already shown he was both shrewd and ruthlessly brave and had been knighted by Robert.[52] Rheinsberg held out valiantly for several weeks, buying time for Robert to launch an attack with his entire force on Doesburg, an important outpost for Parma. Robert demonstrated all his father's bravery. He moved among his men regardless of personal safety, inspiring them to greater effort. Pelham, who was standing in front of him, was shot in the stomach, but the wound did not prove fatal and he left the field praising God that he had protected his commander. This show of strength resulted in Doesburg's surrender, forcing Parma to lift his siege of Rheinsberg.[53]

Buoyed up by this success, Robert now moved on to attack Zutphen, protected by two forts on each side of the Ijssel. Although they were considered almost impregnable, Parma was taking no chances. On 22 September, he sent a relief column to support them with supplies, but Robert sent a force of 500 men under Norreys and Sir William Stanley to cut it off. They were supported by fifty volunteers, including Essex and Sidney. After approaching in heavy fog, they only located the baggage trains after they came within earshot. When the fog lifted, it was realised that the column was supported by 3,000 Spanish troops, and the English force was within range of Parma's arquebuses. The English cavalry under Essex was given orders to charge the Spanish lines. Although it performed with conspicuous gallantry despite facing a fusillade of shots, the baggage train managed to enter the town. Nevertheless, the Spanish troops were routed, leaving their ordnance behind. Although English losses were few, Sidney showed reckless bravery in riding deep into enemy ranks, where his horse was shot from under him. As he remounted another, he was shot in the thigh by a musket ball. Although he should have been protected by his armour, he had given his cuisses to Pelham, only recently recovered from his injury. Sidney was able to ride back to camp, but he had lost a lot of blood and called for a drink. He then, famously, offered it to a dying soldier, saying: 'Thy necessity is yet greater than mine!'[54] Robert arranged for him to be taken in his barge to Arnhem, where he was nursed by his wife, Frances, who was six months pregnant. The wound was not thought to be fatal, and he seemed to have overcome the danger of blood poisoning.

On 30 September, Sidney made a will as a precaution. By this time, both Sir Henry and Mary Sidney were dead, but he was Robert's heir. After providing for his wife, he made bequests for all his Dudley relations. Two days later, Robert wrote to Walsingham: 'He amends as well as is possible at this time … he sleeps and rests well and hath a good stomach to eat.'[55] Despite this the wound would not heal; by 8 October, gangrene had set in and he died nine days later. Robert was distraught, writing to Walsingham:

> The grief I have taken for the loss of my dear son and yours would not suffer me to write sooner of those ill news unto you, especially being in so good hope so very little time before of his good recovery. But he is with the Lord and his will must be done. If he had lived, I doubt not that he would have been a comfort to us both, and an ornament to his house. What perfection he has grown unto and how able to serve her majesty and his country all men here almost wondered at. For mine own part, I have lost beside the comfort of my life, a most principal stay and help in my service here and, if I may say it, I think none of all hath a greater loss than the Queen's majesty herself.[56]

This great tragedy was made worse when Frances gave birth to a stillborn child. Nevertheless, it had been a famous victory in which Robert had personally acted with great gallantry and without heeding the advice of his officers to achieve a result against all the odds. Edward Stanley was knighted for his conspicuous part played at the breach of one of the forts, and Essex had also excelled.

Despite Robert's military successes, Elizabeth remained exasperated at the lack of proper accounts. In October, she sent £30,000, demanding that Robert should provide answers to the utilisation of funding that had so far not been forthcoming. With the political divide between the allies widening, Robert renewed his request for a temporary recall to discuss his difficulties in England. He was now being opposed by Johan van Oldenbarneveldt, a Dutch advocate who was uniting burghers and aristocrats in a plan to seek recovery from Spanish domination without outside assistance. Elizabeth also wanted Robert home. She had never felt more alone. She missed his company and needed his advice on how to deal with Mary Queen of Scots. With Lord Grey de Wilton arriving to relieve him, Robert set out for England on 23 November 1586.

Without Robert's presence in the Netherlands, the situation went from bad to worse. In January, all his military gains were wiped out. Sir William Stanley, who had been left in control of Deventer, conspired with Sir Rowland Yorke, the Captain in charge of a small fortress outside Zutphen, to yield their positions to the Spanish. To the consternation of both English and Dutch, they opened their gates to Parma and took most of their men into Philip II's service. Stanley was a Catholic and held a grievance that he had not been properly recompensed for his services in Ireland. He argued that 'he could no longer act for a heretic Queen against the King of Spain'.[57] As the Spanish quickly realised, their treachery sowed great uncertainty into the relationship between Dutch and English forces. It also enabled Oldenbarneveldt to gain support for Robert's replacement as military leader by Maurice of Nassau. When Elizabeth sent Thomas Sackville, Lord Buckhurst, to voice a strong protest, Oldenbarneveldt confirmed that Maurice's appointment was only temporary and did not 'touch the honour either of the Earl of Leicester or the English nation, or prejudice the authority of his lordship, whose speedy return they so earnestly desired.'[58] Buckhurst had also been asked to assess Robert's achievement in command. He was no ally of Robert and reported that it 'had better been bestowed upon a meaner man of more skill'.[59] Oldenbarneveldt missed no opportunity in seeking a limitation of Robert's powers. Buckhurst reported nothing of this, but Calvinist preachers in the Netherlands thundered against the duplicity of their politicians.

There was never any real doubt that Robert would resume his position as Governor General in the Netherlands. Despite his criticisms, even Buckhurst saw the advantage of retaining the continuity that Robert provided. Burghley and Walsingham also supported his reappointment. If Robert were in command, Elizabeth was more likely to hold her nerve and confirm her wholehearted support for the campaign. Buckhurst was an efficient administrator but no great leader, and he soon found himself calling for more money to pay the English troops still stationed there and for more aid for the States General. Although both Robert and the Queen realised that the Dutch were in a dire situation, they were not going to put up with any more of their lukewarm support shown in the previous year. They insisted that the United Provinces should put together an army of 14,000 men and pay for it themselves. For his part, Robert refused to return until all arrears of army pay had been settled and a royal loan of £10,000 was guaranteed to cover his personal expenses.

Meanwhile, Philip II was considering another line of attack, which had been triggered by the execution of Mary Queen of Scots on 8 February 1587. Despite having recovered control of Deventer and Zutphen, Parma was instructed to curtail his advance over the northern part of Holland and to establish control of the Netherlands' coastal ports in preparation for an attack on England. The much discussed 'enterprise' had now become an 'armada'. To launch an attack on the English coast, the Spanish needed access to Sluis, a fortified harbour at the mouth of the Scheldt and to Ostend, both of which were garrisoned by allied troops. Parma began by besieging Sluis, which was protected by a system of defensive waterways. He was hampered by a great shortage of provisions and the siege went slowly. Sir Roger Williams led a detachment of allied troops, which fought its way into the town. With the garrison now strengthened, Sluis's courageous resistance drew even Parma's admiration.

Elizabeth continued her efforts to negotiate peace, and Parma continued in dialogue with her. She still hoped to gain restoration of the States' charters and a withdrawal of Spanish troops. Philip II made clear to Parma that he would grant no concessions and was making 'abundant provision' for his invasion of England. On 14 April 1587, he wrote to him:

> The peace commissioners may meet. But to you only I declare that my intention is that this shall never lead to any result, whatever conditions may be offered to them ... this is done to cool them in their preparations for defence, by inducing them to believe that such preparations will not be necessary.[60]

Elizabeth could not make up her mind how to handle the Netherlands campaign and to Walsingham's consternation, she sat on her hands. She believed that she had lost financial control and 'in a burst of unseasoned fury',[61] held back the money to fund Robert's return. Robert retired to take the waters at Bath although these provided him with no benefit. On 17 April, Walsingham wrote to him that affairs in the Netherlands were becoming critical and he had asked Elizabeth to summon him back. Robert knew that the allies were having a hard time of it. On 7 June, he wrote to Christopher Blount, his young Gentleman of the Horse, to commiserate with him after being wounded in the hand, but confirming that troops were being mustered for his return. As always, Elizabeth was concerned for Robert's health and did not want him hurriedly recalled from Bath. It was midsummer when she agreed to make an advance, conditional on it being repaid within one year. On 4 July 1587, Robert set out from Margate with 4,000 fresh troops and 400 horse backed by £30,000 in funding. Although Essex set out for the coast to rejoin his stepfather, Elizabeth recalled her new favourite to her side. While the troops were landed at Ostend under Pelham's command, Robert was transported to Flushing in warships commanded by Howard of Effingham. (It must have been an embarrassment that Effingham was Douglas Howard's brother.)

The immediate objective was a combined sea and land operation to relieve Sluis. This was of far less importance to the Dutch than to the English, who wanted to prevent its use for embarking an invasion force across the North Sea. The Dutch lacked any will to take risks. Although an immediate ship-borne attack on Parma's defences might have provided an element of surprise, Maurice of Nassau, in joint command of the fleet, refused to authorise it until land-based forces were positioned. Furthermore, the Dutch pilots, who were needed to guide the fleet though the sandbars in the Scheldt estuary, refused to commit themselves until tide and weather were ideal. Robert resorted to a plan to make a naval assault on the Spanish headquarters at Cadzand. This required flat-bottomed boats, but Justin of Nassau refused to approve their use without States General approval. The land-based attack under Pelham with 4,000 foot and 400 horse was to march along the coast from Ostend, but a broken causeway at Blankenberge prevented any further advance. Although he received instructions with his raw English levies to take Blankenberge, which guarded the rear of Parma's supply chain from Bruges, it was protected by a large detachment of Spanish veterans. Pelham had no choice but to withdraw to Ostend without a shot being fired. From here his men were transported to Sluis by sea and Robert insisted on a frontal attack. With the narrow winding waterways making this difficult, Robert manoeuvred a fireship to engulf a floating bridge that Parma had created across the river, but Parma simply detached the bridge at its centre allowing the fire ship to pass through and burn out harmlessly beyond. Although Robert exhorted the pilots to sail through the gap before Parma could re-join the bridge, they refused to cooperate, fearful of running into a narrow channel without room to manoeuvre. While Robert fumed, Parma reattached the two sides of his bridge and the opportunity was lost.

No further effort was made to relieve Sluis, which surrendered on honourable terms on 4 August after a fearful bombardment. Parma was so impressed with Williams's handling of its defence that he was offered a role in Spanish forces fighting against the Turks, but Williams turned this down. Parma was greatly relieved at the cessation of hostilities. He had lost 700 men with many more having been wounded. With the campaign season over, he needed a breathing space. He continued his ineffectual peace negotiations with Elizabeth, who was blaming the Dutch for the loss of Sluis and could see no reason to provide them with further support. The breach between the allied forces was now too wide to bridge. On 10 November, the States General failed to accept Robert's continuing authority, despite support for him from Calvinist extremists. He was anxious to leave, but when Elizabeth recalled him, no Dutch dignitaries attended his departure. She was still showing him great affection, and Essex reported that 'there was not a lady in the land that should more desire the news of your return than herself'.[62] Nevertheless, she was still demanding a proper account of his expenditure and again refused further supplies until the completion of a satisfactory audit. Soldiers cheated by their captains remained in the direst straits. Thirty of them besieged Greenwich Palace, and Burghley opened a fund to enable them to return to their homes. Elizabeth called two of them before the Privy Council, which established that their captains had been paid in full. On 17 December, the Council sent a notice to the Lords Lieutenant of each county, that if soldiers provided manifest proof that they remained unpaid, they should appeal to the courts for settlement.

Elizabeth still hoped to avoid a Spanish invasion by reaching a peace settlement. Nevertheless, Burghley and Walsingham had warned her that Parma's only interest was to crush the Netherlands before attacking England. This was true. Philip II was advising Parma not to wait for his Armada, but to cross the Channel with all the forces at his disposal, after which the Armada would deliver reinforcements. Parma was indignant and, on 21 December 1587, gave the Spanish King 'an unvarnished account of the enormous difficulties to be overcome'.[63] He was blockaded into Antwerp and Sluis and was having to dig a canal to the open sea. Although he had flat-bottomed boats for a landing, he could not deploy them without the Armada's protection.

English morale was considerably brightened by the exploits of Drake, who had led the first of two lightning raids onto the coast of Spain. The Queen told him that if he succeeded, 'she would applaud him to the very echo',[64] but if he fell into Spanish hands, she could do nothing to save him. In the first of these, in November 1585, he had sacked Vigo and Santiago, commandeering supplies, before flying across the Atlantic to sack the cities of San Domingo and Cartagena in January 1586. He returned 'to thrill the nation with confidence'.[65] Nevertheless, such derring-do lost Elizabeth any hope of being able to deny her aggressive intentions towards Spain. Parma had already assembled a list of England's heretics, naming 'the principal devils'[66] as Robert, Ambrose, Huntingdon, Burghley, Bedford, Hunsdon, Hatton and Walsingham.

Chapter 26

The Execution of Mary Queen of Scots

Almost all members of the Council, including Robert, had held the view that Elizabeth's safety and the protection of the English Reformation made the removal of Mary Queen of Scots a public necessity. Every Catholic plot to depose Elizabeth focused on placing Mary on the English throne, and it was her very existence in England that seemed to be the catalyst for such scheming. It is true that Mary was aware of most of the plotting and was desperately seeking her freedom. Nevertheless, she was being extremely cautious, and, by this time, had probably lost any ambition for the English Crown. The success of any plot depended on Continental Catholic support, and realistically only the Spanish had the will and the military might to provide it. It was always assumed that English Catholics would support a foreign invasion force, but in reality they remained more supportive of their Protestant English Queen than of any potential foreign Catholic monarch. As Parma realised, his prospect of leading a successful invasion force was extremely doubtful and, once enthroned, Mary was likely to ally with French rather than Spanish interests. So long as Mary lived, there was no great Spanish appetite to invade England, as Elizabeth was astute enough to recognise.

Although a Spanish-led invasion might seem unlikely, the English Government remained concerned that if Elizabeth died, Mary was likely to gain the English Crown by dynastic right. Nevertheless, Elizabeth was not going to agree to Mary's execution unless she was demonstrably involved in a clearly defined plot that threatened the English Crown. As she was not English, it was even questionable whether her involvement in a plot against Elizabeth would be treasonable. It was only her enforced presence in England that provided any grounds for an English court to try an anointed monarch.

A way had to be found to protect the Queen. It was Robert's protégé, Thomas Digges, who came up with a mechanism in his pamphlet,

259

Humble Motives for Association to Maintain Religion Established. He proposed 'a formal bond to be entered into by all English Protestants for the protection of their Queen'.[1] Robert put it forward to the Council and in October 1584, Walsingham promoted a Bill for the Surety of the Queen's Person. Englishmen were obliged under oath to pledge their allegiance to the Crown. Under the resultant 'bond of association', they were required to seek the death of those plotting against Elizabeth and of those who would benefit from such plotting. Even a beneficiary's heirs were to be excluded from the succession. A body of twenty-four councillors and peers was to examine the evidence and take control if Elizabeth should die. Elizabeth balked at the execution without trial of any person simply because of another's action and wanted to protect James VI from being barred from the English throne. The bill was redrawn so that, when it passed in February 1585, only those who had consented to a crime could be put to death. In a show of Protestant solidarity, thousands flocked to sign it. Burghley then prepared legislation, which became the Act for the Queen's Safety which passed into law in March 1585. This stipulated that if a claimant to the throne became involved in an invasion, rebellion or plot against the Crown, he or she would be tried by a commission of Privy Councillors and other Lords of Parliament, with the verdict to be given by royal proclamation. A claimant found guilty would be excluded from the succession, with Englishmen being authorised to kill him or her out of revenge.[2] These two Acts taken together, provided the legal framework for Mary's future trial and execution.

Walsingham faced a different problem. His agents had infiltrated all the Catholic hotbeds of dissent and had failed to unearth any plausible plot with which to implicate Mary. He had to resort to entrapping her into supporting a plot put together by his own agents. In October 1585, Gilbert Gifford, a member of a well-to-do Catholic family from Staffordshire, visited Archbishop Bethune's offices in Paris, now thoroughly infiltrated with Walsingham's men. Gifford was an able linguist who had failed to be accepted as a priest after Jesuit training at the English College in Rome and later at Douai. He was interviewed by Thomas Morgan who organised the system for communicating with Mary from Paris. Morgan immediately employed Gifford, who divulged his plans to assassinate Elizabeth and place Mary on the English throne. Gifford's plot also involved his cousin, George Gifford, as well as John Savage, another failed priest, and John Ballard, an ordained soldier-priest, sometimes known as Fortescue. Morgan introduced Gilbert Gifford to Walsingham's mole, Paget, who enticed him with other conspiracies to free Mary. Gilbert was then given the task of providing a new delivery system for Mary's correspondence, which was piling up at the French embassy in London. By this time, Mary was being held under the guardianship of Amyas Paulet at Chartley Hall in Staffordshire, which belonged to Essex. Although Essex had complained vociferously at the stigma of it being used to house her, its water-filled moat provided great security and limited access to her.

While Paget was undoubtedly a double agent acting for Walsingham, in all probability so was Morgan. He was certainly mistrusted by his French colleagues and had spent time imprisoned in the Bastille. Nevertheless, Mary trusted him implicitly. When Gilbert Gifford crossed the channel to Rye in December, he was arrested after a tip-off by either Paget or Morgan. He was taken to Walsingham, who immediately blackmailed him into becoming another double-agent. He seemed to relish his new role as a spy and dropped any further involvement in his conspiracy. He agreed to intercept Mary's correspondence, passing it to Morgan's friend, the master codebreaker, Thomas Phelippes, to whom he was introduced. Gilbert was sent to collect letters from the French embassy. He then passed them to Walsingham so that Phelippes could decode and copy them. When they reached Staffordshire, they were double-checked by Paulet, before being returned to Gilbert who passed them to a brewer in Burton-on-Trent. The brewer placed them in a waterproof pouch, which was pushed through the bunghole of barrels of beer delivered to Chartley. Letters sent by Mary followed the same route in reverse.[3]

Having established this convoluted delivery mechanism, Walsingham sat back to await a plot with which to implicate Mary. He encouraged Morgan or Paget to find someone to implement Gilbert's original plan. With Paris being at the centre of Catholic intrigue, Morgan was visited by the 25-year-old Sir Anthony Babington, one of Shrewsbury's former pages, who had probably met Mary. In June 1586, Morgan confirmed to Mary through the beer-barrel route that Babington was an approved contact. Babington moved to London and gathered round him a group including Gilbert's former co-conspirators, George Gifford, Ballard, and Savage. Remaining unaware of Gilbert's duplicity, they now initiated Babington and other colleagues into the plot's original plans. Ballard communicated with Mendosa but seems to have exaggerated the level of Spanish support available. Morgan also confused things by tampering with messages from Mary's Guise relations, making her doubtful of the level of their support.[4]

Babington was oblivious of the conspiracy developing around him. Although he was the titular leader, the plot was based on Gifford's original plan manoeuvred into Babington's control by Walsingham's agents. The Spanish invasion was apparently to be led by Mary's Scottish supporter, Lord Claud Hamilton, but Philip II was at best lukewarm about it. It was little more than a romantic fantasy.[5] There were various rumours that Elizabeth's life was in great danger. Elizabeth Jenkins records that one of the conspirators, Robert Barnewell, confronted Elizabeth walking with a group of unarmed courtiers in Richmond Park, but lost his nerve after Elizabeth looked searchingly at him. (In my considerable researches on this subject, I have found no mention of this, but it was the kind of rumour that would make the threat seem greater than it was.)

Walsingham wrote to Robert in the Netherlands: 'If the matter be well handled, it will break the neck of all dangerous practices during her majesty's reign.'[6] All that he needed was Mary's written agreement to support the plot, and she duly obliged. She did not realise that both sides of the correspondence were being read and copied and had given instructions for the originals to be burned. She was taking a gamble to gain her freedom, even if Elizabeth's assassination was the price to be paid for it. To make the evidence absolutely clear, Phelippes provided an embellished version of the correspondence, but even the originals show that Mary supported the plot against Elizabeth. All the conspirators were arrested and faced a traitor's execution, but Gilbert Gifford received £40 from Walsingham and was permitted to escape abroad, heedless of the fate of his former colleagues. Mary was moved to Fotheringhay Castle in Northamptonshire. Fearing that she would use the opportunity of her trial to demonstrate her martyrdom (as she duly did), Robert suggested that she should be quietly poisoned, but Walsingham rejected such an underhand plan.

The easy part of the trial at Fotheringhay was to find Mary guilty of treason. The difficulty was to gain Elizabeth's support for her execution. Elizabeth hoped that one of her own citizens would take the matter out of her hands by assassinating Mary in accordance with the bond of association without the need for her authority, but no one would act without her express agreement. Burghley, Walsingham and Robert were at their wits end to find a means to persuade her. If Mary lived, she might yet become Queen of England. Robert, who was still in the Netherlands, needed to return to steady her resolve. When he rejoined her, he was greeted with open arms, but Elizabeth worried about how Mary's execution would be viewed by the Catholic superpowers and by posterity. They held a lengthy meeting in private over supper. It is not known what was said, but she agreed to authorise Mary's execution. By the following morning, she had changed her mind. Nevertheless, Robert was now firmly back in his old position of influence and, progressively, he wore her down. In a letter which demonstrates his close trust in Robert, James wrote to him: 'How fond and inconstant I were, if I should prefer my mother to the title [the English Crown], let all men judge. My religion ever moved me to hate her course, although my honour constrains me to insist for her life.'[7] Elizabeth now knew that James would not stand in her way. On 4 December, she approved the execution, but when the authority was presented to her for signature, she could not bear to sign it.

Burghley turned to subterfuge. He obtained tacit French recognition that her execution was morally justified and spread a rumour of an imminent Spanish invasion. On 1 February 1587, he arranged for the authority to be included in a pile of papers given to Elizabeth for signature by Davison, who was now her secretary. Although she signed it, it was on the understanding that it was not to be acted upon without her express authority. It was a responsibility too painful for her to face. Burghley did not hesitate. He convened a meeting of all available Privy Councillors, including Robert, and persuaded them to act in accordance with the bond of association. Each Councillor agreed to bear equal responsibility.[8] They passed the authority to Fotheringhay for it to be implemented. Mary was executed immediately, poignantly playing her dramatic role as a martyr to the full.

Elizabeth was hysterical, spending hours of weeping that her authority had been outraged. She tried to make out to Catholic heads of state that she had been duped. Davison bore the brunt of her fury. He was fined £10,000 and was thrown in the Tower. The fine was eventually remitted, and he served only eighteen months, during which he lived under a liberal regime. He was released shortly after the Armada, when he received his full salary as a life pension. Burghley was in a better position to remonstrate with her, pointing out that such theatricals might salve her conscience, but would cut little ice with the outside world.

This did not prevent his temporary banishment.[9] Nevertheless, foreign recrimination was muted, and he was soon recalled.

With Mary dead, Philip could launch an invasion of England in support of a Counter-Reformation with a figurehead properly connected to Spanish interests. He was soon mustering a fleet and a huge military force to place his daughter, the Infanta Isabella, based in Brussels, on the English throne. She was a descendant of John of Gaunt.

> English Catholics had to ask themselves whether they would prefer to keep Elizabeth on the throne or have [a foreign Catholic Monarch] put there by Spanish troops; they had only to consider whether they would prefer to remain an independent and prosperous country or be taken over by the King of Spain and ruled as a Spanish province on the lines of the martyred Netherlands.[10]

Chapter 27

Lieutenant and Captain General of the Queen's armies and companies

Robert found that in his absence, his political influence in the Council had waned. It was Hatton who was the rising star and, in April 1587, he was appointed Lord Chancellor, despite having no legal training and being opposed by the legal fraternity. Robert and Burghley escorted him from Ely Place to Westminster to be sworn in.[1] Members of the Whitgift/ Hatton group had now joined the Council and Robert had lost some of his former supporters. Without his presence, it had become easier to gain access to Elizabeth. No longer was royal approval dependent on his role as an intermediary.

In November 1587, Sidney's embalmed body was carried back to Harwich on his ship, the *Black Pinnace*, which was draped in black with black sails. From there it was brought to London to be landed at Tower Wharf and conveyed to a house in the Minories. Uncharacteristically, Robert fell out with Walsingham over the settlement of Sidney's known debts, which exceeded his assets by three times, and there were legal difficulties over selling land to satisfy his creditors. As an executor, Walsingham was under considerable pressure, and Sidney's body lay unburied for three months for lack of funds for an appropriate funeral. Walsingham contributed £6,000, telling Robert 'that it hath brought me into a most desperate and hard state'.[2] Although he appealed to Robert to do the same, he concluded that Robert lacked the will to assist. Admittedly Robert's finances were in some disarray after his expenditure in the Netherlands, but it might have been expected that the sale of a piece of land would have contributed to the funeral of his nephew and heir. This was not the amenable Robert of old. When Walsingham appealed to the Queen for help, Robert refused to support his request. He also failed to back his application to become Chancellor of the Duchy of Lancaster, even opposing him with a rival candidate. It was Burghley who came to Walsingham's rescue, persuading the Queen to provide a substantial grant of land with the Chancellorship in the following April.

Although Robert attended Sidney's elaborate funeral at St Paul's, and sent his heartfelt sympathy to Frances Sidney, his attitude must have presented a 'disagreeable air'.[3] A procession of seven hundred persons bore Sidney's body to the cathedral, preceded by officers, pipers, drummers and trumpeters of Sidney's regiment of horse and a train of his friends, including Drake.

> His war horse caparisoned in black was ridden by a little page who trailed a broken lance. Heralds bore his arms, his helmet, shield, tabard, spurs and gloves. The coffin covered in black velvet, was slung between two poles, each supported by seven yeomen, robed and hooded in black. The chief mourner, his brother and heir, Robert Sidney, walked alone after the coffin; then, riding on horseback two and two, came the Earl of Leicester and Earl of Huntingdon, the Earl of Pembroke and the Earl of Warwick, Lord Willoughby and Lord North. Seven gentlemen of the Netherlands followed, representing the United Provinces. After these came the Lord Mayor and Aldermen, the Sheriffs and the Recorder of London. Four hundred citizens brought up the rear.[4]

Robert seemed to be tiring of public life, disillusioned by the frustration and anxiety of his role in the Netherlands. Elizabeth was unhappy at his failure to implement her objectives, or to marshal the Dutch into a coherent fighting force to challenge the might of Spain. She continued to bicker with him over accounting for the funds expended. He took umbrage that Burghley supported the Queen, despite her requests being entirely reasonable. On 7 February, he told Burghley that he was being asked to do work 'more the province of an auditor or clerk, than one in high position'.[5] Burghley replied:

> I never did say or mean to say that your Lordship ought to be blamed for 'the [auditors'] imperfections in their accounts. I did say, and do still say, that their accounts are obscure, confused and without credit … And I find in truth that they

ought to have been commanded by your Lordship's authority to have reformed the same and made your Lordship more privy to their doings, for which not doing, I condemn them and not your Lordship.[6]

Robert retired to Wanstead from where he wrote to Elizabeth, beseeching her 'to behold with the eyes of your princely clemency at my wretched and depressed estate'.[7] Noting his estrangement with Elizabeth, Buckhurst attempted to call Robert to account for his mismanagement of Netherlands' affairs. It was the general view that he should submit to an investigation by the Council, during which it was normal practice for those being investigated to kneel. Robert appealed to the Queen to prevent this indignity. Elizabeth's 'heart was wrung' and she promised that he would suffer 'no abasement'.[8] During his investigation, he sat down among them and 'would answer only that he had proceeded on secret instructions from the Queen, which he was not at liberty to disclose to them'.[9] He arranged for a medal to be struck with his image on one side and a dog turning away from sheep, saying: 'I forsake, to my grief.' Elizabeth remained loyal to a fault. She scotched any criticism as soon as she heard of it.

Robert was suffering from a stomach complaint, thought to have been gall stones, and he resigned as Master of the Horse, handing the role over to his stepson, Essex. This was not a sudden decision. It had been discussed in the previous May. Essex was already firmly positioned in the Queen's affections and, while Robert was absent abroad, had used his position to provide wholehearted support for his stepfather's interests. It was now he who sat up late playing cards with Elizabeth, or riding with her in Windsor Great Park. He became Elizabeth's constant companion, a position that he was careful not to abuse. When she suggested that he should occupy Robert's lodgings at court, he immediately wrote to seek Robert's approval. In April 1588, Essex again followed in his stepfather's footsteps by being granted the Order of the Garter. There were no signs then of the later jealousy and greed that were to bring about his downfall.

In retrospect, the Netherlands expedition was not a complete failure. It had prevented Spain from gaining control of the United Provinces after the fall of Antwerp, and it had stopped Parma from gaining the coastline of Zeeland and Holland other than Sluis, where navigation through the surrounding sandbanks was difficult. This was to be the

Armada's undoing. When the mighty fleet of Philip II needed to regroup after its buffeting in the Channel, it had no safe haven in which to undertake repairs.

There were already rumours that Philip II was amassing a huge fleet to form his Armada for an invasion of England. Drake offered to lead a second raid to damage shipping along the Spanish coast and Elizabeth gave him command of a flotilla, which included four naval galleons and a further twenty armed merchantmen and pinnaces, financed by a group of London merchants. She was to receive a half of any profit.

Drake set sail from Plymouth on 12 April 1587. Although he faced a storm off Galicia, two Dutch vessels provided him with intelligence that a huge war fleet was being readied to move from Cadiz to Lisbon. Drake's ships entered the bay of Cadiz at dusk on 29 April. There were sixty Spanish carracks and various smaller boats in the harbour. Although the Spanish fleet came out to face the English, it had been caught by surprise and was soon forced back into port where many ships were abandoned by their crews. Drake's men cut their cables and set them on fire. By dawn on 1 May, at least twenty-seven Spanish men-of-war had been destroyed and a further four captured, laden with provisions. As Drake returned north he destroyed any shipping he encountered, including fishing vessels. He landed at Lagos, near Cape St Vincent, in southern Portugal, storming local fortresses and establishing it as a base to disrupt the Armada fleet being assembled at Lisbon. He now made for Lisbon, which was well protected by shore batteries. Although there was an exchange of fire, it was fairly ineffectual; he rode at anchor, 'defying the Spanish with calm insolence'.[10] He then weighed anchor and returned to Lagos to take on water before setting out for the Azores. This last project was undertaken against the advice of Borough, his second-in-command, who had instructions to curb Drake from exceeding Elizabeth's orders. Nothing daunted, Drake relieved Borough – a naval admiral – of his command and sent him back to England with the four royal navy vessels, leaving himself with only nine ships. On 8 June, he sighted the *São Filipe*, a Portuguese treasure ship, returning from the East Indies. After a brief exchange of fire, it surrendered and Drake returned with it to England, bringing its cargo of gold, spices and silk valued at £108,000. He received a hero's welcome for having 'singed the King of Spain's beard', but knew he had not destroyed the Armada. Nevertheless, his action delayed it by a year. He returned in time to travel to the Netherlands to escort Robert back to England after his attack on Sluis.

When it came to the defence of the realm, Elizabeth would always turn to Robert to lead her land forces. During the winter of 1587–8, he frequently attended Council meetings to discuss the imminent Spanish threat. As late as January 1588, Elizabeth was still holding out hope for a negotiated settlement, sending a delegation led by Henry Stanley, 4th Earl of Derby, to Ostend. This included the devious Sir James Croft, who retained her confidence, despite being suspected of Catholic intrigue at various stages in his career. On 17 April, Croft made a secret approach to Parma in Bruges without the knowledge of his colleagues. He proposed that, if the Spanish gave an undertaking not to set up a Spanish inquisition anywhere in the Netherlands, withdrew all their troops and conceded a degree of religious toleration, Holland and Zeeland should be restored to Spanish control. If they gave up all hostile preparations against England, Elizabeth would hand over the garrisoned towns of Brill, Flushing and Ostend. When Elizabeth heard this, she wrote to ask why he had made any such unauthorised proposals and told the other commissioners to disavow his actions. Despite his impropriety, Croft was permitted to remain in post. Meanwhile, Walsingham and Robert continued to argue against diplomacy, preferring to place their reliance on the English navy and army. However, the Council faced the perennial problem of Elizabeth's ambivalence and a shortage of money. There was also a lack of civilian enthusiasm to take up arms. Robert was left struggling to put the nation in readiness for the conflict that was upon them. Although, on paper, local musters raised 50,000 foot and 10,000 horse, those reporting for duty fell far short of this. Veterans of the Irish and Dutch campaigns had to be engaged to knock recruits into some semblance of order. On 24 July, Robert was formally appointed Lieutenant and Captain General of the Queen's armies and companies, the position he had held in the Netherlands, and he took personal responsibility for the defence of the Thames estuary. Even before this he was 'issuing commands, ordering supplies and enquiring into the state of coastal defences'.[11]

On 20 March 1588, Philip wrote to Parma that the Armada was fully equipped and ready to sail from Lisbon with 8,000 sailors and 18,000 troops. The fleet consisted of 130 ships, of which twenty-eight were purpose-built men-of-war, supported by sixty-eight armed carracks and thirty-four light ships. It was under the command of Alonzo Pérez de Guzmán, Duke of Medina Sidonia. Parma was to pick 6,000 of the troops on board to add to his invasion force being prepared in the Netherlands, with the remainder being left to guard the subjugated Netherland provinces. Parma had initially wanted 30,000 men for the invasion, but with England now being readied he considered even 50,000 to be insufficient and predicted disaster. His only hope was to put the English off their guard by promising peace negotiations. Elizabeth alone was taking these seriously, and even Burghley considered war to be inevitable.

Although the Armada fleet set out on 28 May, it took two days to leave Lisbon and was scattered by bad weather in the Bay of Biscay. Although it regrouped at Corunna, only about 123 ships reached the English Channel. News of its departure reached England in early June, but the cumbersome fleet made slow progress. It only passed the Lizard on 19 July, spread out in an undulating crescent seven miles across. The English fleet was well prepared. Although Elizabeth had done little to ready land-based forces for war, she had spent huge sums, like her father before her, on shipbuilding at the dockyards at Chatham. Howard of Effingham wrote to Burghley, who had taken control of the fleet's administration: 'I do thank God that they be in the state that they be in; there is never one of them that knows what a leak means.'[12] Howard had 197 ships under his command, of which thirty-four formed part of the royal fleet. Fifty-one vessels were galleons of between 200 and 400 tons carrying at least forty-two guns each, of which Howard, Sir John Hawkins, and Drake had provided a total of twelve privateers. The English were prevented from making an early attack after a southerly wind held them locked in harbour, but on 19 July, with remarkable daring, they extricated a flotilla of fifty-five ships from Plymouth and, two days later, confronted the enemy off the Eddystone rocks. They used their superior speed and manoeuvrability to gain the weather station while keeping their distance. Although no ships were lost on either side, two Spanish vessels were abandoned after colliding. Drake turned back to loot them, gaining supplies of much needed gunpowder and gold. Without his navigational skills, the rest of the English fleet became scattered and took a full day to regroup. Despite this, it caught up with the Armada within a day and re-engaged it off Portland, but again to little effect. Medina Sidonia had been hoping to create a temporary base for the Armada on the Isle of Wight, but with the English threatening a full-scale attack, he gave orders to return to the open sea from where it headed up the Channel.

On 27 July, the Armada anchored in a tightly packed defensive formation off Calais to await the arrival of Parma's invasion force. This had been reduced by disease to 16,000 men. Parma's land-based forces were expecting to be transported along the coast in a fleet of barges from the Netherlands' coastal ports for embarkation at Dunkirk. Poor communication meant that he needed at least a further six days to deliver them. The ports were being blockaded by thirty flyboats able to negotiate the shallow waters under the command of Justin of Nassau. With the Spanish invasion barges being pinned down in Nieuport and Dunkirk, Parma's men never left dry land. Meanwhile, the Armada fleet remained sitting at anchor. Without access to Netherlands' harbours, Medina Sidonia hoped to revictual at Gravelines in Flanders, close to the French border. He was reluctant to move further east as the Dutch had removed the sea marks from the sand shoals. The fleet was left extremely vulnerable, particularly at night. On 28 July, the English cast downwind eight fireships filled with pitch, brimstone, gunpowder and tar. Although the Spanish towed two of them out of the way and the principal warships held their positions, the remainder cut their anchor cables, scattering in confusion. They were now too far to leeward to regroup.

The English needed to close to a range of less than 100 yards for their guns to penetrate the oak hulls of the Spanish ships and they were short of gunpowder. Nevertheless, they had 'an overwhelming preponderance of gun-power [and] their vessels were altogether superior in sailing qualities'.[13] Reloading of Spanish guns was hampered by the storage of supplies on the gundecks. It had always been Spanish practice for ships to fire once, after which the gun crews jumped to the rigging to prepare for grapple boarding. They were given no opportunity. With their superior manoeuvrability, the English were able to provoke Spanish fire while remaining out of range. They could then close while firing repeated damaging broadsides into the enemy. By keeping to windward, they holed the heeling Spanish hulls below the waterline. With many Spanish gunners having been killed, the guns were manned by foot soldiers, who did not know how to operate them, but the ships moved close enough to exchange musket fire.

By 4.00 pm the English fleet was out of ammunition and forced to pull back, but it had established complete mastery.[14] The mighty Armada was reduced to 'a rabble of battered ships'.[15] The Spanish had lost 2,000 men, but the English suffered only fifty casualties.[16] Five Spanish vessels were lost, often after being forced to beach on the coastal shoals. Many others were severely damaged and faced a storm in the North Sea. Although the English attack had ended any hope of loading Parma's invasion force, the Armada's presence as it moved north along the English east coast still seemed to threaten a landing. Despite their shortage of ammunition, the English fleet continued in pursuit to prevent the Armada from returning south. It only pulled back when the Spanish ships passed the Firth of Forth.

Sightings of the Armada had resulted in levies being mustered along the south coast. A great chain of beacons established on headlands and hills carried the alarm and summoned the militia to their posts. Shore-based preparations were nothing like so well advanced as those of the navy. It was recognised that Parma's first objective would be to gain control of London, so Robert focused his attention on entrenching the camp at Tilbury, guarding the north bank of the Thames, opposite Gravesend. He considered it an entirely suitable location to station the main English force protecting London's approaches. His main concern was the delay in recruitment. The train bands due to arrive from London were not yet ready. On 22 July, he was still doubting whether Tilbury and Gravesend could be made impregnable in time, complaining at a shortage of powder, ordnance, implements and victuals. He supervised the construction of a boom across the Thames but was worried about its adequacy. He complained that most men of substance were moving with their retainers to serve under Hunsdon, who was in command of the bodyguard to protect the Queen and the capital. The men of Essex arrived at Tilbury only slowly and, by 25 July, there were only 4,000 at the camp. By then the Spanish fleet had already passed the Isle of Wight. Robert went about trying to stir up patriotism but maintained an uneasy relationship with his subordinates, Norreys and Sir Roger Williams. He was short of veterans to train his troops and complained when Norreys was sent by the Council to supervise the camp at Dover. A shortage of victuals forced him to stay 1,000 reinforcements in London, until they could bring their own provisions with them. He ordered beer at his own expense and had to send town criers into the surrounding area to appeal for food from local farmers.[17]

By 27 July, Robert had established some semblance of order at Tilbury and he urged Elizabeth to make a personal appearance. She asked his advice on her protection. He recommended that she should move to Havering, about ten miles from Tilbury, with a small bodyguard. In the end she did not decamp from Westminster. Nevertheless, on 8 August, she was rowed down the Thames to Tilbury in her barge by forty men to review Robert's troops, now numbering 11,500 men. This may have created an illusion of military might, but it was another piece of Robert's masterful stage management with tents and pavilions in orderly rows and breastplates gleaming. Elizabeth knew exactly how to react. She was dressed all in white, wearing a polished steel cuirass and mounted on a grey gelding with a page bearing her polished helmet with its white plume on a cushion. Robert was mounted on her right, Essex on her left, and Norreys behind. When she reached the cheering soldiers, she confirmed that she came among them as: 'Your general, judge and rewarder', ready to 'lay down for my God and my Kingdom and for my people, my honour and my blood'.

> I know I have but the body of a weak, feeble woman, but I have the heart and stomach of a King – and a King of England too – and think foul scorn that Parma, or Spain, or any Prince of Europe should dare to invade the borders of my realm.[18]

This was stirring stuff, worthy of Shakespeare, and she commended Robert to them as her Lieutenant General. Her appearance shows that his standing was still paramount. She dined with him and his officers and slept at Ardern Hall nearby, ready to watch her soldiers drill.[19] During dinner she received news that the Armada had been driven by the storms up the east coast to Scotland.

Despite this, rumours persisted that Parma was ready to cross the Channel. Elizabeth was reluctantly persuaded by Robert to move back to London. Respect for Parma meant that some cunning trick was suspected. Huntingdon wrote from Newcastle bemoaning the lack of preparedness, but Robert turned to the Dutch for support. Although his authority had been revoked in March, the Calvinists still looked to him as their leader. Yet further assistance was refused. Killigrew, who was now the ambassador in Holland, found his position intolerable and asked to be recalled, as did Sir William Russell, the Governor of Flushing, who blamed the States General for weakening his garrison.

By mid-August, the danger was past. Robert was required to break up the camp at Tilbury by his money-conscious colleagues on the Council. He must have been thankful. He was considerably weakened by his efforts with discomfort from the pain in his stomach and his continuing malaria. Yet he made a triumphant entry back into London with an escort of gentlemen and 'a picked contingent of soldiers'.[20] None of them had fired a shot, but, in the prevailing euphoria, they were welcomed as heroes.[21] Camden states that, for a second time, Elizabeth contemplated making Robert her deputy with the title of 'Lieutenant Governor of England and Ireland', but to Robert's mortification, Burghley and Hatton talked her out of it. He was still, however, the man she trusted most. She dined with him every day and her confidence in him remained firm to the end. He stayed at court while Essex staged a troop review in the tiltyard at Whitehall, during which Essex took part in two jousts against the Earl of Cumberland, 'two of the best horsemen in the country'.[22] Robert watched with the Queen from a window, but his continuing malaria prevented him from attending other celebrations. He excused himself from the Queen, who readily agreed for him to return to Buxton. She also provided medicine prescribed by her own physicians.

On 26 August, Robert and Lettice left Wanstead by easy stages to make for the Midlands spa. He was 56, feverish and ill. On 28 August, they were the guests of Lady Norreys (the mother of Sir John) at Rycote, from where Robert wrote an inconsequential note to Elizabeth asking after her health and thanking her for some token just received. It was his last letter to her. He was now very ill, but managed to travel on for a further twenty-five miles, with an overnight stop at Oxford, to reach his lodge at Cornbury. On arrival, he took to his bed and died there on 4 September after several days and nights of pain.

Lettice was with him and there were immediate rumours that she had poisoned him so she was free to marry her lover. This is unthinkable, and she much later chose to be buried next to Robert at Warwick. Although there were other rumours that Sir James Croft's son, Edward, was involved in a plot to poison him, this seems another fabrication. The post-mortem showed no evidence of foul play. His massive physique had been undermined by a chronic intestinal complaint and his malaria had taken hold.

Aftermath

There is no evidence that Lettice was remotely unfaithful to Robert during the latter part of their marriage and she retained a strong influence over him. Nevertheless, eyebrows were raised when, seven months after Robert's death, she remarried Sir Christopher Blount, thirteen years her junior. Blount was a Catholic but had acted as a double-agent for Walsingham in attempting to infiltrate the offices of Archbishop Bethune in Paris. He had always been loyal to Robert, being a gentleman of his horse, and his father, Sir Thomas, had been tasked with unravelling the mystery of the death of Amy Robsart. Blount and Lettice were certainly greatly attracted to each other, but she also needed his help in unscrambling Robert's huge debts.

Lettice was appointed as Robert's executrix to be assisted by Howard of Effingham, Ambrose and Hatton. With their help, she obtained probate within twelve days of his death. Robert's will had been written without proper legal advice in the Netherlands and was found to be defective. It began with a personal expression of his Puritan faith. He sought to be buried next to his ancestors in the Beauchamp Chapel at Warwick church, where Lettice later erected a magnificent tomb to his memory. Ultimately, she was also buried there as his 'moeltissum uxor, (most tender wife)', out of her love and conjugal fidelity. Effigies of Robert and Lettice lie side by side.

His bequests begin with a preamble: 'They cannot be great … I have always lived above anything I had (for which I am heartily sorry), lest that through my many debts from time to time some men have taken loss by me.'[1] He left Elizabeth a pendant formed of three great emeralds arranged with diamonds around a large table-diamond hung with a rope of 600 'fair white pearls'. His principal heirs were Lettice, his 'faithful and very loving and obedient careful wife', and Ambrose, his brother. Robert Jr was to inherit some properties when he was 20 or 21, and in some instances, others after the deaths of Lettice or Ambrose. Lettice received Drayton Basset in Staffordshire, Balsall and Long Itchington in Warwickshire, and Wanstead house, park and related lands and tenements. She also received most of the jewellery, the contents of Wanstead and half the contents of Leicester House, which was to be hers for life with the remainder to go to Robert Jr, failing whom to Essex. Lands, the ownership of which was disputed by Lord Berkeley, were to go to Ambrose, from whom they were to pass to Robert Sidney, Philip's brother. At the age of 20, Robert Jr was to receive the house and lands at Aldersbrooke, including the adjacent pond which was part of the manor of Wanstead. On the death of Ambrose, he was also to receive Kenilworth and the manors of Denbigh and Chirke. Nevertheless, any thought that he might marry Arbella Stuart ended with his father's death.

Robert's estate was indebted to the extent of £50,000, of which £25,000 was owed to the Crown. In view of her continuing malice towards Lettice, Elizabeth was not about to concede anything. Inventories were made to prepare the contents of Wanstead, Kenilworth and Leicester House for sale. Not everything, particularly the jewellery, was included in the list. Although the sale raised £29,000, this was insufficient to settle all the outstanding debts. Despite this, by the end of Elizabeth's reign she had been repaid £22,000 of the £25,000 owed and the balance of £3,000 was remitted by James I. The problem for Lettice was not so much Robert's debts, but Blount's profligate dissipation of her remaining jewellery. Although she did not complain, he sold magnificent pieces in every year and parted with valuable property leases to finance their extravagant lifestyle. In 1596 he joined Essex's expedition to Cadiz, followed a year later by an expedition to Fayal in the Azores. He was beheaded in 1601 after his involvement in Essex's ill-fated rebellion.

Although the will provided £200 per annum for the maintenance of the 'Master and poor men' of Lord Leycester hospital at Warwick, Lettice was in no mood to hand out money unnecessarily, and she made no contribution, even though the will had suggested increasing the charity by adding a provision 'for some number of poor women'.[2] Ambrose was left to meet the cost of maintenance, but when he died in 1590, the hospital was destitute. Two years later, Thomas Cartwright, who was still the Master, had to write to Burghley for assistance, after providing money from his own resources. Following Blount's execution, Lettice retired to the country, living at Drayton Basset, as a 'highly thought of old lady', until the age of 92. She was 'a brisk and benevolent grandmother to "the grandchildren of her grandchildren"'. She also showed later munificence. Her epitaph states that 'the poor that lived near, death nor famine could not fear'.[3]

Robert's principal heir, his bastard son Robert who now took the surname Dudley, was only 13 when the will was drawn and it may be for this reason that his uncle, Howard of Effingham, was asked to assist Lettice in handling the will. Robert Jr now took the place intended for the Noble Imp. When Ambrose died in 1590, Kenilworth passed to Robert Jr. Before he could take possession, Blount made forcible entry to occupy the castle. 'It took an order from the Privy Council to dislodge him.'[4] As has been seen, Robert Jr was less successful when he attempted to claim that he was Robert's legitimate heir in 1603. Lettice filed a Bill in the Court of Star Chamber against his claim and against his mother, Douglas, and stepfather, Sir Edward Stafford. This established that his procedure for bringing the action was unlawful, so that the case never came to trial.

Robert Jr bore a strong likeness to his father, but with fair hair and a beard. He shared his father's athleticism, 'famous at the exercise of tilting'.[5] He was an expert horseman and was instrumental in teaching dogs to sit to await the picking up of partridges.[6] He became a skilled mathematician and distinguished navigator, renowned as an explorer and naval architect. Although he married Alice Leigh, by whom he had several daughters, after the Court of Star Chamber case, he left his wife. He was granted leave to go abroad, and was accompanied to Italy by his beautiful cousin, Elizabeth Southwell, dressed as a boy. They never returned.

In the midst of the great rejoicing over the outcome of the Armada, Robert's death had robbed Elizabeth of all happiness. In floods of tears, she shut herself in her chamber alone, refusing to speak to anyone. Eventually, Burghley 'and other councillors had the doors broken open and entered to see her'.[7] It was characteristic that she would want to mourn in private, but she still made a minute examination of Robert's estate, seeking to recover anything owed to her. This apparent insensitivity was aimed more against Lettice than against Robert's memory.

Robert had acted as Elizabeth's consort and, in her eyes, no one ever replaced him. Camden reported: 'The Earl of Leicester ... saw farther into the mind of Queen Elizabeth than any man.'[8] She had been infatuated with him. Even Essex never shared the same intimacy with her. She would not hear a word said against him. When, in 1596, her godson John Harington published a book containing some slightly disparaging comments, she banished him from court 'until he had grown sober'.[9] After her own death on 24 March 1603, the casket of her personal treasures found by her bed contained the letter that Robert had written to her from Rycote. It contained nothing of importance but was annotated: 'His last letter.'

It has generally been accepted that there was no great sense of loss at Robert's death. Even his protégé, Edmund Spenser, in *The Ruines of Times* written much later suggested:

He now is dead and all his glories gone
And all his greatness vapoured to naught
That as a glass upon the water shone
Which vanished quite, as soon as it was sought.
His name is worn already out of thought.
Ne any poet seeks him to revive.
Yet many poets honoured him alive.

Robert has not received a great press from historians, partly, it would seem, because he was Burghley's rival for the Queen's ear, and Burghley is always idealised as the ultimate minister. There are many instances of Burghley's underhand dealing, particularly in blackening the name of Mary Queen of Scots and in fabricating plotting against the Crown to make the Catholic threat seem more real than it was. Robert was certainly not faultless, but he was loyal. This book attempts to redress the balance. It may seem a surprise that Elizabeth, with her shrewd judgement of character, saw so much good in him. It is suggested that her passion and devotion were such that when he was denied to her as a husband, she forsook all thought of matrimony and 'lived and died a virgin'. It seems likely that they enjoyed a sexual relationship in the early part of her reign and, indisputably, he was her only true love. Even when their passion had cooled, she remained unfailingly loyal, but was not above some very public criticism of his shortcomings. In any other circumstance than as Queen she would undoubtedly have married him. In part, her decision was a political one, as the resultant jealousy would have damaged her popularity. It would also have removed her from the international marriage market, which was her strongest political card on the Continent. It would be unfair to blame Robert for having thwarted each royal suit as it materialised. It was always Elizabeth who took her suitors to the brink before letting them down. This left her free to carry on the wooing process just one more time. It may well be that her doubtful fertility played a part in her decision not to marry. She had watched the acute embarrassment of Mary Tudor at first hand. If she did enjoy a sexual relationship with Robert, she certainly did not become pregnant by him, and if she could not achieve it with her handsome paramour, what chance would she have elsewhere? It was better to play the part of the virgin queen than the barren wife. She knew she had a perfectly acceptable successor in her godson, James VI, and always took a great interest in his upbringing. She wrote to him regularly, and although he did not always tow her line, he was always her common-sense heir.

The Dudleys' ambitions made them unpopular. Robert's father and grandfather were both executed for treason, but family members were intensely loyal to each other and proud of their heritage. 'Like his father and grandfather before him [Robert] was a dedicated supporter of the Tudors and wore himself out in their service.'[10] It is thanks to him that Elizabeth survived the uncertainties of the first part of her reign, and by the time of his death was well equipped to stand alone as Gloriana, enduring the strains of office and sifting the advice of her councillors.[11]

Robert's receipt of lavish gifts from his royal patroness caused jealousy and he undoubtedly benefited from kickbacks in return for providing access to the royal presence. Perhaps it was jealousy that brought accusations of him being an inept politician, an incompetent soldier, a meddler in Elizabeth's marriage negotiations and a great lothario, unbecoming to his standing as a committed Puritan. The reality needs to be examined with care. As a politician, he was an important member of the Council, always more hawkish than the rest. His policies ensured that England was militarily prepared and had a well-organised navy. He fought tenaciously to encourage Elizabeth to stand up to superior forces on the Continent. Although he sparred with Burghley, it has been shown that they needed and respected each other.

As a soldier, Robert has been criticised for his failure in the Netherlands. This is unfair. He fought with inferior numbers and resources against Parma, who was the finest general of his age. He had some notable successes and showed great personal bravery and resource. He was let down by uncertain allies, a shortage of money, vacillation from Elizabeth and the States General, and treachery from his own officers. Despite this, he prevented the United Provinces being subsumed under Spanish control and, other than Sluis, secured the coastal ports of Holland and Zeeland, thereby thwarting their use by the Spanish during the Armada.

While acting as a royal intermediary, Robert was almost always sheltering Elizabeth from opportunistic pleas at her own request. There is no evidence that he abused her trust. On the contrary, he was vital to the smooth running of the Household. He was the consummate courtier, performing his duties diligently to put visitors at their ease. If he pocketed money, he used much of it for charitable welfare or to finance protégés, expeditions and other projects for the benefit of the commonweal.

As a devastatingly attractive man, Robert was sought out by a string of beautiful women. It was his great tragedy that Amy Robsart failed to conceive, but there can be no doubt that as his relationship with Elizabeth developed, he tired of his young wife. It was hardly unusual for attractive men at court to look elsewhere when away from home. Robert probably behaved little differently than the other studs of his period. He was careful to conduct his misalliances with great decorum and discretion, avoiding serious contemporary criticism. His relationship with Douglas Howard seems to have become known even to the Queen, but she accepted it as the norm. There is no evidence of him giving any commitment to marry her, making his position clear to her from the outset. His attraction for Lettice was probably more all-consuming. By then his relationship with Elizabeth had run its course and Douglas had become irksome. It is easy to assume that, while her husband was in Ireland, Lettice made much of the running in what became an irresistible love affair. As the probable granddaughter of Henry VIII, she was a catch to appeal to Robert's self-esteem.

Leaving aside political, military and personal considerations, Robert was undoubtedly the greatest Englishman of the Elizabethan age with a plethora of achievements. He was largely responsible for funding Drake's circumnavigation and was a champion of mercantile expansionism. He encouraged the colonisation of the Americas. He was the great supporter of academic endeavour, whether in the fields of navigation, Renaissance poetry and drama, classical study or Puritan scholarship. He financed numerous protégés who are now household names. He was the great upholder of Puritanism, raising its dogma to a place in Christian worship that allowed it to punch above its weight. As Master of the Horse he transformed the bloodline of English equine stock for military and ceremonial use. He was a great equestrian and athlete in his own right, always chivalrous and brave in the tiltyard and magnificently attired on ceremonial occasions. He was perhaps the greatest impresario of his age, showcasing the great pageants of Elizabeth's reign, allowing her to appear to glittering effect before her adoring public. He spearheaded the development of the London theatre, combining classical style with ribald comedy. This created an environment which allowed Shakespeare to flourish. He formed his own team of players, many of whom went on to perform for Shakespeare. In an age burgeoning with the building of fine properties, when fortification was no longer the object of the day, he created Kenilworth, Wanstead and Leicester House as the most opulent mansions in the land, outdoing the rival efforts of Burghley, Shrewsbury, Bess of Hardwick and many others. In 1575, he held a party lasting eighteen days at Kenilworth, which was arguably the most sumptuous event of the Elizabethan age.

Except perhaps in his final few months, Robert was also an easy-going charming companion, whose company was sought by people at every level. Elizabeth was to lose her way without him, and he would surely have stamped on the build-up of future conflict among her advisers. The latter years of her reign demonstrated her military indecisiveness in Ireland and elsewhere, which his presence would have mitigated.

Robert's protégé, the Jesuit Edmund Campion, wrote what makes a fitting epitaph:

> Thirteen years to have lived in the eye and special credit of a prince, yet never during all that space to have abused this ability to any man's harm; to be enriched with no man's overthrow; to be kindled neither with grudge nor emulation; to benefit an infinite resort of daily suitors; to let down your calling to the need of mean subjects; to retain a lowly stomach, with such facility, so mild a nature in so high a vocation … this is the substance which maketh you worthy of these ornaments wherewith you are attired.[12]

Bibliography

Alford, Stephen, *Burghley: William Cecil at the Court of Elizabeth I,* Yale, 2008 ("Alford")

Ascham, Roger, *The Schoolmaster,* Cassell, 1909

Bradford, C.A., *Helena Marchioness of Northampton,* London,1936 ("Bradford")

Braybrooke, Richard, Lord, *Diary and Correspondence of S. Pepys,* Vol. I, Appendix, 3rd. ed., London, 1848 ("Braybrooke")

Bruce, John, ed., *Correspondence of Robert Dudley, Earl of Leicester,* Camden Society, 1844 ("Bruce")

Camden, William, *The Historie of the Most Renowned and Victorious Princess Elizabeth, Late Queene of England,* London, 1630 ed. W.T. MacCaffrey, 1970 ("Camden")

Camden, William, *Annals of Elizabeth* ("Camden - Annals")

Camm, Bede, *Lives of the English Martyrs, Edmund Campion,* Cambridge, 1929 ("Camm")

Campion, Edmund, *History of Ireland*, Dedication, 1571 ("Campion")

Cavendish, George, *The Life of Cardinal Wolsey,* ed. S.W. Singer, Harding and Lepard, London, 1827 ("Cavendish")

Chamberlin, F., *Elizabeth and Leicester,* 1939 ("Chamberlin")

Chapman, Hester W., *Lady Jane Grey,* Boston, 1962 ("Chapman – Lady Jane Grey")

Chapman, Hester W., *The Last Tudor King: A Study of Edward VI,* Jonathan Cape, 1958 ("Chapman")

Collins, A., *Letters and Memorials of State,* 2 vols., 1746 ("Collins")

Commendone, G.F., *The Accession, Coronation and Marriage of Mary Tudor,* ed. C.V. Malfatti, Barcelona, 1956 ("Commendone")

Dee, John, *The Compendious Rehearsal,* 1594

De la Ferrière, Arnaud, *Projets du Mariage de la Reine Elizabeth,* 1882 ("De la Ferrière")

Devereux, W. Bourchier, *Lives and Letters of the Devereux Earls of Essex, 2 vols.*, London, 1853 ("Devereux")

Dictionary of National Biography ("DNB")

Digges, T., *An Arithmetical Military Treatise Named Stratioticos,* Appendix, 1579 ("Digges")

Ellis, H., *Original Letters Illustrative of English History,* First series, Vol.II, London, 1825 ("Ellis")

Foxe, J., *Acts and Monuments,* ed. Rev. S. Seed, VI, London, 1838 ("Foxe")

Furnivall, J.D., *Ballads from Manuscripts,* London, 1868 ("Furnivall")

Grafton, R. *An Abridgement of the Chronicles of England,* London 1564 ("Grafton")

Graham, Roderick, *An Accidental Tragedy, The Life of Mary Queen of Scots,* Birlinn Limited, 2008 ("Graham")

Guy, John, *My Heart is my Own: The Life of Mary Queen of Scots,* Harper Perennial, 2004 ("Guy")

Harrison, G.B., *Letters of Queen Elizabeth,* 1968 ("Harrison")

Hayward, Sir John, *The life and raigne of King Edward the Sixth,* Partridge, 1630 ("Hayward")

Hume, Martin Andrew Sharp, *The Great Lord Burghley; A Study in Elizabethan Statecraft,* Longmans, Green, and Co., New York, 1898 ("Hume")

Jenkins, Elizabeth, *Elizabeth & Leicester,* Victor Gollancz, 1961 ("Jenkins")

Jenkins, Elizabeth, *Elizabeth the Great,* Coward-McCann, New York, 1959 ("Elizabeth the Great")

Klarvill, V. von, *Queen Elizabeth and some Foreigners,* 1928 ("Klarvill")

Lacey, R., *Robert, Earl of Essex: an Elizabethan Icarus,* London, 1971 ("Lacey")

Laneham, Robert, A Letter, wherein part of the *entertainment unto her Queen's Majesty at Kenilworth Castle in Warwickshire in this summer's progress – 1575 – is signified* (Nichol's Progresses of Queen Elizabeth) ("Laneham")

Leicester's Commonwealth 1583 ("Leicester's Commonwealth")

Leland, John, *Collectanea* ("Leland")

Lloyd, David, *State Worthies,* London, 1765 ("Lloyd")

Lodge, Edmund, *Illustrations of British History, Biography and Manners, II* 1791 ("Lodge")

Malone Society, *Dramatic Records in the Declared Accounts of the Treasurer of the Chamber 1558-1642,* Collections, VI, Oxford, 1962 ("Malone Society")

Mattingly, G., *The Defeat of the Spanish Armada,* 1959 ("Mattingly")

Melville, Sir James, of Hallhill, *Memoirs of his own life 1549-1593,* ed.Francis Steuart, 1929, ed. Gordon Donaldson, The Folio Society, 1969 ("Melville")

Motley, J.L., *History of the United Netherlands,* London, 1867 ("Motley")

Naunton, Sir Robert, *Fragmenta Regalia,* 1641 ("Naunton")

Neale, Sir J.E., *Queen Elizabeth I,* Jonathan Cape, 1934 ("Neale")

Neale, Sir J.E., *Elizabeth I and her Parliaments,* 1559–1581, 1953 ("Elizabeth I and her Parliaments")

Nichols, J.G, ed. *Greyfriars' Chronicle,* Camden Society, Old Series, 1852 ("Greyfriars' Chronicle")

Nichols, J.G., ed. *The Chronicles of Queen Jane and Two Years of Queen Mary,* Camden Society, London, 1850 ("Nichols")

Nichols, J.G., ed. *The Diary of Henry Machyn 1550–1563,* Camden Society, Old Series XLII (1848) ("Machyn")

Nicolas, H., *Memoirs of the Life of Christopher Hatton,* 1847 ("Nicolas")

Ödberg, Fridolf, *Om Princessan Cecilia Wasa,* Stockholm, 1896 ("Ödberg")

Peck, D.C., ed. *Leicester's Commonwealth: The Copy of a Letter Written by a Master of Art of Cambridge,* 1584, *and Related Documents,* London, 1985 ("Peck")

Pennant, Thomas, *A Tour of Wales,* London, 1781 ("Pennant")

Pollard, A.F., *History of England from the Accession of Edward VI to the Death of Elizabeth,* Longmans, Green and Co., London, 1919 ("Pollard")

Pollini, G., *L'Historia Ecclesiastica della Rivoluzion d'Inghilaterra,* Rome, 1594 ("Pollini")

Raumer, F. von, *Elizabeth and Mary Stuart,* London, 1836 ("Raumer")

Reese, M.M., *The Royal Office of Master of the Horse,* 1976 ("Reese")

Read, Conyers, *Lord Burghley and Queen Elizabeth,* 1960 ("Read")

Robinson, H., ed. *Original Letters Relative to the English Reformation,* I, Cambridge, 1846-7 ("Robinson")

Rosenburg, E., *Leicester, Patron of Letters,* 1955 ("Rosenburg")

Rowse, Dr A.L., *Ralegh and the Throckmortons,* 1962 ("Rowse")

Stedall, Robert, *Mary Queen of Scots' Downfall,* Pen & Sword Books, 2017 ("Mary Queen of Scots' Downfall")

Stedall, Robert, *The Challenge to the Crown,* The Book Guild, 2012 ("Challenge to the Crown")

Stedall, Robert, *The Survival of the Crown,* The Book Guild, 2014 ("Survival of the Crown")

Stow, J., *Annales, or, a general chronicle of England,* ed. E. Howes, 1631 ("Stow – Annales")

Stow, J., *Historical Memoranda,* Camden Society ("Stow – Memoranda")

Stow, J., *The Chronicles of England,* 1550 ("Stow")

Strickland, Agnes, *Lives of the Tudor and Stuart Princesses,* London, 1868 ("Strickland")

Strype, Sir John, *Annals of the Reformation,* 1824 ("Strype - Annals")

Strype, Sir John, *Life of Sir John Cheke,* Clarendon Press, 1821 ("Cheke")

Strype, Sir John, *Sir Thomas Smith,* 1824 ("Sir Thomas Smith")

Tallis, Nicola, *Crown of Blood: The Deadly Inheritance of Lady Jane Grey,* Michael O'Mara Books, 2016 ("Crown of Blood")

Tallis, Nicola, *Elizabeth's Rival: The Tumultuous Tale of Lettice Knollys Countess of Leicester,* Michael O'Mara Books, 2017 ("Tallis")

Thomas, William, *The Pilgrim,* ed. J. A Froude, Parker, Son, and Bourn, 1861 ("Thomas")

Tytler, P.F., *England under the Reigns of Edward VI and Mary,* 2 Vols., London, 1839 ("Tytler")

Vertot, R.A. and Villaret, C. (eds.) *Ambassades de Monsieur Noailles en Angleterre,* II, Paris, 1763 ("Vervot")

Warner, G.F., *The Voyage of Robert Dudley to the West Indies 1594-1595,* Hakluyt Society, 1899 ("Warner")

Wilson, Derek, *Sweet Robin: A Biography of Robert Dudley Earl of Leicester 1533-1588,* Allison & Busby, 1981 ("*Sweet Robin*")

Wilson, D.A., *The World Encompassed: Drake's great Voyage 1577-1580,* 1977 ("Wilson")

Wingfield, R., *Vita Mariae Reginae,* trans. D. MacCulloch, Camden Miscellany, XXVIII 4th Series, XXIX ("Wingfield")

Wood, Anthony á, *History and Antiquities of the University of Oxford,* Oxford, 1792 ("Wood")

Wormald, Jenny, *Mary, Queen of Scots, Politics, Passion and a Kingdom Lost,* Tauris Parke Paper Backs, 2001 ("Wormald")

Wotton, H., *A parallel betweene Robert late Earl of Essex, and George late Duke of Buckingham written by Sir Henry Wotton,* London, 1641 ("Wotton")

Wright, Thomas, *Queen Elizabeth and her Times,* London, 1838 ("Wright")

Zilletti, G., *Lettere di Principi, le quali si scrivono o da principi, o ragionano di principi,* Venice, 1577 ("Zilletti")

Papers

Baga de Secretis, Pouch IV

British Library, Harley MS ("Harley MS")

British Library, Lansdowne MS ("Lansdowne MS")

Bulletin of the Institute of Historical Research, *Letters of Thomas Wood, Puritan, 1566-77* Special Supplement, No.5, November 1960 ("Letters of Thomas Wood")

Calendar of State Papers Domestic ("CSP Domestic")

Calendar of State Papers Foreign ("CSP Foreign")

Calendar of State Papers Scottish ("CSP Scottish")

Calendar of State Papers Spanish ("CSPS")

Dent-Brocklehurst MS, Sudeley Castle ("Dent-Brocklehurst MS")

Dudley Papers, Longleat

Ellesmere MMS, *A letter from Robert, Earl of Leicester, to a Lady,* The Huntingdon Library, Bulletin No. 9, April 1936 ("Ellesmere")

Hardwicke State Papers

Historical Manuscript Commission ("HMC")

Historical Manuscript Commission, Hatfield ("Hatfield")

Le Report de un Judgement done en Banke du Roi, 1581 ("Le Report de un Judgement")

Letters & Papers of Henry VIII ("Lit. Rem.")

Public Records Office, Baschet Transcripts 31/3/26 ("Baschet Transcripts")

Scottish History Society, *Warrender Papers* ("Warrender Papers")

State Papers, ed. Haynes ("State Papers")

References

PART I: PRE-ELIZABETHAN UPS AND DOWNS

Prologue

1. Letters & Papers of Henry VIII, xiv, part 2, p.141; cited in Chapman p.77
2. Cavendish, *Cardinal Wolsey* ed. Singer p.100; cited in Chapman p.54

Chapter 1: John Dudley, Viscount Lisle

1. *Sweet Robin*, p.4
2. ibid. p.5
3. ibid.
4. ibid.
5. ibid. p.6
6. Jenkins, p.8
7. *Sweet Robin*, p.6
8. ibid.
9. DNB, cited in *Sweet Robin*, p.6
10. Baga de Secretis, Pouch IV; cited in *Sweet Robin*, p.6
11. Jenkins, p.9
12. ibid.
13. *Sweet Robin*, p.6
14. Jenkins, p.8
15. ibid.
16. *Sweet Robin*, p.7
17. ibid.
18. ibid. p.8
19. ibid.
20. ibid.
21. ibid.
22. ibid.
23. Lit. Rem., iii, 3516, cited in *Sweet Robin*, p.8
24. *Sweet Robin*, p.8

25. ibid.
26. ibid.
27. ibid. p.9
28. ibid.
29. ibid.
30. ibid. p.12
31. ibid. p.9
32. ibid.
33. ibid. p.15
34. ibid. p.10
35. ibid.
36. ibid. p.13
37. ibid. p.10
38. ibid.
39. ibid. p.15
40. ibid.
41. ibid.
42. ibid. p.16
43. ibid.
44. ibid.
45. ibid. p.17
46. ibid. p.19
47. ibid. p.20
48. R.B. Wernham, *Before the Armada,* pp.204–7; W.K. Jordan, *Edward VI: The Threshold of Power,* pp.490–3; cited in *Sweet Robin*, p.20
49. *Sweet Robin*, p. 20
50. ibid.
51. Lit. Rem. V, ccccxciii; cited in *Sweet Robin*, p.21
52. *Sweet Robin*, p. 22
53. ibid. p.17
54. ibid. p.18
55. ibid.
56. ibid.
57. ibid.
58. Cheke, p.22; cited in Chapman, p.66
59. Chapman, pp.103–4
60. Ascham, *The Schoolmaster* p.198; cited in Chapman, p.51
61. Jenkins, p.15
62. Neale, pp.24-5
63. Chapman, p.104
64. *Sweet Robin*, p.18

65. ibid.
66. ibid. p.23
67. ibid. p.24
68. ibid. p.25
69. ibid.
70. ibid. p.22
71. CSP Spanish, VIII, p.557; cited in *Sweet Robin*, p.23

Chapter 2: The Seymour brothers' rivalry

1. *Sweet Robin*, p.26
2. ibid.
3. ibid.
4. ibid. p.27
5. ibid.
6. ibid.
7. Elizabeth the Great
8. Hayward, p.195; cited in Chapman, p.86
9. *Sweet Robin*, p.28
10. Chapman, p.84
11. Thomas, p.56; cited in Chapman, p.96
12. *Sweet Robin*, p.28
13. Chapman, p.94
14. *Sweet Robin*, p.29
15. ibid.
16. Crown of Blood, p.61
17. ibid. p.62
18. CSPS IX, p.340; cited in Crown of Blood, pp.63-4
19. Dent-Brocklehurst MS; cited in Crown of Blood p.63
20. Hayward, p.198; cited in Chapman, p.112
21. Crown of Blood, p.64
22. Chapman, p.86
23. Crown of Blood, p.58
24. Lit. Rem. I, pp.56-7; cited in Chapman p.113
25. Hume, p.16
26. Chapman, p.145
27. Lit. Rem. I, p.49; cited in Chapman p.145
28. State Papers, p.99; cited in Crown of Blood, p.67
29. Crown of Blood, p.67
30. Neale, p.35
31. Chapman, p.138
32. ibid. p.139

Chapter 3: Somerset's difficulties in Government

1. *Sweet Robin*, p.30
2. Chapman, p.114
3. *Sweet Robin*, p.30
4. ibid. p.14
5. ibid.
6. ibid.
7. Chapman, p.147
8. *Sweet Robin*, p.30
9. ibid.
10. ibid. p.31
11. ibid.
12. ibid.
13. ibid. p.34
14. ibid.
15. ibid.
16. ibid. p.36
17. ibid. p.38
18. ibid. p.37
19. ibid. p.38
20. ibid.
21. ibid.
22. ibid.p.39
23. Chapman, p.153
24. *Sweet Robin*, p.40
25. ibid. pp.40-41
26. ibid. p.41
27. Jenkins, p.19

Chapter 4: Warwick establishes control

1. *Sweet Robin*, p.41
2. BM, Add, MS. 48126, fo. 16a; cited in *Sweet Robin*, p.42
3. *Sweet Robin*, p.42
4. ibid.
5. ibid. p.50
6. ibid. p.43
7. ibid. p.44
8. ibid.
9. ibid.
10. ibid.

11. ibid.
12. ibid. p.47
13. ibid. p.45
14. ibid. p.52
15. ibid, p.53
16. Chapman, p.213
17. ibid. p.210
18. ibid.
19. Pollard, p.59; cited in Chapman, p.211
20. Chapman, p.214
21. ibid. p.213
22. Jenkins, p.21
23. *Sweet Robin*, p.47
24. Chapman, p.215
25. ibid. p.245
26. *Sweet Robin*, p.51
27. Chapman, p.235
28. *Sweet Robin*, p.52
29. ibid.
30. Machyn pp.13-14; cited in *Sweet Robin*, p.52
31. Chapman, p.250
32. *Sweet Robin*, p.52
33. Machyn, p.103; cited in *Sweet Robin*, pp.53-4
34. *Sweet Robin*, p.48
35. ibid.

Chapter 5: Efforts to circumvent the succession of the Catholic Mary Tudor

1. Tytler, II, p.155; cited in *Sweet Robin*, p.50
2. *Sweet Robin*, p.53
3. Ibid. p.51
4. Chapman, p.264
5. Ibid. p.275
6. CSPS XI, p.8; cited in Crown of Blood, p.127
7. Wingfield, p.249; cited in Crown of Blood, p.126
8. *Sweet Robin*, p.53
9. Crown of Blood, p.126
10. Guy, p.279
11. Hume, p.36
12. Jenkins, p.22

13. Wingfield, p.245; cited in Crown of Blood, p.131
14. Ibid. cited p.132
15. Crown of Blood, p.133
16. Chapman, p.274
17. Jenkins, p.23
18. Grafton, f.159; cited in Crown of Blood, p.133
19. Strickland, p.85; cited in Chapman, p.275
20. Crown of Blood, p.138
21. CSPS XI, p.40; cited in Crown of Blood p.137
22. *Sweet Robin*, p.57
23. ibid.
24. Jenkins, p.24
25. ibid.
26. ibid. p.25
27. Chapman, p.281
28. Jenkins, p.25
29. Chapman, p.277
30. ibid.
31. *Sweet Robin*, p.56
32. CSPS Edward VI and Mary, XI, 46; cited in *Sweet Robin*, p.56
33. *Sweet Robin*, p.59
34. ibid.
35. ibid. p.60
36. ibid.
37. ibid.
38. Pollini, p.355; cited in Crown of Blood, p.152
39. Crown of Blood, p.152
40. Commendone, p.7; cited in ibid.
41. Vervot, p.57; cited in Crown of Blood, p.157
42. Crown of Blood, p.153
43. CSPS XI, p.80; cited in ibid. p.155
44. Zilletti, f.223; cited in ibid. p.156
45. Jenkins, p.27
46. ibid.
47. Nichols, p.9; cited in Crown of Blood, p.161
48. Ellis, p.185; cited in ibid. p.170
49. Wingfield, p.253; cited in ibid. p.176
50. CSPS XI, p.94; cited in ibid. p.170
51. *Sweet Robin*, p.61
52. Cited in Chapman – Lady Jane Grey, p.146; cited in Crown of Blood, p.187
53. Jenkins, p.30
54. Tytler; cited in Jenkins, p.30

55. Commendone, p.24; cited in Crown of Blood, p.203
56. Nichols, p.12; cited in ibid.
57. *Sweet Robin*, p.64
58. ibid. p.62

Chapter 6: Events leading to Lady Jane Grey's execution

1. *Sweet Robin*, p.62
2. Pollini, p. 355; cited in Crown of Blood, p.205
3. CSPS XI, p.232; cited in Crown of Blood, p.215
4. *Sweet Robin*, p.63
5. ibid.
6. Greyfriars Chronicle, p.83; cited in ibid. p.63
7. *Sweet Robin*, p. 63
8. ibid. p.43
9. Crown of Blood, p.213
10. Nichols, p.20; cited in ibid.
11. *Sweet Robin*, p.65
12. ibid. p.64
13. ibid. pp.70-71
14. ibid. p.65
15. ibid.
16. ibid.
17. Jenkins, p.34
18. Wingfield, p.273; cited in Crown of Blood, p.242
19. ibid. p. 279; cited in ibid. p.240
20. Neale, p.48
21. *Sweet Robin*, p.65
22. ibid. p.66
23. ibid.
24. ibid.
25. Le Report de un Judgement; cited in ibid.
26. Foxe, p.1620; cited in Crown of Blood, pp.231-2
27. Robinson, p.77; cited in ibid. p.233
28. CSPS XI, p.366; cited in ibid.
29. Crown of Blood, p.241
30. CSPS XI, p.446; cited in ibid. p.224
31. Neale, p.42
32. CSPS XI, p.416; cited in Crown of Blood, p.241
33. Cheke, p.180; cited in Chapman, p.289
34. Jenkins, p.31
35. Wingfield, pp.279-80; cited in Crown of Blood, p.243
36. Nichols, p.39; cited in *Sweet Robin*, p.67

37. Neale, p.44
38. Crown of Blood, p.249
39. ibid.
40. ibid. pp.257-8
41. Harley MS 2342 ff.59-60; cited in ibid. p.267
42. ibid.
43. Commendone, p.49; cited in ibid. p.268
44. *Sweet Robin*, p.68
45. ibid.
46. Nichols, p.59; cited in ibid.

Chapter 7: Surviving Mary Tudor's reign of terror

1. *Sweet Robin*, p.69
2. Jenkins, pp.35-6
3. Neale, p.45
4. ibid.
5. Nichols, p.58; cited in ibid. p.47
6. Jenkins, p.36
7. Neale, p.46
8. *Sweet Robin*, p.69
9. Neale, p.58
10. ibid. p.59
11. ibid. p.55
12. ibid.
13. Collins, I, p.30; cited in *Sweet Robin*, p.75
14. *Sweet Robin*, p.76
15. Jenkins, p.94
16. *Sweet Robin*, p.75
17. ibid. p.76
18. ibid. p.78
19. Jenkins, pp.37-8
20. *Sweet Robin*, p.79
21. Quoted in Chamberlin, App. IX, pp.92-3; cited in *Sweet Robin*, p.76
22. Alford, p.73
23. Neale, p.57
24. ibid. p.63
25. Jenkins, p.131
26. Neale, p.63
27. State Papers, 12/1 f.12r-v; cited in Alford, p.89
28. Jenkins, p.131

PART 2: ELIZABETH'S FAVOURITE

Chapter 8: Master of the Horse

1. Jenkins, p.41
2. *Sweet Robin*, p.86
3. Jenkins, p.263
4. *Sweet Robin*, p.92
5. Jenkins, p.98
6. ibid. p.193
7. ibid. p.41
8. *Sweet Robin*, p.83
9. ibid. p.84
10. ibid. p.93
11. ibid. p.81
12. Reese, p.159; cited in ibid. p.89
13. *Sweet Robin*, p.94
14. ibid. p.82
15. ibid.
16. ibid. p.85

Chapter 9: Elizabeth establishes herself as Queen

1. Neale, p.64
2. ibid.
3. *Sweet Robin*, p.89
4. Jenkins, p.81
5. ibid. p.58
6. *Sweet Robin*, p.88
7. ibid. p.89
8. ibid. p.90
9. Jenkins, p.81
10. Alford, p.91
11. ibid. p.95
12. Jenkins, p.110
13. ibid. p.81
14. Alford, p.95
15. Neale, p.67
16. Alford, p.95
17. ibid. p.98
18. ibid.
19. Jenkins, p.109

20. Neale, p.66
21. ibid. p.96
22. ibid. p.62
23. Jenkins, pp.45-6
24. Neale, p.64
25. ibid. p.61
26. ibid. p.76
27. ibid. p.96
28. ibid. p.76
29. Jenkins, p.47
30. Neale, p.79
31. ibid. p.77
32. ibid. p.79
33. ibid. p.83
34. ibid. p.79
35. BM, Lansdowne MS 94, f.29; cited in *Sweet Robin*, p.100
36. Neale, p.81
37. ibid.
38. CSPS, I, p.27; cited in *Sweet Robin*, p.98
39. Cited in Jenkins, p.51
40. ibid.
41. *Sweet Robin*, p.101
42. ibid. p.103
43. Neale, p.82
44. ibid.
45. ibid. p.83
46. ibid. p.80
47. ibid.
48. ibid.
49. ibid. pp.80-1
50. Hume, p.88
51. ibid. p.89
52. ibid. p.99
53. ibid. p.90
54. *Sweet Robin*, p.113
55. Ibid. p.115
56. Jenkins, p.76
57. Challenge to the Crown, pp. 115-6
58. *Sweet Robin*, p.117
59. ibid. p.118
60. Jenkins, p.68

61. Neale, p.106
62. ibid. p.85
63. ibid.
64. Jenkins, p.56
65. Neale, p.85
66. Klarvill; cited in Jenkins p.56

Chapter 10: Robert's relationship with Amy Robsart and her tragic death

1. *Sweet Robin*, p.97
2. ibid. p.121
3. ibid. p.122
4. Jenkins, p.65
5. Braybrooke, Vol. I, Appendix; cited in Jenkins, p.66
6. Jenkins, p.65
7. *Sweet Robin*, p.125
8. Hume, p.102
9. Jenkins, p.69
10. *Sweet Robin*, p.125
11. Jenkins, p.72
12. ibid.
13. ibid.
14. ibid. p.73
15. Hardwicke State Papers; cited in Jenkins p.73
16. Jenkins, p.73
17. Neale, p.88
18. Jenkins, p.74
19. Hume, p.103
20. Hatfield; cited in Jenkins, p.176

Chapter 11: The not so virgin Queen

1. Jenkins, p.73
2. *Sweet Robin*, p.133
3. Jenkins, p.78
4. ibid. p.90
5. ibid. p.79
6. Hume, p.104
7. Jenkins, p.79
8. ibid.
9. ibid.

10. ibid. p.80
11. ibid. p.51
12. ibid. p.80
13. ibid. p.57
14. ibid.
15. Challenge to the Crown, p.156 fn.
16. Alford, p.117
17. Challenge to the Crown, pp.156-7
18. *Sweet Robin*, pp.135-6
19. CSPS, I, pp.113-4; cited in ibid. p.104
20. Jenkins, p.55
21. ibid. p.76
22. Ödberg; cited in Jenkins, p.76
23. CSP Foreign; cited in Jenkins, p.77
24. Hume, p.93
25. Jenkins, p.87
26. Hume, p.138
27. Challenge to the Crown, p.159
28. *Sweet Robin*, p.137
29. Hume, p.164
30. Jenkins, p.92
31. *Sweet Robin*, p.138
32. ibid. p.139
33. ibid.
34. CSPS; cited in Jenkins, p.89
35. Jenkins, p.116
36. Jenkins, p.89
37. CSP Domestic, CLIX, I; cited in *Sweet Robin*, p.138
38. Jenkins, p.95
39. ibid. p.96
40. ibid. p.103
41. ibid.
42. ibid. p.104
43. ibid. p.101

Chapter 12: The political background to Elizabeth's European marriage negotiations

1. Melville, p.56; cited in Wormald, p. 163
2. De la Ferrière; cited in Jenkins, p.140
3. CSPS, Elizabeth, Vol. I
4. Hume, p.152

5. Jenkins, p.105
6. Hume, p.167
7. ibid. p.174
8. ibid. p.166
9. ibid. p.170
10. Jenkins, p.109
11. ibid. p.115

Chapter 13: Marriage considerations

1. Jenkins, p.164
2. Elizabeth I and her Parliaments, p. 109; cited in *Sweet Robin*, p.142
3. Dudley Papers, III, f.37; cited in *Sweet Robin*, p.142
4. Sir Thomas Smith; cited in Jenkins, p.77
5. Jenkins, p.92
6. Alford, p.124
7. Wright; cited in Jenkins, p.113
8. CSP Scottish, p.52-9-385; cited in *Sweet Robin*, p.144
9. Jenkins, p.94
10. ibid.
11. Hume, p.162
12. CSP Scottish, 1563-69, 233; cited in Jenkins, p.95
13. Guy, p.207
14. Jenkins, p.110
15. Mary Queen of Scots' Downfall, p.82
16. ibid.
17. Jenkins, p.119
18. ibid. p.107
19. Hume, p.164
20. Jenkins, p.108
21. Guy, p.193
22. Jenkins, p.118
23. Jenkins, p.101

Chapter 14: Patronage and trading projects

1. *Sweet Robin*, p.14
2. Jenkins, p.178
3. ibid. p.268
4. ibid. p.178
5. ibid.
6. ibid. p.143
7. ibid. p.144

8. ibid.
9. Camm; cited in ibid. p.145
10. Jenkins, p.184
11. Dudley Papers, II, f.65; cited in *Sweet Robin*, pp.235-6
12. *Sweet Robin*, pp.152-3
13. ibid. p.153
14. Jenkins, p.205
15. Laneham; cited in Jenkins, p.206
16. ibid; cited in *Sweet Robin*, p.153
17. ibid; cited in Jenkins, 206
18. ibid.
19. Jenkins, p.141
20. ibid. p.161
21. ibid. p.204
22. ibid. p.221
23. Tallis, p.186
24. Jenkins, p.226
25. ibid. p.302
26. *Sweet Robin*, p.148
27. Tallis, p.202
28. ibid. p.205
29. *Sweet Robin*, p.155
30. Jenkins, p.220
31. ibid.
32. ibid. p.219
33. *Sweet Robin*, p.155
34. ibid. p.163
35. Tallis, p.202
36. Jenkins, p.284
37. *Sweet Robin*, p.157
38. ibid. p.159
39. Jenkins, p.77
40. *Sweet Robin*, pp.159-60
41. Jenkins, p.147
42. *Sweet Robin*, p.161
43. ibid. p.157
44. ibid. p.161
45. ibid. p.158
46. ibid. p.156
47. Stow, Dedication; cited in *Sweet Robin*, p.165
48. *Sweet Robin*, p.165

49. Jenkins, p.143
50. *Sweet Robin*, p.167
51. ibid.
52. ibid. p.168
53. ibid. p.151
54. Jenkins, p.163
55. *Sweet Robin*, p.149
56. Jenkins, p.309
57. *Sweet Robin*, p.173
58. Lloyd; cited in Jenkins, p.249
59. *Sweet Robin*, p.174
60. ibid. pp.174-5
61. Pennant; cited in Jenkins, p.238
62. Jenkins, p.241
63. ibid. p.113
64. *Sweet Robin*, p.149
65. Jenkins, p.212
66. *Sweet Robin*, p.258

Chapter 15: Flirtation with Lettice Knollys designed to provoke Elizabeth

1. Jenkins, p.121
2. ibid.
3. ibid. p.122
4. ibid. p.123
5. ibid. p.122
6. ibid.
7. ibid.
8. CSPS, 1558-1567, I, p.472; cited in Tallis p.85
9. Jenkins, p.125
10. CSPS Elizabeth 1558-1567, I, p.472; cited in Tallis p.86
11. Tallis, p.86
12. ibid. p.87
13. Jenkins, p.125
14. Jenkins, p.128
15. Leland; cited in ibid.
16. Hume, p.169
17. Jenkins, p.129
18. Hume, p.170
19. Raumer; cited in Jenkins, pp.123-4
20. ibid. cited in ibid. p.130

21. Hume, p.174
22. Naunton; cited in Jenkins, p.137
23. Jenkins, p.135
24. Stow – Memoranda; cited in ibid. p.138
25. HMC Pepys; cited in Jenkins, p.136
26. Jenkins, p.136
27. ibid. p.139
28. Bradford; cited in ibid. p.139
29. Jenkins, p.128
30. ibid. p.129
31. Raumer; cited in ibid. p.129
32. Jenkins, p.133
33. ibid. p.139
34. ibid. p.133
35. *Sweet Robin*, p.183
36. Jenkins, p.133
37. ibid. p.139
38. Raumer; cited in Jenkins, p.141
39. Jenkins, p.150

Chapter 16: Robert survives political attempts to undermine his standing

1. Wright, p.209; cited in *Sweet Robin*, p.179
2. Jenkins, p.148
3. CSP Domestic, Add.XIII, 8 cited in *Sweet Robin*, pp.183-4
4. ibid. cited in ibid. p.184
5. *Sweet Robin*, p.185
6. ibid. pp.185-6
7. CSPS, I, 415; cited in *Sweet Robin*, p.187
8. *Sweet Robin*, p.187
9. ibid. p.183
10. Jenkins, p.146
11. ibid.
12. Elizabeth I and her Parliaments, Vol. II; cited in Jenkins, p.146
13. *Sweet Robin*, p.195
14. ibid. p.196
15. ibid. p.194
16. Jenkins, p.150
17. ibid.
18. ibid.
19. *Sweet Robin*, p.197

20. ibid.
21. Jenkins, p.158
22. ibid.
23. ibid. p.199
24. *Sweet Robin*, p.197
25. ibid. p.198
26. ibid.
27. ibid.
28. Jenkins, p.153
29. ibid. p.158
30. Raumer; cited in ibid. p.201

Chapter 17: The Northern Rising

1. *Sweet Robin*, p.212
2. Jenkins, p.166
3. ibid.
4. Survival of the Crown, p.102
5. ibid. p.103
6. Neale, p.191
7. Survival of the Crown, p.104
8. Jenkins, p.265
9. Rosenburg, pp.215-6; cited in *Sweet Robin*, p.243
10. Jenkins, p.172
11. ibid. p.266
12. ibid. p.185
13. Neale, p.222
14. Dee; cited in Jenkins, p.204
15. Jenkins, p.300
16. *Sweet Robin*, p.223
17. Jenkins, p.198
18. ibid.
19. *Sweet Robin*, p.217
20. Jenkins, p.176

Chapter 18: Romance with Douglas Sheffield

1. *Sweet Robin*, p.199
2. Jenkins, p.197
3. ibid. p.154
4. ibid.
5. ibid. p.186
6. ibid. p.187

7. Ellesmere; cited in *Sweet Robin*, pp.208-9 and in Jenkins, p.188
8. Lodge, p.17; cited in *Sweet Robin*, p.209
9. Warner, p.vi; cited in Wikipedia
10. ibid.
11. Tallis, p.124
12. ibid. p.122
13. Jenkins, p.217
14. Warner, p.xlv; cited in ibid. p.251
15. Peck, p.82; cited in Tallis, p.121
16. Jenkins, p.249
17. *Sweet Robin*, p.210
18. ibid. also in Tallis, p.123
19. Jenkins, p.190
20. *Sweet Robin*, p.248

Chapter 19: Religious confrontation

1. Jenkins, p.266
2. ibid.
3. *Sweet Robin*, p.243
4. Jenkins, p.268
5. *Sweet Robin*, p.199
6. Jenkins, p.164
7. *Sweet Robin*, p.199
8. Baschet Transcripts f.207; cited in *Sweet Robin*, p.200
9. *Sweet Robin*, p.200
10. ibid. p.199
11. ibid. p.200
12. ibid.
13. ibid. p.203
14. ibid. p.202
15. ibid.
16. ibid. p.204
17. ibid. p.202
18. ibid. p.205
19. ibid.
20. Letters of Thomas Wood; cited in Jenkins, pp.215-6
21. *Sweet Robin*, p.271
22. ibid.
23. ibid.
24. ibid.
25. Strype – Annals, III, p.333; cited in *Sweet Robin*, p.271

26. *Sweet Robin*, p.271
27. Nicolas, pp.371-2; cited in *Sweet Robin*, p.273
28. *Sweet Robin*, pp.202-3
29. ibid. p.272
30. ibid.
31. Read, p.295; cited in *Sweet Robin*, p.272
32. *Sweet Robin*, p.272
33. Jenkins, p.299
34. ibid.
35. ibid.

Chapter 20: Royal visits to Dudley homes

1. *Sweet Robin*, p.221
2. Jenkins, p.207
3. ibid.
4. Collins, I, p.48; cited in *Sweet Robin*, p.221
5. Jenkins, p.205
6. ibid.
7. ibid.
8. ibid.
9. *Sweet Robin*, p.221
10. Laneham p.162; cited in *Sweet Robin*, p.222
11. Jenkins, p.264
12. *Sweet Robin*, p.223
13. Jenkins, p.209
14. ibid. p.210
15. ibid. p.211
16. ibid. p.212

Chapter 21: Marriage of Lettice Knollys

1. CSPS; cited in Jenkins, p.212
2. Tallis, p.129
3. ibid. p.144
4. Jenkins, p.203
5. ibid. p.202
6. Devereux, p.120
7. *Sweet Robin*, p.227
8. Jenkins, p.217
9. *Sweet Robin*, p.227
10. Jenkins, p.203
11. Tallis, p.143

12. ibid. p.153
13. ibid. p.155
14. Camden, p.80; cited in ibid. p.159
15. Peck, p.76; cited in ibid. p.160
16. Tallis, p.157
17. Malone Society, p.14; cited in Tallis, p.157
18. Graham, p.376
19. ibid. p.375
20. Jenkins, p.221
21. ibid. p.213
22. Survival of the Crown, p.136
23. Ödberg; cited in Jenkins, p.223
24. Jenkins, p.227
25. *Sweet Robin*, p.235
26. ibid. p.236
27. Jenkins, p.230
28. Dudley Papers, III, f.190; cited in *Sweet Robin*, p.232
29. Jenkins, p.229
30. ibid. p.230
31. ibid. p.233
32. ibid. p.234
33. ibid. p.235
34. *Sweet Robin*, p.230
35. Tallis, p.280
36. *Sweet Robin*, p.249
37. Jenkins, p.247
38. ibid. p.281
39. ibid. p.282
40. ibid. p.252
41. Tallis, p.206
42. ibid. p.207
43. *Sweet Robin*, p.249
44. CSP Scottish 1584-85, VII, p.248; cited in Tallis, p.210
45. Jenkins, p.245
46. Tallis, p.210
47. ibid. p. 214
48. *Sweet Robin*, p.230
49. ibid. p.249
50. Wotton, p.1; cited in Tallis, p.211
51. Tallis, p.212
52. *Sweet Robin*, p.250

53. Jenkins, p.263
54. *Sweet Robin*, p.250
55. Tallis, p.191
56. ibid. p.193
57. Lansdowne MS, 885, f.86; cited in Tallis, p.194
58. Jenkins, p.277
59. ibid.
60. ibid.
61. ibid.
62. *Sweet Robin*, p.243
63. Jenkins, p.280
64. ibid. p.281
65. ibid. p.300
66. CSPS, Elizabeth, 1580-86, III, p.451; cited in Tallis, p.196
67. ibid. cited in ibid. pp.196-7
68. Tallis, pp.198-9
69. Jenkins, p.300
70. ibid.
71. Warrender Papers; cited in Jenkins, pp.300-1
72. Tallis, p.180
73. Peck, p.128; cited in Tallis, p.182
74. Jenkins, p.286
75. ibid.
76. ibid. p.283
77. Tallis, pp.200-1
78. ibid. p.133
79. ibid. p.183
80. ibid. p.204

PART 3: POLITICAL ADVISER AND MILITARY COMMANDER
Chapter 22: Negotiations for Elizabeth to marry the Duke of Anjou

1. Jenkins, p.227
2. ibid.
3. *Sweet Robin*, p.224
4. Jenkins, p.240
5. ibid. p.233
6. *Sweet Robin*, p.241
7. Jenkins, p.233
8. ibid. p.241
9. *Sweet Robin*, p.234

10. ibid.
11. Jenkins, p.242
12. CSPS, XI, p.681; cited in Tallis, pp.175-6
13. *Sweet Robin*, p.234
14. Jenkins, p.240
15. Neale, p.241
16. CSPS, I, p.592; cited in *Sweet Robin*, p.235
17. *Sweet Robin*, p.235
18. Neale, pp.241-3
19. Jenkins, p.228
20. *Sweet Robin*, p.236
21. ibid. p.237
22. ibid.
23. Furnivall; cited in Jenkins, p.246
24. *Sweet Robin*, p.236

Chapter 23: A more aggressive approach to international diplomacy

1. *Sweet Robin*, p.238
2. ibid. p.239
3. ibid.
4. ibid. p.240
5. Neale, p.236
6. CSPS, I, 486; cited in *Sweet Robin*, p.226
7. *Sweet Robin*, p.241
8. Jenkins, p.222
9. Neale, p.237
10. Jenkins, p.303
11. ibid. p.222
12. ibid. p.241
13. ibid. p.222
14. *Sweet Robin*, p.237
15. Wilson, pp.191-204; cited in *Sweet Robin*, p.237
16. Hume, p.347
17. Wilson, pp.191-204; cited in *Sweet Robin*, p.237
18. Jenkins, p.264
19. *Sweet Robin*, pp.237-8
20. ibid. p.238
21. Neale, p.246
22. *Sweet Robin*, p.242
23. ibid. pp.250-1

24. Jenkins, p.269
25. ibid.
26. Hume, p.389
27. Neale, p.254
28. ibid.
29. *Sweet Robin*, p.260
30. Jenkins, p.270
31. *Sweet Robin*, p.242
32. ibid.
33. ibid. p.254
34. CSP Domestic, CLXX, p.88; cited in ibid p.255
35. *Sweet Robin*, p.254
36. ibid. p.251
37. Jenkins, p.279
38. ibid. p.278
39. ibid. p.284
40. ibid. p.268
41. ibid. p.288
42. ibid.

Chapter 24: Leicester's Commonwealth

1. *Sweet Robin*, p.255
2. Jenkins, p.296
3. Jenkins, p.290
4. *Sweet Robin*, p.267
5. Tallis, p.213
6. *Sweet Robin*, p.252
7. ibid.
8. Jenkins, p.290
9. *Sweet Robin*, p.253
10. ibid.
11. ibid.
12. ibid.
13. Jenkins, p.290
14. *Sweet Robin*, p.268
15. ibid. p.254
16. Jenkins, p.298
17. Leicester's Commonwealth, p.47
18. *Sweet Robin*, p.261
19. ibid.

20. Jenkins, p.292
21. Leicester's Commonwealth, pp.19-20
22. ibid. p.44
23. Rowse, pp.73-4; cited in *Sweet Robin*, pp.258-9
24. Jenkins, p.294
25. Leicester's Commonwealth, p.50
26. Jenkins, p.294
27. ibid.
28. *Sweet Robin*, p.254
29. Jenkins, p.294
30. ibid. p.296
31. *Sweet Robin*, p.264
32. Jenkins, p.296
33. *Sweet Robin*, p.263
34. ibid. p.268
35. ibid. p.269

Chapter 25: Governor of the Netherlands

1. Motley; cited in Jenkins, p.301
2. *Sweet Robin*, p.274
3. Jenkins, p.304
4. ibid.
5. ibid.
6. Bruce; cited in Jenkins, p.305
7. *Sweet Robin*, p.275
8. ibid.
9. ibid. p.276
10. Jenkins, p.308
11. ibid. p.306
12. ibid. p.302
13. Lacey, p.35; cited in Tallis, p.218
14. Jenkins, p.301
15. Nicolas; cited in *Sweet Robin*, p.273
16. Jenkins, p.307
17. *Sweet Robin*, p.278
18. ibid. p.273
19. ibid. p.274
20. *Sweet Robin*, p.274
21. Neale, p.232
22. Jenkins, p.311

23. Digges; cited in *Sweet Robin*, p.279
24. *Sweet Robin*, p.276
25. ibid. pp.276-7
26. ibid. p.278
27. ibid. p.279
28. Stow – Annales, p.112; cited in *Sweet Robin*, p.280
29. Harrison, pp.174-5; cited in *Sweet Robin*, p.280
30. Jenkins, p.312
31. *Sweet Robin*, p.281
32. Jenkins, p.312
33. ibid.
34. *Sweet Robin*, p.283
35. Tallis, p.224
36. Jenkins, p.315
37. *Sweet Robin*, p.283
38. Bruce, p.209; cited in *Sweet Robin*, p.283
39. Harrison, p.179; cited in ibid.
40. *Sweet Robin*, p.284
41. Bruce, pp.365-6; cited in *Sweet Robin*, p.284
42. Jenkins, p.320
43. ibid.
44. Bruce, pp.367, 312, 426, 378 and 394; cited in *Sweet Robin*, p.285
45. Jenkins, p.320
46. *Sweet Robin*, p.284
47. Jenkins, p.320
48. ibid. p.321
49. ibid.
50. ibid. pp.321-2
51. *Sweet Robin*, p.287
52. ibid.
53. ibid. p.288
54. Jenkins, p.322
55. ibid. p.323
56. Bruce, pp.445-6; cited in *Sweet Robin*, pp.288-9
57. Jenkins, p.329
58. Mattingly, p.60; cited in *Sweet Robin*, p.293
59. Read; cited in Jenkins, p.337
60. Motley; cited in ibid. p.336
61. Jenkins, p.338
62. ibid. p.342

63. ibid. p.345
64. ibid. p.326
65. ibid.
66. ibid. p.345

Chapter 26: The execution Mary Queen of Scots

1. *Sweet Robin*, p.355
2. Survival of the Crown, p.216
3. ibid. pp.218-20
4. ibid. pp.220-1
5. ibid. pp.221-2
6. Cited in Guy, p.477
7. Neale, p.278
8. Jenkins. p.332
9. Survival of the Crown, p.246
10. Jenkins, p.333

Chapter 27: Lieutenant and Captain General of the Queen's armies and companies

1. *Sweet Robin*, p.292
2. Jenkins, p.330
3. ibid. p.331
4. ibid.
5. *Sweet Robin*, p.293
6. Read; cited in Jenkins, p.330
7. CSP Domestic, CXCVIII, p.19; cited in *Sweet Robin*, p.298
8. Jenkins, p.344
9. Camden – Annals; cited in ibid.
10. Neale, p.293
11. *Sweet Robin*, p.299
12. Jenkins, p.347
13. Neale, p.295
14. Neale, p.297
15. *Sweet Robin*, p.301
16. Tallis, p.236
17. *Sweet Robin*, p.300
18. Neale, p.298
19. *Sweet Robin*, p.302
20. ibid. p.304
21. ibid.
22. CSPS, Elizabeth, 1587-1603, IV, p.418; cited in Tallis, p.237

Aftermath

1. Jenkins, pp.363-4
2. ibid. p.367
3. Tallis, p.202
4. Jenkins, p.367
5. ibid. p.368
6. Wood; cited in Jenkins, p.368
7. CSPS, IV, p.431; cited in *Sweet Robin*, p.304
8. Jenkins, p.370
9. *Sweet Robin*, p.305
10. ibid. p.311
11. ibid. p.312
12. Campion, *History of Ireland*, Dedication

Index